FREE-LANCER AND STAFF WRITER

Newspaper Features and Magazine Articles

Titles of Interest from the
WADSWORTH SERIES IN JOURNALISM AND MASS COMMUNICATION

FREE-LANCER AND STAFF WRITER

Newspaper Features
and Magazine Articles

WILLIAM L. RIVERS

Stanford University

FIFTH EDITION

WADSWORTH PUBLISHING COMPANY
Belmont, California
A Division of Wadsworth, Inc.

Communications Editor: Kristine M. Clerkin
Editorial Assistant: Nancy Spellman
Production: Greg Hubit Bookworks
Print Buyer: Martha Branch
Designer: Christy Butterfield
Copy editor: Patricia Harris
Compositor: G&S Typesetters, Inc.
Proofreader: Dorothy Wilson
Cover: Stuart Paterson

Printed in the United States of America
1 2 3 4 5 6 7 8 9 10—96 95 94 93 92

Library of Congress Cataloging in Publication Data

Rivers, William L.
    Free-lancer and staff writer : newspaper features and magazine
articles / William L. Rivers. — 5th ed.
      p. cm. — (Wadsworth series in journalism & mass
communication)
  Includes index.
  ISBN 0-534-15996-6
  1. Authorship. 2. Feature writing. I. Title. II. Series.
PN147.R59 1992
808'.02—dc20   91-16581
                                          CIP

CONTENTS

A s have earlier editions, this fifth edition of *Free-Lancer and Staff Writer* includes sample articles with marginal editing and comments. Students who give these articles and points careful attention will understand how to shape and refine their articles. I also continue to include the varying perspectives of free-lance writers, staff writers, and editors of magazines. Students are shown how all of these workers' tasks combine to produce magazines. A chapter on voice, tone, and flow enables students to work out their own style.

This edition is designed, however, to meet students' needs in a new way. The Introduction contains long anecdotes and stories that focus on central aspects of the subject of this book. The anecdotes and stories teach at least most students something new. Also, in each chapter, a professional writer—David Halberstam, John McPhee, Joyce Carol Oates, Gloria Steinem, Stephen King, Gay Talese, Elie Wiesel, and others—contributes words to this book. Because each writer writes of at least one aspect of a subject in a way that I have never considered, I have learned much from each contribution. In most cases, a short profile of the writer is included immediately after his or her words to make certain that students know something about the writer. As for the quotations within each chapter, they are placed so that those who like them can read them and others can ignore them.

Chapter 6 is a highly important chapter because it links listening with observing. This is followed by chapters on interviewing, using libraries, and legwork. This group of chapters combines listening, observing, interviewing, library research, and legwork in such a way that students will be surprised to see how these abilities work together.

During the past twenty years, newspapers and magazines have faced strong competition from television and radio for advertising and for the public's attention. As a consequence, newspapers have become more like magazines. Almost any medium-sized or metropolitan newspaper will publish stories that run at least 3,000 words. Some of these stories read as though they were published in leading magazines. Some newspaper reporters for the larger newspapers work as magazine writers do, turning in their features only after days or weeks of work.

Let me thank those professors who read the manuscript of this book and offered many valuable suggestions: Warren "Sandy" Barnard, Indiana State University; Gilbert L. Fowler, Jr., Arkansas State University; Laura Widmer, Northwest Missouri State University; Robert C. Willson, George Washington University.

WILLIAM L. RIVERS

FREE-LANCER AND STAFF WRITER

Newspaper Features and Magazine Articles

SCENES OF WRITERS

Words differently arranged have a different meaning, and meanings differently arranged have different effects.

BLAISE PASCAL

W hen professional writers think of their writing, they may conjure up the most beautiful words they know. Or they may parody the work of some people they know—or deride the habits they developed while working for a magazine. In fact, it could be that at times they will make fun of themselves. The following words introduce writers at work as they think, wonder, and write.

MOUTH-FILLING WORDS

In *Vogue* magazine, Caroline Duerr wrote in praise of mouth-filling words:

> A *blunderbuss* seems to me much more explosive than a pistol, and *Beelzebub* twice as alarming as the Devil. To *bamboozle* must be more fun than to cheat, and less likely to land one in prison. *Buxom* conveys a charm which fat entirely lacks, and *beholden,* a graciousness in accepting favors which is missing in thankfulness. *Lackadaisical* has a delightful sound, conveying much more than languid. *Rascal* and *rapscallion* were used by my two grandfathers, generally when referring to old acquaintances. *Scalawag* belonged in this group, I think, as did *nincompoop, numbskull* and *curmudgeon.* In the nursery, *rambunctious* and *cantankerous* rumbled; also *pandemonium*—which was used to describe unnecessary squabbles of which the *Powers Above* were growing heartily tired.

Dean Walley wrote in *All Things Glad and Beautiful* that he had romances with tongue-twisting words, gentle words, and dim, shady words:

> I like big, rambunctious words that come tumbling out of your mouth—*sassafras, Mississippi, abracadabra.* And I love soft, flowing words—*luminous, rendezvous, quintessence.*
>
> And there are words that practically bloom when you say them—*daffodil, anemone, hyacinth.*

"What are so wild as words are?"
ROBERT BROWNING

Thunder is a dark word that rumbles in my mind.

The very best words convey meaning, and sound like what they mean. That's why I've always been a little dissatisfied with the word *love*. It's too short, too clipped, to encompass such a big emotion.

But the French have a word for it that works beautifully— *amour!*

Perhaps the journalist with the most enviable reputation for his writing ability is Leslie Whitten, a Washington, DC, reporter, translator of French poetry, and novelist of startling dimensions. In Washington, where Whitten spends most of his time, he has often contributed to Jack Anderson's reports on the odd financing that entangles high officials. His exposés have caused several members of Congress to be defeated and others to retire. But Whitten thinks his best work was a story about Senator Everett Dirksen of Illinois, who died in office. Whitten showed that Dirksen had put one of his aides on the board of a bank with the help of Roy M. Cohn, a former aide to the notorious Senator Joseph McCarthy of Wisconsin.

Now, let us enjoy Whitten's use of words and phrases:*

Lest the new bureaucrat find the complexity of applied logic and Washington "in" knowledge too cumbersome a means of reading between the lines, there is a shorthand method available. It's called Adjectival Gush Analysis.

For example, when a columnist calls anyone "brilliant," "conscientious," "dependable," or "enterprising," you can safely wager your Secrecy Stamp that the subject leaked or is on the verge of leaking a good story to that columnist.

The same *may* be true of lesser adjectives such as "hard-working," "able," "capable," "earnest," "zealous," or the Affability Series: "affable," "amiable," "good-humored," "friendly," "good-hearted," and "kindly."

A column might read, "*Earnest* Rep. Sorghum R. Mediokra (D-Ala.) is locked up in a do-or-die battle for reelection with a man convicted in 1951 of illegal cotton-ginning."

Between the lines, the columnist is telling you that Mediokra leaked the column to him. But the columnist is also saying that the "earnest" Mediokra is a bumbler not much better than the crook he is running against and unworthy of the adjective "effective."

Before you condemn this artfulness, consider who profits by it. It's true that Mediokra gets a cudgel to use on his opponent ("Ah would not stoop to such an attack mah-self, but since this Washington cahlumnist has raised the issha, perhaps mah opponent would cayuh to answer the charge"). But the public also learns something more about the challenger—and gets a chance to vote for the lesser of two evils.

There is one important caveat in Adjectival Gush Analysis. Like everyone else, columnists fear legal suits, even ones they can win. And at trial, fairness is always an important factor.

---

*Reprinted by permission of Leslie H. Whitten, Jr.

By inserting a favorable adjective in an unfavorable story, the columnist may be buying a little libel insurance: "*Affable* Ivan Repressovich hardly seems the kind of federal judge who would molest children, but. . . ." Or, "One of the nation's most *hard-working* anti-Semites is Charlington Goering-Smythe. . . ."

Next, we consider a little-publicized device known as the Non-denial Denial. Let us suppose that Senator Hamlet has just spilled the beans to a columnist about his worst enemy. Hamlet does not want his leak known, however obvious it may appear.

So he asks the columnist to ask him *on the record now* for comment. The columnist asks and Hamlet says "no comment," or "I hate that kind of charge, even against an adversary."

The columnist dutifully prints the denial to steer the curious away from his source. Think about that, new White Housers, the next time your bureaucratic rival is quoted as "huffily denying" or "uttering a sharp 'no comment'" on a story that cuts you off at the jugular.

LESLIE WHITTEN

The Devil works at me. The Devil does not tire;
He floats above me like the air, impalpable.
I gulp him down, I feel him set my lungs on fire
And fill me with desires, endless and culpable.
—Charles Baudelaire

These lines show another Leslie Whitten, escaping his adversary chores as investigative reporter and former Jack Anderson partner by assuming one of his private roles: translator of Baudelaire for literary magazines. Whitten also follows the more traditional pursuits of teacher of creative writing and author of children's books, mysteries, biographies, and political novels. Since graduating magna cum laude from Lehigh University in 1952, Whitten has done many kinds of reporting—for Radio Free Europe, United Press International, the *Washington Post,* the Hearst newspapers, and Jack Anderson—and has been tested in most of the reporter's crucibles: strikes, trials, floods, hurricanes, suicides, murders, and wars. "Used-car hoodlums and militant revolutionaries have threatened me physically, and I was gassed and pushed around by the Chicago cops at the 1968 Democratic National Convention," Whitten said. But Whitten's worst panic came when navy ships put on a show for the press off the coast of Cuba: "One of their missiles got out of whack and was pointed at the ship I was on only a couple of hundred yards away."

Somewhere along his reporter's route, Whitten developed investigative techniques to match his instincts. He broke key elements in the Billie Sol Estes scandal, and his story on an insurance man's gift of a stereo set to President Lyndon Johnson was one of the better stories in the Bobby Baker criminal case. Such work led Jack Anderson to make Whitten his junior partner. When Anderson was away, Whitten broadcast Anderson's daily radio program and ran the Anderson team: three other reporters, two reporter-interns, and two secretaries.

Although Anderson often gave credit to his assistants, his column was sometimes such a mix of teamwork that readers could not always tell who dredged up what. In his years with Anderson, Whitten turned up hidden information in Laos, Cambodia, and Vietnam, and sometimes interviewed Vietcong as they came from battle. He has reported from Israel and from Egypt, and he once searched the waters off uninhabited Florida Keys for treasure buried by the CIA.

Whitten so often reports, or is involved in, conflict or controversy that some of it inevitably turns up in his other life of poet, biographer, and novelist. In his readable novel *The Alchemist,* a flexible attorney and a seductive female official who schemes for the vice presidency are both crooked and surrounded by crooks. At one point, the attorney says that there are "splendid exceptions" among the crooks, cowards, and liars in politics, but . . .

"She belongs in jail," the attorney said flatly.
"They all do," I said quietly.
"They all what?"
"They all belong in jail. All politicians."

Even more subtle is the use of a "beard" in an interview. Imagine that Secretary Schmack wants to destroy his undersecretary. He calls in his personal lawyer and the columnnist. Without ever looking at the columnist, much less shaking his hand, he tells his lawyer—under the flimsiest of lawyer-client privilege—all about the undersecretary's affair with the assistant secretary.

When the story blasts the undersecretary out of his chair and into unemployment, Schmack can swear to him, "Gary, I never met that columnist bastard, much less talked to him. How *could* he have known about you and Hortense?"

WRITER MATCHES HER SUBJECT

Jennifer Koch, a free-lancer whose writing has been published in *City Sports* (San Francisco) and *Sports Illustrated,* wrote the following words to show how gymnasts practiced:*

Randy Besosa's concentration, calculation and extraordinary focus on the apparatus is evidence that he does have everything "figured out." When performing on the floor exercise, he looks directly at the audience—and directly through it.

In the extreme corner of the mat during his floor routine, Besosa gently lifts one leg behind his body, straining to extend it straight towards the ceiling, his upper body slowly pushing forward until it is parallel to the bright blue carpet. His mouth is tight with anticipation of his next tumbling run, and although his eyes are clear and bright, he sees no one.

Besosa's movements are overwhelmingly elegant and obviously designed to please the crowd, but he often appears unaware of where he is and who is watching. Coach Sadao Hamada described Besosa's practices as "efficient"; the intensity displayed in competition is always present in the training room as well. When practicing or learning a difficult trick, he tumbles to the mat dozens of times, the same introspective expression always on his face—no relief, no smile.

Even when the move is exquisitely executed, Besosa meets Hamada's approval with only the briefest of nods before mounting the equipment to repeat his performance. Perhaps the only indication to the crowd that Besosa realizes he has left the practice room is his expression when he has completed his dismount cleanly, with no extra steps—a slow smile that rapidly widens, holds and culminates in a satisfied and exuberant hand clap high over his head.

Hamada, although sympathetic to Besosa's highly individualistic behavior and lack of experience in team situations, says, "He wasn't used to being told what to do and he didn't like it. I gave up on him a few times."

"When I first got to Stanford, I had no sense of competing with somebody else or of representing something. It was a hard transition

---

*Reprinted by permission of Jennifer L. Koch.

for me," Besosa says. "When I came here I did it for myself and had no space for anybody else."

This impatience is evident to anyone watching Besosa just before he begins a routine. He stands perfectly still, almost too still, the slight tensing of his locked arm muscles and the overly focused gaze revealing a not-so-subtle resentment at having to wait his turn.

Even when poised in an effortlessly graceful handstand atop a high bar, Besosa gives the impression that he relinquishes his balance only because the anticipation of the next move has become unbearable for him.

Besosa's next move on the high bar might be one of his original tricks—a straddle one-arm giant, pirouette, full turn gienger in gymnastics terminology, and one of the most difficult release moves attempted on this apparatus. The completion of this particular move consists of a release from the bar, a complete turn in the air and then a regrasp of the equipment.

The move fits in his routine without a single slip or hesitation, but Besosa appears almost to have perfected his timing to induce an added element of sensationalism in the trick. Besosa's hands stretch confidently for the bar, eyes looking upward with an instinctive sense of his position in the air, and very, very rarely do his hands fail to firmly connect and to instantaneously prepare for his next movement. But for the audience, time and time again, there is an involuntary gasp, an intake of breath, shock at the thought that he will not, cannot, find the bar in time. It is then that Besosa re-grasps the high bar.

John Brecher, formerly the city editor of the *Miami Herald,* once worked as a writer in New York for *Newsweek.* In Brecher's following words, he tells how *Newsweek's* writers—and *Time's*—put together their stories:*

Essentially, as a writer at *Newsweek,* I worked Tuesday through Saturday with all the rest of the writers in New York. On Tuesday, the writers—there were six in the foreign department when I was there—got together and decided what stories should be done that week. Then we sent out queries to the reporters in the field, telling them what stories we wanted. There was usually nothing to do the rest of Tuesday, Wednesday and Thursday.

The reporter's files came in on Friday, usually. The writer was always bombarded with a hundred times more information than he or she could possibly include in the story. The idea, however, was all of that information would "inform" the story, so that the writer could put the piece together with a real air of authority.

The trick of *Newsweek* writing is that it looks so simple. Pick up any *Newsweek*—or *Time*—and see how simple the writing appears. That's one thing that makes it so damn difficult.

There is a clear formula as to how a *Newsweek* story is written. Every paragraph should be 20 lines long, and every graf should have one major thought. So say you are given 140 lines to write. The idea is

*Reprinted by permission of John Brecher.

to crystallize your story into seven major thoughts. Each one of those thoughts will be the first sentence of the paragraph. The next sentences will back up that first thought. The last sentence of the paragraph will be a punchy quote.

It's a lot harder to write than it looks. A classic newsmagazine story will give you an enormous amount of information in a small amount of space. Take apart a good newsmagazine piece and you'll find more facts strung together in one sentence than you'll see in a whole newspaper paragraph. There is even a phrase for that at *Newsweek:* a freight-train sentence.

Writing a story for *Newsweek* is an intense experience. You truly are trying to set five pounds of, um, material into a three-pound bag.

When I was there at *Newsweek,* at least, writers closeted themselves in their offices throughout Friday and deep into Friday night. They finally crawled out, pale and emaciated, in the wee hours and handed their copy to their editors.

Unfortunately, the editors had read all of the same files from reporters. So each editor, of course, liked different parts of reporting. So the foreign editor would rewrite my story using the information he liked best from the files; then the managing editor would rewrite the rewrite; and then the editor-in-chief would rewrite that.

No kidding.

Meantime, researchers checked all facts in the story, and inevitably found themselves in the worst position: the reporters, who didn't like the way the story turned out, demanded that the researcher change it; the writers, defending the rewrite of the rewrite to the death, demanded that their stories be untouched.

And then, finally, on Saturday, when all of the kinks had been ironed out and the reporters had been mollified and the facts corrected and the story rewritten just one more time, I'd work with the layout artist to fit my story onto the page—and discover that it had to be cut in half.

Now, aren't you sorry you asked how the sausage was made?

WRITING—OR PLAYING NERF

Danny Pearl sits in his North Adams, Massachusetts, apartment. He is writing a feature article for a newspaper. He is writing it under the lousiest conditions he can.

The desk faces out a bay window. The stereo is an arm's length away. The refrigerator always holds something enticing enough to lure him from his writing.

Danny Pearl does not look over any of his notes before he begins, for fear that he will be able to read or understand only a small fraction; "that would be too discouraging."

Danny Pearl does not even set aside time to write. "It would never work. Instead, I trust in the law of obsession and impulse."

> "Having precise ideas often leads to doing nothing."
>
> PAUL VALÉRY

Pearl writes his lead. He looks at it. He succumbs to an urge to fiddle with it, another no-no. He screws it up.

"With this realization, the obsessive force within me begins to dissipate, and I start to feel a nervous tension that could only mean one thing—the Nerf hoop is calling me."

The Nerf hoop resides in the living room. A breathtakingly simple object, the hoop is Pearl's destination in times of stress; a mental Bahamas, if you will.

Or that is the idea. Stretching, throwing, performing an activity that demands little or no thought. Returning to the desk refreshed, clearheaded, unencumbered by stress.

Danny Pearl starts shooting Nerf hoops. Again and again, he bops the ball into the basket.

Danny Pearl's mind starts counting the baskets. One, two, three. Pretty soon, Danny Pearl is in pursuit of a world record and new personal best in Nerf hoops with a twenty-five-shot limit.

"Finally, I say to myself, 'This is stupid. I am not getting paid to play Nerf basketball, and if I did this in a newsroom I would probably get fired.'

"So, I return to my desk with anger and self-flagellation added to the stress. This is the perfect frame of mind with which to fix a lead."

Pearl makes a couple of the obvious changes that had been so evasive to his mind ten minutes before. Fired by new momentum, he races ahead with the article. Pangs of guilt for his excursion to the living room remain, but the writing flows more easily now.

Danny Pearl leads dual lives as a staff writer and free-lancer in Massachusetts. That is to say, his life is rather muddled. He researches endlessly, sometimes using information found in the course of his "normal" job to write free-lance articles.

When an article idea appears, Pearl sets about to sell it, even though he admits, "Free-lancing is a difficult thing for me, because I am a lazy person. Give me a job on a newspaper and a good beat, and I'll come up with great story ideas. But when it comes to selling story ideas to editors I don't work for, I usually don't do as well."

Pearl has a gift, though, for tying things together and looking at anything as a possible story. He lets his interest and ingenuity lead him. Sometimes he ends up writing on the same subject for two papers. Sometimes he chases after an idea only to find that his writing and the editors' uses for it do not match up too well. But he is always writing stories.

Pearl graduated in 1985 with a degree in communication from Stanford University. He has been a staff writer for the *Indianapolis Star,* the *Transcript* in North Adams, and the *Springfield Union-News.* He has published articles in the *Boston Herald,* the *Boston Globe,* the *Berkshire Business Journal,* and the *Greenfield Recorder.* A long list for someone who describes himself as lazy.

As the stories vary, so does the pay. A check for $100 after three hours of writing may later be counterbalanced by five hours with no pay or eight hours of research and writing for a mere $50.

The conditions under which Pearl must gather information vary also. In a letter from February 1987, Pearl writes:*

> Now I am working on a first-hand account based on events from last night that are already hazy in my memory. The city of North Adams got its first exposure, as it were, to male strip-dancing, and since I have the vice beat, I had to be there. The problem is, the bar had a strict "ladies only" rule, so I had to wear makeup, lipstick, and a wig. I got past the doorman, but none of the women were fooled. Still, they let me stay, and they even let me take their pictures. My only fear is that the police will seize my film to bust the poor fellow who had his loincloth ripped off by some overenthusiastic vixens in the front row. We have strict laws about such things here in Massachusetts.

While things are not always this bizarre, Pearl does perform a daily juggling act with angry officials, sticky court cases, note trading with other reporters, and even threats to his person by scary people named "Rocko."

All this makes for a career resembling a roller coaster, but Pearl is of a type that feeds on incident. As with any line of work that calls for self-motivation and initiative, a career in journalism demands an enormous amount of self-control. Why, Pearl even provides himself with guidelines for knowing when the Nerf hoop is too close to becoming a crutch:

1. If he is heading for the living room when faced with a word he can't spell.
2. If the letters on his computer screen begin to resemble bouncing or rolling Nerf balls.
3. If he searches for the ball for an entire day, and if it is not found he calls in sick.

Exercises

1. List the five most beautiful or most rambunctious words you know. Turn in your list to the instructor at the next class meeting.

2. Try to match the length of Jennifer Koch's writing on the gymnast by watching and writing about any male or female while he or she is practicing any sport. It is difficult to write as much as Koch did, but this exercise may help you a bit in stretching your writing to magazine length (many newspaper feature writers are writing at almost magazine length).

3. Using Danny Pearl's writing as an example, think and write of the various methods that allow you to procrastinate about your writing for classes. Limit this exercise to two typed pages.

---

*Reprinted by permission of Danny Pearl.

ONE

UNDERSTANDING WRITERS AND EDITORS

America is par excellence *the land of magazines.*

FREDERICK LEWIS ALLEN

I n a 1982, *New York Times Magazine* article on the *Atlantic* magazine, Diane McWhorter wrote:

> Meanwhile, in response to the growing sophistication and immediacy of television journalism, newspapers of the 1970's turned into daily magazines, with fat feature sections and slick designs; their long, investigative pieces were not simple reactions to events, but magazine-like analyses of the forces behind the news. Papers like *The Wall Street Journal* and *The New York Times* assumed the national editorial mandate that was once reserved for weeklies and monthlies.

Although her observation was not quite true in 1982—only most of the metropolitan papers had adopted the role formerly played by magazines—some medium-sized newspapers are beginning to publish magazinelike articles. Grant Dillman, formerly bureau chief at the United Press International headquarters in Washington, DC, said recently, "At least 25 percent of our effort now goes into in-depth, magazine-type stories." Many daily newspapers subscribe to UPI.

Addressing about thirty professional newspaper reporters and editors in February 1982, one speaker assumed that they knew about the magazine-like articles appearing in newspapers. Unfortunately, not *one* journalist there had ever heard of magazining newspapers. One reporter stood up and said, "I don't write for magazines. I'm a *newspaperman.*" Then he sat down, no doubt pleased with himself.

Like many other journalists and journalism students, these reporters and editors are affected by these facts:

In the *Syracuse Herald-Journal,* readers can find in almost any issue at least one or two stories that run at least 3,000 words.

In almost every issue of the *New York Times,* there are at least two or three stories that run more than 3,000 words.

The method by which the *Wall Street Journal* has accumulated its wide circulation has been to publish three long stories daily beginning on the front page, all of which are written and edited carefully.

Residents of Seattle saw in a Sunday edition of the *Seattle Post-Intelligencer* a front-page headline that clearly illustrates what is happening: "FOUR SUNDAY MAGAZINES IN TODAY'S PI."

David Shaw of the *Los Angeles Times* writes not five or six stories a day but eight stories a year. His stories usually run at least 5,000 words, and nearly all of them are gathered through his travels over most of the United States. Other *Los Angeles Times* reporters also write about eight or nine stories a year.

To write a 5,000-word story about then-senator Pete Wilson, Keith Love of the *Los Angeles Times* observed Wilson five times in five different settings. For example, he observed Wilson singing a solo at a campaign stop, singing along with a car radio, and on and on. Love also interviewed nine people who knew Wilson; most of the sources supported Wilson, but some did not.

To illustrate what is and has been happening, here is the beginning of a front-page story in the *Los Angeles Times.* It runs more than 3,000 words.

COMMENTS

Observe especially how the first sentence begins: the pace is almost leisurely, compared with the way feature writers once wrote their stories. Robert Jones feels no pressure from editors to write a captivating first sentence.

Readers know that the writer is promising them a good, serious story. The beginning of this story lays a foundation for a highly readable long feature.

Notice that the one-sentence paragraph common in traditional newspaper stories no longer obtains.

STORY

By Robert A. Jones, Times Staff Writer

CEDAR RAPIDS, Iowa—About 250 persons crowded into the Holiday Inn here recently for the annual convention of Iowans for Life. They wore tiny embroidered roses on their collars, offered prayers for the speedy end to legalized abortions, and then broke into small groups for a series of workshops. One of the most popular was titled, "Fetal Pain."

"We now know that the fetus develops the mechanism to feel pain early in the pregnancy," Dr. Robert Hedges, an obstetrician and medical adviser to Iowans for Life, told the workshop attendees. "That mechanism involves skin receptors, a spinal column and the thalamus of the brain. All of these become functional somewhere between eight and 13 weeks after conception."

As Hedges flashed slides of. . . .

Had you read this entire story, you probably would have said that the writer is a wonderful fashioner of stories. Wait! Think of the editor (whose name you will never know). The *Los Angeles Times* has some great editors, and you must credit these unknown people, along with the writers they guide, for crafting good stories.

MAGAZINING OF NEWSPAPERS

"There are two motives for reading; one, that you enjoy it; the other, that you can boast about it."

BERTRAND RUSSELL

The public's desire for printed news has not been diminished by the success of television's incursions into territory once claimed by newspapers and magazines. Some observers claim that television actually whets the viewers' appetites for more news. Since 1950, the number of daily newspapers published in the United States has lost much ground. These dailies try to do in their pages what television cannot do—to offer readers tightly written stories that cover subjects in depth, using formats that enable readers to choose from among many different kinds of stories in the order of their interest and at the time of their choosing. No matter how it tries, television will never be able to duplicate these functions. Viewers will always have to watch news stories in the order the program uses for presenting them, and until every home has a video recorder, they will have to watch the programs at times chosen by the stations.

The Rise of the Feature Story

Both suburban and metropolitan newspapers have upgraded the feature story as they attempt to keep up with television magazines.

What is the difference between a news reporter and a feature writer? One anecdote illustrates the point. A young woman who planned to leave a small newspaper asked her managing editor for a reference. He wrote one praising her intelligence, diligence, and warmth, and added this sentence: "She has a wonderful flair for feature writing, and she has been working hard on her news reporting and writing." Obviously, the managing editor was also saying that she had a long way to go before her ability to gather and report news would match her feature-writing ability.

Like a good many who work for newspapers, this young woman was a natural feature writer, although editors normally seek the writer who can blend a feature touch with reportorial ability. Feature writers are becoming more prominent with time, particularly as a result of the great interest among young newspaper staffers in investigative reporting, which got a new impetus during the reporting of the Watergate scandal. As Jim Reed of the *Topeka Daily Capital* said, "any news story—a fire, an automobile accident in which someone dies, an act of heroism—is used regularly. Good feature stories are *always* wanted. Unusual hobbies, success stories, inventions, interviews, personality stories, human interest stories—all can be used." This statement keynotes the trend among newspapers.

Another change in newspapers that has fostered feature writing is the demise of the "Women's Page" or "Society" sections. In their place have risen sections with names like "Style," "Living," and "View." These pages are generally filled with feature stories that are of interest to both sexes. As a result, one newspaper's feature editor noted that many of her readers are men, and that men today are more interested in feature writing than they ever have been. Features are no longer regarded by newspaper professionals as the "soft" news stories.

Journalists are also finding feature writing more attractive because it provides greater freedom of style than is found in straight-news reporting. The distinction between the two is obvious, as this excerpt from a feature article illustrates:

> When Herman O. Tolson first came to town, the restrooms at the fairgrounds were marked "white" and "colored."
>
> That was in the mid-1960s. The signs are gone now. Mexico, Missouri, has changed quite a bit since then, especially for a town that calls itself the capital of "Little Dixie"—a band of counties through the heart of central Missouri that traditionally have considered themselves a part of the South.
>
> The biggest sign of change is Tolson himself. The forty-four-year-old assistant high school principal and ordained Baptist minister became the town's first black mayor this month. . . .

If this same story had been written in straight-news style, it might have begun like this: Herman O. Tolson, 44, this month became the first black mayor of Mexico, Missouri. A former assistant high school principal and ordained Baptist minister, Tolson has been a resident since the mid-1960s. . . .

Even when the news is sad, writers may often lure their readers with a quiet note instead of straight reportage:

> The Post Office manager sat in his cubicle munching on a sandwich, a solitary figure behind a row of wickets marked "closed."
>
> Where is everybody? he was asked.
>
> "They're all sick—again," he said.
>
> When will they get well?
>
> "They're all supposed to recover tomorrow," he said. "But who knows how long they'll stay well."
>
> The illness that periodically infects this city's 4,000 residents. . . .

Certainly, the writer who has a feature touch can see the distinction between this kind of writing and the kind that opens most news stories.

THE MAGAZINES CHANGE

The great philosopher Immanuel Kant is a striking example of how intellectuals can become preoccupied with things of the mind. After considerable internal debate, Kant decided to get married. However, when he called at the young lady's house, he found to his intense disappointment that she had left town—twenty years ago.

Unfortunately, Kant was unaware of many important changes that had occurred as years passed. Likewise, over the decades magazines have gone through a significant transformation that should not be overlooked. First, we must recognize *how* the magazine world has changed during the past thirty-five years. The fact that it *has* changed is indicated by the laments of some veteran writers who say that the article market has shrunk dangerously. They maintain that the deaths of some leading magazines and the trend among others to hire staff writers who work full-time for a magazine rather than relying on independent free-lancers has reduced opportunities for the independent writer.

They argue persuasively, and in a sense they are right. But to consider only their lamentations is to misunderstand what has happened, and is happening, in the world of magazines. In his valuable history of American magazines, John Tebbel points out that during the decade of the 1960s, a total of 162 periodicals disappeared through sale, merger, or suspension, but 676 new magazines appeared.*

This growth does not mean that there has been an increase in free-lance opportunities. The article market is quite different today from what it was in the fifties. The key difference is that the number of general magazines has decreased significantly and the number of special-interest publications has increased significantly. Most of the longer-lived special-interest magazines pay writers more than they once did, and many of the new ones pay more than the most openhanded publications in their fields paid ten or twenty years ago. But the old-time free-lancers were accustomed to dealing with a dozen *general* magazines, and they were often able to work up an article that might be published in any one of half a dozen of them if their first choices turned them down. Now they find so few general magazines left that their range is restricted and their margin for error is slender to the point of invisibility.

To understand what has happened in the magazine world, it is necessary to look again at the role of television. To the extent that it is an *information* medium, television is primarily useful in reporting spot events. As we have seen, though, television magazines are usurping functions that once belonged almost exclusively to the newspaper. This usurpation has pushed many newspapers into assuming part of a function that was once almost exclusively the magazine's—reporting at length and sometimes in depth. Although most newspapers continue to provide a startling range of information on many subjects, mostly in short items, many are giving at least a few reporters the leisure to pursue stories in depth and to write in the fluid style of magazines. The result has been turbulence in the magazine world.

Since radio, television, and newspapers are primarily general media that aim at the broadest possible audience, the magazines most affected by them are the general magazines. It is not at all surprising, then, that the mass-circulation general magazines suffered first, and most, from the change in the

---

*John Tebbel, *The American Magazine: A Compact History* (New York: Hawthorn Books, 1969), p. 249.

roles of the mass media brought on by television. *Collier's,* long one of the most popular weeklies, moved to fortnightly, then died. Several monthlies—notably *American Magazine, Woman's Home Companion,* and *Liberty*—also died.

Magazines for Special Interests

Author James A. Michener believes that his literary career stands as a great tribute to the American way of life, explaining:

> Because I did well in school, I received scholarships and fellowships, and ultimately attended nine of the world's best colleges and universities, always at public expense. If I'd been born in a country with a caste system, I might never have been discovered and would have spent my life counting gasoline drums. I was the product of America's dedication to free public education.
>
> Some years ago a tax man calculated that America had spent about $11,000 educating me and had, at that time, taken back in taxes upon books, plays and television shows I had initiated more than $68 million. Not from me personally, you understand, but from the flow of money made possible by my works. That is the splendid gamble made by free societies.

The magazine industry is another example of the workings of a free society. Only the most competitive, well-managed magazines can succeed. In contrast to the general nature of the magazines that have died during the past two decades, the successful magazines that grew up during this period emphasize special interests and seek particular audiences—*Sports Illustrated, American Heritage, Horizon, TV Guide,* and others, including dozens of "city" magazines like *New Orleans, San Francisco, Dallas, Atlanta, Milwaukee,* and *New York.*

One of the most convincing illustrations of the need to address a special audience was provided by *Rolling Stone.* Created with a borrowed $7,000 by twenty-one-year-old Jann Wenner, it began as a rock magazine in 1967. Dozens of magazines had discovered rock and were covering it then. But Wenner and his young staff soon proved that their belief that music *was* the youthful counterculture, combined with their ability to speak to a youthful audience in familiar and convincing terms, could make *Rolling Stone* a success. In 1991, *Rolling Stone's* circulation was 1,150,000.

And, of course, hundreds of religious, occupational, fraternal, farming, business, and professional magazines were born during the same period. In his excellent book *Magazines for Millions,* James L. Ford complains that the consumer publications are given enormous attention while the thousands of specialized publications are "produced by an enthusiastic army of 100,000 men and women."* He points out that there are nearly 1,700 magazines

---

*James L. Ford, *Magazines for Millions: The Story of Specialized Publications* (Carbondale, IL: Southern Illinois University Press, 1969), p. 4.

in religious publishing alone, and perhaps as many as 17,000 company publications.

Some of these specialty publications have become too specialized for almost any audience. A new magazine, launched in Tokyo, is being published by Yasuhiro Nakasone, Japan's former prime minister. Strangely, the magazine is all about Nakasone: his haiku poems, his painting, his philosophy and thoughts, and gossip about the Nakasone household (provided by his wife). But readers get more than that. One issue contained a two-page spread on the in-flight menu offered during one of Nakasone's trips—complete with four full-color pictures of food trays.

Will this magazine find an audience? Although many specialty magazines are launched each year, most do not last a decade. *Divorce, The Magazine for People Starting Over,* is one such example. After introducing the magazine at a glamorous New York press conference, the publisher spent over $250,000 within one year, during which time the magazine failed. Media experts say that divorce was simply a poor topic for a magazine.

Of course, every generalization is undermined by at least one glaring exception. In this case, it's *People* magazine, begun by Time-Life, Inc., in 1974. If *People* specializes in anything, it has to be celebrity journalism, but it also devotes half of its pages to stories about interesting but unknown personalities. Its stories are superficial, but the magazine's success is not. It began with a remarkable starting circulation of 1 million and in five years boosted that figure to a total circulation of 18.3 million. Its audience is 42 percent male and 58 percent female, a rare distribution in magazine readerships, which usually are dominated by one sex or the other.

Part of the key to *People's* success has been its marketing strategy. About 85 percent of its circulation is single-copy sales through grocery stores, drugstores, or convenience chains. The shift away from reliance on mail circulation was a deliberate strategy developed to combat the 400 percent increase in second-class postage rates that occurred between 1970 and 1974. It was this increase that shrank the size of many magazines and forced others, such as *Look* and *Life,* to fold. (*Life* has been revived.)

In conclusion, it is clear that both magazines and newspapers are responding to external forces that are beyond their control. Yet they are surviving through a long process of adaptation that is changing both their appearance and content. How these changes affect the people who write the newspapers and magazines is a subject this book will discuss in detail in subsequent sections.

If writers yearn to write for national magazines, they must study them carefully. Some of the most talented writers fail. Paradoxically, this is *because* they are so talented. Knowing that they can put one word after another attractively, they stint on research and lean much too heavily on writing, which makes it mere writing. Some of their plodding contemporaries, who recognize the limits of their own talents, are more likely to succeed because they dig for facts, insights, and ideas.

Perhaps one who digs deeper than anyone else is David Halberstam. Here, we present Halberstam's words, then his profile:*

The only thing I've ever been is a reporter and it's all I aspire to be. A. J. Liebling was once asked the secret of his success and he said, "I write faster than those who write better, and I write better than those who write faster." I've amended it slightly: I work harder than people who are smarter and I'm smarter than people who work harder. But in both, I never want anyone to outwork me.

You want a certain density in what you write, and so you keep interviewing until you get it. There are no short cuts. When you're there, you know it. I tell young writers to be dogged, to keep going back to their interviewees for second and third and fourth and fifth interviews. The last question I ask everyone I see is, "Who else should I see?"

You go to see the smaller people first, so that when you see the larger people you are better informed and your questions are better. Let's say, for example, that the issue was CBS cutting back the second special report on Watergate. If I just called up the principal figures cold, they might stonewall me. But if I went to see them, having already done eight or nine interviews, and asked very specific questions, mentioning names and incidents, it encouraged candor immensely. Doing your homework is crucial. You talk in a way that rekindles their memo-

---

*Reprinted by permission of David Halberstam.

DAVID HALBERSTAM

David Halberstam is a reporter accustomed to the idea that people in power do not like him. Moreover, it does not seem to bother him much. He has candidly referred to the press as a "flexible instrument with self-evident mechanical weaknesses which favor the strong against the weak, the in against the out, the traditional against the new," and he has described journalism as a profession in which "tartness, skepticism, irreverence, fatalism are much more valued . . . than is open liberalism."

A highly successful and exceedingly prolific reporter and writer of books, Halberstam is certainly qualified to say that American reporters are "more alienated and skeptical than many of the men they cover." On graduating from Harvard, Halberstam worked for two years as a reporter for the *West Point Daily Times Leader* in West Point, Mississippi, one of the smallest newspapers anywhere. He spent the next five years at the

Nashville Tennesseean before James Reston, then the Washington bureau chief of the *New York Times,* lured him to Washington.

When Halberstam initially flopped there, Reston suggested that he needed "a hotter climate and darker people." Halberstam fared much better in the Congo, winning a Page One award for his eyewitness accounts of fighting. The *Times* then transferred him to Saigon, and he probed so relentlessly into official intrigue there that the struggle for Vietnam became known as "Halberstam's War." Many of his stories contradicted the reports of U.S. officials. As he stated in an *Esquire* article, "I was profoundly depressed about the war; at best it was hopelessly stalemated and I had a strong sense that we were, in fact, losing and that no one in Saigon knew we were losing, which was by itself a very dangerous combination." Later, when it became clear that Halberstam had been right all along, he won a Pulitzer Prize in reporting.

ries, and they realize you know, you understand. Often you get information by giving information.

I talk to everybody. I don't just see the generals—what I call the four-star interviews where everything is set up for you. I start with the privates so when I get up to the top, I know what I'm talking about.

But when you consider the traveling, the interviewing, it's really physical labor. You have to love doing it. There has to be the thrill you get when you're interviewing someone and you lock in some piece of critical information. It remains after all these years exhilarating and exhausting. There is no short cut to legwork. Sometimes I felt just like Willy Loman in "Death of a Salesman," waking up in strange motels and really having to wonder for a minute where I was.

WRITER-EDITOR RELATIONSHIPS

Columnist Don Freeman remembered:

Once I interviewed the great songwriter Irving Berlin. "Mr. Berlin," I began, "is there a question that you'd like to be asked?"

"Young man," replied Berlin, "there *is* one: 'What do you think of the many songs you've written that did *not* become hits?' The answer is: I still think they're wonderful."

Freeman's words should comfort the many writers who send articles to magazines only to have them sent back with a polite note. On any given workday, professional and amateur writers and reporters produce about

At this time, Halberstam was far more successful as a reporter than as an author. None of his first four books was very memorable. However, he was on his money-strewn way in 1972 with the publication of *The Best and the Brightest*.

Halberstam has since become known for his technique of interviewing someone again and again, looking not only for what the interviewee knows but also for facts that only Halberstam wants to know. After years of confronting mound after mound of notes, books, magazines, and newspapers bearing any relation to his subject, Halberstam will produce a huge manuscript at which an editor will sigh, and sigh again. After cutting page after page for nearly forever, the editor will then fuse the remaining pages into a wonderful book and have it published.

After seven years of research and writing, Halberstam's *The Powers That Be* was brought out by Alfred A. Knopf, Inc., in 1979. In keeping with his propensity for producing unwieldy

manuscripts, Halberstam thanked Charles Elliott in the Acknowledgments for taking "an immense and complicated manuscript and help[ing] fuse it together." Richard Rovere of the *New York Times Book Review* called the book a "prodigy of research and of tendentious but sharply focused narrative and analysis" that "will remain stirring history."

Although Halberstam has referred to his profession as one in which "even the best reporters can only react," it is clear that he has great respect not only for journalists but also for those who appreciate the work that journalists do. Explaining why John F. Kennedy was so popular with reporters, Halberstam stated: "In part they got along unusually well with Jack Kennedy not so much because he was handsome or served them good food but because he understood them and their work . . . and he could understand why a man who had other professional possibilities in his life might instead choose to be a journalist."

2,000 magazine articles. In any given year, they write at least one-half million articles. From this mass of manuscripts, only about 5 percent will ever be published—most written by professional writers. The writers of the other 95 percent will receive rejection slips ("Unsuited to our present needs") or, if they are lucky, notes of regret from an editor ("Sorry, this didn't quite make it"). Many of the losers assume that article writing is a closed corporation.

The truth is that magazine editors *do* want, need, and seek new writers. Most issues are released with perhaps one excellent article, five others that are reasonably good, two or three that are competent at best, and usually one or two that got into the magazine simply because nothing better was available. To imagine an editor rejecting the work of a writer solely because he or she is an amateur is to imagine a prospector kicking away a gold nugget because he is searching for silver.

Magazines cannot be published unless, month after month, the editors are able to count on their authors' meeting deadlines with articles coming in at the prescribed length. A typical case is described by a series of letters from an editor to an author who had suggested writing an article on how bombers are used to fight fires. The first letter ran:

> Thank you for your outline, "Here Come the Flying Fire Engines." This sounds like an interesting story, but I wonder if you could give me a little information about it? Do you suppose you could arrange to ride in one of the bombers fighting an actual fire, or at least on a trial run? I have an idea that an actual experience such as this would provide you with usable color and details. Could you also spend some time with a group of the pilots at their base, in an effort to dig up anecdotal material about actual fire fighting? Could you get a quote for me, either on or off the record, from the top fire authority in California, attesting to the efficacy of this new method of fighting fires? Before we go all out in saying that this is the most effective method of forest fire fighting yet developed, I should like to be sure that top authorities agree with us. If you can provide this extra information, I feel there is a good chance that I can give you a go-ahead with the piece.

The author replied by letter that he could provide the kind of reportage and detail the editor wanted. The next letter from the editor ran:

> Our Washington Office has obtained permission for you to fly on one of the fire-fighting jobs. Now that this has been cleared, I hope you will go ahead with the story. We are glad to guarantee you $250 for submitting a manuscript and we shall of course pay your expenses. The piece seems to be shaping up in most promising fashion. I hope you will set yourself to producing the most complete and definitive article that could possibly be done. Please feel free to travel to any places where you think you can dig up additional material. I would concentrate on California until you had everything available there, and by that time you ought to know where else you should go. Remember that it is anecdotal material which we must have—little stories of action, drama and characterization. There can't be too many of them.

The author plunged into the research and writing, submitted the article, and received this letter:

> You have certainly done a big and careful research job on this subject, amassing an impressive amount of material. I am sure it is the most comprehensive job that has ever been done on the subject. In its present form, however, the manuscript is too long. And you need to be more selective. A good deal should be cut out of the piece; much of what remains should be sharpened up, made more dramatic. You have got to keep the reader keenly interested in every paragraph from beginning to end.
>
> I have taken the liberty of making a number of suggested deletions and changes on the manuscript—in a very rough way—which may be useful to you in rewriting. I feel sure that, when you read the article over again in the light of these suggestions, you will see how much it can be improved by general tightening and specific heightening of effect. My pencil markings, of course, are meant as suggestions for revision, not as hard-and-fast editing changes. Their main purpose is to help the piece move faster from your opening lead up to your dramatic conclusion.
>
> In that conclusion, incidentally, would it not be possible for you to introduce yourself as a passenger in the scout plane? Or is that not for publication? If you could describe your own emotions when flying over a fire, as well as the conversation of the fire boss, I am sure the reader would get a greater sense of participation. This section must be dramatic and memorable—it is what the whole article builds up to. I hope you will make it just as vivid as possible.

How Editors Work

Here is Erin Cooperrider of *Sunset* magazine explaining how editors labor:

> The editing process at *Sunset* is best characterized by the word *thorough*. The department editor of food, travel, garden, or building is the first to see a story after the writer is finished with it. This first review gives the writer a chance to take care of any of the department editor's questions and problems before he or she files the story.
>
> Filing the story means that the layout is finished, the photographs (if there are any) are printed, and the copy has been approved by the department editor. The writer turns in all of the above to the production department and sends the electronic copy file to be "filed." The writer will also send out "checking copy" at this time to people who have been involved with the story so that they can check the copy for accuracy.
>
> After being reviewed by the managing editor, each story gets a first and second read by a copy editor. Copy editors often have additional questions for the writer, and many copy editors sit down with the writer and discuss any changes they have made in the story as a matter of course. One of the senior copy editors usually does the second read. The story then goes to the editor for headlining. Then pro-

duction pages the story (composes text and captions into formatted pages) and transmits the composed electronic file to the typesetter for page proofs.

The writer gets the page proof back for a last reading, makes any final changes, and signs it off. The final page proof of every story makes the same last rounds: writer, department editor, copy editor, editor, production for final formatting.

In the editing process at *Sunset* every story is read at least five times by at least four different editors, excluding the writer, and proofread at least twice by the production staff. However, each writer has ultimate responsibility for the accuracy of the story when it appears in its final form in the magazine.

Editor Versus Writer

A young man who regularly wrote for a magazine on sailing finally became incensed after the editors had made many small changes in one of his articles and published the changed version without consulting him. He sent a long letter to the editor in chief, complaining:

> The manuscript of "Instructive Mistakes" begins: "Experience," said Oscar Wilde, "is the name everyone gives to their mistakes." The printed article begins: "Experience," said Oscar Wilde, ". . . is merely the name men give to their mistakes."
>
> First, how can a professional editor possibly change a direct quotation taken from the works of an author as famous as Oscar Wilde? The quotation is taken from Wilde's *Lady Windermere's Fan*, Act III. Second, the published quotation is punctuated incorrectly. Ellipses are correct only if some part of the quotation has been left out; Wilde's complete sentence is in my manuscript. Third, the meaning has been subtly changed; and fourth, the new quote is flatter than Wilde's original.
>
> For a second example, in my June article on the Class Racing Committee, the manuscript paragraph on Bill Winters began: "Bill Winters, gold medal crew for John Benson at the Olympics last summer, will be. . . ." Someone changed that sentence to: "Bill Winters gold medal Soling crew for John Benson in the Olympics last summer and in FDs in 1976, will be. . . ." The structure of that sentence isn't parallel and is therefore confusing. The most obvious interpretation of the sentence is that Benson also won a gold medal in 1976, which is not correct.

This letter illustrates a fairly typical problem in writer-editor relations. After citing these changes, the writer mentioned another that disturbed him and then added: "I won't bother you with further examples of this sort, but there have been about half a dozen similar changes that alter the thrust of what I am trying to say." Many writers send letters reciting in paralyzing detail how their works have been "butchered." At least a few fail to add, as this writer did, "I'm not saying that my writing doesn't need any editing." Many *do* doubt that their writing needs editing.

This particular author had reason to complain: his arguments are valid.

> "The relation of the editor to the writer is the same as that of the knife to the throat."
>
> ANONYMOUS

And he is also correct about another change in the article entitled "Instructive Mistakes." The original sentence read: "But if you will make the right kind of mistakes, and lots of them, you will gain valuable experience which will sharpen your racing skills." An editor had changed it to: "But if you make the 'right' kind of mistakes, you will gain valuable experience which will sharpen your racing skills." The quotation marks around "right" surely seemed to some readers pretentious; it is condescending to point out to them that "right" should not be defined in its usual sense.

The editor's worst error was failing to clear these changes with the writer before publication. The American Society of Journalists and Authors states:

> Editors may correct or delete copy for purposes of style, grammar, conciseness, or arrangement, but may not change the intent or sense without the writer's permission.

In Defense of the Editor

All editing, bad as it can be at times, is based on certain practices, some laudable, others indefensible.

First, consider the Oscar Wilde quotation. The writer was correct in arguing that the exact quotation should have been left as he had written it, but the editor who made the change had followed a laudable practice: checking on the writer to make certain that the quotation was accurate. Unfortunately, like many other writers, Wilde often used an adage in one form in one piece of writing and in a slightly different form in another. The writer quoted from one of Wilde's works, the editor quoted from another. Praise to the editor for taking the trouble to check—damnation to him for checking the wrong source!

Next, the editor added information to the sentence about Bill Winters. While this is sometimes a good practice (depending on the length of the sentence and the amount of information it already includes), it was wrong in this instance because the added information made the sentence confusing.

Third, the editor was trying to clarify meaning when he put quotation marks around "right"—trying to make certain that readers would not misunderstand or be confused. The change the editor made did ensure clarity; surely no reader could misunderstand "right" in quotation marks. In this case again, though, the writer was correct; the condescending tone in those quotation marks made clarity for every reader too expensive.

As for the editor's failure to check changes with the writer, many editors argue that they seldom have time to check small corrections with writers who live some distance away—especially because so many writers miss deadlines. Besides, some editors think that most writers are far too possessive about every word they have written and every bit of punctuation they have used and become defensive about *any* change. Telling them about minor changes often leads to endless arguments over small incidents. This time, however, the writer was indeed correct once again; he was not unreasonable about most changes that the editor made.

Rejecting an Article

Both to demonstrate that writers are not always right and to show other functions of magazine editors, let us examine an instance in which an editor encouraged a talented young free-lancer, Michael Pollock, to write an article. Pollock had sent the editor a query, a short article proposal submitted to discern whether or not a subject that a writer wants to undertake might fit an editor's needs; query writing is a common and useful practice. Queries save time for both writer and editor. If the writer's queries in a subject fail to interest any editor, the writer can drop the project without wasting further work. An editor who is flooded with manuscripts can decide quickly from a well-written query whether or not a subject may be worthwhile. That is the theory; sometimes it backfires.

In this case, although the editor did not promise to buy and publish the article (editors are usually careful not to make such promises), he replied that he would like to consider it. Pollock did his research and wrote the article carefully—no doubt counting the cash in his imagination while he worked—and mailed it. The editor rejected it.

There are scores of reasons to respond positively to a query and then to reject the article. This time, the editor was attracted by the query, which began:

> A young woman is reading from a hand-scrawled paragraph to others sitting around a table:
> "I'm walking on a beach and I see the wreckage of a car or something . . . twisted metal and a mangled body inside. Then I see two other people standing by the wreck, and they're laughing at the body."
> The woman is a participant in a Jungian dream workshop. . . .

The letter went on to provide a brief description of the workshop, which was led by a social worker who lived in the city where the magazine was published. The writer made it clear that the workshop leader was not a psychologist or psychiatrist—and that some of the five hundred area residents who had taken the course were not convinced that it worked. The writer pointed out that many participants had gone on to more advanced workshops and into psychiatric treatment. The writer also suggested that some of the pictures drawn by workshop participants to describe their dreams might be published with the article.

So far, it sounds interesting. But the article the editor received began:

> "I've spent more than half a century investigating natural symbols, and I've concluded that dreams are not stupid and meaningless. On the contrary, they provide the most interesting information for those who take the trouble to understand their symbols."
> These are the words of Swiss psychologist Carl G. Jung. When he died in 1961, he bequeathed to the world a method of delving into the unconscious mind through dream analysis.
> But until a few years ago, few nonprofessionals cared. Now things have changed, perhaps for the same reasons which fostered movements such as. . . .

The contrast between the beginning of the query and the beginning of the article suggests one reason for the rejection: the query is more readable than the article. Although magazine articles can begin at a more leisurely pace than newspaper features, those written for city magazines should not begin with a general statement that only gradually comes to the point or the local angle.

The lead could have been changed, but the writer could not change another aspect of the story that he had mentioned in the query but that seemed like a real problem area: some participants had considered the dream-analysis workshop a failure. If the social worker were a recognized authority, the article might have been worth publishing nonetheless; he was, however, an amateur.

Often editors think and hope that a writer will be able to revise an article successfully. But what if the revision does not work? If the editor promises to pay the writer a "kill fee"—a guaranteed sum whether the article is eventually used or not—it may strain the editorial budget. If payment is not promised, how much additional work can the editor ask the writer to do on speculation? In either instance, continuing to work with a writer who may not satisfactorily complete an article will eat into the time that the editor might devote to more promising articles. All editors complain that hours and days are too short for everything they have to do, and wasting time can only result in strained relations.

An Editor-Writer Reversal

For another view of the editor-writer relationship, consider the situation at *Fortune* magazine. Some of the editors at *Fortune*, like many other editors, prefer to be staff writers, even though they make less money, because most staff writers must turn in only four or five articles a year. During the rest of the time, they can free-lance. One basic problem emerges: staff writers must face the story editor after they submit their articles. Several years ago, the managing editor of *Fortune* decided to step down to become a staff writer. Although he was an excellent writer, he had to rewrite his own articles. As with most writers—good or bad—the succeeding drafts were better than the originals he had submitted.

For twenty years, Ken Purdy was an editor and a writer. He worked as a reporter for three newspapers and an editor of one, an associate editor of *Look* magazine and two other magazines, managing editor of one magazine, an editorial consultant to two magazines, and an editor in chief of four magazines. During these years, he was also a free-lancer who sold short stories and articles to twenty-odd magazines, and he published two books. Because he had extensive experience as a writer and as an editor, he said the following:

> The relationship between editor and writer is, now and then, a happy one. Now and then, indeed. A warm, pleasant, long-standing relationship between an editor and a writer is a rarity. By the very nature of things, it must be. These two people, the editor and the writer, do not begin to understand each other.

WHY MAGAZINES NEED EDITORS

Editors best serve their writers when they represent the reader, so the best editors try to ask questions readers might ask: Why is this point made at the beginning of this paragraph when it might better round off the paragraph by ending it? Why don't you explain where Taiwan is? Why is all this garble included about African-American English when most readers—including African Americans—don't understand what it's about? When all this historical stuff is put together, it becomes so tedious that the reader will stop reading; why not change it by breaking it here, then end with the rest of the historical stuff, plus a better ending?

Editors must have an engineer's eye for the structure of an article. They often have to read an article many times to understand what the writer is attempting to do. When an editor sees what a writer is trying for, the editor should explain to the writer how to reassemble the article. In some cases, the editor should actually reassemble the article—not try to explain in words how to do it.

Many writers are convinced that copy editors exist only to make the writer's life difficult and his or her prose unreadable. Yet the perceptive editor will grasp the essence of an article and improve it. One news magazine editor encountered this line in an article: "Winston Churchill, half British, half American. . . ." He demonstrated his understanding of the enigma of Churchill with a few strokes of his pencil, so that the line read, "Winston Churchill, wholly British, half American. . . ."

It is also true that the copy editor, whose value rests in the fresh eye given to an article, is crippled when he or she attacks flabby writing. Cutting heavily into several ballooning sentences almost invariably halts the flow of the writing and makes sentences too choppy or too decisive. The editor may recognize the failing but simply be powerless to do much about it. After all, the writer has all the information; the editor (who in this circumstance has become a rewrite person) seldom knows enough about the subject to add the fact-filled clauses and phrases that make writing rhythmic. Correcting this failing usually requires that the editor and writer work together.

WHY NEWSPAPERS NEED EDITORS

Unfortunately, most newspapers have no editors who have the painstaking time needed to put together an excellent story from mediocre writing. In fact, many of them have been trained to edit, say, a ten-page story in half an hour.

For example, read the attached story, which is both excellent and deplorable. This story is about Sissy Spacek, a movie star. Observe how the writer has chosen good quotations but placed them near the end of the story. Notice especially the number of comments and questions inserted. (Because this piece was distributed to many newspapers by the Associated Press, there are no long paragraphs.)

COMMENTS

In a truck? Why? I don't know much about her, but I know she's rich because she's a movie star. A *truck*? And the verb "rolls," which doesn't match the sentence's subject, "Spacek and family," is distracting.

Now she's speaking of mattresses. I guess she's spent all her money. If she says "spreadin'," wouldn't she also say "thinkin'"?

Oh, she could have flown. That means she still has money. The question is still there: Why a truck?

Oh, now I see: "suburban-style truck." If the writer had written that earlier, I (and my fellow-readers) would have understood.

Another grammatical error: it's Spacek and Fisk, not the coffee, who is up every day by 6:30.

Now I've finished reading ten paragraphs and the writer has never described Spacek. I know, there's a picture of her. That tells me very little—just a generalized clue to what she looks like. How does she walk and gesture; how does her voice sound?

STORY*

NASHVILLE, Tenn.—Over the Appalachian Mountains from her beloved Virginia home rolls actress Sissy Spacek and family in a truck bound for the country music capital of the world.

She hits the pavements of Nashville, not as an Academy Award–winning actress, but as country music's newest singing sensation.

"We put a double mattress in the back with pillows," Miss Spacek says in an accent that ties her unmistakably to her East Texas roots. "On the way, I kinda chuckled as I was spreadin' up peanut butter sandwiches, thinking, 'Oh boy! Here we go!'

"We could have flown, but it was so much more exciting to have the radio tuned to a country station, rolling into Nashville in our truck. Oh man, to see that Nashville skyline!"

The family was in Music City so Miss Spacek could plug her first solo LP, "Hangin' Up My Heart."

But after two packed days of interviews, she found it hard to keep her mind on anything but loading the family's suburban-style truck for the overnight drive home.

As Miss Spacek finished her interviews, husband–director Jack Fisk took care of their one-year-old daughter, Schuyler, and packed the truck for the trip home.

More and more, Miss Spacek's life is beginning to revolve around the family's seven-acre horse farm in northern Virginia.

Up every day by 6:30 a.m., there's coffee on the front porch swing with Fisk while a round-faced and smiling Schuyler knocks back the first of several boxes of raisins.

"For kicks we just sit around and watch her grow," Miss Spacek says. "Then there's the horses, our second love."

---

*Reprinted by permission of the Associated Press.

At 34, she still enjoys making films and is scheduled to begin shooting "The River" with Mel Gibson next month.

"I'm lucky, because I don't have to be in Los Angeles hitting the pavement. But look at me now—hitting the pavement in Nashville . . . trying to sell an album."

There is no transition between the two preceding paragraphs. Having to figure out the relationship between the two ideas takes my attention away from what the writer is saying.

Singing country music is not entirely new to Miss Spacek, who won her Oscar for portraying country star Loretta Lynn in "Coal Miner's Daughter." She also received critical acclaim as the disturbed teen-ager with telekinetic powers in "Carrie" and Jack Lemmon's distraught daughter-in-law in "Missing."

No transition from the above paragraph to the next one. What's the relationship?

Born Mary Elizabeth Spacek on Christmas Day, 1949, she saved up baby-sitting money to buy her first Silvertone guitar from a Sears, Roebuck and Co. catalog.

Her first performances—singing and dancing—were in front of her family and later at school and civic association concerts before the 1,500 residents of Quitman, Texas, where she grew up.

"That's one of the good things about small towns: it's easy to excel," she says.

•

Miss Spacek soon moved to New York and eventually made her film debut in "Prime Cut" with Lee Marvin and Gene Hackman. Her role as the naive girl in "Badlands" displayed her deep talents. Last year, she starred in "Heart Beat" with Nick Nolte.

Once again, my attention is pulled away by lack of a transition.

Country living suits the entire family, she says. While Fisk tends the livestock, Miss Spacek and Schuyler water the tomatoes, squash, corn, and cucumbers in the garden.

Then there's breakfast and a nap for the baby. During those quiet times, Miss Spacek catches up on reading scripts or listens to a Rosanne Cash record.

"Seems like I'm always behind two or three books and four or five scripts," she says. Still, part of her contentment comes from a feeling of artistic accomplishment.

"It's the little, everyday stuff that makes me happy now," Miss Spacek says. "Having Schuyler deepened me. I'm more patient, more tolerant. It's intensified everything.

"I feel like I've moved into another phase. Like I've got a new knowledge. More than anything else in my life, it's affected me."

Her *mother* was pregnant?

Miss Spacek's mother died the day after she found out she was pregnant.

"It was almost like I went from child to mother in one day—like a baton being passed in a relay race," she says.

This last section flows smoothly and pulls me in. I wonder how many readers made it this far, though.

Part of the reason for the move from the West Coast to the East was to find a healthier environment to live in, Miss Spacek says.

"But it's a rude awakening when you see there really is no place that is safe," she says. "You can't hide from it (uranium radiation). The idea of being genetically damaged freaks me out. I didn't used to worry about it until I had Schuyler. Until then, I never thought much beyond my own life."

Last year, she testified before the Virginia General Assembly to lobby against a uranium mine in southern Virginia.

If her fears run to the destruction of the environment, she finds solace in the artistic accomplishments of others, such as artist Georgia O'Keeffe, whose frank portrayal of southwestern life reminds Miss Spacek of the warmth and toughness of Texas life.

She also admires "selfless people, like . . . women who, at the turn of the century, had the guts to have 10 children and live in the middle of nowhere.

"If I seem down to earth it's because I can afford to be," Miss Spacek says. "I'm artistically satisfied. I get my ego stroked all the time. It's easy to be a regular person. . . . They're the ones who really deserve to be admired."

The editor of the Spacek story operated like someone who is late catching an airplane flight.

Exercises

1. To investigate for yourself whether the large newspapers are becoming more like magazines, read the features in the nearest metropolitan newspaper and the articles in one of the national magazines *People* or *Cosmopolitan*. After reading one of the newspaper features and one of the magazine articles, choose which you prefer. Be prepared to defend your choice at the next class session.

2. See the next episode of "60 Minutes" and choose one of the "magazine" chapters. Then read a magazine article that will take you about twenty minutes to read. An hour after you've seen "60 Minutes," write down what you remember of the "magazine" chapter. Then, an hour after reading the magazine article, write down what you remember of that article. Finally, match what you remember of each of those with what your fellow students remember in the next session.

3. Choose a topic for a feature story, then describe how the story might be handled by a newspaper, a magazine, and a television news show. Who would be interviewed and how would quotes be presented? How would the story be handled visually? How would the information presented differ among the three media?

4. This chapter describes situations involving the writer and the editor. Discuss in writing the differences between the writer's goals and the editor's goals. Remember, writers often are writing for themselves. On the other hand, editors must keep in mind that they are not just working for themselves; the magazine must be first in their minds.

5. Make a list of four articles on your community that might capture a national audience

and therefore be suitable for publication in a general-interest magazine. Write one or two sentences of description for each story; then match it with a magazine that publishes that type of article. *Writer's Market* may help you select suitable publications.

6. Find an "offbeat" publication—a house organ or trade magazine, for example—and read it carefully, looking for the *worst* article. Ignoring grammatical and spelling errors, criticize the article on the basis of structure. Ask yourself these questions: Is the article focused? Does it hang together? Does it flow? Is it labored, dull, or hackneyed? Write a 500-word summary of your critique, including specific examples to support your conclusions.

TWO

STUDENTS HAVE SUCCEEDED; MARKETS AND JOBS

Success nourished them. They seemed to be able, and so they were able.

VIRGIL

riters who aim at reasonable targets usually develop their talents faster than those who aim too high at the beginning. Impatient novices who shoot for riches receive rejection slips. What they learn from *that* experience is only that their writing has been rejected. They are not likely to be told why their articles were unacceptable, what the shortcomings were, or how they might have improved them. Even if a long shot is published, the writer learns little—which helps explain why a writer may sell an article to a respected magazine, count on hitting it regularly, then go for years without selling again to the same magazine. Perhaps only then will writers become aware that their early successes were happy accidents. Patient writers who move from one attainable target to another, however, learn with each upward movement. The mere fact of changing from one magazine to another will teach them about varying audiences. More important, writing for local publications will give them ready access to criticism. And criticism, whether it comes from editors or readers, helps writers learn self-criticism, which is the central necessity of all writing. All writers need the views of others because they are always too close to their own work to see it with the proper detachment. But they must develop a self-critical attitude or they will never be able to improve even their first drafts. It does not matter whether self-criticism takes the form of setting aside a period for measuring what has been written against a checklist of writing techniques and devices or whether it is in the form of a vague dissatisfaction that pushes writers into tinkering with this paragraph, rewriting that one, or discarding two others. In either case, the writers have learned to be critical. If they have listened carefully to informed critics, their dissatisfaction will result in effective action.

Accepting criticism is difficult for everyone, and it is especially difficult for writers because they are likely to be so personally involved in their work.

But learning to accept criticism is pivotal, and it may be the chief value of courses in writing. Thoughtful novices learn to *weigh* the critical comments of their teachers and classmates rather than react defensively. Having learned that important lesson, writers are ready to learn from editors, which makes it vital that they submit their work to editors who will offer criticism and advice.

The chief danger in aiming at reasonable targets is that the talented writer soon finds that they are easy to hit. The alumni magazine, the local Sunday supplement, the little political or literary journal with a scattered national readership—each may, in time, become a wide-open market for talented writers who work their way up through them. The more receptive they become, the greater the hazard, for writers are likely to dash off a piece with a careless flourish for magazines that are eager for their work. Instead of exercising their talent and requiring it to grow by making new demands on themselves, writers may allow their talent to atrophy by calling on it to do only what it can do easily. One way to avoid this trap is not to write for a magazine that has become too easy to hit. But a better rule is to rewrite and reshape and polish everything, no matter what the market. It is all very well for writers to tell themselves that a minor magazine will publish their second-rate stuff. The return on sloppy writing does not match the cost to the writer.

After graduating from college, Rich Jaroslovsky began working for the *Wall Street Journal,* first for the Cleveland bureau, then for the *Journal's* bureau in Washington, DC. In the fifteen years Jaroslovsky has worked for the *Journal,* no other story of his has caused as much joy as this one, published on October 11, 1976:*

Petroselinum crispum probably appears on more plates in more restaurants than any other vegetable. And although health-food addicts adore it and nutritionists sing its praises, it remains untouched on more plates than any other vegetable.

Petroselinum crispum is parsley, and it has been around for centuries. Ancient Greeks used it as a breath-freshener. The Romans thought it an aphrodisiac. Britons more recently used it to make parsley pies.

Even today, parsley is celebrated in story and song. For instance, a story:

Waiter: "How did you find your steak, sir?"

Customer: "I looked under the parsley and there it was."

As for the song, there's the Simon & Garfunkel hit, "Parsley, Sage, Rosemary and Thyme."

Such praise of parsley is patently justified. Can you imagine a hit record called, "Swiss Chard, Sage, Rosemary and Thyme"?

Parsley also is one of the eight key ingredients in V8 Juice, and it may or may not be one of the 11 secret herbs and spices used in Colo-

---

*Reprinted by permission of Rich Jaroslovsky.

nel Sanders' Kentucky Fried Chicken. ("If it was, we wouldn't tell you," a spokesman says. "That's why it's a secret.")

Unloved Herb

But the ungarnished truth is that parsley these days is largely unloved and unappreciated—used for its color and eye-appeal and then relegated to the far edge of the dinner plate. "Parsley is garsley," wrote Ogden Nash, the poet.

Even the government, which ought to know better, largely overlooks parsley production. The Agriculture Department refers questions to the Census Bureau. But the Census Bureau says it lumps parsley output in with such other key crops as rutabagas and dandelion greens. In 1964, the last year for which separate figures are available, some 2,764 acres of parsley were cultivated, mostly in California, Texas, Florida and New Jersey.

The Census Bureau says it doesn't get many requests for information on parsley. In fact, after a spokesman offered a few facts about parsley, he hurriedly called back to apologize. "I'm awfully sorry," he explained. "All that stuff I gave you was about parsnips, not parsley."

RICH JAROSLOVSKY

Easily the best thing about being a reporter in Washington," says Jaroslovsky of the *Wall Street Journal*, "is the opportunity it provided for a front-row seat at the great events of our time."

So, naturally, he became an editor of the *Journal* and doesn't have his front seat anymore.

Jaroslovsky, a native of northern California, joined the *Journal* in 1975, straight out of Stanford University. He spent fifteen months covering business in the paper's Cleveland bureau—an experience that he says gave him a healthy appreciation for cold beers and warm coats—before being transferred to Washington. His education began almost immediately. On his first night in town, he was sitting quietly in the lobby of his hotel when the immediately recognizable figure of a major congressional leader lurched drunkenly by, demanding, "More ice, more ice!" (It turned out that his daughter's wedding was being celebrated in the hotel.)

Within a week or two, Jaroslovsky was sent out on his first major assignment: covering a 1976 campaign trip by President Gerald Ford. The first words Jaroslovsky heard a president of the United States utter in person were: "It's great to be here at Ohio State." Unfortunately, Mr. Ford was at *Iowa* State at the time.

After covering several other beats, including energy at the time of the 1979 oil shortage, Jaroslovsky became the *Journal*'s White House correspondent in 1981. Here he witnessed firsthand such memorable moments as:

President Reagan falling asleep during a meeting with His Holiness the Pope.

President Reagan at a state dinner in Brazil, offering a toast to his hosts as "the people of Bolivia."

And President Reagan greeting Samuel K. Doe, head of the state of Liberia, as "Chairman Moe" (leading to speculation about whether his top aides were named Larry or Curly).

During his White House tenure, Jaroslovsky won the Aldo Beckman Memorial Award from the White House Correspondents Association for his coverage. His 1984 story about the effects of Mr. Reagan's age on his performance as president touched off a national debate on the subject.

In 1985, Jaroslovsky became Washington political editor of the *Journal*, handling congressional, White House, and political coverage and coauthoring the paper's weekly page-one Washington Wire column. He has held that job ever since, in addition to writing occasionally for such magazines as *Psychology Today*, the *Washington Monthly*, and several computer publications. Jaroslovsky is married to Mindy Seltzer; has a son, David; and lives in Chevy Chase, Maryland.

STUDENTS WHO HAVE SUCCEEDED

A few students have succeeded in selling their articles to national magazines, and many others have succeeded in selling articles to regional and local magazines. In this section, you can read statements by two students who have sold their articles to many different magazines and newspapers.

Jack Liebau, a beginning senior when he wrote the following passages, earned more than $5,000 from writing for magazines and newspapers before he ended his junior year at college.

My first experience in journalism came from an unlikely source: church. The production manager of the San Marino Tribune, *a local weekly paper, also worked with the church altar boys. Thus, my fellow workers and I comprised the talent pool for part-time work at the paper. Every Wednesday night, several of us would operate badly outdated and worn Addressograph machines, which would imprint a subscriber's name on the paper. Though the work was rather tedious—even for a grade-schooler like me—it marked my first job and my first exposure to news-paper work.*

After a few Wednesday nights on the job, I became curious about the other aspects of the newspaper. After speaking to the city editor (who also served as sports editor, writer, and part-time secretary), I got a few assignments to write stories. Despite still being in grade school, I cockily thought I could write articles as good as those that were published (which speaks less for my writing ability than the paper's editorial quality). One of my first stories covered in depth the repainting of the local rose arbor. My stories were certainly not newsworthy in my mind, but they were for the Tribune, *which placed my rose arbor story as number two. It became a thrill to see my articles the day before the paper came out when I worked on Wednesdays. I soon realized that I enjoyed writing more than manual labor. Besides, my mother did not disagree with this con-clusion, since she did not appreciate printer's ink on my clothes.*

Spurred on by the journalism experience that had started at the Tribune *at the age of 15, my first action in high school was to join the student-run weekly newspaper. I probably learned more about journal-ism and writing in general from my student editors than from any other source, though I did spend one productive summer taking a seminar for high school journalists at the University of Southern California School of Journalism. I immersed myself completely in writing, spending more than ten hours a week my first year. In my senior year I was named news editor and now admit to having loved my power over editorial quality and content, as well as over the twenty or so reporters.*

During my senior year I also tried my hand at selling articles. Many of my fellow editors and I enrolled in a course called Free-lance Writing, mainly because it sounded easy. It did prove easier than cal-culus, but the course actually intrigued many of us into selling articles, rather than just writing for a newspaper. (Besides, a published article could also constitute important "college suck" for getting us into the college of our choice.)

The first class assignment was to write query letters to several publications, to be chosen from Writer's Market. *I proposed profiling a publicly held company for a business magazine. I wrote queries to more than ten publications, from* Forbes *and* Fortune *to* Northwest Business Review *and other small magazines. One week later, I received a reply from* Barron's *(the weekly publication of Dow Jones, which also brings us the* Wall Street Journal*), which said they might be interested in my story in the future. At least I received a response, I thought. Shortly thereafter,* Forbes *and* Fortune *wrote to request a copy of the article (both later rejected it). After two months passed, I phoned the smaller publications from whom I hadn't received a reply. In almost every case, an editor said (when I could get through to one) that he was too busy to respond to query letters from free-lancers. That particular episode taught me not to be afraid of contacting large and respected magazines; in fact, I was more apt to receive a response from the biggies than from anybody else.*

A postscript: after I had given up all hope of ever peddling a business article, an editor at Barron's *called to say he liked my earlier work.* Barron's *paid a kill fee and bought the article, though it ended up not publishing it.*

For the free-lance writing class in high school, I also wrote a story on my day-long experience walking precincts and registering voters for the Reagan-Bush campaign in 1980. Again, my conclusion was comparable to my previous experience in selling articles: the big publications proved more likely to reply to query letters than the smaller magazines. I wrote to National Review, *the publication of Young Americans for Freedom, and, shooting for the moon,* Reader's Digest. *I was shocked when my one and only response came from the source I least expected:* Reader's Digest. *More surprisingly, they expressed interest in the article and asked to see it. I was less surprised to face eventual rejection from them, but felt that at least I made it through round one while still in high school.*

Even though sending out query letters has a low success rate (along with an even lower probability of even receiving a response), it was certainly a worthwhile venture, which led to publication of several articles and gave me an "in" with Barron's.

The summer between high school and college, I worked as a reporter for a suburban section of the Los Angeles Times. *This proved an altogether different writing experience from selling articles as a free-lancer. Instead of worrying about potential topics to write about, I usually found an abundance of story ideas at the* Times. *Unfortunately, for the first few weeks, my work was largely devoted to learning how to master the word processor and writing news briefs and items for the Calendar of Events. After I had finished these tasks with flying colors, my editor decided I was ready for some stories. I wrote profiles on area citizens, including former football player/actor Merlin Olsen, jockey Bill Shoe-maker, and former Libertarian Party presidential candidate Ed Clarke.*

Here is the lead of my story on Shoemaker, published on July 23, 1981:

> In Hollywood Park's Jockey Room, jockeys and officials are watching television, playing cards and reading the Racing Form.
>
> But when the world's winningest jockey, William (Willie) Shoemaker, walks in, he is noticed by all, despite his 4-foot, 11-inch, 95-pound body.
>
> At 49, Shoemaker says he maintains a full daily schedule, working about the same hours as when he began riding 30 years ago. "If I work with horses in the morning, I get up early, about 6 or 6:30. I get up early anyway, because my little daughter wakes me."

This story ran about 1,500 words.

This is the lead of my story on Merlin Olsen, published on September 20, 1981:

> Having survived the transition from retired football player, Mer-lin Olsen of San Marino is successfully wearing three hats—as a football commentator for NBC, an actor and the owner of a car dealership in Encino.
>
> Olsen, a Los Angeles Ram for 15 of his 40 years, is regarded as one of the best football commentators on television. And after four years of appearing on "Little House on the Prairie," he is star-ring in a new NBC series, "Father Murphy," scheduled to pre-miere this fall.
>
> Four years prior to retiring from football, Olsen negotiated with the major networks about a broadcasting job, then drafted his own contract to give him freedom to do some acting. He signed the contract a month after he retired at the end of the 1976 football season.
>
> "Little House" had a vacancy that needed filling by "some-one with a physical sense to take over," Olsen said.

This story ran about 2,000 words.

My entree into interviews was considerably easier now, since I was a staff writer for the Los Angeles Times *and not just an eager student hoping to sell an article. Writing a number of articles created more de-mands, especially to meet deadlines, but the paychecks were also a lot more regular than during my free-lancing career. More importantly, that summer experience gave me an opportunity to write on a broader array of topics than I had before and gave me some real journalistic credentials.*

During my college years, I wrote for Barron's. *In my first three years in college, I had four articles profiling companies published in their Investment News and Views section. These articles averaged about*

1,500 words in length, and they paid $200 each for them. I also wrote one long article on a favorite topic of mine: Horse racing. This feature ran about 3,000 words and earned my biggest paycheck to date: $500. I was still a junior.

This excerpt is from my horse racing story in Barron's *(November 18, 1983), entitled "Tearing up the Turf":*

> In California, they're off and running! The state is fast becoming the center of horseracing, the nation's most popular spectator sport.
>
> The odds are, moreover, that California will continue to cash in on the sport of kings and surfers, thanks to possible off-track betting, year-round racing in a mild climate, aggressive promotions and improved breeding. The state's winning form is sheer delight to the four publicly held California racetrack companies: California Jockey Club, Hollywood Park, Los Alamitos, and Santa Anita.

*For my profiles, I would often talk to the president of a company and then write an article. Here is a paragraph from an article called "Retail Recycler" (*Barron's, *March 7, 1983):*

> Consumers haven't been on a spending spree of late, but Jamesway Corp., a discount retailer with 68 stores in the Middle Atlantic region, has weathered the recession in fine form. In fact, while competitors have fallen by the wayside or shuttered many outlets—Woolco, King's Department Stores and Two Guys among them—Jamesway has been mapping plans to add stores.

Julie Jacobs, the second successful college writer, traveled to China to research two articles. She writes:

I decided to major in engineering in college because a number of significant adults convinced me that I could always read and write on my own time. I had decided at the age of eight that I would be a writer, chiefly because I couldn't paint or sing or speak intelligently. I thought I already knew how to write and even type, so I should do something lucrative and disciplined like engineering.

I began the engineering track, but also took a class in poetry and a job at the student newspaper. I quickly realized, or was informed, that I don't like engineers and would never like to work with them, and that I am a lousy poet.

I worked at a fairly predictable sequence of papers. The first, the Palo Alto Weekly, *felt like a family that happened to get together in an old barn every week under the rallying cry of, "Hey, kids, let's put out a paper!" At that point, the paper's editorial standards were very high, and there was a degree of smugness and insularity that I found comforting. My editor was as much my older brother as my boss: he let me share a room with his two-year-old son when I needed a home for a summer and prodded me past every form of writer's block known to humanity.*

He essentially threw me out of the paper to take my second internship, because I never wanted to leave that snug environment.

The second internship, at the Peninsula Times Tribune, *was a quantum step up economically and professionally. The* Weekly *saw the PTT, a daily, as its major competition. The* Weekly *maintained higher standards, or so my code of honor told me, and was a better institution. How can those ad reps sell that thing, my friends in the* Weekly's *ad department wanted to know.*

Unfortunately, I loved it. The paper was seriously understaffed and needed whatever I could produce. I plunged into fifty-hour weeks (eight of them at $25 each), trying to get over my fear of deadlines and my inability to cut off a story. I revised one story forty-three times, according to the computer's annoying tally. Every editor in the place looked at it, or at least five or six of them. Everyone gave me different input, an important lesson in itself; one man, especially, insisted that I quit caring so much about the subject and issue involved and just write and pare the story like a professional. I wasn't one, but I tried, because he made me.

The story concerned a man whose MediCal benefits had been cut. A victim of emphysema caused by his job as a welder, Paul Mitchell was hooked up to oxygen tanks twenty-four hours a day. Because of the cuts, his limited income, and his inability to work, he essentially had to choose if he would breathe or eat.

I felt strongly about his struggle to live and about the injustice it represented. And it was my story; I had dragged it out of a phone call to someone else that I had happened to answer. I wanted to see this man helped.

I used an embarrassingly soft lead:

> "I'm used to putting in eight hours a day in the office and feeling productive," said Paul Mitchell, a former welder and computer software specialist.
>
> "Now I'm 46 years old and I'm sitting here playing computer games. When you've worked a number of jobs and all of a sudden you can't work, it's really something."

Because our circulation area was computer-rich Silicon Valley, I decided to try to snare the man a computer so he could work out of his home. My last grafs:

> In the meantime, Mitchell plans to recover and go back to work. If he had access to a computer terminal and modem, Mitchell said, he could work out of his home and get himself off MediCal entirely.
>
> "I'm determined to turn this whole thing around and be working this time next year," Mitchell said.

I loved this story.

Sitting next to me at the PTT *was a woman who also had graduated from the* Weekly, *except into a real job and not an internship. She complained about the* PTT's *seeming policy that no story be more than 15 inches; at the* Weekly, *she had done a number of very successful longer pieces. But she agreed with me that our friends at the* Weekly *would not understand the simple fact that a community paper seemed terribly provincial, even from the next step up, a not-so-terrific daily for a slightly larger community.*

To escape, I decided to leave the country. In fact, that's not literally true; I had applied for an internship at a paper in Tokyo months before I ruined my chances for work at this outstanding daily. But by the end of the summer, I felt that the Foreign Legion would have been a good way out and was relieved to have a chance to redeem myself with strangers.

The year turned out to be mixed, of course. The internship was with Pacific Stars and Stripes, *the military's paper for personnel stationed in the Far East. One noteworthy event occurred, however, in that I was allowed to go to China to do a story.*

It still is astonishing to me, and funny, that a paper would be so disorganized as to let an intern go to China for a story. I wasn't paid for the two weeks I was there, but then I wasn't supposed to get any vacation time during my internship. The paper ended up by paying me almost half the cost of the trip in free-lance salary for the two stories I did. Since the trip was probably less than half of what I would have paid for a similar tour out of the States, I felt I had found a very good deal. I figure it cost me about $800 to go to China for 18 days on a study tour; since I also earned college credit and a good clip, I felt lucky. And amused, as I said.

The two stories and my photos occupied eight full tabloid pages in Stripes' *Sunday magazine over two weeks.* Stripes *has no advertisements, so there was nothing to distract from my attempts to fill a lot of space with very little information.*

The key to my story, to me, had been two interviews, one with a Chinese student who spoke frankly about his parents' ordeals during the Cultural Revolution and one with the U.S. defense attaché from the Beijing embassy. I had made one error, however; I had failed to identify myself as a reporter when the attaché addressed our study tour and so couldn't use any of his quotes, as he had presumably been speaking off the record. He hadn't said anything revolutionary, of course, but he was articulate and he gave me about half of my story.

The first interview was fascinating to me, because the student was skillful enough in English to compensate for my ignorance in Chinese. My editor, still dumbstruck by my mistake in not identifying myself to the attaché, read my notes and determined that I had discovered nothing new about China, the Cultural Revolution, or even this one student's family.

I tried, though:

. . . Zhou is the oldest student in the international relations department because during the Cultural Revolution he was assigned to a coal mine for eight years instead of to a university.

"My family suffered a lot during the Cultural Revolution," Zhou says. Hunched in his coat in the unheated meeting room, he speaks with a disarming openness, as if to bridge the language gap with sincerity and humor when we can't cross it verbally.

"My father was beaten a lot. He had to stop work and was sent to a farm in Anhain Province. It's a very poor province, and far away. He was there for four years."

I tried to get Deep:

. . . "I think, [social standards] will go back to the way they were before the Cultural Revolution," Zhou said.

"During those years, whether you worked or not, you got money. Now good workers are respected again."

These old-time Chinese values, I tell him, sound similar to capitalist law-of-the-jungle standards. . . .

"In recent years, our country is taking good care of its intellectuals, because the party leader now considers them important to our country," Zhou says. "So it's not a privilege for our family (to own these luxuries). It just gives us more convenience."

And, more often than not, I just got in over my head:

. . . What's left of the Wall snakes across the barren hills like a serpent's spine, deceptively small in the distance but colossal close up. Bands of tourists from inside and outside China line up on its broad back, shivering, waiting for the shutter to snap.

We're here, well north of Beijing, after a two-hour bus trip. And it's cold, too cold for a leisurely stroll. We hop around like chilly fleas and end up spending our time over hot lunch and souvenir counters, where we buy mock certificates and T-shirts, to prove we were actually at the Great Wall.

We've flocked here to see an emperor's failed dream of isolation, a barrier against the nomads of the north who insisted on coming down anyway. Despite the Wall's bulk, as a fortress it was a flop.

We've heard the Chinese are practical—that they will eat an entire Peking duck, leaving only the quack. Now, we see another example of efficiency: the Wall, no longer useful at keeping out foreigners, is used to lure us in. More than 2,000 years after the first segments were built, almost 700 years after the ancient chunks were united, the Wall now welcomes invaders. It has become another Chinese E-ride.

A friend of mine who is an Army colonel and much better educated than I informed me that my stories were superficial and condescending to a people I didn't understand. He's right. But someone chose the stories to be used as the final chapter in a 40-year retrospective on

Stripes. *Like everything else, the China stories are partly an embarrass-ment and partly a step forward. I still lack discipline; I still can't control a story and stop writing when it's finished; I still leave out the wrong things and focus on the trivial. But I'm working on it, because I'm reasonably certain writing is the only thing I'll ever have a shot at do-ing well.*

JOB OPPORTUNITIES

A pamphlet published in 1969 by the American Newspaper Publishers Asso-ciation Foundation contained a caption that read: "Reporter at work—all it takes is concentration, speed, accuracy—and talent." More than twenty years later, most journalists would still agree with that prescription, but many would add an additional item—luck. Today, the number of journalists seek-ing jobs far exceeds the number of openings in the field.

Despite this overcrowding, journalism's popularity among college stu-dents continues to increase. In 1990, there were more than 147,000 journal-ism students studying in U.S. colleges. At a time when enrollment in human-ities courses is declining, students are turning to journalism because of its vocational possibilities. This movement is the logical outcome of the in-creased presence and importance of the media in American life.

There was a time when newspapers couldn't find enough qualified staff members. In the early 1960s, *Editor & Publisher* estimated that there were three positions open for every graduating journalism major. A study under-taken for The Newspaper Fund indicated that two-thirds of all the daily news-papers in the United States regarded human power as their major problem. According to this survey, newspapers had to attract 3,500 new employees every year to fill news and editorial positions alone. But colleges and depart-ments of journalism were graduating fewer than 3,000 journalism majors a year, some of whom did not go to work for daily newspapers.

By 1984, the number of journalism graduates had increased to more than 60,000. Their job-hunting endeavors have resulted in a flood of applica-tions both at newspapers and magazines. It is not unusual for a publication advertising a single job opening to receive hundreds of applications. Even when no openings are announced, applicants submit their résumés and clip-pings. An associate editor at *Women's Sports* estimated that he had accumu-lated a file of over five hundred unsolicited applications for staff jobs and re-ceived an average of two per week. A Seattle newspaper features editor said that her paper received over two thousand applications annually.

Edwin Haroldsen summed up the situation this way:

Over the country, news executives are being flooded with job applica-tions. This is shown by the responses of 30 representative U.S. daily newspaper and broadcast news executives recently surveyed for the *Quill.* The *Chicago Sun-Times* alone receives 1,000 a year, approxi-mately 700 of them from young persons fresh out of school.

The *New York Times* gets approximately 40 applications a week, but has had only two or three reporting positions open so far this year.

And another report tells us the *Philadelphia Inquirer,* with 1,800 applications on file, sends a monthly list of candidates to other papers. A promising applicant to the *Washington Post* might be referred to a paper as far away as Colorado.

THE QUALIFIED APPLICANT—NEWSPAPERS AND MAGAZINES

Here are a few comments managing editors have made about the qualifications they seek in applicants who would like to fill openings on their staffs:

Preferably experience on another newspaper, or at least internship on papers of comparable size. Where a person comes to us directly from school, the minimum requirement is nearly always good campus publication experience, part-time work on a newspaper, or summer interning elsewhere. Solid educational background, not limited to journalism schools or departments, demonstrated writing talent and reportorial experience, a strong commitment to newspaper journalism.
—Ralph Otwell, managing editor, *Chicago Sun-Times*

Deep dedication to daily newspaper work, intelligence, wide range of interests, ambition to advance, skills, thoroughness, accuracy, ability to meet deadlines, excellence in grammar and spelling.
—Paul McKalip, editor, *Tucson Citizen*

Must be able to type, spell, show a talent for writing . . . should indicate he/she can get along with other staffers and contacts. . . .
—Jerald A. Finch, managing editor, *Richmond News-Leader*

A person who is well-grounded in liberal arts, insatiably curious, well-mannered in person and on the telephone, a skilled researcher on the street and in the library, and with a basic knowledge about back-shop operations.
—Harvey Jacobs, editor, *Indianapolis News*

Must have a strong interest in one of our subject areas, which are food, travel, gardening and home building projects. We do occasionally hire people right out of school and train them. The gardening and building areas are the most difficult to staff because of the lack of qualified people with knowledge about those subjects.
—Bill Marken, editor, *Sunset* magazine

FIRST PRINCIPLES OF GOOD WRITING

The "first principles" do not mean something that is to be taken care of while typing; instead, these words mean think of these during planning an article.

Organizing the Material

It is far better (if extraordinarily difficult for some writers) to organize the material first than to start a first draft without planning. Impatient writers can force themselves to plan by telling themselves that they must work efficiently rather than temperamentally. They may have to submerge their artistic egos, but doing so will enable them to use all their time, energy, and talent effectively.

Patient writers will stay away from the typewriter for as long as is necessary to organize facts and thoughts. Although individual writers work at different speeds and no system will transform a plodding writer into a fast one, anyone will benefit from organizing the attack on research material. Consider four levels of organizing, each of which lends itself to variations.

Level 1 is almost ridiculously simple. It involves nothing more than reading the research material. Yet some writers *never* reach this level. Itching to write, they simply try to remember the clippings they have read and the releases and passages from books they have scanned, referring to their notes and to a clipping or a passage only when they want a direct quotation. The occasional need for one item or another leads them on a time-wasting, frustrating search through the stack.

In general, writers should be so familiar with their material that they can put their hands on the right source for a particular item in a matter of seconds. This means that not only should you read your material once, you should reread it two or even three times.

At least a few writers reach the first level and stop there, too impatient to go on to Level 2. This level requires arranging notes, clippings, releases, pamphlets, and books by placing similar materials together—descriptive passages here, anecdotes there, and so on—and by marking the items that are likely to figure heavily in the article. Writers who work at this level often surround themselves with research, using not just desk space but spreading notes and clippings in an arc around their chairs. The more careful the writer, the greater the probability that he or she will organize the material rather than merely open it to view.

Level 3 of organization, after reading and arranging the material for easy access, involves outlining the article. Among professional writers, this is seldom the academic outline made up of roman and arabic numerals and capital and lowercase letters. It is more often a simple, general-subject outline that starts with a thematic sentence and indicates how and when the various elements—anecdotes, statistics, incidents, descriptions—will be used to point up the theme and flesh out the characters.

Level 4 is a quantum jump. It calls for organizing research material in a way that many might consider extravagant. One variation has the writer jotting sequences of his projected article on index cards, then putting the cards in order to firm up the pattern of the article. Another has the writer putting sequences on sheets of paper that are then fastened to the wall above the typewriter. Perhaps the most elaborate method is used by an extremely successful free-lancer. He describes it as "the perspirational system of writing":

> This is purely mechanical, and it's a fine warm-up exercise for writing. First, I cut up the small pocket notebooks that I use in note-taking and paste the pages on sheets of typewriter paper, four pages to a sheet.

Then I add to that stack of sheets whatever notes I've made on tablet paper and organize the releases, tear sheets, bulletins, and books, which also go on the stack. My live field notes—most of my best stuff from interviews and on-the-scene reporting—go on top of the stack. Then I go through all this and number each sheet and item.

By this time, I'm warming up to the task ahead of me and am eager to get to the writing. But I don't start beating any typewriter. Instead, I take a large sheet of paper, about the size of a newspaper page laid sidewise, which is divided into four columns, and which has a space at the top about three inches deep for random notations like lead sentences or titles that might occur to me. I use so many of these special pages in my work that I have them printed.

Then, reading through my notes and the other material, I jot down sequences in my prospective story in the columns on that big page. I number each sequence to correspond to the page number in the stack of notes. This is for quick reference when I'm writing, so I won't have to thumb through a wilderness of notes for a fact, a figure, an anecdote, or a quotation. After I've outlined all the material, I scan the whole sheet for what seems to be a lead, then mark that sequence with a red pencil, "1." Then I look for the next sequence and mark it "2," then "3," and so on. Soon my story is organized on that big sheet of paper right down to the last paragraph.

At this point, I back off and look at the sheet of sequences and say to myself, "Do I have a story or don't I?" If I decide that I do, I'm almost ready to start writing. If I decide that I don't, I know that I'll have to do some more research. It's much better to learn this before I start writing rather than after I've spent hours or days pounding the typewriter only to discover that my piece is too thin to send to an editor.

Even when I have everything I need, I hold off on the writing until I answer this question: "Exactly what am I trying to say in this piece?" I try to answer in one sentence, which I then condense into a few words or a phrase. This serves as my working title, my guide as I write. I jot them down in the space at the top of my page of sequences, and sometimes I have twenty titles before I'm through. I pick the one that looks best, knowing that the editor may decide on another. After all, he may think, he's a better title-writer than I am—and he probably is. Why don't I just forget all about titles? Because a title, even one that's rejected, gives me a mental picture of my story. And I must have one or I can't write.

This is a complex system, and it is doubtful that many writers have the patience for it. More writers use a simpler approach that pivots on subtopics. This requires making a list of important subtopics that the article must cover (the length of the list varying with the length and complexity of the article). The writer numbers each research item (notes, clippings, and the like), reads each item to decide which topic it concerns, then places the appropriate number next to the relevant topic on the list. Next, the writer organizes the list into an outline. When ready to write a subtopic, the writer can prepare a small pile of relevant materials by referring to the outline.

How carefully each writer organizes his or her material will vary with temperament, willpower, habit—indeed, with all the qualities that make a writer one kind of worker or another. It would be absurd to suggest that every writer attempt to adapt to any one pattern of work. But a writer must read and organize his or her material in some way before beginning to write.

Basic Writing Considerations

For the beginner, there are other considerations before starting to write. We might group them under the following headings: (1) mechanics, (2) forms, (3) style, and (4) market.

Mechanics

Some beginners worry endlessly over whether they should use longhand, type, or dictate. Each method has been used successfully, often by the same writer at different times. A writer should adopt the method that suits him or her. Writing in longhand has one striking advantage: it cuts down verbosity. Most free-lancers find that their handwritten articles are seldom flabby with words. But longhand can be slow and tiring. Typing goes faster for almost everyone, especially those who have learned to "think on a typewriter." Ernest Hemingway, who was a newspaper reporter for years, eventually turned to longhand for much of his writing, but he usually typed dialogue because it came to his mind so rapidly that he felt the need to get it on paper as fast as possible. But some writers avoid the typewriter because they believe typing requires too much time and energy feeding pages in and yanking them out. They suspect that the speed of typing encourages them to write too many sentences that find their way into the wastebasket. For those who work from detailed outlines, dictating is undoubtedly the fastest method, but one who does not outline carefully can become lost in his or her own sentences. Dictation can turn out a smooth article that flows well from point to point. But few writers are really capable of dictating well, and even those who develop a talent for it often find that the result is startlingly verbose. One writer who turned to dictating said, "I've always had dictated manuscript transcribed with a wide margin, usually a third of the page, so that I can condense and refine the story—sometimes through as many as six or eight revisions."

Forms

Another question that troubles most beginners is the form of the magazine article. Those who have been told that there is a structure for the news story and a structure for the formal essay and various structures for various kinds of poetry worry about "the proper form of the article." There is none. One can analyze *categories* of articles. Profiles, descriptives, narratives, personal experiences, informatives, how-to-do-its, analyses, and essay-reviews are among the categories identified and illustrated in the chapters of this book. But the structure of each article varies with the material. That is, even within a single category, the articles begin differently, develop their themes differently, and end differently; the possible variations are limitless. This is suggested by one of the best articles written by *Life*'s Robert Coughlan.* A profile of a controversial assistant secretary of defense named Roger Kyes, the article was in the form of a trial, with those Coughlan interviewed speaking for and against Kyes, much as they might have had they been on a witness stand. Was Coughlan wrong to cast his article in this eccentric form? No. There are no wrong forms. There are only ineffective forms—and they, too, are countless. Ultimately, the material and the writer's ideas about it determine the form the article should take.

Style

The fact that the mechanics of writing and the forms of articles are numerous may seem to suggest that anything goes in article writing, that it is idle to try to establish general rules. But when we consider style and content, the focus sharpens. Although there are certainly exceptions to almost any rule one might propose, one may generalize confidently about the style and content of most magazine articles.

Rather than devoting page after page to questions of style (in the traditional and stale manner), this book is arranged so that you will learn primarily by covering the high points of style in this chapter and by analyzing the articles reproduced in later chapters. Study the sentences. Note that the writing is hardly ever in the choppy style common to many news stories (most of which are designed to do little more than impart information). Nor is it the leisurely prose of most essays or the specialized jargon of articles in scholarly journals. Magazine prose does vary from article to article and from magazine to magazine because subjects and audiences differ. Without being formularized, however, magazine writing is a distinct body of prose, usually made up of words the reader can understand without a dictionary and information he or she can absorb without being gravely purposeful about self-improvement. Vivid writing is prized, but the writer must use the restraint dictated by taste and common sense.

The general style favored by most magazines consists of crisp, original phrases made up of familiar words. It seeks to avoid the trite. Where possible, the words and phrases are concrete and visual rather than intangible and abstract. Where numbers will help, they are not piled on one another in a statistical morass; they are used infrequently for maximum effect. Pointed quotations are sprinkled through most articles to change the pace, to enliven the reading, and to present facts and ideas distinctively. Although long articles may be broken into sections (much as a book is broken into chapters), the general rule is that the writing flows from beginning to end through smooth transitions. Because the reader is not automatically interested in hard fact and analysis, she is *led* to them. For example, a profile never begins with the

---

*"Ugliest Man since Abe Lincoln," *Life* (August 10, 1953), pp. 86–94.

vital statistics of the subject's birth and parentage. These are worked in only after the reader has been given so many interesting facts, incidents, and insights that she wants to know about the person's beginnings.

Market

The writer must study each magazine he or she is considering writing for, and that means much more than reading a few issues. Whether he is a beginner or a professional, the free-lancer must devote hours, even days, to analyzing a particular market. One highly successful writer says that he aims at a magazine for the first time by reading all the issues of the preceding year. He analyzes the style and tries to understand the essence. "The feel of the articles," he says, "is just as important as the mechanical analysis."

Use the techniques described in Chapter 4 of this book to help you analyze the magazines you are aiming toward; then use that information to help shape the content of your articles.

Some Guidelines for Writers

In summary, these are some of the techniques involved in successfully writing a magazine article.

The audience   One must write for an audience, not for oneself at one extreme or for the entire universe at the other. In the magazine world, the audience one writes for is fairly easy to discern: it is made up of the readers of a particular magazine. This seems simple, and yet failing to write for a magazine's audience is probably the most common fault among beginners.

Theme and tone   Speaking of the "angle" or the "slant" of an article refers to its theme. Whatever term is used, the requirement is the same: the writer must decide what she is going to say *about* her subject—what aspect she will emphasize and develop fully—and write a title or a thematic sentence that will guide her.

The theme and the audience together will help the writer determine the tone—sinister, serious, straightforward, light, flippant, or whatever. It is fairly common for beginners to change the tone of an article inadvertently. Although light elements can appear in articles that are essentially serious, the article that seems never to be able to make up its mind about tone leaves readers puzzled. The problem of varied tones does not usually arise for the writer who selects a magazine to write for and a theme to write about at the beginning.

Anecdotes, examples, concrete versus abstract   Anecdotes (*little* stories, not necessarily *funny* stories) are among the most compelling devices in writing. Properly used, they point up; they illustrate. Their value is suggested by the difference between merely *saying* that an attorney is "like a tiger in the courtroom" and relating an anecdote that proves the point.

Anecdotes are actually examples of behavior. There are other kinds of examples, of course. One can write that some U.S. senators have been demagogues and yet not be especially convincing. But citing Senator Joseph McCarthy of Wisconsin offers a persuasive example of demagoguery. It is useful for anyone who writes a generalization to pause and ask himself, "Can I give two examples of this?" Then he should supply them.

Few techniques in magazine writing are as pivotal as *showing* the reader a point rather than merely telling about it. (Anecdotes show.) It is one thing to tell the reader that the subject of an article is a great humorist. It is another, and much better, thing to show the person's humor by recounting some of his or her jokes.

It is nearly always true that the specific is more readable and interesting than the general ("She has two billion dollars" is better than "She is rich"), and the concrete is more readable and interesting than the abstract (writing about a wealthy person is better than writing about the idea of wealth).

Description   Following many of the preceding suggestions will help the writer describe people, places, and things more vividly. It should also be emphasized that describing routinely ("He weighs 210 pounds, has blue eyes, and smiles often") invites yawns. It is far better to color in a person as a distinct personality. How does he walk? How does he talk? What are his distinctive mannerisms and gestures? Similarly, describing a place or thing requires that the writer focus on its distinctive qualities. What is it about Boston (or the Florida Keys or a Kansas wildflower) that makes it interesting and worth reading about?

Words and phrases   Writers should shun the trite. They must try endlessly to fashion evocative and memorable phrases. Instead of using clichés, they must strive to make phrases so captivating that they will *become* clichés— phrases that are so attractive that other writers will steal them and use them over and over to the point of exhaustion (which is exactly how the current clichés became trite). Not every sentence can, or should, be so captivatingly fashioned that it calls attention to itself. But a sentence that is not fresh and lively should at least be written in straightforward English rather than in clichés.

Rewriting   A first draft is never as good as a second. A second draft is never as good as a third. Perhaps there is a point in rewriting at which improvement ceases. It may even be true that an article begins to deteriorate with too much rewriting, but it is easy to suspect that if this occurs it is during the thirty-seventh rewriting, or the fifty-fifth, and is thus not much of a threat to many writers.

It is important, of course, to know what to *do* in rewriting. Going at it aimlessly merely because one has been persuaded that a revision is necessary seldom improves an article. It may be necessary to put the writing aside for a time and return to it with a fresh eye and attitude. It should be possible to improve a piece by analyzing it against the items in this checklist and against the many other suggestions about writing offered in this book.

Grammar, spelling, punctuation   The literary genius may not need to bother with these mundane matters. If you are not certain you are a genius, however, these "mechanical" matters do require your attention. Editors certainly notice them. In fact, editors are likely to wonder whether a writer who spells shoddily and writes drunken sentences is similarly careless with facts. Before you write your final draft, make sure your sentences are correct.

BREAKING IN AS A FREE-LANCER

"You can get your cues from all your senses—sight, touch, smell, and taste as well as hearing. Pass them on to the readers."

IVAN ROBINSON

The typical student is accustomed to writing for himself or for a professor and has not yet had the chance to master the knack of writing for a large audience. Ill equipped to aim for a high-paying national magazine, he or she may nonetheless do exactly that. Success is doubtful at best. The more effective course is to write for the college newspaper or magazine, then for a publication with a larger and more varied readership—if not the alumni journal, perhaps the Sunday magazine of a nearby metropolitan newspaper.

Such work not only gives the beginner the experience of writing for an audience but also emphasizes the value of *reporting*—gathering facts through interviewing and observing as well as reading and thinking. The typical undergraduate term paper is based on library research and thought. It is therefore no surprise that many students rely almost exclusively on these techniques in free-lancing. Only a small percentage of magazine articles are based on library research, though; most are more demanding.

This does not mean that a student must always compete with professional writers on *their* terms. In fact, the alert student may use a course assignment as the basis for an article, as we have seen earlier. Unfortunately, students often assume that an "A" term paper can become an article with no more effort than retyping. Two experiences Frank Allen Philpot had when he was a graduate student in communication at Stanford are instructive. Philpot had been editor of the campus newspaper at Vanderbilt and had later worked briefly for a professional daily and a television station. In a course at Stanford, he studied the changing technology of mass communication and decided that the subject was valuable not only for a term paper but also for a magazine article. He queried *San Francisco* magazine, and the editor was interested. But Philpot tried to make one piece do double duty, both as an article *and* as a term paper. His work pleased the professor, but not the editor. The article was rejected—a fairly predictable fate for a piece that attempts to appeal to two such different audiences.

In another course, Philpot learned that three new UHF television stations would soon begin operations in San Francisco. He wrote a term paper on the potential economic impact of the stations. Later, he queried *San Francisco* magazine and received a go-ahead. Then he interviewed the general manager of each station and fashioned a manuscript that borrowed something from the term paper, a bit from his own experience with a UHF station, and a great deal from the interviews. The article, which was published, can serve as a model for using course work in free-lancing.

Leonard Sellers had a similar experience with a student piece that led to a published article. When he was editor of the campus daily at San Francisco State College (now State University), a campus confrontation was at its height. Sellers was asked by the editor of *Seminar*, which assesses the mass media, to describe how a student newspaper handles a student strike. Using his own experiences and interviews with strike leaders and faculty members, Sellers put together a piece that touched on staff dissension, newspaper production under stress, the importance of objective information, the background of the strike, and the founding of a new campus newspaper. The editor deleted the strike background and published the rest of the article.

On another occasion, Sellers wrote a long memo of observations and advice to the student who was to succeed him as editor of the campus paper. He pinned it to the board behind the editor's desk so that his successor would see it. Professor Bud Liebes saw it first and sent a copy to *Quill,* the magazine of the journalism fraternity Sigma Delta Chi. Sellers's memo was published.

The successes of Philpot and Sellers show how young writers can use college experiences and how writing for a publication that is certain to be interested in the subject can be valuable.

BREAKING IN AS A MAGAZINE STAFF MEMBER

Erin Cooperrider, whose story of writing at *Sunset* magazine was quoted in Chapter 1, won her job while looking for an internship:

> I had written to many, many other publications and had gotten several offers. I followed the same procedure when I wrote to *Sunset*: I wrote a cover letter to accompany my resumé, including jobs and experiences that were not on my resumé but that I thought might be interesting to the people at *Sunset.* It was too late, I was informed; interns for the summer had already been chosen.
>
> Several weeks later, however, I got a letter saying that there was a position open. *Sunset* needed someone to fill in for several staff editors who were going on long vacations. At the time I didn't know what I was getting into, but I took the job. My duties, to begin with, consisted of typing, filing, answering phones, taking reprint orders, and cutting checks. Not glamorous work, but it did allow me to be right in the middle of the editorial wing where I could see who was doing what and how the whole magazine was put together.
>
> After a while I began doing some research and checking for some of the writers, and by the end of the summer I was doing some of my own small stories while continuing to research and check stories for other writers.

The techniques and devices of the free-lancer are also those of the staff writer. Many magazine staffers work with and sometimes guide free-lancers. Before seeking a staff job, one should first try free-lancing, not only because the experience will give the staffer a firsthand view of free-lancing but also because writing successfully for the magazine whose staff one wants to join is persuasive proof that one understands the magazine's purpose and can reach its audience. Further, prospective staff members who have been published elsewhere—the more respected the magazines, the more respected the writer will be—have demonstrated at least that they are at home in the world of magazines. In either case, applicants who have free-lanced have a significant advantage over most of those seeking staff positions: they need not begin in a flunky job and spend months or years proving that they deserve important assignments; they have already proved themselves, and they will begin higher on the ladder.

The value of free-lancing first is suggested by the hiring practices of a little magazine called *Plane and Pilot.* June Chase, assistant editor, said that most of the staffers are college graduates with majors in journalism and English. "After learning to fly, they free-lanced for us and other aviation magazines and then moved in as staffers."

National Geographic also looks for those who have proved that they can write for magazines. Associate editor John Scofield says:

> After screening by our personnel office to assure at least minimal professional qualifications, the applicant is interviewed by at least three assistant editors. In their evaluation they weigh heavily the applicant's previous writing—preferably magazine articles in fields we normally cover. In the past few years no staffer has been hired without undertaking a trial assignment, usually a short- to medium-length article, often on a subject suggested by the candidate himself, and often on a "minimum-guarantee" basis.

Thomas Griffith, former editor of *Time,* said that several of his staff writers began by "writing pieces for us, having a track record, and then being signed on. We often see something people write elsewhere and begin by asking them to do a book review for us, where we get the first measurement of their talents and adaptability to length, tone, frequency, and speed."

Another important path to staff writing offered by *Time, Newsweek,* and many other weeklies calls for working part-time as a stringer. Needing coverage of campuses, state capitals, and large metropolitan areas that full-time correspondents cannot always provide, many weeklies and not a few monthlies retain students and young newspaper reporters. Griffith points out that most *Time* staffers "rose to the top by the same method: they began perhaps as stringers in our Time-Life News Service or on the way up from office helpers and summer fill-ins; proved reliable, fresh, talented; and got better and better assignments. The final stage—doing signed text pieces—is a very difficult last hurdle, for we have few available spots, and here writing talent, reportorial quality, judgment are decisive."

Moving from Newspaper to Magazine

Newspapers represent another important path to high-level magazine work. John Adams, former editor of *U.S. News & World Report,* said, "As a general rule we require five years or more of prior experience on a press association or metropolitan newspaper." Few other magazines are so stringent, even in setting general rules, but newspaper experience is prized in the magazine world, and not only by news magazine executives. Bryon Scott, first editor of *Today's Health* and then executive editor of *Medical Opinion,* said: "Of the eight members of the *Today's Health* staff who held editorial posts, only two had not 'served time' on a daily newspaper. Over many a beer we agreed that newspaper experience imparts to the magazine writer a sense for accuracy, conciseness, and speed. These become an excellent base for the qualities of style, depth-reporting, and creativity required of a magazine type."

CHECKLIST: RULES FOR MAGAZINE WRITING

1. First, do not automatically omit the comma before the final "and" in a series. In newspapers, no comma before the last "and" in a series is *the* rule. Not in most magazines. Perhaps twenty magazines—*Time* and *Newsweek,* among others—hold to the newspaper rule, but many do not. When you submit an article, make certain that your cover letter (which should accompany your article) also does or does not obey the newspaper rule, as appropriate.

2. Read very carefully the magazine for which you are writing before submitting your article. If, for example, you are writing for the *New Yorker* or the *Atlantic* (the latter edited by William Whitworth, who was an editor, year after year, for the *New Yorker*), be certain you are using the kind of sentence the editors of those magazines welcome: long, properly punctuated, and involved, yet clear. Not every writer of an article published in either magazine obeys this rule, but most do. Read as carefully as you can *any* magazine you are writing for.

3. *Always* observe the length of your paragraphs. Many magazines will run paragraphs so long that any newspaper would shun them. At least one magazine editor says that newspaper people who attempt to write for his magazine are "illiterate." This comment may not necessarily refer to the length of paragraphs, but one- and two-sentence paragraphs—paragraph after paragraph— *will* set him and other magazine editors afire.

4. Always gather more information than you can use in your article. If you are uncertain whether to include worthwhile material in your article, nearly always do so. If you cut good pages, no editor can possibly add them.

Direct Application and Internships

For varied reasons, not all those who become staff writers have either the opportunity or the inclination to work their way onto magazine staffs by beginning as free-lancers, as stringers, or as newspaper reporters. Indeed, so many are impatient for staff positions that they simply apply, and perhaps more staff writers are trained and developed on the job than in any other way. For a long time, the process of working up to important assignments was frustrating. Beginners did secretarial work and simple clipping, filing, and research. A full opportunity to demonstrate reporting, writing, and editing ability was often agonizingly slow in arriving. Such frustrations still exist on many magazines, and novices should consider the possibility that getting a few writing credits through free-lancing may enable them to bypass the tedium of low-level staff work. But in recent years, many magazines have recognized that personnel policies must be revamped. Some companies, especially those like McGraw-Hill that publish many magazines, have set up training programs that make use of beginners' talents and also help to develop them. The Magazine Publishers Association has established a summer internship program that gives about fifty journalism students a ten-week taste of magazine staff work. Accredited schools and departments of journalism are invited to nominate an outstanding junior every year. In many cases, the interns prove their talents so well that they are given responsible positions on graduation.

Students who work as interns are generally regarded as trainees. They sometimes receive minimal wages for their work, but more often they work for free in exchange for the knowledge and experience they acquire. Many journalism departments award college credits for internships because they recognize their educational value.

Internships need not be at national magazines to be valuable. In fact, it is often easier to find them at local publications because the competition is less keen. A small publication can actually be a better place for a beginner to learn because it is less likely to limit an intern's activities to filing and typing letters. But even those chores can be instructive because they help a novice gain insight into the way a magazine operates. Interns are often asked to perform clerical tasks that may seem unrelated to the business of becoming a journalist, but it is important to realize that beginners are expected to start at the bottom. Those who are willing to do so usually are offered more challenging assignments sooner than are those who complain about their work.

Unorthodox Beginnings

Occasionally, too, editors use unorthodox methods for hiring. When he was an editor for *Esquire,* Harold Hayes announced in his "Editor's Notes" column that he was looking for a junior editor:

> We would like for him to be resourceful, intelligent, and committed to high purpose. But mostly what we need is somebody with a sense of humor. No rush. We can wait until the right man comes along. If you are under twenty-five and interested, just give a try at rewriting the titles and subtitles in this issue. Where you see an opportunity to be funny, seize it. No phone calls or personal appearances, please. Just send in the stuff with your name and address. If you make us laugh, you can come tell us a joke and see how you like us.

Two years later, in a letter to an author of this text, Hayes said that he had written that invitation in some despair of finding a suitable applicant, but "the wife of one young writer saw the column and persuaded him to apply. He proved to be the best of some 75 to 100 applicants, and is today thriving as an Associate Editor here at *Esquire.* His name is Lee Eisenberg."

TWO MAGAZINE STAFFS

A rough notion of how some magazine staffs are formed can be gleaned from reports by two editors. First, associate editor John Scofield of *National Geographic* magazine, which is published by the National Geographic Society, writes:

In pondering how our writers and editors joined the staff, I am somewhat surprised at the random pattern that emerges. The most consistent thread seems to be that writers *apply* to the National Geographic Society for employment rather than being actively recruited from other publications. Only rarely have we resorted to advertising in the trade press. In general we have tended to hire talented young (under thirty-five) writers, some of whom have demonstrated considerable editing talent and have moved up the ladder. Thus all of our editors are capable of undertaking writing assignments, and they frequently do.

Of some forty people actively engaged in the writing, editing, and production of *National Geographic,* the majority have had staff experience on other publications. Thirteen came directly from newspapers, wire or feature services, public relations, or related enterprises. Nine left the staffs of other magazines (among them, *Life, Holiday, U.S. News & World Report, Changing Times,* and *Pathfinder*). Nine have transferred from the Society's other departments or publications, although most of these, too, have had newspaper or magazine experience. Seven came from other fields—government, science, or directly from college, for example. Only two present staffers were full-time free-lance writers when we hired them. (Several others in this category are no longer with us.)

Thus one might fairly conclude that the applicant with the best chance for a staff position at *National Geographic* is currently holding down a writing job with another magazine or newspaper; has an impressive scrapbook to show us; and is willing to undertake a trial assignment, on speculation if necessary.

I think, understandably, staff openings on the magazine itself do not occur frequently. Thus an applicant might have a better chance if he aimed first at one of the Society's other publishing activities: our Book Service, Special Publications, News Service, or School Service. As I have indicated, a number of our magazine staffers have moved up (or over) from other departments.

Former assistant managing editor John Tibby of *Sports Illustrated* reports:

Sports Illustrated began publication in August 1954 under the assumption that about one-third of the magazine would be produced by staff writers, the remainder by free-lance and contract writers. But it was soon judged that a pattern quite suitable to many monthlies was inadvisable in a weekly that undertakes to be as timely as any other newsweekly. *Sports Illustrated* began the gradual development of a "senior editor" system, with departmentalized responsibilities in certain clusters of sports assigned to such editors. In addition, the title senior editor was awarded in a number of cases to persons who did not prefer to specialize in story planning and editing; these are in effect senior writers.

Today about 80 percent of *Sports Illustrated* is staff written, and of the remainder about half comes from contract writers (e.g., Jack Olsen) and the other half from usually well-established writers not under contract.

In addition to the managing group, we have forty-one staff editors and writers ranging in masthead designation from senior editor through associate editor to staff writer. These are supported by an auxiliary group with masthead designations ranging through writer-reporter and senior reporter to reporter. These individuals help research stories, help check them, and often accompany writers on story locations. All are encouraged to show writing ability, and a good many in the senior and intermediate writing groups have risen from the reporter divisions.

In general, appointments to junior staff (reporters) go to men and women in their early to mid-twenties. The competition for the relatively few openings in any year is especially severe for men, since the largest number of applications or inquiries reach us from men (up to 100 a year). As a result *Sports Illustrated* is inclined to choose from among those with the best writing samples of their professional work. One or two years of professional writing is not an absolute requirement, but such experience helps to show something more than latent talent.

We use no form letters in correspondence with people inquiring about staff opportunities. We are always glad to have such men and women introduce themselves to us in person. We regret that we have no means of conducting job interviews except in New York City.

To summarize, the clearest paths to magazine staff work are free-lancing, working as a stringer, working as a newspaper reporter, and simply applying for a job. Some have followed *all* these paths, and many have reached high-level magazine positions by combining newspaper reporting and free-lancing.

Exercises

1. Look over the critical comments on articles you have written as class assignments. On the basis of these criticisms, compile a five-to-ten-item checklist made up of the most valuable or most frequently repeated negative comments on your work. Keep this checklist, use it as a guide in revising future stories, and add to and delete from it on the basis of future criticism and mastered difficulties.

2. Reread the stories of successful student journalists told in this chapter. As you do so and reflect on how their experiences apply to you, write a plan for selling articles during the rest of your college career. Be sure to say specifically where and when you plan to try to sell your work, and aim for clusters of similar publications rather than single magazines or newspapers.

3. List five campus publications, alumni publications, and local publications from your area. Make an appointment to talk with the editors of these publications, agree on a story idea, write to the editor to confirm this agreement, and submit a story. If you repeat this exercise—and you should—try a college publication if you tried one in your town or city first, a community publication if you began with a school publication.

THREE

FREE-LANCERS AND STAFF WRITERS

No man is an island, entire of itself;

every man is a piece of the continent,

a part of the main. . . .

JOHN DONNE

Free-lancers were, year after year, in a category envied by many prospective writers. Some still are, but magazine staff writers have achieved a new envy: they are certain to publish in their magazines. Here are their joys and controversies.

THE MAGAZINE STAFF WRITER

Rather than relying on free-lancers, some publishers have moved to staff-written products, in part because many have learned from the example of the news magazines that a tailor-made quality is most evident when a closely knit staff produces a magazine. The move toward staff writing was not designed to cut costs. In fact, staff-written articles are usually much more expensive to produce than free-lance articles.

Although later chapters will deal extensively with staff writing, it might be helpful here to suggest some of the reasons for the trend. When one considers the flaws of the free-lancer from the editor's point of view, the reasons for using staff writers become clear. Not long after he became managing editor of *World View,* a prestigious magazine that reprints serious articles from leading newspapers and magazines around the world, Barry Golson, then twenty-five years old, wrote to the author of this book:

> One of the more amazing things I've found about free-lancers, to judge by the letters and queries we receive here, is their lack of discrimination. They seem to whip off queries without pausing to consider the nature of the publication. Some guy sent us an unsolicited manuscript on beauty aids for children. Others deluge us with constant hot tips, ambitious projects, political essays, revolutionary tracts—none of which have the slightest bearing on "Best from the World Press," our clearly marked subtitle.

Rather than devote hours to considering unsolicited articles and letters from free-lancers, many editors prefer to spend their energies on staff writers who have a clear notion of the needs of the magazine and possess the ability to write for it. This does not mean that getting a job as a staff writer is easy. In fact, landing a job as a magazine staff writer is a bit like trying to hop aboard a moving merry-go-round; the real problem is in getting on, but once you do, it is easy to change horses. In particular, the New York publishing world is a place in which staff members move frequently from one publication to another. The same names appear over and over again on different mastheads and in different combinations. As in many other fields, the key to landing these jobs is experience.

Acquiring that experience has lately meant starting at the bottom of the magazine staff heap. College students, and even some nonstudents, who work as interns on magazine staffs get the best chance to demonstrate their abilities. They often perform research tasks or even clerical assignments for little or no pay, but in exchange they may learn a great deal about how magazines operate. They may also be given opportunities to write short articles or to take responsibility for magazine departments like "Letters to the Editor." The lucky ones may be offered staff jobs as editorial assistants based on their experiences as interns. Such jobs are usually the first rung of the editorial ladder and are followed by positions like assistant editor, department editor, associate editor, and so on. *Newsweek* even has a position called "senior editorial assistant."

The specific responsibilities of people in these positions vary among magazines. Perhaps the most significant difference between a magazine staff job and a feature-writing job at a newspaper is that the former usually involves many tasks in addition to article writing. This chapter describes magazine systems for handling editorial material, reviews the activities of people in different kinds of magazine staff writing jobs, and then discusses the general role of the staff member.

Magazine Systems

According to Charles F. Kettering, "virtually nothing comes out right the first time. Failures, *repeated* failures, are finger posts on the road to achievement. The only time you don't fail is the last time you try something, and it works. One fails forward toward success."

When you mail your articles to magazines, keep Kettering's words in mind. Most people fail many times before earning a success. Every magazine develops its own system for handling articles that are submitted for publication. Usually one or more people are assigned the task of reading unsolicited manuscripts and deciding whether or not they merit consideration by an editor. Commonly known as "the slush pile" in New York editing circles, these articles rarely pass beyond this initial review. Most are not written by professionals, who rely primarily on query letters to pave the way for articles they want to write.

An assigned story usually goes directly to the editor with whom the writer has corresponded. Often this will be the person in charge of a particular department of the magazine, such as profiles, how-to's, and so on. The procedure from this point varies greatly from magazine to magazine, depending on the size of the editorial staff. The department editor may read the article first and decide whether or not it is publishable material. If not, it will probably be sent back to the writer with either a rejection slip or a request for revisions. If the piece passes the first editorial review, it may then be given to other editors for their comments or to the editor in chief for a final decision. Or the person with final authority for accepting articles may be the department editor.

Once the article has been accepted, it is then edited by one or more people. If major changes are made, an editor may contact the writer for approval, but the writer cannot assume that this will happen. During this stage, a person called a fact checker may also be assigned the task of verifying all of the objective facts and direct quotations contained in the article. To facilitate this process, some magazines ask writers to provide a list of their sources of information, including the telephone numbers of the people they interviewed. Most writers welcome the services of a fact checker because they ensure that no easily correctable errors will appear in the published versions of their stories.

While the article is being edited, it may also be under consideration by the art department. If photos were provided with the manuscript, the art director will decide whether or not they are adequate. If an illustration is to be used, the art director will either assign it to an assistant or commission a freelance artist to do the job. Sometimes the editors consult with the art director concerning the visual appearance of an article. This is especially likely to occur when the article will be featured as a cover story.

Some Unusual Staff Writing Jobs

At the home of *Sunset* magazine in Menlo Park, California, thirty-five miles south of San Francisco, many staff writers serve a diversified clientele. By any estimate, *Sunset* is the most successful magazine in the West, with more than one million subscribers. *Sunset* serves the entire nine-state region of the western United States and has several writers working in other cities. All *Sunset* workers have a mission—to concentrate on food, travel, outdoor recreation, gardening, or home-building and decorating projects. One of the staff writers, Mary Ord, has drawn a sharp picture of the work of the staff writer.

> At *Sunset* a staff writer functions somewhat like an in-house free-lancer. His job may bear little relation to "staff" except that he uses the magazine's resources and conveniences (files, photographers, art staff, darkroom, checking facilities, etc.). Like a free-lancer, he attempts to put his prose into the magazine's style—that is, he writes to serve the magazine's avowed purpose to the reader, in our case—how to make it, bake it, grow it, visit it. People in *Sunset*'s "outer" offices—Seattle, Los Angeles, Honolulu—sometimes work at home, checking in by phone.
>
> Like a free-lancer, a staff writer proposes article ideas to the edi-

"Two roads diverged in a wood, and I/—I took the one less traveled by,/And that has made all the difference."

ROBERT FROST

tors. He should have done enough research into the topic (and perhaps have scouting photography in hand) to determine if the subject can be handled in such a way as to be interesting to the magazine's specific audience. He must have enough information on the subject and a clear enough idea of a suitable approach so he can "sell" it to the editors. He must convince them that *he*, not another staffer, is the one to do such a story. I once had the go-ahead to do a story on shopping in Los Angeles museums for Christmas gifts. A writer in the Los Angeles office suggested a different way to handle it—covering just three museums and keying gift ideas to their current shows. He got the nod and I lost out. The writer should be able to suggest timing (perhaps tying the story to a news event) and photographic possibilities.

Then there is the same sort of give-and-take that might happen between editor and free-lancer, with the editor possibly suggesting different timing, other aspects to consider, other photo possibilities. The editor might also bring up other story ideas he has had in mind along the same lines and ask the writer to help research them or take them over completely for future stories.

The writer then goes out to get scouting photography (if he doesn't already have it and if the story calls for pictures). He does more in-depth research, reporting in as things develop. The story may change shape or focus as research or photos turn out better or worse than expected. . . .

Among free-lancers and staff writers there is competition for stories, and you win some, lose some. Unlike a free-lancer, a staff writer must learn to have a give-and-take relationship with other staffers—face to face, day to day. Free-lancers, I think, are more removed, having only to hear over the phone or by letter, "We already have someone working on that."

At *Fortune,* the staff writers are so independent of office routine that a man who was once managing editor described the system as "subsidized free-lancing." The subsidies can be substantial, including comfortable salaries and expense accounts as well as the help of capable researchers. The freedom is equally substantial. In fact, few *Fortune* writers visit the office very often, most preferring to write at home. Between assignments, a staff writer may be given other chores, such as helping to produce the magazine's regular sections and departments. But the limited demands imposed by such supplementary work are suggested by the fact that one *Fortune* writer was in the office only sixty days one year. He described this as typical. (The office is not deserted, of course. Editors, artists, and writers who produce special departments are routinely on hand.)

Gene Bylinsky, who was once a free-lancer and is now one of the best *Fortune* writers, described the operation:

You do have deadlines, of course. They come maybe six or eight weeks apart. But once you have started on a story you are on your own. *Fortune* is unusual in its researcher help, especially in serving as another reporter on the story. That's how the researcher and I worked on the computer peripherals story in the June issue. We started by interviewing sources in Boston together. Then I went on to upstate New York while she flew to Dallas to interview companies there. We then met in San Francisco, where we interviewed a large number of people, separately. Later, even as I was writing the story, she continued interviewing, in Philadelphia, Washington, and other cities. (In addition, by the way, a great service provided by researchers is that they transcribe notes for the writers.)

I get a much faster response to stories as a staff writer than I got as a free-lancer. The editors have to respond quickly because the way things are organized at *Fortune* a writer's story *has* to work out—it's scheduled for an issue.

A number of people at *Fortune* act as "story editors" (from time to time), although the managing editor actually runs the magazine. After a writer turns in his manuscript to the typing room, it is mimeographed and distributed to the editors. That's the first draft. The managing editor reads it, scribbles comments on it, talks to the story editor, then the story editor talks to the writer. There's usually at least one rewrite. Interestingly enough, when one managing editor voluntarily stepped down to become a writer again, *he* had to rewrite *his* stuff. This probably illustrates the subjective nature of writing. This system certainly isn't a bad idea. I know that most second drafts turn out a lot better.

Assuming that the second draft gets by the managing editor, the "closing" starts. It's almost like publishing a book, but on a smaller scale. The manuscript is checked by the researcher, who calls sources to check on quotations, figures, etc. Then the manuscript goes to the proof room and is set in type. We get one proof of "the front of the book"— the major part of the article that runs near the beginning of the issue. The checking and double-checking results in a magazine that has very few errors—typos or otherwise.

After the staff writer is finished with the story, he goes on to the next one. It can be his idea or the editor's idea.

Regardless of how many staff writers work like those at *Fortune,* Bylinsky's work for *Fortune* and Mary Ord's work for *Sunset* represent only a small percentage of the sorts of staff writing jobs available on American magazines. What might be termed the more conventional staff writing work is quite different. But there are too many varieties of the "conventional" to describe all of them.

The best way to understand all the varieties of staff writing is to consider a few that are fairly common.

Traditional Staff Writing Jobs

Traditional staff writing jobs may differ as much as news magazines vs. the many magazines. While reading, remember the heading over each set of paragraphs.

The News Magazines

Hal Bruno, formerly the news editor of *Newsweek,* has said that "a news magazine is a place where reporters report, writers write, and a person contemplating a career in this field should have some idea as to which of these skills he or she does best and enjoys most." In the sense in which we are considering the term, "staff writing" refers to both reporting and writing. But it certainly is necessary to be aware of the distinction Bruno makes. One aspect of that distinction is that *Newsweek* writers (and editors) work in New York; almost all the reporters work in twenty-two foreign and domestic bureaus. Basically, the writers fashion most of the stories that appear in news magazines by using the research pieces that are sent to New York by the reporters. Very rarely do free-lancers provide any of the material that goes into news magazines.

In recent years, news magazines have begun to quote long passages from their reporters. It has thus become possible for news magazine reporters to consider themselves writers as well.

How the work of news magazine bureaus is carried out is described by Peter Sinton, who was a reporter in the San Francisco bureau of *Time:*

> The bureaus, national and international, are tied very closely with New York; a teletype-telephone umbilicus ties the bureau with the great mother organization in New York. In the case of *Time,* and I suppose *Newsweek,* the umbilicus is never broken, and New York is sort of the revered and hated parent. Relationships with New York tended to be rather impersonal, quite businesslike, terse and efficient. Telephone calls are brief, not by edict from New York, but by understanding of the big news magazine process and how things operate. If you can't grasp this, you can't very well work for the magazine. . . .
>
> There were usually enough exciting stories to go around, many times even more than we could handle, and this made the job especially interesting. No obituaries or fires or gossipy trash, the staple of many dailies. The stories at *Time* were of a higher level, of national importance or interest. It was especially satisfying suggesting a story to New York, having it accepted, working on it alone, and having it published, in brief, but still intact. . . .
>
> As for sources, we didn't have enough writers and researchers to spread around the city or our territory. We had some stringers on campuses but we couldn't cover a beat like a newspaper reporter could. We didn't have men stationed at the Federal Building or the Police headquarters. So we depended a lot on the newspapers and the leads they offered. The *Examiner* and *Chronicle* and *Palo Alto Times,* and the *New York Times* and *Wall Street Journal,* were all searched for important news leads. Our minds were programmed to scan the papers, the daily flack mail, etc., with the sections of the magazine turning over in our minds like IBM cards. Would the story have appeal for its oddity, for its national news value, etc.? We'd send the idea off to New York and the maze of hallways and offices and the final judgment, the word from above. Sometimes we could argue a certain story was worthwhile, but we couldn't press it too far. We were outflanked and outnumbered by the huge New York operation.
>
> Thinking was also useful for dreaming up stories, things that the papers hadn't touched. Things of wider scope, thought pieces. One had to raise his mind above the day-to-day repetition of events. It was

drummed into us that we should read widely, get out and talk with sources, and develop sort of an individual think tank. . . .

Groups of Magazines

The trend toward grouping many publications under one ownership is noticeable throughout the magazine world, but it is especially strong among business and industrial publications. One of the most successful groups is McGraw-Hill, which publishes nearly fifty business and scientific magazines. Like the news magazines, all McGraw-Hill publications are produced almost entirely by staff writers (who are known as editorial assistants, correspondents, assistant editors, and the like). Some of the most prestigious magazines in the McGraw-Hill group—most notably *Business Week*—maintain their own bureaus, but most are served by bureaus that also serve many other McGraw-Hill magazines.

How this system works is indicated by the organization of the Los Angeles bureau, one of the largest in the McGraw-Hill World News Service. It has six correspondents and one editorial assistant who divide responsibilities for covering much of California for more than thirty magazines. As a rule, each staff writer in the bureau is designated as the local correspondent for five or six magazines. There are two exceptions. If a correspondent who is busy with important assignments receives still another assignment from one of his or her magazines, it may be passed on by the bureau chief to another correspondent. Second, most correspondents become specialists—one has become expert in air and water pollution, for example—and handle most of the assignments in their special areas regardless of which magazine the story is slated for.

For the most part, this is an excellent system. One former staffer commented: "Work for McGraw-Hill was remarkably pleasant, and was excellent training for a young journalist. Work conditions were, and apparently still are, very interesting and rewarding."

There are inevitable problems, however, in any system. McGraw-Hill may be on the way to solving one that irked staffers—the "inch-count system" that measured bureau performance. The memories of it nurtured by one former Los Angeles bureau correspondent, Jerilyn Sue McIntyre, are worth recounting because they reveal the difficulty in determining efficiency in a large organization that encompasses many magazines and many writers:

> The mechanics are simple: each month we tabulated the number of inches in print contributed by members of our bureau to each of the magazines covered by the bureau. At the end of the year, statistics were sent to each bureau chief, indicating the inch-count total for all bureaus in the World News organization and comparing the totals with previous performances. Apparently, each magazine is assessed for the amount of coverage done by the bureaus; and eventually, or so we were led to believe, these totals probably have some effect on budget allotments for individual bureaus. . . .

Occasionally, there may be issues larger than economics involved in publishing groups of magazines. Among physicians and others who know it well, the *Journal of the American Medical Association* (familiarly known as the *AMA Journal* or *JAMA*) is a prestigious publication. It is sometimes criticized because of the policies of the association itself, and, as one staffer has said of all AMA publications, "It isn't always easy to practice freedom of the press in an institutional setting."

Small Magazines

A young journalist who has worked for newspapers and for large and small magazines makes this observation: "There seems to be an inverse relationship between the size of the magazine and the staff relations with editors. The bigger and better known the magazine, the less likely it is that the top editors are going to be close to the staff." Although there are certainly exceptions, a moment's reflection should suggest that this observation is almost certainly accurate. Few sizable organizations are noted for close relations between executives and workers.

But if the observation is a truism, it may also suggest to one who yearns to work for a big magazine that a few years on smaller publications may be better training. Just as one who begins work for a giant manufacturing firm is likely to find that her experiences are specialized and limited, the young magazine staffer who takes a job with a giant publication is likely to find the spectrum of her tasks quite narrow.

Normally, the reverse is true for those who work for small magazines. Indeed, if the magazine is small enough—and hundreds are published with staffs consisting only of an editor, an assistant editor, and a secretary—a staffer may find that he is getting a good bit more experience than he can absorb comfortably in a short time.

A young writer described the operation of *Ski* magazine:

An unbelievable amount of time is spent on researching stories and checking on facts. Many writers at *Ski* seem to spend most of their time on the phone—tracking people down, conducting interviews, confirming details, etc. Actual time spent writing is much less than time spent researching.

There is a big emphasis on coming up with the unique ideas that appeal to many people. With the speedy competition from radio, TV, and newspapers, magazines have to come up with things these other media can't do.

The story is the responsibility of the writer right up to the time it is "closed" in page proof, but a lot of other people share the responsibility. At *Ski*, the managing editor reads everything and goes over it with the writer. The writer writes the head for the story as well as the two- or three-line display lead-in. Though these are subject to change by the managing editor, more often than not they're left alone.

At some magazines, checking copies of articles are sent to all sources and to all people involved in the article. At *Ski*, showing copy to any outsider is strictly forbidden. Bill Berry, the executive editor, commented, "Nothing can compromise the integrity of a magazine more quickly than this."

Each monthly issue is kind of the baby of everyone involved. There is a freshness with each copy of the magazine that's lacking in the newspaper world. If you make an error which slips through, there is rarely a tomorrow to rectify it. The entire staff seems dedicated to making every story on every page as appealing, accurate, and original as possible.

The Staffer as Jack-of-All-Trades

For no clear reason, magazines have never developed titles that adequately describe staff duties. On a newspaper, the work of the editor, the managing editor, the city editor, the political reporter, and the other news and editorial employees is fairly well defined. The work of a city editor for a large newspaper may differ from the work of the city editor for a small paper—the former is likely to be more an executive in the sense of leading and directing operations; the latter probably spends much more time with pencil poised over news stories—but their tasks are at least similar. In the news departments of radio and television broadcasters, the work of the news director, the assignment editor, and the reporters may vary with the size of the station and other factors, but again the similarities are more apparent than the differences. But in the magazine world, anyone hoping to find the kind of order represented by titles and duties neatly defined is likely to be disappointed. On one publication, a "contributing editor" may do no editing; he is actually a staff writer who ranges over the world and writes at home. On another, a "contributing editor" may be a contract writer who gives only half her time to the magazine—and that time is devoted to writing rather than editing— while the other half is given to free-lancing. "Associate editor" may be similarly misleading because one who holds such a title may write articles, article titles, and picture captions and also may edit or supervise production.

All this would be inconsequential if it simply meant that the duties of a staffer on one magazine differ from the duties of a staffer holding the same title on another magazine. These differences are important, however, because they indicate the immense diversity of staff work. Many who are considering magazine careers may think of staff writing jobs as being limited to those outlined in the first section of this chapter. It is doubtful, for example, that beginners ever wonder who writes the captions for the illustrations in picture magazines and even more doubtful that they consider caption writing important training for the kind of writing represented by 4,000-word articles. One staff writer described caption writing as:

> . . . fitting headlines, text blocks and captions to the spirit and content of pictures—"writing square sentences," as we sometimes called it in times of desperation. Writing for pictures—with the words meant to illumine the picture rather than the other way around—enforces a spe-

cial set of disciplines: economy for one (you don't waste many words when you are working within a framework of two lines precisely forty-three characters long—no more, no less). And you acquire a deep respect for the narrative power of the photograph or illustration . . . they are there as an integral part of what the piece has to say—heart and guts rather than mere decoration.

Nor would a beginner be likely to think of a magazine researcher as a writer. It is certainly true that few *are* writers in the sense of producing by-lined pieces. Many researchers do little more than check manuscripts for accuracy. But some who have earned the confidence of writers and editors contribute measurably to the final product that carries the byline of one whose label is "staff writer." How this works has been described by Ann Scott, a former *Fortune* researcher who became a writer for *Newsweek:*

> Sometimes the writer–researcher team splits up, dividing parts of the story to cover more ground. This can be most useful, especially for the lengthy, in-depth story that *Fortune* should be doing. The better researchers contribute a great deal to the thesis of their stories, too, and this can include writing memos to writers and editors about positions that should be taken, points that should be included, and the like. Sometimes, too, a researcher does a full written report on some aspect of a story, as I did once on the European chemical industry for a piece on big business in Europe.

In 1971, the more than fifty *Time* researchers became "reporter–researchers." As Publisher Henry Luce III pointed out, the new title describes more fully and precisely what they do. Every week, they help shape articles and send queries to more than four hundred *Time* correspondents and stringers around the world. They cull the magazine's extensive reference library. Some routinely search for information in Manhattan's offices and institutions. Several have traveled far afield to interview and observe.

These tasks suggest other dimensions of staff writing. When the author of this book was a staff writer and Washington correspondent for *Reporter* magazine, most of the work was writing. But about 15 percent of it consisted of discussing article ideas with other correspondents who wanted to write for the *Reporter;* editing and rewriting some articles and considering, accepting, and rejecting others; and providing information for other *Reporter* writers who were based elsewhere.

Editorial Functions

To obtain a broad view of the many possible tasks of the staff writer, it might help to consider the functions of the editor, for staff writers on many publications are assigned some of these functions or are assigned to help with them:

1. Creating the formula or pattern for a new magazine or reconsidering the formula or pattern for an existing one.

2. Long-range planning and planning of individual issues.

3. Procuring and selecting articles.
4. Editing articles.
5. Preparing layouts and dummies.
6. Selecting, sizing, and cropping pictures.
7. Coordinating the work of specialists.

The Editor Makes Assignments

Staff writers often succeed in winning assignments over free-lancers. In some cases, of course, staff writers work side by side with free-lancers. And when an editor learns to trust the work of a free-lancer, the difference in making assignments is usually slight. Here, for example, Lucille Enix, editor of *Dallas* magazine, has written one assignment memo to a trusted free-lancer, Carolyn Barta, and another to the magazine's associate editor, Jenny Haynes:

Carolyn Barta

Cover article for the September *Dallas* magazine
Subject: What makes Dallas a top convention city?
Length: Approx. 4,000 words
Deadline: August 1

At this time the city of Dallas is ranked as 8th largest in population in the U.S. Yet, according to the book "World Convention Dates," Dallas ranks something like 4th in conventions. You'll need to get the exact rating and sources from Wes Young of the Convention Bureau on convention ratings. The question is, why does Dallas seem to draw a larger share of conventions as compared to the size of the city?

Part of the answer is in the sales force now working with the Dallas Convention Bureau. Ray Bennison, manager, will introduce you to the sales staff and they will explain their responsibilities.

Another part of the answer is the services available in Dallas to groups holding conventions here—air transportation, hotel and motel rooms available, persons to run registration desks, services of decorators to set up booths and lay out exhibit space, audiovisual equipment rentals, transfer companies to move and store equipment, printers for daily house organs, newsletters, reports that come out of conventions, security guards, business machines and office furniture to run convention business, special telephone services, catering services, special Dallas bus services, florists—Bennison can name more.

The city itself draws some conventions: the climate, citizens, and convention center and market hall complex.

In sketching what the city has to offer for conventions, describe some of the personalities, inside looks at how the services work immediately on the scene and future planning.

How many persons attended conventions in Dallas last year, what's projected for this year? How much money was spent by persons attending conventions? Both for services and personally? How much business becomes repeat business from conventions held here?

What is the city's potential in the convention business?

Jenny Haynes

Article for the September Visitor's Guide
Subject: Exploring the Dallas Health and Science Museum, Planetarium, and Aquarium
Length: Approx. 3,000 words
Deadline: July 27

This is the visitor's exploration through three museums that illustrate and explain the wonder of life and the universe. It is primarily a descriptive piece with anecdotes of exhibits, objects and events within each museum. It is not a history of how the museums came to be.

What can the visitor find when he visits? Can he participate with the content in the museums? How? Where are the museums located—the highway number, not the local name of the highway, helps get the visitor there.

H. D. Carmichael is in charge of the Health and Science museum and the Planetarium. The Dallas Park Department is in charge of the Aquarium.

In the Aquarium, you might describe some of the sea life, why certain species were selected for Dallas and how they live.

These memos are rich in lessons. First, they represent the kind of work that staffers do on some magazines. That is, one who devotes much of his or her time to writing or editing manuscripts may also be assigned to write memos of this kind to free-lancers and to other staff writers.

Second, although one memo is to a free-lancer and the other to a staff writer, it is obvious that the editor has confidence in both writers. Because Carolyn Barta, the free-lancer, had already written perceptive articles for *Dallas*, the editor knew that she could handle the convention article capably. Perhaps, though, if editor Lucille Enix had been assigning the article to an untried free-lancer, she would have written in much greater detail.

Third, note that both memos focus on the length and substance of the articles. Carolyn Barta's article should carry this fact about Dallas conventions and answer that question for the readers. The article by Jenny Haynes should cover this aspect of the museums and describe these features. In neither case is the editor attempting to dictate writing style or technique. The writers are professionals; and, although the editor's perspective is likely to aid them in revising before their articles are published, the writers decide on approach and treatment.

Some of the current arrangements editors make with writers resemble the system developed by Harold Ross. Shortly after his *New Yorker* was established in 1925, Ross put a few free-lancers on generous "drawing accounts" that paid them regularly. In effect, they owed the magazine, but the debt was erased when their articles were published. They were not quite staff writers, but they were certainly not free-lancers in the conventional sense.

Such arrangements suggest where many of the free-lancers have gone. Although some are still free-lancing and others have become full-fledged staff writers, still others are in the ill-defined area between free-lancing and staff writing. They are likely to work at home, and they are tied to magazines by contracts that call for a few articles a year, with some time left for conventional free-lancing. Only successful free-lancers are likely to be offered writing contracts of the sort described here, but one need not be successful as a free-lancer to become a staff writer. Indeed, it is likely that a majority of the magazines now published in the United States employ staff writers (and editors) who have never sold a free-lance article. As indicated in Chapter 2, free-lancing (even with only moderate success) is a good avenue to a job as a staff writer or editor.

Some free-lancers, of course, remain free-lancers. Some publications still rely largely on their work, and a great many editors believe that at least part of their magazines must be produced by free-lancers, because magazines produced solely by staff and contract writers often seem stale and lacking the freshness of view that outsiders can provide. Due to the special demands of modern magazines, free-lancers are likely to write for fewer publications than they did in the past. Further, the writer must keep in close touch with editors, usually by visiting magazine offices for story conferences, rather than merely reading and analyzing magazines from a distance.

THE FREE-LANCE WRITER

> "Patience, diligence, painstaking attention to detail—these are the requirements."
>
> MARK TWAIN

The late, great writer Ernest Hemingway made a statement that has had neophyte novelists repeating his words over and over:

> A writer's problem does not change. He himself changes and the world he lives in changes, but his problem remains the same. It is always how to write truly and, having found out what is true, to project it in such a way that it becomes part of the experience of the person who reads it.

Would-be novelists love these words, but what of the nonfiction writers? Although few of them may have heard the Hemingway quotation, all nonfictionists should make it a familiar saying, for it is more applicable to nonfiction than to fiction.

In fact, novelists and short story writers work much as nonfiction writers do. Here is a young novelist whose work habits are like those of many professional writers. Michelle Carter wrote her first novel in 1985. Here are her words about writing that novel:*

> The narrative voice of *On Other Days While Going Home* (William Morrow & Co., 1987) originated in a short story I wrote in 1982. The next year, I worked at Simon and Schuster in New York—nothing sucks the creative juices dry like working in publishing. But the following year, at the Fine Arts Work Center in Provincetown, I returned to

---

*Reprinted by permission of Michelle Carter.

that voice, that character, her general predicament in the world. 1984 was a good, important, productive year of writing pages and throwing them away. In the summer of 1985, after a year of teaching at Stanford, I was ready, at last, to set down a complete draft. Since I'd gotten a lot of false, ingenuous material out of my system (kindly old curmudgeons saying colorful things like "Well kiss my ass and call me Mildred"), I felt pretty confident that I had now arrived at something *concrete.* I realized that one shouldn't sit down to write about, say, quirky people and places, any more than one should set out to write about truth and justice, or good vs. evil, or loyalty, or love. I needed, rather, to start with a particular young woman who, due to the peculiar nature of her personality, couldn't figure out quite how to live.

That first-draft summer, I set a weekly page quota. My goal was ten readable pages a week. Though that draft was to go through four major revisions, I had to get the story on paper in some form before I could bring the characters and their world fully to life in my imagination.

Here follows a day in the life of draft number one, reconstructed from journal entries.

July 13, 1985

10:30 a.m.   Coffee, *San Francisco Chronicle.* Eye catches horoscope: "Heed the counsel of friends and advisors."

11:15 a.m.   Search pants-pockets, find napkin with notes jotted yesterday during coffee with John L'Heureux. Rest napkin beside computer.

11:30 a.m.   Read through yesterday's pages: the book's only real sex scene. Decide characters are unhappy enough with each other to keep readers from cringing. Make cosmetic corrections—cut excess flab, enliven some verbs.

1 p.m.   Turn on computer, open journal. Today: the climactic fire scene. While Annie and Nelson are making love, Tom the villainous Hell's Angel will set the building on fire to remind everyone who's boss. Consult journal notes based upon discussion with firefighter about sounds, sights, and smells from inside burning building:

>—Bad smoke inhalation makes you cough up black stuff
>—You see heat waves rise from floor
>—Floor, walls get hot, smoke
>—Eyes water, sting; lungs ache
>—Burning walls can boom, or crackle like bacon frying
>—Flames can travel quietly inside walls
>—Fire creates wind, sucking
>—Ash can fall in solid sheets
>—Flames can skid down stairs, skate over surfaces
>—Etc.

Skim lists on next page of journal: *Fire- and smoke-related words*

fume	soot	burn	flare	smother
vapor	pitch	scorch	flicker	
gas		scald	glow	
cloud		swelter	smolder	
plume		blaze	sweat	
steam				

Scan random notes beneath word lists:

—A. should lose something in the fire, maybe something Jotta gave her

—Men and women from the gay bars could be partying in the firelight

—Nelson locked up dog before he and A. went to bed; rescue dog? fry dog?

—Irony maybe if, before fire, Nelson uses line, "Love sneaks up on you, sort of like freezing to death." Maybe not.

Remember friend Deborah said the name Nelson made her think of wimpy second-grade boys. Remember horoscope. Call Deborah; no answer. Consult notations on napkin:

The more vague the threat, the more terrifying

Especially chilling when what seemed casual turns out to have caused the inevitable

Napkin yields exciting applications in coming Tom confrontation, but not relevent to fire scene.

MICHELLE CARTER

A San Francisco Bay Area native, Michelle Carter is a young writer whose "career is going to be an interesting one to follow," according to a *Glamour* magazine reporter. While teaching fiction writing at Stanford University, Carter has published short stories in national magazines and lectures in fiction writing.

In a short story, "The Things That Would Never Be Mine," Carter writes: "Now thirty-seven, I've migrated the length and breadth of California like a cut-rate local airline. As a kid in Bakersfield, I thought the city got its name because the sidewalk looked dusted with flour." This story is printed in an anthology titled *The New Generation*.

Carter's work has been called "appealing, original, and stylistically deft" by *Booklist* and has earned Carter numerous fellowships and awards, including a grant from the National Endowment for the Arts. From 1980 through 1982, Carter was a Mirrielees Fellow in the graduate program at Stanford, where she also completed four years of a Jones Lectureship.

In a passage that demonstrates her talent for description, Carter describes one of her characters: "In our eleven years, I've never seen Peter reveal an ugly emotion in a gesture. Peter is a man who runs water in the ice tray after using three cubes, who would never leave a grocery cart in the middle of the parking lot or eat the chocolate vein out of the Fudge Ripple."

By using such descriptive language, Carter illuminates her characters; a few pages later in the story, she explains: "Peter's care and planning afford him the luxury of composure in front of strangers, the appearance of casual, indifferent, spontaneous charm. This is one of the things I work hard not to hate in him."

In 1985, after working at Simon & Schuster for one year and completing a writing fellowship at the Fine Arts Work Center in Provincetown, Massachusetts, Carter turned to writing longer works and finished the first draft of her first novel. In July 1987, her novel, *On Other Days While Going Home,* was published.

Early reviews uniformly praised the book for its skill,

1:45 p.m. Get up and change kitty litter. Notice dust-devils gliding across bathroom floor. Mop floor, scour shower and sink. Run out of Comet, none left for toilet or kitchen sink. In car, head toward Payless—might as well hit the Safeway and stock up all round.

5 p.m. Friend Jessica calls for no particular reason. "Say," I wonder aloud, "you doing anything about dinner?"

11 p.m. Line up four new napkins beside computer. Five pages later: draft of fire scene.

Beginning free-lancers have one advantage over prospective staff writers: they do not need to persuade anyone to hire them full-time in order to start writing. In fact, many free-lance writers have eased into staff positions by becoming frequent and reliable contributors to a magazine. A full-time position may not be your goal, especially after you have experienced the freedom and independence of free-lance writing. Along with the flexibility of free-lancing, however, go a number of constraints.

How a Free-Lancer Operates

A few years ago, William Least Heat-Moon went on a journey to such places as Brooklyn Bridge, Kentucky, Klickitat, Washington, and Ninety Six, South Carolina. His book, *Blue Highways*, took its title from the old maps, which showed major roads in red and back roads in blue.

Those two kinds of road reflect two different ways of getting some-

---

vitality, and originality. It is the story of eighteen-year-old Annie, a smart, tough teenager who was raised in her aunt Marie's bail bond office in San Francisco. Annie goes on a journey of discovery, looking for a way out of childhood and for life, adventure, and freedom.

According to Doris Ober, the characters are "on the fringes of society, on the edge of trouble, with marginal resources and plenty of street savvy." Ober continues: "Although their world may be foreign to many readers, their humanity, or lack of it, is always believable."

Critic Ron Hansen describes the novel as "charming, forthright, true, revealing; and little orphan Annie is one of the most likeable and unlikely ingenues to have appeared in recent fiction."

Carter's writing has been called refreshing, reflective, and compelling. In her first novel, Carter writes:

"You want to live on that dark side you've read about in books and heard about in songs. But what I'm telling you to remember is that it's not there for us—sleeping in bus stations, hitching rides with truck drivers, sharing stories shoulder to shoulder, living dime to dime. The streets are all about power, Annie, and the closest we can get is the back of a motorcycle. . . ."

Because of Carter's special handling of her subject, John Irving wrote that she brings "new vigor, grace, and sympathy to the old subject of women suffering the many disillusionments of that old American dream—family happiness, making peace with the past, a sense of belonging."

On Other Days While Going Home has been included in Penguin Books's Contemporary American Fiction series.

where, Heat-Moon asserts. "A tourist is a person to whom the ends are important—to reach a goal, like Yellowstone, by a set time. A traveler, on the other
hand, is after the means, driving the blue highways and going slower, entering the lives of people. It's a case of sightseers versus people-seers."

Heat-Moon traveled again last year, "just poking along and looking into
things. I've got no schedule," he says. "My favorite kind of trip is one with a
simple pretext for traveling someplace. Then, before I arrive, all sorts of
things happen."

Unlike Heat-Moon, who travels at a leisurely pace, watches things happen, makes no plans, and follows no deadlines, free-lancers must be disciplined, organized, and efficient in order to succeed. Many aspiring journalists
do not realize that free-lance writing is a business that, in order to be successful, must be run efficiently and economically. The commodity for sale is
magazine articles. In most cases, the free-lancer will be the business's writer,
reporter, typist, accountant, advertising director, and salesperson. Beginners
often expect to spend most of their time in the first two roles and are surprised when they discover that the last four can require as much or more
effort. It is important to realize that being successful in these roles will enable a free-lancer to devote more time to writing and reporting.

The beginner should be aware that free-lancing articles is not the most
profitable work a talented and industrious person can pursue. Nothing is
more essential, perhaps, than conditioning the mind for disappointment. Of
sixty-four members of the American Society of Journalists and Authors who
participated in a survey, eight made more than $30,000 a year, but eleven
made less than $10,000.

Free-lancing should first be thought of as a game the writer plays. He is
pitting his wits and resourcefulness against a hundred other writers who may
have hit on the same idea on the same day, or perhaps the week before. So he
plays it as a game, knowing that he cannot win all the time. Many beginners
cannot stand the defeats and disappointments—some veteran writers are
eventually crushed by them—and they should not play the game. Those who
are sensitive and easily hurt by rejections discover that it is a cruel contest.

The necessity for businesslike procedures envelops the free-lancer's
life. She must make herself write regularly and during the same hours every
day. "It's a brutal discipline," one holds, "and you have to stick to it. If you
make the mistake of trying to write fiction in your spare time or fix light bulbs
around the house, you're finished."

Getting Paid

Magazines pay either "on acceptance," or "on publication." Because a magazine may not publish an article for many months after accepting it, payment
on publication can put quite a strain on the free-lancer's monthly budget.
Unfortunately for beginning writers, most small magazines pay on publication
because they operate on strict monthly editorial budgets and do not have the
resources to pay now for articles they will publish later. Even worse, the mor-
tality rate among small magazines is very high, which means that one may fold

having accepted an article but without having published it. The writer may get back the article, but it isn't likely to be accompanied by a check.

Payment for articles varies widely. Most large national magazines pay more than small regional or local ones do. Some pay a flat rate per word of the published article. That means a writer whose 2,500-word article is cut to 1,500 words by an editor is losing more than space in the magazine. More often, however, magazines agree to pay a specified amount for an article and do not change that amount if the story is heavily edited or cut. Beginners may earn as little as $50 for a story in a small magazine or a short item in a large one. More experienced writers earn hundreds of dollars for their articles, and very well established free-lancers may earn thousands for a single piece. It's a long road from the hundreds-per-article to thousands-per-article stage, one that few writers travel very quickly.

It doesn't take much calculating to see that free-lancing is not a lucrative occupation for beginners. Most have to rely on part-time jobs or other sources of income to supplement their earnings as writers. However, this necessity has the advantage of forcing the free-lancer to get out of the house and into the world, which is where most good ideas come from. Skillful free-lancers seek part-time jobs that either provide them with other kinds of writing or editing experience or may produce material for articles. One free-lance writer, Shelley Smolkin, worked part-time as an editor and writer at a contract research organization concerned with issues in social science. Published articles came directly from subjects she encountered in her work there, and many of the research scientists she met have proven to be valuable sources of information for other articles.

The Advantages of Free-Lancing

The disadvantages in a free-lance writing career may seem enormous. Fortunately, the magazine publishing world also gives the free-lancer some advantages.

Magazines Need Free-Lancers

Many magazines want national coverage but must operate with very limited staffs. They *need* free-lancers to give their publications the national focus they cannot achieve from their editorial offices alone. They do not have the bureaus of Time-Life, Inc., to gather information from different parts of the country, so they must rely on stringers or free-lancers to send them stories.

And look at the financial arrangement from the magazine's point of view. When an assignment is given on spec, the magazine gets an article on a subject that the editor has declared to be of interest to it for an initial outlay of the cost of a postage stamp. If the article is rejected, the magazine hasn't lost any money. Even if a kill fee is involved, the cost to the magazine is minimal. If the article is accepted, the magazine has acquired a publishable story, and that, after all, is what magazines need. From a financial standpoint, there is no reason an editor should not ask to see an article on spec, provided the free-lancer can convince him or her that there's a good chance the final product will be publishable. While these arrangements may be a hardship to the writer, he or she is also being given the chance to make it into print.

The Finances of Free-Lancing

An important part of running a free-lance writing business is keeping records for the Internal Revenue Service. This is no mere bureaucratic detail; it is the free-lancer's primary means of protecting his or her income from being eaten away by taxes. As in any business, the goal in free-lancing is to make a profit, but at tax time your primary objective will be to whittle it away as much as possible. This is done by deducting legitimate business expenditures from the total amount of payments received from magazines. The amount of income tax you owe is a percentage of that final figure; it is to your advantage to reduce that number as much as possible.

In general, any expense you incur that is *directly* related to your work as a free-lance writer is deductible. The list of legitimate deductions includes the costs of such items as postage for query letters, editorial correspondence, or mailing articles; long-distance phone calls to editors or sources of information; office supplies, such as typing paper, ribbons, and so on; magazines you buy for the purpose of your work; miscellaneous expenses such as photocopying charges for research materials, parking garage fees paid during reporting expeditions, or tapes for interviewing. One of the greatest boons to a mobile free-lancer is the mileage deduction allowed for use of your personal car for business purposes. The rate changes from year to year, but it has been as high as 26 cents per mile.

Perhaps the largest deduction for many free-lancers is that allowed for home offices. Writers who qualify for this deduction can include expenses such as percentages of their mortgage payments or rent, property taxes, utility bills, and phone bills. However, there are very strict limitations on who qualifies for these deductions. The best way to find out if you do is to consult a knowledgeable tax accountant.

The only way you'll know how much you've spent on your work at the end of the year is to keep accurate, ongoing records. A journal divided into categories in which you record the expense, its purpose, and the date it was incurred accomplishes this task quite well. It is also important to keep receipts whenever they are available. An envelope stapled into the journal is a convenient way to collect them until tax time. As an additional form of documentation for the IRS in case you are ever audited, you should keep copies of all your letters to editors and sources, as well as your manuscripts.

The experiences of one free-lance writer illustrate how the finances of free-lancing operate. While working part-time as an editor at a research organization, Shelley Smolkin learned about the activities of groups whose purpose is to help women reenter the job market after many years as homemakers. She also found that a national conference was scheduled that would bring together people working in these "displaced homemaker" programs from various parts of the country. The conference was in Baltimore, Maryland; the writer was in Seattle, Washington.

The free-lancer queried *Working Woman* magazine on an article about displaced homemaker programs, emphasizing the job-oriented thrust of most of them. In the query, she also mentioned the upcoming conference and suggested that attending it would help her write the article. The reply was favorable. *Working Woman* agreed to assign the story and to pay $500 for it on publication. The editor also specified that while the magazine would pay the conference registration fee of $30, it would not pay for the writer's airfare or other travel expenses.

The writer decided to combine attendance at the conference with a trip to New York to talk with editors at several magazines about future assignments. Most free-lance writers find that an occasional trip to New York for face-to-face exchanges with editors they correspond with regularly is well worth the expense. And she convinced the research organization to fund a third of the expenses of her trip to the conference in exchange for a fact-finding report on her return.

While on the trip, the writer kept a daily record of her expenses. She arranged to stay with friends in both Baltimore and New York, so there were no hotel charges. Here are the items she recorded:

Airfare	$260.00 (discount rate)
Conference fee	30.00
Taxi fares to and from conference	7.50
Meals	25.00 (Baltimore)
	40.00 (New York)
Train fare from Baltimore to New York	22.00
Taxi fares in New York	10.00
Mileage to airport to Seattle	8.50 (.17/mile, 50 miles)
Bus to airport in New York	4.50
TOTAL	$407.50

When the trip was over, the writer divided her expenses into three categories: (1) to be paid by *Working Woman,* (2) to be paid by the research organization, and (3) to be paid by the writer herself. As agreed, she sent the magazine a bill for $30 along with the completed manuscript. She then billed the research organization for one-third of the expenses incurred in relation to the conference, except for the registration. That came to $100. The remaining expenses, $277.50, were recorded in her accounts book as business expenses to be deducted from her total receipts at the end of the year.

Of course, one way to view the financial outcome of this situation is to say that the writer earned only $222.50 for writing the article ($500 fee minus $277.50 expenses). But that does not take into account the assignments she generated while in New York. At least one article for which the writer was paid $500 came as a direct result of meeting with an editor there, and others came indirectly, aided by the personal contacts she made during the trip. The adage "you've got to spend money to make money" applies as much to free-lancing as to any other business. The writer's task is to decide when and how to take that risk.

Compiling the information you need for income tax purposes will tell you how well your business is doing from a financial standpoint.

In addition, journal and letter copies can serve as reminders of when you sent queries or manuscripts and how long it was between your submission and the response. And once you are a successful, prosperous free-lancer, you will be able to look back on those lean early years and chuckle over the empty-looking "payments received" page. But for the present, concentrate instead on offsetting those few precious payments with all the deductions the government allows.

Exercises

1. Based on your interest in the subject it covers, purchase a copy of one of these magazines: *Sunset, Fortune, Newsweek, Time, Business Week, Ski, Rudder,* or *Dallas.* Read the entire issue and write 500 words to describe what was wrong with that issue. Were the articles too long? Too short? Have the editors chosen the wrong articles?

2. Create the formula for a new magazine by listing ten subjects you would include in the first issue.

3. You are the editor of a small specialty magazine published in New York but distributed nationally. There are four other people on your editorial staff. Choose a focus for your magazine (a sport, a hobby, an industry, and so on), then discuss how you will organize your staff to provide national coverage without leaving New York. How will you get information from other parts of the country?

4. If you decided to become a full-time free-lance writer, how many queries and articles would you expect to write each month? How would you organize your activities? How much time would you spend researching and writing a query?

5. Assume you are the editor of a national magazine that relies heavily on free-lance writers. How would you organize your exchange of ideas with them? Consider some of the problems you might face, such as two good writers who want to do similar stories, a usually reliable writer who turns in an unpublishable piece two days before deadline, or staff writers who resent your giving choice assignments to free-lancers. How would you handle these situations?

6. Examine the financial difficulties of free-lance writing by projecting how many articles you would need to write each year, and how much you would have to be paid for them, in order to make what you consider a reasonable living. Don't forget to deduct federal and state income taxes from the gross amount.

FOUR

GENERATING AND DEVELOPING IDEAS FOR ARTICLES

The eye of the master will do more work
than both his hands.

BENJAMIN FRANKLIN

The ability to generate magazine article ideas is really the ability to see the world from a writer's point of view. When photographers walk down the street, they visualize the scenes before them as though they are looking through a camera lens. Architects see the spatial relationships between the objects around them. Similarly, skillful magazine writers regard the everyday experiences of life as being full of story ideas just waiting to be discovered.

Beginning writers are often discouraged by their apparent inability to churn out ideas. What they do not realize is that this kind of thinking is an acquired skill, one that it is possible to develop. After three years of practice, one free-lancer remarked that she was never dismayed when she discovered that one of her ideas had already been published by someone else; she regarded such events as evidence that her skill in generating marketable ideas was improving.

Because of the sharp competition among magazines for the reader's time and attention, nothing is quite so critically important in the magazine world as a good idea. Before he was elected to the United States Senate, the late Richard Neuberger of Oregon was one of the best-known free-lancers in the West. Editors welcomed his articles, but not because he was a richly talented writer. In fact, Neuberger was little more than a competent writer. More often than not, his phrases were somewhat matter-of-fact, and his sentences did not sing. Magazine staffers often had to rework long sections of his articles (and sometimes the articles themselves) to put them in shape for publication. But Neuberger had interesting ideas for articles and techniques for developing them, and he supported both with careful and wide-ranging research. Several of his pieces—notably "They Never Go Back to Pocatello," "The Decay of the State Legislature," and "My Wife Put Me in the Senate"— have been reprinted widely.

ANALYZING MAGAZINES

Before beginners can view the world from a writer's point of view, they must be able to see magazines that way. Detective Sherlock Holmes could deduce a person's occupation, character, and even recent activities simply by observation; likewise, astute magazine writers can glean a great deal of information about a magazine simply by looking at it. Holmes's expertise was in knowing what to look for and how to interpret the information once he had it. The same skills can help a writer both to generate ideas and to market them.

Covers

You can't judge a book by examining its cover, but you can learn a lot about a magazine that way. What kind of identity is the magazine trying to establish through its logo and cover artwork? Imagine a newsstand and the magazines a person would be able to spot on it right away. Magazines like the *New Yorker, Life, Time,* and even *Cosmopolitan* are among the first that come to mind because each has established a clear, distinct identity that separates it from the dozens of other magazines on display. A buyer would never mistakenly pick up the *Atlantic* if he or she meant to buy *Sports Illustrated.* The former uses covers that illustrate ideas, while the latter generally relies on action shots that virtually scream "SPORTS!" at the reader.

Look at the cover lines. How does the magazine try to lure readers inside its pages? Are the cover lines informative or tantalizing? Are they characterized by "A Guide To . . ." or "25 Ways To . . ." or "How to . . ."? Some magazines that rely on formulas to fill their pages month after month seem to run the same headlines regularly. A parody of *Cosmopolitan* published by *Harvard Lampoon* caught the spirit of that publication's cover with a photograph of a model posed in a revealing evening dress, Cosmo style. Only one detail of the picture was amiss—the model's eyes were crossed. A headline printed in the standard Cosmo type style read, "How to Tell if Your Man Is Dead."

Finally, note whether or not the article titles displayed on the cover are followed by the author's names. If they are, there's a good chance that the magazine relies on well-known writers and may not be very receptive to considering the work of a newcomer.

Mastheads

Take a look at the magazine's masthead. Study the organization of the editorial staff. Are there many layers of associate editors, department editors, assistant editors, writers, researchers, or editorial assistants? If so, the magazine is probably written mostly by staff. But if the number of editors wouldn't even comprise a volleyball team, there's a good chance they have to go outside their own offices for articles. Check to see where the editorial offices are located. Although most national magazines are located in New York, there are some scattered throughout the country. A beginning sports writer living in Bellingham, Washington, was amazed to discover that the offices of one of her best potential markets, *Young Athlete*, were less than 50 miles away. The advantage, of course, was that the writer was able to visit the editor in person rather than rely strictly on letters to transmit ideas.

Tables of Contents

The most important information available on the table of contents page is how the articles in the magazine are organized. Often magazines arrange stories into regular departments that appear in each issue. Sometimes these are always written by the same person, but an examination of a few back issues should reveal whether or not the authorship of departments changes. If it does, and the names are not those that appear on the masthead, the magazine is probably using free-lancers.

Advertisements

Magazine advertisements can indicate who reads the magazine. If the ads are for Mercedes-Benz, Chivas Regal, or Saks Fifth Avenue, the audience is likely to be an upper-income group. It is safe to assume that these advertisers try to place their ads where people with money to spend on such goods will see them. Who uses the products advertised in the magazine? Are they old, young, male, female, athletic, middle class, or highly educated? Advertising salespeople sell ads not only on the basis of a magazine's circulation but also on the demographic characteristics of its audience. They get this information through readership surveys and use it to show prospective clients that their readers are the people who buy the clients' products.

Are any of the articles related to the advertisements? Magazines do not allow advertisers to influence editorial content, but they do sometimes try to attract advertisers by publishing articles that are related to their products. Salespeople carry around lists of upcoming articles to show clients. At *Women's Sports* magazine, the advertising staff was sure to contact Bausch & Lomb, a leading manufacturer of optical supplies, anytime there was an article on how to protect eyes from the sun. Advertising was sold by position in the magazine, so a client like Bausch & Lomb could specify that its ad should appear next to the relevant article. The idea, of course, was that readers interested in the subject of eye protection would be exposed to the advertisement as they read the article.

Articles

Now have a look at the articles. Are they long or short or both? Count the words in a line and figure out how many words there are on a page. Translate that into a typewritten manuscript and see how many pages the writers are generating to produce each article. The trend in recent times has been toward stories that are "short and snappy," which means that an editor needs a greater number of articles to fill a single issue.

What types of articles are there? Do they tend to be serious, light, or both? Does the magazine rely on an eighth-grade vocabulary, or are the articles written in a more sophisticated style? A clue to the overall tone can be found in the headlines. Are they informative, catchy, or both? It's unlikely that a headline published in *New West,* "A Wok on the Wild Side," would ever appear in *Good Housekeeping,* even if the articles were on identical subjects. Do the articles cover subjects on a national, regional, or local basis?

Finally, who are the authors of the articles? Are their names on the masthead? Check the endings of stories for biographical information about the writers, such as "Jane Smith is a free-lance writer living in Oklahoma who specializes in topics related to health and medicine." Occasionally, magazines devote an entire page to descriptions and photographs of their writers. Read these for clues about the level of expertise the magazine expects from its free-lancers.

Here is a free-lancer who measures up to almost anything any magazine editor could want. His name is Richard ("Dick") Harris. Here, he has traveled a long way from home on an article-writing trip: *

> In Atlanta's Ridgeview Institute I was interviewing drug and alcohol abusers. They were not derelicts, skid row bums, criminals, social outcasts, the poor or the ignorant. They were men and women you'd consider least likely ever to become drunks and drug addicts.
>
> They were some of society's brightest, most gifted, envied and admired, universally honored. These victims of booze and drugs were medical doctors, ages ranging from 30 to 60, from big cities and small towns, clinics and hospitals throughout the United States and Canada. They represented the entire spectrum of modern medical specialties: anesthesiology, pediatrics, cardiology, orthopaedic surgery, obstetrics, ophthalmology, internal medicine, urology, psychiatry.
>
> Intrigued by a poignant letter from Dr. William Kennedy of Cleveland, I had made the trip to Atlanta (from my home in San Diego). The doctor had written eloquently on addiction, a subject that he knew only too well and about which he felt compelled to share with the public through a major magazine.
>
> Kennedy was a "graduate" of Ridgeview, a center for treatment of physicians whose lives and careers were going down the drain because of their addiction to drugs and alcohol.
>
> "Very few people are aware of this unique institution," Kennedy wrote. "It graduates the equivalent of a regular medical school senior class every year."
>
> Although he described his own problem and recovery candidly and in considerable detail, Kennedy was more interested in telling me about the miracles that were taking place at Ridgeview and the work of its director, Dr. G. Douglas Talbott, himself a recovered alcoholic. After achieving sobriety, Talbott had dedicated his life to helping fellow physicians recover from addiction and getting their family affairs and medical practices back in order. Ridgeview was the culmination of Talbott resolve.

---

*Reprinted by permission of Richard Harris.

"It may sound absurd to speak about gratitude for an addiction," Kennedy said, "but after having spent six months being treated and learning how to treat addicts, I can only say that my world and that of my family is more complete than it has ever been before." Like so many others, Kennedy's career had been salvaged, his life turned around by a loving, caring fellow doctor.

The letter was an unfeigned tribute to Doug Talbott—friend, brother, mentor, esteemed healer of healers. Kennedy acknowledged that the medical profession was experiencing a serious drug/alcohol abuse problem and that Ridgeview, under Talbott, was treating addicted doctors openly, actively as though they suffered from diabetes, heart trouble or any other "respectable" disease. Further, that if black lung disease is an occupational hazard to a coal miner, then alcohol and drug abuse are occupational hazards to a physician.

My interviews in Atlanta with Talbott and both recovering and recovered physicians left me convinced that Kennedy had put me onto a good story. So good, I thought, that I fired off an outline query to *Reader's Digest.* Then, with full confidence, I started writing the piece.

The reply to my query arrived a month later, just as I was finishing the 4,000-word manuscript.

Reader's Digest editors write the nicest rejection letters. This one arrived complete with tear stains. "I feel just terrible. . . . I hate to tell you. . . . You came so close. . . . A terrific story, but. . . ." The editor even confessed that he couldn't understand why my proposal didn't make it. "Please," he implored, "try us again."

So there I was, looking at a completed manuscript ready to submit, and already it was being turned down by my favorite magazine. I was tempted to abandon the story, chalk it up to experience and faulty judgment.

No, I had too much invested in the Ridgeview story. I decided to look for a different angle and offer it to another magazine (advice I always give my students). But it would involve a second trip to Atlanta, and I'd have to do it immediately while my hopes were alive.

On my second visit, I got acquainted with Dr. Martha Morrison, who I had missed the first time around. A brilliant, 34-year-old psychiatrist and Ridgeview "graduate," she was now head of a treatment facility for drug and alcohol addicted adolescents. I spent most of the day recording details of her dramatic, tragic, heroic story.

Could this incredible story be true? Dr. Talbott confirmed the details and added more: "Martha was as far into addiction as one can go— and still live. Her treatment was long, the suffering profound, but her recovery has restored to medical practice—and to the community—a talented, sensitive, beautiful human being whose special skills and experience are now being directed toward the huge and growing problem of adolescent addiction. She is demonstrating that the best way to grow in sobriety is to give away her recovery and her coping skills to help others."

Here was my story—the struggle of an attractive, promising young woman doctor, trapped in addiction, going down the drain, even planning suicide, until she meets the healer of healers at Ridgeview.

I put a new, graphic lead on the story proposal—with Dr. Morrison as the focus—and sent it to *McCall's*. Two days later, I got a phone call (to save time, he said) from Don McKinney, *McCall's* managing editor. He had read my outline, but wondered if I was offering fiction. He had questions: "Are you sure of all those details? Is it all true?" When I told him I had verified everything, he asked, "How soon can we get the story?"

The story was on McKinney's desk three days later. Three months later it was on the *McCall's* cover: "MY SEVENTEEN YEARS AS A DRUG ADDICT: A Woman Doctor's Shocking Story."

It was not long before I got a call from *Reader's Digest* requesting permission to pick up the story. Permission granted. After all, that's where it was supposed to be. It appeared two months later as a lead feature.

Then a literary agent called. Would I put together a book proposal? She had a publisher in mind and was sure it would sell. It did. Another publisher wanted the *Reader's Digest* version in a college psychology text anthology.

So the Ridgeview story, told through Dr. Morrison's struggle for survival, then sobriety, has gone full circle.

I'm glad I went back to Atlanta.

Graphics

Graphics can make a small magazine look big but can't make a poor magazine look rich. Color is the key component—how much is there, and where does the art director put it? If there are lots of color photographs and illustrations with the articles (don't include color ads—the advertisers pay for them), the

DICK HARRIS

I had bought a one-way ticket to Atlanta because I knew that either I would find help there, or I would kill myself. I was just 29 years old, but I had reached the end.

For 17 years, beginning in 1964, I'd been using almost every mind-altering drug then known to man. Now my highs lasted only a few seconds; then I was trapped again, with an irresistible urge for more. I finally knew that I could no longer live with drugs—and I couldn't live without them.

My story is not a pretty one. I will tell it with the hope that it will help others recognize drug and alcohol abuse in time to save themselves or their loved ones.

Although these paragraphs were written by Dick Harris, they are not part of an autobiographical account. Instead, Harris has produced an authentic rendition of Martha Morrison's personal story by using what he learned during interviews. Consequently, the article, published in *Reader's Digest* and *McCall's*, flows naturally and evokes deep emotional responses.

After receiving his master's degree in journalism from Stanford University in 1948, Harris worked for ten years reporting, writing, and editing for three California daily newspapers: the *Grass Valley Union*, the *San Mateo Times*, and the *San Francisco News*. Then Harris moved on to publishing as an editor of Meridian Publishing Company, one of the nation's largest publishers of specialty magazines. For many years his writing has been published regularly in national magazines, such as *McCall's*, *Family Weekly*, *Reader's Digest*, *Golf Digest*, and *Business Today*.

Repeatedly, Harris has illustrated concern for public issues. Interested in highway safety, he has written numerous articles on safe driving, one of which won a Highway Safety

magazine is probably in good financial standing. Color is a very expensive part of art production, but because it enhances the visual appeal of the "book," as magazines are called in the publishing industry, everyone wants to have as much as possible. Articles regarded as the most important or most popular are the ones illustrated with color.

A seasoned writer can size up a magazine simply by glancing through it. For beginners, the process must be more deliberate and detailed. Information gathered in such analyses can be used either to match an idea to a particular magazine or to help the writer generate ideas for that magazine. Here are some additional tips to round out your analysis of magazines and to generate article ideas:

Think in headlines Editors use headlines to help sell magazines; writers can use them to help sell articles.

Ask questions as the basis for a story Is the private university a dying institution? Why can't Americans read? Who really controls our supply of gasoline?

Examine the other side of an issue Why public universities are growing. Why Americans can't add. How to use less gas.

Don't limit ideas to subjects that have never been covered before There aren't many left. Try to develop new angles for old subjects, or new markets for subjects that have been covered elsewhere. Of course, if a new subject comes along, approach it from as many different angles as possible.

Think in terms of magazine departments That's what editors of

---

Journalism Award from Uniroyal in 1976. The following year, his article "The Truckers' Greatest Menace" appeared in *Commercial Car Journal.* Here is an excerpt:

> "It's a lot like watching a horror movie. The difference is that it's real—and I'm in it!"
>
> Munching a sandwich at a motel coffee shop at the end of his Akron-Columbus run, Jack Wagner of Addison, Ill., was describing how it feels maneuvering a fully loaded, 40-ft. trailer through fast, heavy traffic on a rainy night just after the bars close.
>
> Wagner is only 33-years-old, but he says: "Already, I've seen enough drunk drivers to last me a lifetime."

In addition, his insightful article "How to Survive the Drunk Driver" was published in *Family Weekly* in 1978. Based on interviews with more than 100 truck drivers, Harris compiled a list of twenty life-saving tips to prepare people for handling drunks on the road. In this article, Harris described the painful events leading to his desire to promote awareness of the hazards of drunk driving.

Involved in *Reader's Digest,* Harris was one of its consultants for ten years. In the field of education, Harris was a member of the journalism faculty at Utah State University and is currently a member of the journalism faculty at San Diego State University. Today he is the owner and editor of Harris & Associates Publication Division, a features syndicate. A talented writer in many fields, Harris's specialties include public affairs, aviation, medicine, business, and sports. He belongs to Sigma Delta Chi, the Society of Professional Journalists, and the Association for Education in Journalism and Mass Communication.

magazines that are organized into departments do. Writers who can suggest ideas for particular segments of a magazine that appear regularly often find their work being published with comparable frequency.

Cherchez la femme   Or, as one California free-lancer put it, "Look for the Lithuanian." In virtually every story there is another story, often one that appeals to a slightly different audience.

Think in terms of illustration   A dramatic photograph can often provide the basis for a good magazine article. Art directors have been known to suggest article ideas to editors after seeing the work of a photographer, and there is no reason why writers should not do the same.

PHOTOGRAPHS

For a long time, magazines have had to compete for readers' attention with the color and allure of photographs. As a result, they have been much more visually innovative than newspapers, and magazine writers have learned to coordinate their efforts with those of photographers. For example, *People* is basically a picture magazine. Some have described it as television in print. It runs about 15,000 words an issue (*Time* runs three times that many), and its text and photographs offer a flashy, quick look and read into the lives of celebrities. Although most magazines cannot be described as "picture magazines," editors are more and more aware that photography is as powerful a tool as the words it accompanies.

Many free-lancers work with photographers on article assignments; most staff writers do. In fact, unless the staff writers are employed by magazines that do not publish pictures, they may spend a large fraction of their time on aspects of photography—anything from hiring free-lance photographers to making layouts of their own words along with the photographers' pictures.

Should a writer try to shortcut this process and *become* a photographer? The prospect may be especially attractive to a free-lance writer; perhaps his income would double if he could illustrate his own articles. A staff writer, too, might enhance her income by learning to take pictures. These are alluring prospects. Unfortunately, they are seldom realistic. The experiences of many who have tried to become true photojournalists by developing talents in writing and photography suggest that striking a balance is almost impossible. A journalist is likely to be so much more skilled as a writer than as a photographer—or so much more skilled as a photographer than as a writer—that one talent far overshadows the other. A photographer whose pictures satisfy the exacting demands of the picture editor is not likely to write well enough to satisfy the text editors; but his or her pictures are almost certain to be light-years ahead of those taken by anyone who writes regularly for the magazine.

There are related dangers. The talented writer who tries to develop photographic ability may be stealing time from writing that is actually needed to develop his or her primary talent. It may be, too, that one who develops both talents to the point of publishing words and pictures regularly could have written (or taken pictures) for more demanding and prestigious publications if he or she had been content to develop one talent or the other. If this assessment is negative, it is nonetheless drawn from the experiences of many journalists. Most writers must learn to work *with* photographers rather than working *as* photographers, and vice versa.

In the following quotation, Mary Ord of *Sunset* presents a point of view on the relationship between magazine writer and photographer—and on how the two can work together effectively:

> The quality of the photographs makes the difference between a two-column and a two-page story, no matter how worthy the topic. So the writer chooses the photographer whom he thinks can do the job best. Some photographers are best at studio shots, some at wildlife shooting, some at house photography, and some at photographing children.
>
> The writer tries to tell his photographer as much about his story as possible. If the story calls for going out of the studio to work, the writer tries to give the best idea he can what the situation will be, what lighting there is, what distance the photographer may be shooting from, how much legwork may be involved in getting the shots. The writer should say if he just doesn't know what they'll find, or if he has specific shots in mind.
>
> Doing your own photography is encouraged. If you are competent at it, you are more useful. It is good if a writer can take at least adequate scouting photographs to help him sell his story to editors, to help determine if it is worthwhile to send a full-time photographer back, and also to show that photographer what kind of conditions he will find. Writers often do their own photography if the story is some distance away and is not of certain enough value to warrant the expense of a photographer's time.

In some cases, you, as a free-lancer or staff writer, may be assigned by a magazine's editors to accompany the photographer to produce an article. There must be a meeting of the minds as to whether words or pictures will determine the direction of the story. If the article is primarily a visual story, the photographer should have the right to chart the course. But if the words will dominate the published story, you should demand the right to shape it.

Even if you're not at all certain that you should be a photographer, taking a beginner's course in photography will help you understand its language, problems, and joys.

Writing to Pictures

When writers have worked with photographers, their next task comes into sharp focus. Mary Ord suggests the best procedure for those who are writing to pictures. She speaks of the *headline,* which is the title of the article; the *display wording,* which refers to any type that is larger than the body print of an article; and the *captions* (sometimes called cutlines), which are the explanatory words accompanying a picture:

> Writing to pictures is an important element of staff writing. We are told that when *Sunset* readers turn to an article, they look at the pictures first, read the headline and any other display wording second, read captions third, and then—if they are still interested—they'll read the lead (hopefully more). From these few elements the reader should get the gist of the article. *Sunset* articles have boldface kick-ins in captions and leads to draw the reader's eye. So these words are especially key ones. They should say as much as possible; it's no time for leisurely writing. We try to void *a, an, the,* and prepositions as the first word so the reader gets to the key words quickly.
>
> The headline, captions, and lead should be written out of the pictures. The headline should summarize the situation most directly; that is, the reader should be able to look at the pictures, then look at the head and have it sum up the point the pictures are making.
>
> For example, in a story you see a map of a road running the length of Baja California and four pictures of different Mexican-looking scenes. The head says, "Should you try the Baja road this year? Now or soon is the best time. Here is *Sunset*'s report." The reader knows what he is getting. In another story, photographs show different baskets woven from flat strips which could be clay. They hold rolls and bread. Three other pictures show step by step the weaving of the strips which here look like some kind of dough. The head says, "The bread basket looks good enough to eat. (But don't nibble.) You roll, weave, and bake baker's clay." If the pictures were at all puzzling, the reader now knows what the story is about.
>
> After the headline, the next chance the writer has to attract the reader is in the captions. Caption writing requires that the writer really know what is going on in the picture, and more. The caption should *not* just restate what is obviously happening in the picture. Here's a simple example. With a picture of a hillside blooming with ice plant and daisies, the caption could have said just "Ice plant and daisies cover a Southern California hillside." But instead it said, "Purple ice plant and daisy have been in bloom since midwinter." Now, besides knowing what is in the colorful picture, the reader gets a little more information to start him thinking. The caption writer should acknowledge what is going on that's clearly visible in the picture, then give more information or point out something less apparent in the photo to make the reader look more closely. The caption should draw the reader *in* to the photo.
>
> The boldface words of the caption demand thought on the part of the writer; generally, here is the place for whatever clever writing you can muster, some alliteration or metaphor, for example, as long as it's used to amplify the photograph . . . and as long as it's done in the space allotted. Sometimes, when a series of pictures show the steps in a project, it is a good idea to start the caption for each picture with a boldface number to show the sequence clearly. This helps the reader know exactly what the pictures are telling him.

Writing Picture Stories

Meaningful picture stories are essays. They must be planned. In fact, it is doubtful that a great picture story can be composed unless its producers have arrived at a theme or a central idea *before* the photographer starts work. Happy accidents have been known to grow out of haphazard shooting, but the weight of experience is on the side of the picture story that is developed rather than the one that is stumbled on while going through batches of photographs. The role of the writer in building a picture story is not merely accessory to that of the photographer, as this step-by-step description of the process should make clear:

1. Develop an idea.
2. Present the idea to an editor for discussion.
3. Plan the picture story on the basis of the discussion.
4. Research the story.
5. Brief the photographer on the general plan, then assist him or her during the making of pictures.
6. Select and organize the pictures.
7. Help an artist make a layout.
8. Write the cutlines and text that fuse word and picture into a graphic presentation.

A finished picture story is usually made up by:

1. Choosing a dominant picture.
2. Facing pictures toward the related text.
3. Avoiding the "rivers of gray" that are caused by captions meeting irregularly near the same level.
4. Arranging similar captions in the same width, type, and number of lines.
5. Focusing simultaneously on a subject or personality as well as a theme or mood.

Writing to a picture story differs markedly from writing to a single picture. The writer must at once focus on a single picture as he or she writes and remember to preserve continuity from photograph to photograph. This can be accomplished by:

1. Providing a central copy block that relates to all the pictures and echoes the spirit of the pictures as a group.
2. Ruthlessly holding captions to a minimum. (The reader likes to leap rapidly from picture to picture.)
3. Avoiding superfluous words in direction as well as in description; captions can be related to pictures by proximity, keyed letters or numbers, or arrows.

A perceptive writer can observe a scene and describe it keenly, in rich or simple prose. But few written descriptions can compete for truth with pictures. As the philosopher Suzanne K. Langer has observed: "The correspondence between a word picture and a visible object can never be as close as that between the object and its photograph." The ancient Chinese had another way of expressing it: a picture is worth ten thousand words.

FINDING TOPICS

French author Colette was a life watcher. She heard, she touched, she breathed the world in; she stared with intense care, hypnotized.

Look at flowers, she would say. Look at the white gardenia that after three days resembles a "white kid glove that has fallen into a stream." The tulip—a painted Easter egg, its heavy posterior sitting on its stem. The black pansy—the velvet of it.

Look at people; recognize them; accept them as they are, without wanting to change them. She looked at love most of all, determined to define its nature and worth. "The heart can begin again," she said with authority.

"We will never look enough," summed up Colette, "never accurately enough, never passionately enough."

How do you go about finding good topics? The strength of your writing will rely directly on the strength of the topic you begin with. One professional writer, Kurt Vonnegut, has suggested: "Find a subject you care about and which you in your heart feel others should care about. It is this genuine caring, and not your games with language, that will be the most compelling and seductive element in your style."

To find a subject worth caring about, you must be receptive to the world around you. The germ from which a piece of good writing grows is usually commonplace: a chance remark, an experience had by someone the writer knows, a picture in the newspaper, an article read, or an incident that was part of the writer's everyday life. A huge ocean of stimuli for good writing surrounds you: talk to the people around you, read widely, and use your senses. Constant curiosity is the most valuable habit a writer can have, and there is no good writer who isn't curious.

As you seek to understand the environment you and your readers live in—whether you're exploring your school or global politics—you should look for relationships. When the answer to a question you asked or an article you read leads you to seek more information, you will discover patterns. Those patterns, supported by details that made you recognize them, provide the best topics for writing.

How can it be, then, that so many students find themselves protesting "I don't have anything to write about!" when everyone is surrounded by rich resources for articles? First, many beginning writers fail to value their own experiences. Years of writing school compositions that simply reword material from the library or comment only on the work of other writers can lead students to believe that what they know from experience is not worth putting into writing. Actually, though, the strongest beginning for writing is what you have discovered in your own surroundings; when you write about what you have figured out yourself, you bring to your readers events and ideas they don't already know and can't understand without your help.

A second obstacle to recognizing the worthwhile subjects for writing that surround you is failing to observe fully. Unless you wonder at and about the world around you, you can't focus on the parts of your experience that will enrich other people's lives when you put them into words. If you ride a bus to school or work, you can screen out the conversations around you and glance at other passengers' faces without really concentrating, or you can give your surroundings your full attention: see the frayed, gray lace on the edge of her slip when the woman beside you sits down and crosses her legs, wait a few minutes and see the makeup that has collected in a crease on her cheek, and make a connection; listen to what the three boys behind you are saying—the words they choose, the sound of their voices, the interplay among them as camaraderie deepens or a fight brews; smell and feel the warm, stale air that surrounds you and the stickiness of the floor against the soles of your shoes; ask, tactfully, that woman beside you the question that will satisfy your curiosity about her; read the graffiti. The most important experiences you have are the easiest to miss. Test yourself often: Did I really listen to what that person just said to me? Did I ask questions to find out what I'd like to know? Did I really *see* the people around me today—my family, my friends, the strangers at the market or at the corner waiting for the light to change? By consciously observing—talking with people, using your senses fully, and reading widely—you will discover the unique experiences readers respond to.

You also need the initiative to seek out experiences that are accessible to you but not part of your routine. No matter how small the community you live in, there are facets of it you have never explored. When you take the time to find out what is happening beyond your home, work, and social life— when you have the initiative, for instance, to visit the trade fair at your community center or to talk with the people who congregate at a local diner every morning—you will enrich your idea bank and come across many good topics for stories. Good writers know that experience is essential to lively writing. William Faulkner, winner of the Nobel Prize in literature, acknowledged the value of observation in his writing when he said: "I always write out of my personal experience, out of events I've been present at, out of stories I've heard from people. . . . All [any author] is trying to do is tell what he knows about his environment and the people around him in the most moving way possible. He writes like a carpenter uses his tools."

Once you learn to observe skillfully, to search for connections, and to value your insights, only one obstacle to finding worthwhile subjects remains. How can you *remember* all the details you notice so that you can use them later to show your readers what you have perceived?

Most writers keep written records of their experiences in files, on cards, or in a journal. Many famous writers, including Nathaniel Hawthorne and Franz Kafka, have used journals to collect material for writing. Excerpts from their journals show how keeping written records of experiences will help you write.

Collect many observations and ideas in notes to yourself. You will find that some of them are dead ends; others, though, will turn out to be the ideas you need to make your writing work.

When your instructor assigns you to write, say, an article on a football game, think of the people and things that appeal to you. The author of this book has remembered for thirty years a student who returned from a football game and wrote a captivating piece about how the salespeople sold soft drinks. In fact, she did more: she asked the sales manager how many bottles of soft drinks his employees had sold. When your class has much the same assignment, think about what most interests you.

Ideas from Reading

Nearly everyone who goes into free-lancing seriously becomes a careful reader, and clipper, of newspapers. Charles and Bonnie Remsberg, formerly a husband-wife writing team in Evanston, Illinois, subscribed to the two major Chicago papers. When these seemed to be yielding few items, the Remsbergs subscribed to as many as six out-of-town papers, searching for local features and news items that were not carried by the wire services. They spotted in the *Chicago Sun-Times* a report that the Gallup Poll had discovered that six out of ten Americans favored establishing a system through which the inno-cent victims of violent crimes (such as when a mad killer shoots wildly at everyone he meets) would receive government compensation for physical, mental, and economic suffering. After doing extensive research in their own heavy files of clippings as well as in legal periodicals, libraries, and law en-forcement offices, the Remsbergs produced "Should Crime Victims Be Paid?" which was published by *Family Weekly.*

This experience is an excellent example of what reading can do for writers—and what writers must do for themselves. That is, the Gallup Poll story was published so widely that thousands of professional writers must have seen it. It was simply a fact, not a magazine article sitting there for the plucking, until the Remsbergs thought imaginatively *about* the fact and how it might serve as the cue for an article. It is equally important to note that the writers thought of their article in relation to a particular magazine. They said that they were "aware from carefully studying the magazine that *Family Weekly* often runs stories anticipating burgeoning public issues." If they had not studied the magazine, they might have dismissed the Gallup Poll report as a profitless item. This underlines a vital aspect of generating ideas that was emphasized earlier: writers must read and analyze magazines to get a feel for what the editors want. It follows that writers should aim at magazines they enjoy reading. To attempt to write for a magazine one does not read is to send an engraved invitation to failure.

When reading newspapers for ideas, writers must see more than the facts; they must see their implications. A story in the *Wall Street Journal* about the weather service led Frank Taylor, a leading free-lancer, to two *Reader's Digest* articles on jet streams. Another *Wall Street Journal* story on the business of building swimming pools for Hollywood stars led him to a search for the leading builder and eventually to write an article titled "Those

High Jinks in Hollywood Pads." Still another mentioned the problems of finding homes for newly rich stars. This posed the question "Is there someone who's tops in this field?" There was—a live-wire realtor on Sunset Strip named Al Herd. From Herd's experiences came Taylor's "He Sells Houses to the Stars." Prosaic news stories about California's great irrigation projects resulted in a Taylor article for *Nation's Business* on how Californians were "moving the rain."

These experiences should clearly demonstrate that an article writer's imagination must always be at work. A newspaper item about a zoo's swapping kangaroos for a polar bear is just an amusing little story to the general reader. To the article writer, it is an invitation to look for a larger story. One did, and found that the San Diego Zoo had become one of the world's best zoos by astutely swapping seals (which could be caught nearby) for many kinds of animals other zoos considered surplus. The article that resulted was "Swapping Zoo Keepers."

Although metropolitan newspapers can be mined by imaginative freelancers for scores of articles, professional writers often read much more widely. Some focus on publications that are not so likely to have been culled by their competitors. An article in a local farm publication led to "Lazy Man's Orchard." Another farm-paper story, this one on a young beekeeper who rented bees by the millions to orchardists to pollinate their blossoms, became "Hundred Million Bees for Hire" in *Reader's Digest*. Company magazines—especially the house organs of aerospace, oil, and electronics companies—are sometimes heavy with facts that can be used profitably by freelancers who venture out on the growing edge of technology. Like university magazines, which are a similarly rich source of material, these publications are usually available free to a writer who asks to be placed on the mailing list.

One eminently successful free-lancer began early in his career to subscribe to numerous obscure journals, looking for leads. An item in *Engineer's Digest* reported that many people are electrocuted every year because they think it is safe to handle a high-voltage wire with ordinary rubber gloves, when the fact is that rubber gloves will protect the wearer only from 110-volt wires around the house. He promptly wrote to the safety heads of such organizations as the American Red Cross, the National Board of Fire Underwriters, the National Safety Council, and the American Medical Association, asking, "What are the most popular fallacies concerning safety that imperil the public's life?" From the 60 pounds of literature he received, the writer fashioned a manual for survival titled "Safety Rules That Can Kill You."

SOURCES OF IDEAS

Article ideas are everywhere, but it helps to narrow the field somewhat. Here are some fertile sources of ideas that beginners should consider:

Ideas from campus The campus can be an excellent source of ideas and information for articles. If your school maintains an alert news bureau, its

> *"An original writer is not one who imitates nobody, but one whom nobody can imitate."*
>
> FRANÇOIS-AUGUSTE-RENÉ DE CHATEAUBRIAND

staff can usually provide leads to dozens of article possibilities. However, the imaginative student writer seldom needs news bureau help.

Ideas from trade journals These are not the kinds of ideas or sales that make a writer rich, of course, but they enable the beginner to break into writing—to learn how to develop ideas and turn them into publishable articles. Some young writers go on from there to publish in prestigious magazines. Others make a career in what are known as secondary markets, which include trade journals.

Ideas from observing Writers who are truly observant look into their own experiences and surroundings with the clear eye of a newcomer. It is not necessary to live in an area that most magazine readers would consider colorful or exotic to generate article leads from one's surroundings.

Ideas from experience Experiences need not be unusual for you to write about them. In fact, commonplace experiences properly packaged by a deft writer often provide article ideas with which many readers can identify. Experience articles that are cast in how-to form are often the most widely read pieces a popular magazine can publish. Advice is a staple of many widely circulated magazines, some of it from experts, but much of it from diligent article writers.

Ideas from publicists Although it pains some writers to admit it, publicity and public relations workers are often the richest sources of ideas. For a journalist to ignore all publicists or treat their suggestions cynically because of some lofty or "holier-than-thou" attitude is unfair. A worthy article is a worthy article even though the person who suggests that it be undertaken may benefit from its publication. The writer need only guard against being used for unworthy purposes.

Ideas from editors When a writer has begun to sell fairly regularly to a magazine, he or she can expect the editor to begin suggesting ideas. In time, half the writer's ideas may come from editors. This is the most important source to develop, since an editor who suggests an idea has a vested interest in it, wanting it to become a published article.

PREPARING TO WRITE

Flannery O'Connor would go into her writing room faithfully for four hours every morning and not be bothered at all if she came out without getting a syllable onto the page. "I go in every day," she would explain, "because if any idea comes to me between eight and noon, I'm there all set for it."

A blank piece of paper—or an empty display screen on a computer—can thoroughly intimidate the writer who doesn't know how to prepare to write. Experienced writers, though, expect to spend much of the time they put into writing just discovering what they want to say. Ernest Hemingway, for example, said: "My working habits are simple: long periods of thinking, short periods of writing." Conscious exploration is what helps good writers get started and keep going, first figuring out the plans that help them write their first drafts and then doing the actual writing.

People may have told you in the past that writing an outline is a good way to start writing. Outlines can be tremendously helpful, but formal outlines don't work well as tools for *starting* to write. Before you can decide on an order for your ideas, you have to come up with good ideas in the first place.

To start writing, you should deliberately *explore*, seeking out a wide range of possibilities. By discovering many options before you commit yourself to a particular, limited plan, you can later settle on the *strongest* of the choices available to you. The thinking you should rely on as you start to compose, then, should not be critical. Instead of criticizing your ideas too early, concentrate on collecting as many ideas as you can.

Simply talking about your topic is one technique that will help you prepare to write. As you talk with another person, in a group of people, or even into a tape recorder, ask yourself what you already know about the topic you plan to pursue and then what additional information you'll need to collect.

These nine questions are worth asking your listener(s) or yourself:

1. What subject will I write about?
2. Which aspects of the subject will I include, and which will I ignore?
3. What incidents do I know about that illustrate my particular topic?
4. Where can I find out about aspects of my topic I'm not already familiar with?
5. What questions can I ask about my topic?
6. What are the answers to these questions?
7. Do I have any problems with this topic?
8. What are the problems?
9. Who is my audience?

If you take notes while or just after you talk about your topic, you will have a collection of ideas that is much less cumbersome to sift through than a tape recording and one that you don't have to worry about forgetting. "Notes," here, means not just complete sentences but whatever *you* need to have on paper in order to remember an idea later. Note taking is also at the heart of two other dependable techniques for exploring a topic: free writing and brainstorming.

Free writing is uncensored, nonstop writing. With your subject in mind, begin writing and do not allow yourself to stop, even for a second. Don't let yourself go back to something you have already written to revise it; just keep writing—new ideas or versions of ideas you've already used that you like better than what you came up with earlier. If you get stuck, write the last word over and over until a new idea occurs to you. And when you free write, don't let yourself be distracted by trying to write in complete, correct sentences. Halfway through a sentence, you may think of a better idea and start a new sentence. Or you may find yourself writing phrases and leaving out unimportant words. Free writing is for your eyes only and should be a messy collection of ideas: brilliant ones, useless ones, and mediocre ones, all mixed together. By putting off criticism until later, you will compile the richest possible group of ideas from which to choose the material you'll actually use.

For the same reason, brainstorming also demands that you compile ideas and put off criticizing them until later. Brainstorming consists of generating all the ideas you can, getting them down as you go. One way to brainstorm is to write the general idea for your composition in the center of a piece of blank, unlined paper. Then, suspending the impulse to question, jot down randomly—all over the paper—all the ideas you can think of that are related to your general idea. As a third step, use arrows or lines to join related ideas.

Some writers use index cards or separate pieces of paper for brainstorming. If you jot down ideas and details one to an index card, later you will easily be able to set aside material you don't plan to use and also experiment with different plans for organizing your writing. You will be able to group related cards in piles and choose an overall order for the piles that works as an outline to guide your writing.

As you can see, exploratory techniques like brainstorming ease the difficulty of the rest of writing. They give you good answers to the questions "What am I going to write about?" and "What do I have to say about this topic?" They also give you the resources you need to come up with a strong plan for your writing, saving you anguish and wasted effort.

Combine and vary these techniques for exploratory thinking in whatever way fits your personality. No one of them is magical or indispensable. What *is* essential, though, is that you harness your experience—gathering the ideas you already know and searching out whatever additional material you need—before you write. As Kurt Vonnegut advised student writers, "Your own winning style must begin with ideas in your head."

Composition and Audience

Now that you have used curiosity, a sense of relationships, and exploratory thinking to compile a rich stockpile of ideas and observations, you are almost ready to assemble the material for a specific composition. Choosing the content of a written composition is like deciding how to compose a photograph within its frame. You must decide what to include within the frame and what to leave outside it before you can convey your vision to others.

The photographer and the writer both have to know their audiences to decide what to capture on film or in words. The success of any article depends on how well the composer has identified his or her audience and responded to its needs. You may discover you have already started thinking about your readers as you collected ideas for writing. Or you may find that, for you, exploring and observing first and then figuring out who your readers will be works better. Either approach—subconscious or conscious—is fine. Be sure, though, that you wait to plan and draft until after you know exactly who your readers will be and have thought about what they will need and want.

Every piece of writing you have ever produced has had a specific audience: the students, faculty, and staff members who read your campus newspaper; a professor, teacher, or teaching assistant; classmates; a friend or relative; or even just you, the writer. Professional writers also write for a specific audience whenever they submit an article for publication.

Many beginning writers are at a disadvantage because they have written almost exclusively for the teachers who have taught them what they are writing about and then assigned their grades. This kind of writing is poor training for professional writing, for several reasons. First, professional writers usually write for people who know less than they do about the subject of an article. Second, professionals write for people whose goal as they read is understanding or entertainment rather than evaluation. And third, professional writers usually aim toward groups of people rather than a single individual. Studies have shown that high school teachers' preferences diverge from those of newspaper and magazine readers. Anyone who picks up a periodical wants to be able to grasp the meaning of articles without straining unnecessarily to understand and enjoy them. In contrast, it has been shown that some high school English teachers tend to rate poorly reasoned compositions written in exotic vocabulary as better than simply written, logically organized papers.

The audience you have written for in school, then, may have been an artificial one. Unless your teachers have valued clarity in your writing and provided you with assignments written for a variety of audiences—classmates, students in other classes and grades, parents, other adults in your community, and teachers not primarily concerned with grading your work—you will need to learn now to write as professionals do: to inform and entertain.

DEVELOPING YOUR IDEAS

William Allen White, writer and renowned newspaper editor, explained:

> I have never been bored an hour in my life. I get up every morning wondering what new, strange, glamorous thing is going to happen, and it happens at fairly regular intervals. Lady Luck has been good to me. I fancy she has been good to many. Only some people are dour, and when she gives them the come-hither with her eyes, they look down or turn away. But me—I give her the wink, and away we go.

Articles often begin as little more than passing thoughts, images, or statements. Only in the process of developing an idea into one that is marketable does the writer decide on the angle from which to approach the story, the form in which to write the story, and the possible sources of information for researching the story. It is not unusual for the final product to have little rela-

> "Writing is not hard. Just get paper and pencil, and write as it occurs to you. The writing is easy—it's the occurring that's hard."
>
> STEPHEN LEACOCK

tion to the original concept, and writers must be flexible enough in their thinking to allow for that adjustment.

Beginners often have difficulty asking the questions that help to develop ideas. Here are two examples of story suggestions and how they could be turned into publishable articles:

Art as an investment   The originator of this idea was not really certain who her audience would be. Serious art collectors or people interested in making large investments would probably not be interested in advice from anyone who is not an authority on the subject. But what about the average person? Is art a good investment for someone with $500 to $1,000 to spend? What kind of art could such a buyer invest in? Where could he or she go for help? How do relatively small investments in art compare with other types of investments available to people with the same amount of money, such as savings accounts or stocks? The answers to these questions could form the basis for an article that would be marketable to a wide range of magazines.

Controversy over the initiative to limit construction of high-rise buildings in San Francisco   The writer who thought of this idea knew that the story would be thoroughly covered by the local press. Her best chance for developing it was to examine the related issues from a national perspective. Have other cities passed similar initiatives? Have such initiatives been defeated elsewhere, and why? What are the long-range implications of such restrictions on the survival of urban areas? How do businesspeople in different parts of the country view the issue? What do urban planners have to say on this subject? Is there a clear-cut division between various national groups that are for or against these initiatives? A well-researched article on this subject would have obvious appeal for many national magazines.

One Idea Leads to Another

Another factor working in the free-lancer's favor is that there are no restrictions on squeezing every last drop out of research on a particular subject. You can't sell the same article to more than one magazine, but you can sell different articles that use the same material. Usually this involves approaching the subject from a different angle, appealing to a different audience.

Sometimes one article simply leads to another if the writer is observant enough to notice the path. While covering a ski race for *Women's Sports* magazine, one writer met a contestant in the race who she felt would be a good subject for a *Women's Sports* profile. She sold the idea and traveled to a freestyle skiing training camp in order to interview the skier. She wrote the article and then decided that a piece on freestyle training camps would be suitable for another magazine, *Sportswoman.* The editor accepted the idea, and the writer went to one of the country's top freestyle training camps to do some interviews. While there, she met another skier, a young woman whose coach claimed that she could already do tricks that no other woman on the freestyle circuit was able to do. Not one to miss an opportunity, the writer interviewed the girl, took her picture, and sold both to *Women's Sports.*

Perhaps the ultimate example of how a writer can exploit a subject was described by Bruce Bliven, Jr., in an article titled, "My Table Tennis Racket" that appeared in the *Atlantic*. As a beginning free-lancer, Bliven had managed to extract an assignment from *Life* to do a story about the national Ping-Pong champion. *Life* bought the article for $1,000 but never published it. Bliven took the piece to *Look* after updating it and was rewarded by a check for $500. *Look* subsequently ran a one-page photo of the champion with a 200-word caption. Bliven then sold his story to *Esquire* for $400. This time, the entire piece was printed. Several years later, he suggested another story on the Ping-Pong hero, who had managed to retain his title, to the new *Sports Illustrated*. They bought it for $750. At the time Bliven wrote the *Atlantic* story, the champion had finally retired, but the intrepid author still hoped for one more comeback.

Timeless and Seasonal Articles

Time can also function on the free-lancer's side—not the time it takes to get a query answered but the time it takes for a magazine to be published. Most monthly magazines have lead times of two to three months; that is, they are produced in the editorial offices two to three months before they are sold on the newsstands. This means that a magazine has to appear timely without actually being timely. Such magazines have to relinquish coverage of breaking news stories to weekly or daily publications and instead concentrate on material that has enduring newsworthy characteristics. For example, a monthly magazine like *Women's Sports* cannot publish a story about who won a particular tournament in June because in June the editors are working on their September issue. By the time the magazine hit the stands, the story would be old news. Instead, the magazine might try to cover the same event from a different angle—such as what the future plans of the winner might be or whether there was some promising newcomer there to watch for in the future.

Because of the long lead times, editors have a great need for two kinds of articles. Seasonal stories are written long before the relevant season arrives. Free-lancers should think like department stores and advertise their Christmas specials in July. Editors also need stories that are not time-bound, stories that could be published at any time of year without losing their newsworthy qualities. Many magazines try to keep a supply of such articles on hand to use in emergencies when an assigned piece does not come in on time or arrives in unpublishable condition. Free-lancers should not hesitate to point out this aspect of articles they propose to editors in query letters.

Exercises

1. Choose three magazines of the same genre and analyze them according to the criteria outlined in this chapter. Then compare the three and discuss how each tries to establish a unique identity.

2. Using an issue of *Cosmopolitan* or *National Geographic,* read the captions for the pictures, then come to the next class prepared to discuss whether the writers have observed the rules for writing captions in this chapter.

3. After rereading "Writing Picture Stories" in this chapter, purchase an issue of *People.* Do the writers observe the rules for writing to pictures? Can you edit the captions by taking out unnecessary words?

4. Choose two of the general subject headings listed below and suggest five topics related to each that could be the basis of magazine articles.

health	personalities
sports	art
money	politics
hobbies	minorities
environment	religion

5. Choose one of the topics listed below and discuss how it might be developed into an article. Include possible interview subjects and other sources of information.

alcoholism among teenagers	antique collecting
pottery making	declining enrollment in college human-
health care cooperatives	ities courses

6. In order to learn more about how magazines handle certain topics, do the following:
   a. Examine how three women's magazines handled stories about Christmas.
   b. Examine how one magazine handled a specific topic over a three-year time span.

FIVE

LANDING ASSIGNMENTS

You can't plant a seed and pick the fruit the next morning.

JESSE JACKSON

avid Brinkley's news career began during his high school days in Wilmington, North Carolina, where he started out working for the *Star-News* without pay. He had a flair for news, and finally he was put on the payroll. The salary? "Not bad for 1939," says Al Dickson, his former boss. "I think it was about $11 a week. He seemed very happy about it. Then, three weeks later, he asked for a raise. I was stunned! After he'd been working free for years, and finally was getting a salary, why a raise? 'Mr. Dickson,' Brinkley replied, 'it's all your fault for introducing me to money.'"

It's difficult to imagine Brinkley working for free, but all writers must begin somewhere—usually with the postal system. A universal horoscope for all beginning free-lancers might read: "A stranger wearing a uniform will soon assume an important role in your life." That person is the mail carrier.

Anyone who engages in the business of selling magazine articles long distance soon discovers that a well-written query letter is the most effective selling device. It offers advantages to both the editor and the writer. Editors prefer to receive queries rather than unsolicited manuscripts for two reasons. First; queries can be read more quickly, and editors generally have little time to spare. Second, a query enables the editor to participate in the process of developing the article. In reply, the editor can suggest an angle, specify a length, and discuss treatment of the subject. This has obvious advantages for the writer as well because it tells what kind of article the editor would like to receive, and it reduces the likelihood that the writer will spend a lot of time and effort to produce an article that no editor wants.

QUERY LETTERS

Once a query is in the mail, the free-lancer must be prepared to do a lot of waiting. Although some do reply sooner, it's not unusual for a national magazine to take six or eight weeks to respond to a query. Of course, in the interim, an industrious free-lancer expects to be working on other articles and other queries, because there is no guarantee of when the response will arrive.

When the important letter finally comes, it will either make all the waiting worthwhile or make the free-lancer wonder whether another career might be in order. Many magazines rely on form-letter rejection slips, which often provide little or no information about why a query was turned down. A proposal may be rejected for any number of reasons, including these:

1. The query letter was poorly written.
2. The idea was not suitable for the magazine.
3. The editor has already assigned a similar piece to another writer.
4. The magazine has covered the subject in a recent issue.

Some editors do take the time to explain why they have rejected queries; such responses can be very instructive to free-lancers who read them carefully. Consider the following rejection letters and how the free-lancer who received them might feel:

> Thank you for giving us the opportunity to consider your article proposal. We appreciate your interest in contributing to *Ms.*, but unfortunately we cannot assign your proposed piece because it does not fit in with our current editorial plans.
>
> Our editorial decisions are based on space allowance, material already covered or scheduled for future issues, as well as the projected interests of our readers.
>
> Due to the number of articles, stories, and ideas coming into the magazine each week, it is impossible for us to send you a personal and detailed reply. We want to assure you, however, that the time saved on letter-writing has been spent on careful consideration of your idea by members of the *Ms.* staff.

> Thank you very much for your inquiry about writing an article for HADASSAH MAGAZINE.
>
> While we would like to answer every letter personally, the volume of our correspondence makes it impossible to give you a personal reply.
>
> HADASSAH MAGAZINE, as a matter of policy, does not assign articles to authors who have not previously written for us. We do, however, give a careful and considered reading to all manuscripts submitted to us. Many articles which appear in HADASSAH were unsolicited.
>
> The optimal length for our articles is 1,500 to 3,000 words. We pay 12¢ a word with a maximum of $300.00. Payable upon publication of the article. If you have pictures related to your story, include them. We pay $35.00 for each black and white photo we use.
>
> We would welcome hearing from you.

> Thank you for your article query on behavioral therapy. Although we cannot use this particular idea for the magazine, we do hope that you will send any other ideas that may be suitable for FAMILY HEALTH; we'd be happy to take a look at them.

P.S. Along with your next query, could you please include a few current writing samples? Standard procedure for free-lance writers who are new to FAMILY HEALTH. Thanks.

I'm afraid the answer is No on your proposal for an article about ——— That's one of the problems: I'm not sure what the article is about. The fact that women live longer? That's hardly news. Besides, the real point is that we almost never do articles *about*. We're doing a much more personal and anecdotal kind of journalism, as I explained to you when you came by. That's why we liked the birds. No articles about phobias— but a good piece on someone who overcame one. That's the path.

The first letter gives the writer little indication of why the query was turned down, whereas the last one contains a great deal of information. The writer who received this rejection knew three things right away:

1. The article idea wasn't presented effectively. The editor wasn't even sure what the story was about.
2. The magazine was not interested in that kind of story.
3. A previous article the writer had submitted to the magazine was more the sort of article the editor was looking for. Other suggestions for stories of a similar nature might be well received.

Writing Query Letters

In writing a query, try to accomplish three things:

> "He who fears being conquered is sure of defeat."
>
> NAPOLEON BONAPARTE

Give the basics   of the story. Do this by explaining not only what the story will be about but what your sources of information will be and whom you plan to interview. It is not necessary to have already done the research and interviews; it is necessary to have decided what topics you will cover and how you will do it.

Show why this is a good story   for this magazine. Use your skills as a magazine analyst to point out the relevance of the subject to the magazine's audience or how the article fits in with the magazine's editorial policy. If you have a particular department in mind for the article, say so.

Convince the editor   that you are the person to write this story. Think of the query as a short article, written by you in your best style. It is a sample of your writing that you know the editor will read. Including additional clips from previously published articles is also a good idea, but beginners often have none, so the letter itself must do the job. More experienced writers simply mention the names of the publications in which their work has appeared. Show the editor that you are in an especially good position to do the story because you have access to some key information, are well informed about the subject, or know someone who is an expert.

Although it is unethical, editors have been known to assign an article to a staff member based on a free-lancer's suggestions simply because they do not have confidence in the free-lancer's ability to produce a publishable manuscript. Unless the free-lancer can prove that this has happened, he or she has little recourse. When the editorial offices are in New York and the free-lancer is in Omaha, the chances of his or her knowing the full story behind the "Sorry, but we've already assigned a piece on this subject . . ." replies are slim. The best way to avoid such disappointments is to write a good query.

A query letter should never exceed two single-spaced typewritten pages. If it does, that is evidence that the writer really does not have a clear idea of what the story will be about. It's a good idea to include your phone number in the return address; magazine editors, especially those with access to WATS lines, often like to telephone writers to discuss articles. Make sure the editor doesn't have to search for your number.

The elements discussed above are the yin and yang of query writing because they must be in balance for harmony to exist in the letter. A good idea that is poorly presented, either by sloppy writing or by insufficient reporting, won't stand a chance. Likewise, a well-written query about a good idea could be rejected if the editor lacks confidence in the writer's ability to cover the subject. The idea, your sources, and your style must work together for the query to be successful.

In a few special cases, querying an editor to suggest an idea may be difficult. For example, some articles cannot be outlined, among them very short features. Most humor pieces depend too much on the *way* they are written—the charm of the writing—to be outlined successfully. Some heavily editorial articles—the kind in which the writer is getting something weighty off his or her chest—may be similarly impossible to outline. Still, the query letter to an editor is one of the writer's most valuable tools. Why this is true is illustrated by the following letter:

> I have run across a character who would provide material, I believe, for a lively story. He is a voluble and energetic little Italian fellow with an Irish first name, Patrick Lizza. His enthusiasm is fireworks, and he is the largest fireworks manufacturer in the country. Lizza puts on fireworks shows at state and county fairs, American Legion gatherings, the Hollywood Bowl, and any other place that will be an excuse for lighting up the heavens.
>
> Lizza lives down at Redondo, a seaside town in Southern California, and has two fireworks plants, one at Saugus and another at Redondo Beach. Never satisfied with just putting on a display of colorful illumination, Lizza specializes in telling stories with fireworks. Last summer, for example, I saw one of his unusual shows, an engine and a train that moved, done in fireworks. He also put on portraits of famous people. One of his prides is his Niagara Falls. He has flying saucers, the flag raising at Iwo Jima, the aurora borealis, and the fountain of youth, to mention only a few of his spectacular ideas.
>
> A good deal of Lizza's success has been due to his ability to go before the Board of Directors of a fair or some other pageant and talk

them out of a few extra thousands of dollars to try out one of his new ideas. He gets them all laughing over his excitable Italian-English, and usually comes away with the money.

The big payoff in Lizza's business is his assignments from the Army and Navy to load rockets which are used to turn wartime no-man's-land and any enemy territory into artificial daylight. His two plants are going full blast on this, and while he is up to his ears in war work, Lizza has not let up on his fireworks displays and has a series of shows lined up for this summer that will be bigger and better than anything he has ever done before.

If you wanted to make a try at it, I think we could get set and line up some color of some of these displays. If successful in kodachrome, it ought to make a most spectacular layout.

In view of the fact that Lizza is such an effervescent and entertaining character, I think there would be ample material for an amusing human interest story about him and his unusual game. How does it look to you?

Note especially that although this is the query letter—the first correspondence on this subject—the writer has already done some of the research for this article. Much more fact gathering lies ahead, but the query is fairly detailed. The writer does not say merely that he wants to fashion an article on an interesting man who manufactures fireworks. Instead, the editor learns *why* the subject may interest millions of readers. And, although the writer and the editor are friends, the writer does not presume on the friendship nor even on the fact that he has already written many articles for the magazine. In short, he *works* at writing an attractive, informally phrased query—exactly as he might had he never met or written for the editor. The result was this go-ahead.

Patrick Lizza seems a good bet for a piece. We'll be glad to have you go ahead on this one whenever you can get to it.

One minor word of warning: Please make it quite clear that this fellow's business is selling fireworks for community displays and not to kids. As you know, there is high feeling in many parts of the country against the indiscriminate sale of fireworks to young fry, and many towns and cities have laws against it.

Such direction from an editor can be very helpful to a writer, particularly when it comes in detailed form, as illustrated in the following excerpt from a query and reply. Note that in this case the writer and editor had already discussed the article in person, but the editor had still requested a written proposal before giving the "okay":

One of the subjects we spoke about was a first-person account of how I overcame my phobia of birds. By coincidence, just two days after we met, I faced the most severe test imaginable of my freedom from fear. I was walking down 37th Street toward Madison Avenue when suddenly I noticed something falling from above, slightly in front of me and to the right. It landed with a thud on the sidewalk, followed by the scraping sound of wings against pavement. Imagine a claustrophobic caught in an elevator and you'll know how I felt.

The odds of a wounded bird falling from the sky onto one's head are quite slim; the odds of one falling inches away from a bird phobic are even slimmer. An estimated one in ten people suffer from phobias of some kind. Each could describe a terrifying scene in which all their worst fears come true. Depending on the degree to which a phobic believes what he or she most dreads will happen, the problem can rule the individual's life. A person with fear of heights cannot go into tall buildings or ride in airplanes; an agoraphobic cannot leave the house; a car phobic must walk to go anywhere.

A year ago the episode that took place in New York would have sent me screaming and crying hysterically into the nearest bird-free place. Shaking and panic stricken, I would have imagined it happening again and again. I'm happy to say that because of therapy, my reaction was far less dramatic. I just kept walking. Moreover, I was able to remain calm and did not conclude that the sky was about to rain dead birds down upon me.

My other accomplishments as a former phobic may sound less exciting, but they represent real progress. I can walk down the street without crossing to the other side if I see a bird on the sidewalk ahead of me. I can sit in a restaurant where there are birds in cages and enjoy my meal. I can walk around in my backyard without searching the grass for dead birds. Sometimes, I can even enjoy the graceful picture of birds in flight, or laugh at ducks sliding on a frozen pond.

The treatment that helped me overcome my fear was a brief, relatively simple process. It lasted less than three months, involved only half a dozen sessions, and cost about $300. My therapist was Dr. Gerald Rosen, chief psychologist at Providence Medical Center in Seattle and author of *Don't Be Afraid.* The behavior modification techniques Dr. Rosen used to help me can be applied to any severe, irrational fear, whether it is of snakes or of public speaking. Unfortunately, most people who suffer from phobias are either too ashamed to seek help, are unaware that such help exists, or believe that it would be too expensive. In fact, visits to a clinical psychologist are covered by many health insurance plans.

I would like to write an article about my experience for *Good Housekeeping.* The story is one I'm certain would strike a common chord among your readers, for almost everyone is truly afraid of something that the rest of us find only mildly unpleasant or downright nice. The article would also represent an unusual treatment of the subject— though I have seen stories about phobias, I have never seen one written by a phobic who had been cured. As a service to your audience, the story might provide some phobics with the information they need to get help. Naturally I would obtain the advice and approval of Dr. Rosen before submitting the article.

Thank you for your consideration. I look forward to hearing from you.

The following response was received just one week later, breaking all previous records for response time to this free-lancer's queries:

> I remember your visit and your mention of the bird phobia piece. I do think it would make an interesting article—especially if you can do it in a light, conversational style. Since you have never written for us, we would have to request that you do the piece on speculation. That means that if it proves satisfactory for use in *GH,* we pay you $1,000. If it doesn't work out, you get it back. The piece should not run more than 1,200 words. I suggest you save the episode of the falling bird for the end—a kind of clincher to prove that your cure really worked. You might start the article by saying how glad you are to be cured of your phobia, then describe the phobia and how your fears interfered with your life, how you found out about the treatment, what the therapy was like and how it worked out for you. When you're talking about the behavior modification techniques, please be very specific and don't burden the piece with a lot of theories. We look forward to receiving the manuscript from you by the middle of February.

Here is a long, successful query Shelley Smolkin sent to the article editor of *Working Woman:*

> This year for the first time, the Comprehensive Employment and Training Act (CETA) being considered by Congress cites "displaced homemakers" among the list of economically disadvantaged groups eligible for a wide range of government assistance programs. As defined in the national legislation, a displaced homemaker is one who "has not worked in the labor force for a substantial number of years but has, during those years, worked in the home providing unpaid services for family members . . . ," who has been dependent upon a source of income that is no longer available (such as a deceased or ex-husband) and who is either unemployed or underemployed.
>
> The inclusion of displaced homemakers in the list is no accident—it is the direct result of the efforts of many women, most of whom could have been described by the above definition at some point in their lives. Three years ago the term "displaced homemaker" did not exist. It was coined by Tish Sommers, a California divorcee who decided to do something about the plight of the millions of women who, for whatever reason, suddenly are compelled to seek employment outside the home after many years as homemakers. Implicit in Congress's definition of a displaced homemaker is the recognition that a woman who has spent most of her adult life caring for others is extremely disadvantaged when she tries to reenter the job market. The skills she may have acquired years ago are outdated; her paid working experience is not considered recent enough to qualify her for many jobs. Displaced homemakers are of every age, but many are older women who are ineligible for government-sponsored apprenticeship or training programs.
>
> Together with Laurie Shields, a widow, Tish Sommers set out to do something about this appalling situation. The two enlisted the help

of Barbara Dudley, a young attorney, and drafted legislation that was passed by the California state legislature in 1975, authorizing funds for the establishment of the first Displaced Homemaker Center in the country to be located in Oakland, California. They formed the Alliance for Displaced Homemakers, organized a national letter-writing campaign, and took their message cross-country to legislators, women's groups, and anyone else who would listen. Within two years, 16 states had enacted displaced homemaker legislation. From an idea in the mind of one woman, the displaced homemaker movement had gained national momentum, culminating in the CETA legislation. In a recent speech before Congress, Assistant Secretary for Employment and Training Ernie Green promised to allocate $5 million in the coming year to programs to help displaced homemakers. In October, the first national conference on displaced homemakers will take place in Baltimore, Maryland.

I would like to propose an article on the displaced homemaker movement for *Working Woman.* In addition to describing how it began, the article could provide information on the many displaced homemaker centers already operating in the country. Programs like the one here at Bellevue Community College offer a variety of services, including vocational guidance, counseling, and job referral. Once the CETA legislation passes, many other government-sponsored programs will also be open to displaced homemakers. Of particular interest in the story would be an interview with Evelyn Farber, a labor economist in the Women's Bureau of the Department of Labor, who is an expert on the subject of displaced homemakers and who is instrumental in authorizing funds for the establishment of programs throughout the country.

Over a month later, Smolkin received the following reply:

We are indeed interested in your proposal for an article on displaced homemakers, CETA, the countrywide programs, the women who started it all and the October meeting.

Your approach, as outlined in your query, seems very sound and thorough to us, and we'd like to add just one other ingredient to be included in the article: namely, Why should the younger, employed woman be much concerned about it at all? The answer, as we see it, is twofold: 1. She can learn something from any woman or women who successfully initiate and run a program of this scope and 2. (without being too dour about it) the possibility that any of us at some time in our lives could find ourselves in a similar situation.

Giving emphasis to these points, we think, will involve the *Working Woman* reader in an issue that, in the main, she herself doesn't now face.

Unfortunately, we can't pay travel expenses, so the October meeting part of the piece will have to depend on whether you are planning to come east on your own.

I'm enclosing a contract herewith. If there's anything further you'd like to discuss, please phone me collect.

Note that the editor took this opportunity to offer some advice to the writer on the angle she thought the story should take. She also specified what financial arrangements the magazine was willing to make: first, that it would not pay travel expenses to the conference, and second, that it would assign the story on contract.

Smolkin signed the following contract and returned it to the magazine:

This is to confirm that we will pay on acceptance *$500.00* for your grant to HAL Publications, Inc. of certain rights to the contribution entitled *"DISPLACED HOMEMAKERS."*

You hereby grant to HAL Publications, Inc. (a) exclusive North American serial rights; (b) the right to reprint said contribution from WORKING WOMAN magazine or to authorize third parties to make such reprints; (c) the right to use said contribution in publicizing, promoting or advertising WORKING WOMAN; and (d) the right to include said contribution in any volume of WORKING WOMAN material published or authorized by HAL Publications, Inc.

You represent and warrant originality, authorship and ownership of said contribution, that it has not heretofore been published, that its publication will not infringe upon any copyright, proprietary or other right and that it contains no matter which is libelous, obscene, or otherwise contrary to law.

If the foregoing terms are acceptable, kindly sign and return the enclosed copy of this letter.

Common Problems in Query Writing

Because a query letter is a bit like a short article, it presents similar problems to the writer. There is no room for words or paragraphs that are not essential to either presenting or sellng the story. Here is an excerpt from a query written by a beginner that illustrates some common difficulties:

Clay Felker, Editor
Esquire
1790 Broadway
New York, New York 10019

Dear Mr. Felker:

Recently, I had occasion to reflect upon the past brilliance of the late, great American motor car industry. To clarify, a motor car carries the distinguished marque of a Duesenberg, Stutz, Cord, Mercedes, Rolls, or Bentley, to name a few quality machines from the golden era of classic machines. An automobile is the throughway vehicle built by Detroit, subsequent to World War II.

Last month as I shopped for a new car, immersed in cloudy thoughts about the fuel shortages and even gloomier thoughts about the uneven craftmanship so evident in post-war American automobiles, I really tried to buy American. It was no use; after driving ten new cars, I ended up doing the inevitable: I bought a foreign car. What a shame!

The United States dominates the aircraft industry, because our airframes and engines are the very best available, yet we can't build a competitive quality motor car.

Our motor cars, at one time, were among the very best. Stutz and Duesenberg racing machines gave many a European race team heartburn during the early decades of the century because of their speed and stamina. As a youngster, growing up in New England—the mecca of classic cars, with the net assets of one canary yellow straight-8 Stutz roadster, I developed an early appreciation for fine machinery. Today, I begrudgingly drive my father-in-law's Seville. It doesn't have 20-inch red wire wheels, it doesn't have a one-shot lube system, and worst of all, it doesn't even have a menacing set of exhaust cut-outs protruding from the hood—at the exact height of the average Radcliffe girl's bicycle seat. Essentially, our best has neither elan nor character; it's a eunuch in the company of fine motor cars.

Aside from the obvious need for editing in these opening paragraphs, there is another problem that detracts from the writer's presentation of his idea. After reading these three paragraphs, the editor still will not know what the subject of the article is. Does the writer intend to produce a story about why American cars aren't what they used to be, or does he want to do a nostalgic piece about the classic automobiles of the past?

Here is another query written by a beginner:

Gini Alhadeff
Normal magazine
597 Fifth Avenue
New York, New York 10017

Dear Ms. Alhadeff:

Some unfortunate soul once said, "Those who can, do, those who can't, teach." Obviously, this person never met Nathan Oliveira.

Like an explorer who crosses many different boundaries, Oliveira traverses the line between actuality and academia. Unwilling to make a clear division between the roles in his life, Nathan Oliveira keeps a proverbial foot on each side of the fence, and thus grounds himself in both his art and his teaching. One never can predict where or how one might find Oliveira on any given occasion. One person may know him as the formidable Bay Area artist, dressed to the nines in a black tuxedo, holding a glass of white wine, leading admirers around an opening of an art show. Another may find himself staring at the tortoise-shell-rimmed eyes of a Stanford art professor intensely explaining the meaning of composition and placement. Still another may pass a mustached man in sweats and Reeboks hiking up the foothills behind campus with his wife, searching for oddly shaped rocks and tree branches.

Such versatility and adaptability, valuable qualities especially in the risky world of art, mark Oliveira as a man capable of surviving and succeeding. His prolific and critically acclaimed career has yet spanned over a period of close to forty years. These years have undoubtedly enriched Oliveira with a treasure of knowledge about art itself; yet, at the same time, and possibly more importantly, they have given him an insight into the best ways to promote an artistic lifestyle. That is, Oliveira has found a way to live art to the fullest: he produces and exhibits his own work; he shares his creativity and knowledge with students to further their pursuits in art; and, therefore, he can find art in every aspect of his existence.

His talent for "living art," I believe, makes Nathan Oliveira a most intriguing personality. His dedication and devotion to art inspire his students and friends and validate his opinions about the subject. It is for these reasons that I believe an interview/profile of this artist/ teacher would provide an appealing nonfiction segment for *Normal* magazine. Previous articles on artists, such as photographer Robert Mapplethorpe, prove that an avid interest prevails in the readers for modern and contemporary figures of the art world. Coupled with reprints of Oliveira's work, this article would be a festive visual piece as well as an informative sketch.

Naturally, I would be contacting Oliveira and his colleagues for interviews, as well as observing him in a figure drawing class which I am presently taking. The research will be, as they say, "at my fingertips."

In conclusion, I would like to emphasize my enthusiasm about getting to know Nathan Oliveira and letting your readers get a tangible feel for the artist, teacher, and man. I hope to hear from you soon. Thank you for your consideration.

Notice how the writer leaves no confusion about what the subject of his article will be. However, problems with this query are its lack of brevity and its sales-pitch tone. The writer stresses only the best characteristics of the subject, leading one to believe that the resulting article may read like a public relations piece.

CHECKLIST: WRITING QUERY LETTERS

1. Address the current editor by name, if possible. If you can't tell whether an editor is male or female, address the editor by a full name (such as "Dear Chris Jones:").

2. Include your telephone number in the return address.

3. Do not exceed two single-spaced typewritten pages.

4. Use a strong opening to catch the editor's attention.

5. Include the basics of your story. Give your sources of information, and explain whom you plan to interview and which topics you will cover.

6. Specify why your article is appropriate for the magazine's audience.

7. Persuade the editor that you are the best person to write this article. If possible, mention contacts who will give you access to important information.

8. If possible, include clippings from previously published articles.

9. In your closing paragraph, request to write the article for the magazine. You may specify the date the manuscript can be completed and an approximate length.

10. Do not discuss fees or request advice from the editor.

The Lead

Like magazine articles, query letters should have leads that grab the reader's attention. Like newspaper articles, they should present the most important information in the opening paragraphs. Many beginners tend to take a long warm-up before the pitch; in writing a query, it is essential to get the point across quickly. Here are some that do:

> Who decides which trees are cut? Right now an apparent deadlock exists between the lumber industry and environmentalists. Housing shortages and an expanding economy are demanding an increase in production of timber. But people all over the U.S. are reacting with horror and disbelief to the possibility of a treeless future. Is there an answer to the dilemma?

> Most people are familiar with the McDonald's Restaurant chain, but few realize that the company has concerns that extend beyond the realm of the Big Mac. Owners of McDonald's Restaurants in Northern California and Northern Nevada together with the Children's Hospital at Stanford Parents Group have recently completed construction of Ronald McDonald House, a home away from home for families of catastrophically ill children at the hospital.

> At a time when Disco Fever is sweeping the country, I fear we may be overlooking a much older but no less serious disease which afflicts thousands of college students yearly: Potomac Fever.
>
> The symptoms are many and varied: a burning interest in public affairs and governmental policy, an itch to see Ted Kennedy in person, a phobia of that contradiction in terms—"summer school," and an uncontrollable urge to find out what people really do in a cloakroom besides hang up coats.
>
> Over 3,000 young people descend upon Washington, D.C., every summer to visit the healing waters of the Potomac. Everyone is treated differently, and some are cured—permanently. Many others find that the condition is chronic, but controllable.

These queries, also written by beginners, have poor leads. Notice how they struggle to get to the point:

> It appears that readers/subscribers to magazines, whether they be news magazines, special interest magazines, or even fashion magazines, are constantly bombarded with ads that tell them to buy certain products without the benefit of being told why. Oh, yes, the slogans of the ads themselves tell them why. They may read, "Wheaties: the breakfast of champions," "Toyota: Oh, what a feeling!," or "Arrowhead, water from a higher source." Though the reader is succinctly told in a few words to buy the product, there really is no clear elucidation why that product is the best buy. For instance, why is Wheaties the breakfast of champions? What feeling does Toyota elicit that probably no other car can produce? What makes Arrowhead's water so special? The taste? How is the taste?

Recently, Seana Linnehan, a Boston native, attended the Red Sox's opening home game. While the national anthem played, she cried so hard that she could not sing. She bought three Fenway Franks: one to eat, one to freeze, and one to shellac. During the Seventh Inning Stretch, she, a grown woman of considerable size, yelled and clapped while standing on her foldable seat. When the game ended, her sobbing resumed.

Seana is getting married. Her mate-to-be, however, is not a starting player for the Red Sox. Rather, he is a foreigner, and Seana is preparing herself for a move to his homeland. Although her foreigner fiancé hails from the island we once considered our "mother country," Seana has braced herself for a move to a far, distant, and strange land. This tall, blonde American Catholic of Irish descent is finding that giving up Mom and Apple Jacks is making her sad and soggy.

I am a young, unpublished writer. I don't have a mile-long list of credits with which to impress you . . . I haven't even completed college yet! I do, however, have something extremely valuable to offer you. I have some excellent ideas, fresh insights and definite writing skill. I firmly believe that my lack of experience and professional instruction makes my writing all the more believable to your audience. I am only nineteen years old—the feelings and dilemmas of your reading public are very real to me. I experience the same emotions daily. All right, if I must confess, I still read *Seventeen!!!*

AN ARTICLE IDEA IS ACCEPTED

If the response to a query is an acceptance, it generally comes in one of two forms. The editor may make the assignment entirely "on spec" (speculation); meaning that he or she indicates interest in seeing a manuscript, usually of a specified length and by a specified date, and agrees to pay a certain amount for the article if it is accepted, zero if it is not. Or the editor may make the assignment on contract with a provision of a "kill fee" of 10 to 20 percent of the acceptance price if the article is rejected. In the first case, the writer takes all the financial risk in doing the article; in the second case, the magazine shares some of the risk by guaranteeing the writer a minimum payment. Editors also may indicate whether or not they will pay research expenses for an article, such as long-distance calls, travel costs, or other related out-of-pocket expenses the writer may encounter. If the editor does not provide this information, you should inquire about it before starting work. If you have to pay expenses yourself, that may affect the kind of research you choose to undertake.

THE NEXT TASK: MORE CORRESPONDENCE

For many writers, correspondence with editors begins with one mailing and ends with another: first, a query letter suggesting a subject; then, if the editor has answered affirmatively, an envelope carrying the article.

But there is reason to believe that a free-lancer should undertake much more correspondence. A writer who once gave relatively little attention to correspondence, contenting himself with a query letter and an article mailing in each case, found that nearly half his manuscripts were coming back with rejection slips saying, "Sorry, we can't use this." Deciding that a full dialogue with editors might help, he began to work more industriously at correspondence. He not only wrote an original query letter outlining an idea but also followed up, after doing much of the article research, with another letter—sometimes two or three—sketching his progress and asking for the editor's reaction to the shape the article was beginning to take (which was sometimes quite different from the shape suggested by the initial query). The result was that fewer manuscripts came back, and the writer was almost always able to modify those that did to the editor's specifications. Sometimes two or three rounds of correspondence—after as well as before the first submission of the article—were necessary before an idea would jell at both ends of the correspondence line.

The value of this process should be apparent. Correspondence helped the writer involve the editor in the project. After two or three letters, the editor had a stake in the writer's success. Sometimes the idea became more the editor's than the writer's; the idea the writer had originally proposed to the editor evolved into an even better idea—at least from the editor's point of view.

One value that is less apparent is that editors are part of an editorial team on most magazines. Few of them can or will decide independently whether an article should be published. Editorial conferences are often a process of argument and compromise. When an editor has become deeply involved in an article, he or she is much more likely to argue strongly for it and is much better able to present it winningly. Of course, not all editors have the time or inclination to engage in a dialogue by mail, but those who do can be a great help to writers.

Here is an example of a follow-up letter—not a query—that was written to an associate editor after the writer had received a go-ahead on an article and had completed much of the research. The article that eventually grew out of this correspondence was titled "His Millions for the Big Outdoors":

> By way of a report on the story line for the Rockefeller story, the theme seems to be that it calls for more sweat and tears to give the public a hundred million dollars' worth of outdoor and historical treasure than it did to make the hundred million to pay for it. The Rockefellers have carried out what is probably the most magnificent one-family conservation program in history, and they are still going strong in the face of attacks on their motives that would have deterred a less single-minded family.
>
> Laurance Rockefeller is the brother who picked up the play started by John D., Jr., four decades back. The five brothers are more scientific givers than their father was. They have a partnership, Rockefeller Brothers, Inc., to make the millions, and another, Rockefeller

Brothers Fund, to give them away. However, to keep themselves out of the spotlight, they work largely through other organizations such as Jackson Hole Preserve, Inc., and American Conservation Association. However, Laurance R. frequently plunges on his own, if he thinks an outdoor treasure is in danger, just as John D., Jr., did.

The total of gifts for conservation is well over the $100,000,000 mark, but the canny Rockefellers have doubled this ante by matching federal, state, or other private funds wherever possible. Laurance says they are not "wilderness boys" and they don't propose to invest in virgin areas to "put them in deep freeze for future generations." They think the people should be using the natural recreational areas now. In fact, the Rockefellers talk as much about human resources as about natural resources, when they are on the subject of conservation.

The natural and historical gems they have saved, in many instances in the nick of time, pretty well blanket the country. They range from Williamsburg to Grand Teton Park to Corkscrew Cypress stands in Florida; from the Calaveras Grove of Sequoia gigantea and the Bull Creek Grove of Sequoia sempervirens on the Redwood Highway, to the Great Smokies, Acadia National Park, stands of sugar pines along the roads to Yosemite, museums at Mesa Verde and other parks, roadside cleanup in Yellowstone, "seed money" for a survey in Mt. Rainier to find a way to provide facilities for the public, one of the Virgin Islands now a national park, and numerous others. There is a story behind nearly every one of these projects.

My plan is to put the story together in the rough and have it checked by Horace M. Albright, who acted as front man for the family in lining up many of these purchases. Robert L. Hoke, Room 5425, 30 Rockefeller Plaza, has gathered together many photographs, both color and black and white, and these are available if you want to use any of them. If you can let me know when you would like to have copy, I'll shoot at that deadline.

If you're still not convinced of the value of correspondence, this report from a prominent free-lancer should win you over:

Early in my article-writing career, I hit on the idea of keeping a box score on a large sheet of paper of my article suggestions submitted to editors. The best average I could achieve that first year and the next was one acceptance out of ten ideas submitted. Of course, I could rewrite the letter about a rejected idea and try it on another editor or another magazine. The first year of the box score I submitted ninety ideas and got nine go-aheads. These were not exactly assignments; they were merely the editor's word that he was interested in seeing the manuscript and that nobody else was doing that story for him. He had staked out the idea for me and would give me a reasonable amount of time, usually up to six months, to send him the manuscript. If he wanted it in a hurry, he would tell me and I could put on a night shift (myself) and rush it.

Gradually, as I learned what the different editors did not want and quit submitting sure-fire duds to them, I worked the average down to one acceptance in five ideas submitted, and eventually down to one in three—which is about the best I've been able to achieve. But just because one editor turned down an idea didn't mean that another wouldn't go for it. Editors' choices are as variable as the winds. All this time, as the go-ahead rate improved, the article acceptance rate was zooming until I was batting around .900—selling nine of every ten articles I wrote, and at top rates. All this proves that it pays to write good letters—good sales letters.

TALKING IDEAS OVER WITH EDITORS

Part of the cost of free-lancing is financing trips to the magazine publishing centers, especially New York, to discuss ideas with editors. A writer who lives far from his editors must rely primarily on correspondence, but he cannot rule out travel simply because it is expensive. He learns too much on these "apple-peddling expeditions," as one editor calls them, to forgo them. He acquires insights into what the magazine may want for months ahead. During a lunch with two or three editors, an idea may strike a spark with one even though it may not interest the others. Often, an idea a writer suggests is developed in conversation, enabling the writer to refine his understanding of an approach to a subject in a way that could not have been accomplished in ten exchanges of letters.

Talking to editors, however, is not automatically valuable. Like the other aspects of free-lancing, discussions must be planned. Several general principles are involved in the planning. First, the writer must make appointments well in advance—a month or more, if possible—because many editors travel and because other writers are also making appointments. Writing short notes and making phone calls can enable a writer to set up a schedule that will allow him or her to talk with editors at several magazines during one trip. The beginner must write letters that will persuade editors that a face-to-face discussion is worth their time. (Practices vary from magazine to magazine. On some magazines, a beginner is not likely to be able to meet even the most junior editors. In any case, it is usually wise to ask for an appointment only after your query letters or articles have brought a stronger response than a printed rejection slip.)

The second, and most important, principle is to be prepared to talk specifically about article subjects. A writer's asking vaguely whether there is anything in an area he might cover for the magazine is almost certain to waste everybody's time. Be prepared to discuss your ideas as carefully as you would prepare an extensive query letter. In other words, some of the research must have been accomplished before you visit magazine offices.

One veteran writer began early in his career to prepare for talks with editors as though he were on a campaign:

> Before taking off on an expedition, I always sifted through my ideas and jotted down enough facts in a pocket notebook to talk about each story intelligently. If I didn't have enough facts to talk up the story, I got on the phone or did some in-person interviewing to case the story idea. I

also checked *Readers' Guide to Periodical Literature* to make certain that the magazine had not recently run an article that I was proposing. It's most embarrassing to have an editor advise you to look at an issue two months back and read the story you're proposing—written by another man. No matter how carefully a writer tried to keep up, he'll probably miss a few articles in his magazines. And these are the ones that trip him up. Checking *Readers' Guide* is his protection.

The pocket notebook invariably intrigued my editors. Before we had downed the first cocktail, one of them would say, "Get out your little notebook, and let's see what's in it." Some topics would win a go-ahead right away. The editor might want more information on others. That was my cue to say, "How would you like to have me case the idea and send you a report?" The answer usually was, "Okay, we'll protect you on the story until you can give us an outline." Often, editors offered to pay my expenses while I was casing a story, and sometimes they would pay for my work even if they eventually decided against giving me a go-ahead.

As soon as I return from one of these expeditions, I write to the editors to thank them for their time and to outline the story ideas they want me to turn into manuscripts and those that I am to case. This firms up the assignments and guards against misunderstandings.

Here is another highly successful writer. Because Steve Allen does so many writing chores gracefully and rapidly, he is quoted here discussing his daily duties:*

I suppose the most noteworthy fact about any one more-or-less typical day of my writing is that it never is limited to one project. Having abandoned the typewriter 15 years ago and never having gotten around to using a word processor, I do all my writing by dictating into a pocket-sized hand-held tape recorder. The average produced per day is twenty pages. Since I work seven days a week, not the conventional five, this means that in a year I crank out about 7,000 pages of material. I would be fortunate if all of it consisted of novels, short stories, poetry, essays, social criticism, plays, film-scripts and assorted instances of humor. Some of it does, but mixed with this purely creative flow there are personal and business letters, office memos, letters to admirers, answers to interviewers' questions and reminders to myself to do one thing or another.

I have always envied writers who work on a time schedule. On a visit to Jamaica a few years ago I was shown the home of Ian Fleming of James Bond fame. Mr. Fleming reportedly sat every morning, precisely at 9:00, at a small, triangular table set into a corner of his bedroom and remained there, pecking away, until noon, at which time his day's work was over, after which he could enjoy the glories of the tropical surf lapping outside his door. Ernest Hemingway, it is said, wrote in longhand standing up and leaning on a refrigerator. Parenthetically that has

---

*Reprinted by permission of Steve Allen.

always seemed to me the dumbest writer's regimen imaginable, although Hemingway was a great artist.

If I had to do the transcribing of 20 pages daily, the procedure would collapse of its own weight. Fortunately, staff people have the dreary task of listening to my ramblings and typing them up. There is many a slip, of course, in this process, but I catch the errors at the next stage when the freshly typed pages are presented to me for editorial revision.

Each separate bit of dictation is prefaced with a brief instruction as to its target. If a philosophical observation occurs, for example, I say "The next item is for *Ideas.*" After the entry has been transcribed, edited and re-typed, it is then filed in three-ring loose-leaf notebooks in which I keep such pensées. This particular category is frequently mined; portions of it, over the years, find their way into assorted speeches, magazine articles, novels or television commentaries.

Humorous items are introduced as "for *Funny Stuff*" and, like

STEVE ALLEN

Steve Allen, star of twenty-two television shows, author of twenty-nine books, composer of four thousand songs, and radio comic genius since the 1940s, looked at his Uncle Steve's dolled-up dead body as it lay in a coffin.

"Then I stood and spoke to the others gathered around. A few of the people were flustered at talking to a television entertainer and quite forgot to mention Steve at all, but I understood their nervousness. For the most part, though, those present seemed to be actively, personally saddened by Steve's death. To one side of the room stood a middle-aged man in the uniform of the Chicago Fire Department. It was good to know that Steve had had friends who cared enough about him to cry at his funeral."

Allen is hysterical. Best known for his ad-libbed, witty repartee and monologues, Allen is a prolific author who writes as a way to remember, to express his own opinions, and to make people laugh. Allen would probably explain his knack for wit by referring to genetics. Both his mother and father were vaudeville performers. Unfortunately, the scientific genetic proof lags behind the human hunch. A less debatable fact is that to make people laugh at themselves, at others, or at all, the comedian must have a working understanding of people. And this comes from *observing* them.

The comedian walks down a city street as if he were walking through a wild animal park. Listening, watching, smell-

ing, and then remembering. At Uncle Steve's funeral, Allen was in a wild animal park.

The most important raw skill for a comic is the same crucial raw skill for a writer. Allen recognized this early in his career and since has had little problem translating his observations to the written, spoken, or even sung, word.

"Yes," you might say, "but he must be sick to find something funny about a funeral. And, besides, his words quoted above are not funny."

Woody Allen has pounced on the notion that there is a fine line between emotional opposites. Playing off Tolstoy's classic *War and Peace,* Allen titled a movie *Love and Death.* Steve Allen, who, if given the chance, would point out that he recognized this fundamental connection years before Woody was born, writes that "the raw material of comedy is tragedy." And this realization comes from careful human observation.

As Allen walked the South Side of Chicago's streets on his way to Uncle Steve's funeral, he wore dark sunglasses and a pulled-down hat. While he deterred people from looking in, he was looking out. Listening, watching, smelling, and remembering. Allen has given the world a recollection of Uncle Steve by writing about his own trip to Steve's funeral. Many of the anecdotes are humorous; some are very sad. All of them come from sensitive observation.

—Lisa Caron Bierer

the *Ideas,* later are apportioned out to various comedy monologues, sketches, scripts or books.

I bitterly resent the fact that the bulk of my dictation consists of correspondence. Only a small portion of this, alas, is the sort that might one day be published; much of it is simply a matter of being courteous enough to respond to the enormous barrage of mail that hits our working-premises each morning.

A beautiful element of the method is that it makes theoretically the entire universe of one's workplace. No longer is the writer bound to his office or home work-desk. During the average day, therefore, I may dictate in bed, in the swimming pool, lounging at poolside, at the breakfast table, at my office desk, in restaurants, on planes and—particularly in Los Angeles—in my car. For some mysterious reason, automobiles and airplanes are favorite working places, not from any rational intention but simply because my brain automatically revs at high speed in such settings.

HOW ABOUT AN AGENT?

"The worst cynicism: a belief in luck."

JOYCE CAROL OATES

Perhaps the worst malady that can afflict the beginning writer is "agentitis." All the vexing details, she may think, would be taken care of if only she could hook up with a sharp literary agent, especially one who would take over the "business" aspects while the free-lancer devotes her genius to the serious work of writing. This is a dream.

There are a few agents—very few—who can and will shoulder much of the business load for *established* writers. For 10 or 15 percent of the earnings of a writer who has proved that she can turn out profitable prose, agents will try to do the selling. Some agents have developed such close relationships with their writers that they occasionally serve as confidant, idea generator, and, when their writers are in slack periods, money lender. Some writers consider their agents as essential to success as vigorous verbs.

The pivotal point, however, is that topflight agents will almost never take on beginners as clients. A good agent can afford to give little time (if any) to a writer who is just learning his trade. The agents who specialize in helping beginners charge reading fees (their ads can be found in writers' magazines). They may be able to help a writer get started, but few of them are held in high esteem by editors. In short, the neophyte should cultivate his or her own relationships with editors.

Further, it is questionable whether one who specializes in article writing for magazines should ever hook up with an agent. Some successful article writers have developed mutually profitable relationships with agents. But agents are far more useful to writers who concentrate on fiction and books. Article writers are primarily reporters. Their work with magazine editors resembles the relationship between newspaper reporters and their editors. In addition, neither a writer nor an editor wants to convey messages through a third party.

A highly successful article writer summed up his experience with agents as follows:

> Over the years, I have worked with three literary agents, two of them of high caliber and one not so good. None was of any great help in selling article ideas, although it was reassuring on occasion to talk over ideas with them before talking with the editors. Agents are sometimes able to line up new markets for a writer, but when it comes down to the hard business of selling ideas, the writer must do it himself. In all three cases, after working with these agents for from one to eight years, we have terminated the relationship by mutual agreement, and with good feelings.
>
> Where the agents were able to do good, and justify their 10 percent commissions, was in persuading editors to raise my rate of pay. They may have pushed some editors a little too hard. Most editors are alert to the need of raising rates after eight or ten articles. If they forget, I'm not squeamish about calling it to their attention in a letter. That usually does it.
>
> In principle, agents are supposed to check manuscripts before they go to an editor and suggest revisions. But I've found that agents' guesses as to what editors want are not much better than my own, and sometimes not so good. Also, I've found that agents hesitate to go to bat for a writer if there is a misunderstanding with an editor, for fear of jeopardizing their other clients.

Mark Stephens, author of *Three Mile Island* and many newspaper features and magazine articles, tells about his agent:

> My agent is Liz Darhansoff, who lives in New York, where it seems most literary agents live. My association with Liz began about five years ago when an editor rejected my book proposal, then suggested I get an agent—Liz. Using the same rejected proposal, she sold the book for several times what I had expected to get. And that's why writers have agents.
>
> Liz represents me in most of my projects. She is in her late thirties and has been a literary agent for about ten years. Before becoming an agent, she worked in the promotion department at Random House. Apparently there is no particular training to become an agent. You just do it, learning as you go.
>
> Liz is an independent agent and is not associated with a major firm, as some literary agents are. Working with two part-time assistants, she represents about eighty writers, including several with national prominence. She sells both books and magazine pieces, though she clearly prefers books. I think this is because her 10 percent of my magazine income still does not amount to much. I think she does the magazine work mainly as a favor to her clients, like me, who also do books.
>
> There are some very good reasons for having a literary agent. They have access to editors—access that most writers could never hope to have on their own. They can be good critics of queries and proposals, helping to decide what is worth trying to sell and what is

not. They can negotiate book contracts, which I used to think was either a science or an art, but now I know is a religion. They can get nasty, asking for money or enforcing some contract provision, while not endangering *your* rapport with the editor. They can be near the publishers when you are living in California.

But having an agent is not all positive, either. Sometimes they judge projects too quickly, urging you to give up good ideas. They insert a delay, and often a layer of noise, between you and the editor. They tend to sit on your money, which always comes from the publisher late anyway.

Having Liz as my agent costs 10 percent of my income, but my guess is that my gross income is twice as much for having an agent as it would be without. It's worth it to me.

Obviously, if you plan to work through an agent, you must choose one carefully. Perhaps the best approach is to ask magazine editors to recommend an agent they respect. But if you think that working with an agent will solve all your business problems, you are certain to be disappointed.

BUSINESS AND ETIQUETTE

Many beginners don't know how to handle various situations that can arise after they have mailed a query letter or an article to a magazine. Editors of *Writer's Market* have published these questions and answers to help you learn about the business of writing:

What should I do when I don't get a reply to my query or manuscript in the listing's stated reporting time?   Wait three or four weeks beyond the stated reporting time and send a polite letter inquiring about the status of your manuscript. Sometimes writers are quick to send accusatory letters when a delay can mean that the manuscript is making its way up the ladder and being considered seriously for publication. Delays do happen, however, and occasionally material is lost or misplaced. To cut down on these problems, always submit your work in the way the magazine or publisher prefers; never send your only copy, and remember that most editors will not return manuscripts without a self-addressed, stamped envelope.

Is it okay to call an editor?   Rarely. The few editors who are willing to accept phone queries say so in their listings. Editors you work with regularly may not object to phone calls; some actually *prefer* a phone call on timely pieces that can't be delayed. You probably will be encouraged to call if you're sending your article by modem because you'll need to discuss compatibility and requirements of the systems.

What do I do if the publication doesn't pay on time?   If you don't receive your payment within two weeks of the time you expected it, follow up with a note to your editor. Sometimes it's an honest mistake, a backup in paperwork, a cutoff date that wasn't met, and so on. Most problems can be corrected with a simple inquiry note. If you still don't receive payment, you may find, as some writers do, that sending an invoice to the accounting department works well.

What rights do editors buy for articles?   The most common purchase of rights for articles is first North American serial rights. That means the publication has the right to publish your article for the first time in any periodical. All other rights to the material belong to the writer. Some magazines use this purchasing technique to obtain the right to publish first in both the United States and Canada, since many U.S. magazines are circulated in Canada. Some magazines will buy both first serial rights and second serial or reprint rights, allowing them to print the article for the first time and also to reprint it another time. If you do not sell reprint rights with the first sale, you can market the article's reprint rights to another publication. Some magazines buy all rights. If you sell all rights to an article, you cannot sell it again, but occasionally an editor who has bought all rights will reassign rights to the writer. Finally, some publications ask writers to sign work-for-hire agreements. This is the worst deal for writers, since they sign over the copyright to the article and do not retain any rights to the work. For a complete discussion of rights, see the section titled "The Business of Writing" in *Writer's Market* and *A Writer's Guide to Contract Negotiations* by Richard Balkin (Cincinnati, OH: Writer's Digest Books, 1990).

Can I sell an article for publication more than once?   Yes, if you haven't sold the rights already. If you have sold first North American serial rights, first rights, or one-time rights to an article, you can sell the exact article for reprint to other publications. When you submit the article, send a fresh copy marked with the rights you are selling (usually second serial rights or one-time rights).

To what rights am I entitled under copyright law?   The law gives you, as creator of your work, the right to print, reprint, and copy the work; to sell or distribute copies of the work; to prepare "derivative works"—dramatizations, translations, musical arrangement, novelizations, and so on; to record the work; and to perform or display literary, dramatic, or musical works publicly. These rights give you control over how your work is used and assure you (in theory) that you receive payment for any use of your work.

MARKETS FOR STUDENTS' WRITING

Years ago, nine-year-old Rawson Stovall of Abilene, Texas, had his heart set on an Atari game machine. So he picked pecans from trees in his family's backyard, sold them door to door, and earned the money.

Dick Tarpley, editor of the Abilene *Reporter-News,* remembers the next step in Rawson's career. "This little fellow in a suit walked in carrying a briefcase. He said, 'I want to write a column.'" Rawson presented Tarpley with a stack of sample columns and letters of recommendation from two teachers and a video game repairman. Tarpley offered Rawson a spot in the paper.

Rawson's computer reviews have brought him as much as $1,200 a month. Doubleday has published his book, and television viewers in more than five hundred cities see him regularly on "The New Tech Times." Says Rawson, "It beats shelling pecans."

As Rawson did, it is wise for would-be writers to begin with smaller aspirations and move to bigger ones later. First, Rawson wrote a local column; eventually, he was able to appear on television and have a book published. Students who are certain they can write publishable articles should nearly always begin with campus newspapers and magazines, alumni magazines, and local publications. If the student writer talks to editors of these publications and then writes letters to the editors to make certain that they agree on what will be written, he or she can proceed with confidence.

Students who fail to write these letters *may* find that everything goes well. In many cases, however, students who only discuss their articles with editors may find that what they think are their finished articles are not what the editors had in mind.

The trouble with almost all conversations is that people rarely remember what was said. In some cases, writers will hear only what they want to hear. They may remember only "Your idea is a possibility," forgetting that the editor added: "Widen your interviews to include . . . ," or "But we've got a lot of articles to publish in the next few issues." In other cases, editors may not want to end a willing writer's ambitions and so will pause short of bad news.

Discussing their plans for articles with campus or local editors, then writing letters to the editors, and finally writing and selling articles, may take students days or weeks. Students should never think of the time they have spent as wasted, because these sometimes tedious chores will form a strong foundation for writing. After selling campus and local articles, students should begin to explore national magazines.

The most appealing magazines are probably those that pay at least $2,500 to professionals for full-length articles. Although most of the following magazines will pay a bit less than $2,500 to new writers, students can look forward to becoming established writers and earning full payments. Here are a few of the best-paying magazines for professional writers:

Esquire. 1790 Broadway, New York, New York 10019. Buys a wide range of subject matter, which should be for sophisticated and intelligent readers.

Family Circle. 110 Fifth Avenue, New York, New York 10011. Buys articles for women and wants to see query letters on unique or problem-solving aspects of family life.

Fortune. 1271 Avenue of the Americas, New York, New York 10020. Mostly staff written, but will buy a few articles about business and finance.

Ladies' Home Journal. 100 Park Avenue, New York, New York 10017. Buys articles submitted by literary agents.

Life. Time and Life Building, Rockefeller Center, New York, New York 10020. Although *Life* buys articles, only one or two are published in each issue.

McCall's. 230 Park Avenue, New York, New York 10169. Buys articles about women that focus on women's lives.

National Geographic. 17th and M Streets NW, Washington, DC 20036. Buys mostly first-person narratives, largely about places.

Playboy. 680 N. Lakeshore Drive, Chicago, Illinois 60611. Buys timely, topical pieces, most of them on contemporary men, sports, politics, sociology, business and finance, music, science and technology, and games.

Reader's Digest. Pleasantville, New York 10570. Buys articles of general interest for the largest possible audience.

Woman's Day. 1633 Broadway, New York, New York 10019. Buys articles on all subjects of interest to women—marriage, family life, child rearing, education, home-making, money management, careers, family health, work, and leisure activities.

After reading the above descriptions, most students can probably think of at least one article that will answer at least one magazine's needs. But students' articles will have to compete with hundreds of articles, many of them written by professional writers. Moreover, many professionals will have worked on their articles for a week, a month, or many months. Although a few students write as well or better than some professional writers, students have too little time for research. They have classes and ordinarily cannot take trips to write articles. The professionals can and do.

If students aim at these top magazines initially, they will almost certainly be answered by rejections. After succeeding with campus and local publications, student writers should take the next step: write for regional or national magazines that are not the highest-paying publications.

Consider what Jack Liebau, the student whose firsthand account was printed in Chapter 2, did while he was a college student. He wrote for *Barron's* (actually, *Barron's, National Business and Financial Weekly*—200 Liberty Street, New York, New York 10281). *Barron's* needs articles from various locales to complete its mission.

It's impossible to include in this book the more than four thousand markets listed in *Writer's Market* (1507 Dana Avenue, Cincinnati, Ohio 45207). If you are interested in becoming a free-lance writer or staff writer, you should have a copy of *Writer's Market* near at hand.

Writer's Market is the free-lancer's bible and is a vital source of markets for your work. Although it is updated regularly and includes thousands of listings, it does not include all publishers and magazines. If you find a potential market that is not listed in *Writer's Market,* you should write to the magazine and ask for its writer's guidelines. Some magazines are entirely staff written, and others do not accept outside submissions.

To guide beginning free-lancers, editors of *Writer's Market* compiled a set of the most frequently asked questions and their answers. Here are a few of them:

Is it better to send a query letter or a complete manuscript? The best submission is the one that the listing in *Writer's Market* specifies. This is the way the publisher, editor, or agent prefers to receive material; some will not even consider material submitted another way. Most magazine editors prefer a query for nonfiction and a full manuscript for short fiction.

Can I submit queries and manuscripts simultaneously? It depends. Some publishers and editors don't object to simultaneous submissions. Their listings indicate that with the statement "Simultaneous submissions OK." Simultaneous queries to magazines are not usually necessary, since they generally report back on queries sooner than book publishers and agents will. If you do send simultaneous queries to magazines, you need to decide what you'll do if more than one editor accepts the article. Will you go with the first one to call or the highest-paying and risk the editor's anger? Will you try to write two different articles from the same material? We do not recommend sending complete manuscripts to magazines. The exception to this may be literary magazines, which often have long reporting times.

How do publishers, editors, and agents handle unsolicited manuscripts? Unsolicited manuscripts are handled in a variety of ways. Some review unsolicited material just as they would solicited manuscripts; some give it a cursory review; others will not review it at all and will return the material only if a self-addressed, stamped envelope is enclosed. Although they would like to do so, most publishers, editors, and agents receive too many manuscripts to offer personal letters or constructive criticism. Most will send a form rejection, and some will simply return the material without comment.

What are some keys to finding the right magazine market for my articles? Before submitting, study magazine listings for those using the type of articles you write. Then look at several issues of the magazine to get a feel for its approach and style. You may have to send for sample copies of magazines not circulated in your area. This will help you determine whether or not your article and style of writing fit with the current editorial content. Magazine editors, like the rest of us, have pet peeves, and one of them is submission of material that is totally inappropriate. Before you send a query or manuscript, you should send for a copy of the magazine's writer's guidelines if the magazine supplies them. When you're considering a magazine, also look for payment rates, payment on acceptance, kill fee, rights purchased, payment of expenses, and additional payment for photos. Most writers simply look at total payment, but these other factors should influence your choice, too.

MARKETING YOUR MANUSCRIPTS

Although some writers choose a topic that interests them, write about it, and then search for an appropriate magazine for the article, this tactic reduces the chances of success. Beginners should try the following: decide which writing categories (listed in *Writer's Market*) interest you, then select several listings in *Writer's Market* that you consider appropriate for your kind of writing.

These beginners followed this advice and wrote proposals for articles based on their intended markets. Although it isn't necessary to limit your article ideas to only one magazine, this is a good way for the novice free-lancer to get started. Read these brief proposals and notice how each writer focused on marketing and the magazine's intended audience:

Intended market: *Seventeen*

This article will be a compilation of particularly bizarre or uncomfortable dating situations encountered by various college students. The stories will be collected through personal interviews of approximately one hundred students across several Northern California campuses.

I believe this will be an extremely fun-to-read group of stories, linked by the common bond of their characters, who are all college-age people. By submitting it to a magazine such as *Seventeen*, I will be able to reach the reading audience (composed mostly of young women, ages 16–20) with identifiable, sometimes-funny, sometimes-heartbreaking stories about real life in situations with which they are not only familiar but directly involved.

Intended market: *Glamour* or *Mademoiselle*

There are some people in this world who always seem to know exactly where they are. Blessed with some kind of internal compass forever oriented on North, they rarely lose their way and, if desperate, can rely on the position of the sun or, better yet, the stars. But at the other extreme is a select group with another innate talent: give us a set of directions to a place, written or spoken, and we can, without fail, confuse them, mess them up, get them totally backwards, and end up wandering around in circles in another town. You know who we are—the navigationally inept, the chronically lost, the eternally directionless . . .

This article would continue as a treatise to, or glorification of, those who are perpetually lost, not because of unfamiliarity with location or memory loss, but through some natural and inexplicable luck. It would contain personal anecdotes about getting lost in various countries and offer some tips on how to survive in a world that seems prejudiced against those who simply cannot find their way.

For example:

1. Never believe people who say "You can't miss it." You can.
2. When traveling with someone else, never admit to being lost until the number of times you've passed the same landmark becomes suspicious.

I would include comments by psychologists about how it feels to be one of the navigationally inept, and explain how much healthier such people are for maintaining such constant optimism—always hoping that after hours of wandering, the place for which they are searching will suddenly appear.

Intended market: *Rolling Stone*

I want to trace the history of drugs (including alcohol) in the entertainment world, starting with the initial beginnings of drug use (i.e., alcoholism in the early years of Hollywood), through the abusive drug practices in the sixties (focusing mainly on musicians and performers and the culture which they created), up to the outspoken disapproval of substance use exhibited by members of the industry today. I think I will emphasize the role of drugs in each of these stages of development, discussing such issues as whether drugs were always just a crutch or if certain drugs did, in fact, induce ultra-creative work on the artists' parts. Furthermore, I plan to discuss the public reaction to, and the public awareness of, the drugs in the entertainment world, and how those opinions affected the role of drugs in the society. Finally, in discussing our contemporary situation, I will try to find reasons for the turnaround in the entertainment industry's attitude toward drugs, as well as some ideas as to where the main concentration of drug use has been transferred (i.e., perhaps the business world).

CHECKLIST: MARKETING YOUR MANUSCRIPT

1. Choose a writing category in *Writer's Market.*

2. Select several listings that you consider good prospects for your writing.

3. Develop several ideas for articles.

4. Make a list of potential markets for each idea.

5. Continue developing ideas and approaching markets with them.

6. After sending a query letter to a magazine's editor, don't contact the editor again until you have received a response.

7. Prepare for rejection and the sometimes lengthy process of publishing.

8. If an editor gives reasons for not accepting your query or article, consider making revisions.

9. Do not take rejections personally. A rejection means only that your particular piece did not fit the needs of the publisher at that time.

Exercises

1. Write two queries based on one of your story ideas to two different magazines. Explain how you tailored your subject for each one.

2. Exchange your two queries with one of your classmates. Tell him or her which of the queries you would prefer if you were an editor and why.

3. Assume that you are a full-time free-lance writer who earns an average of $500 per article and has a total income of $12,000 per year from free-lancing. How many queries will you need to write each month to maintain your income if 30 percent are accepted? Calculate this figure for other acceptance rates.

SIX

LISTENING AND OBSERVING

A good listener is not only popular everywhere, but after a while he gets to know something.

WILSON MIZNER

The most important things a writer does include listening and observing, but he or she hardly ever thinks about listening—and few writers think of observing. There are lessons in this chapter that everyone should learn.

LEARNING ABOUT LISTENING

Although listening is the first step in learning how to gather information, beginning writers—like most people—find talking easier than listening. We introduce ourselves more easily than we remember the names of those to whom we're introduced, and most of us have asked a question only to break into the first sentence of someone's response with another question or a response of our own.

Many of us have had some training in effective speaking, but most people still haven't been taught to listen well. Listening requires at least as much effort as speaking does. Listening ability can be cultivated and gained by anyone who chooses to reshape poor listening habits, though.

To listen well, put aside the impulse to concentrate on speaking. The biggest obstacle to listening is failing to concentrate on someone else's ideas. To develop the desire to listen, develop the desire to learn. If you make a habit of learning as much as you can from everyone you talk with, you'll find that not only have you become well informed, you have also started to listen easily, free from the habitual impulse to present your own ideas.

Look at the person you are listening to as much as possible. As a writer, you will need to take notes while you listen, but you must also regularly meet the speaker's eyes. Your eyes will convey more strongly than anything else your interest in what the speaker is saying, and looking at the person you're listening to will also help you concentrate on his or her actions.

The look in your eye, your alert posture, your tone of voice, and your manner of speaking should all reflect a sincere desire on your part to hear what the speaker has to say. If you have developed the habit of listening to learn, you won't send out physical signals—like shifting in your chair or fidgeting with a pencil, pen, or paper clip—that indicate you're not interested in listening.

Allowing speakers to express complete thoughts also shows them you respect them and want to understand what they think. When you refrain from interrupting a speaker and focus instead on listening to what he or she has to say, you protect yourself from missing important information or ideas and also from inhibiting your source. Sometimes writers do have to interrupt to ask for clarification or, when an interview is being broadcast live, to keep a speaker on track. Unless you have a reason for interrupting that serves your audience's interests, however, let sources complete their sentences and thoughts.

Even when you have allowed a speaker to state his or her thoughts without interruption, you will often need to ask questions in order to make sure you've understood the source's meaning. Every question you ask should have a purpose: either to get specific information or to determine a speaker's ideas and feelings. Summarizing the main points a speaker has made can also give you and the speaker a chance to make sure you haven't overlooked valuable information or distorted what the source has said.

Your job as a writer is to understand as well as possible what a source has to say. In school or elsewhere in our competitive society, you may have developed the habit of starting to compose a response as early in someone else's comments as possible. You do need to keep in mind the purpose of your conversation with a source as you listen to what the source says and respond with questions that will help your audience understand what the source knows. You should not, however, focus on your words more than on your source's.

Most people are good at pretending to listen while they decide what to say next or even daydream. Many can nod at appropriate places, respond with "um-hmm," and look at a speaker without paying attention to what the speaker is saying. This habit is hard to break and is dangerous for writers. If a source asks you a question while you are faking attention, you risk alienating the person when you show you've been ignoring him or her. And while your mind was elsewhere, the source may have provided information your audience needs.

Be careful also not to tune out because you don't like a source's looks, manner, or affiliations. Sources you don't like are just as useful to your listeners, viewers, or readers as are sources you find appealing. Make an effort to respect and try to understand everyone you speak with.

When a source's ideas disagree with your own, remember that you are listening as a large audience's representative and have a responsibility to listen dispassionately. Willingness to listen to someone whose views contradict yours shows self-confidence on your part. Listeners who can't face the possibility that their beliefs may be flawed also signal fear that their positions are vulnerable. Those who are confident that their views are reasonable and who would rather be flexible than misguided can afford to listen to opposing ideas.

As an example of many listeners who don't like what a speaker says, consider what Henry Seale, a student at the University of Florida, recalled about a visiting writer. One summer during the height of her fame, novelist Marjorie Kinnan Rawlings taught a course in writing at the University of Florida at Gainesville. Students flocked to enroll because the summer crowd favored what looked to be courses for easy credit.

The first day, the classroom overflowed. Rawlings cast a disgruntled glance over the crowd. Calling for order, she announced casually, "In all fairness, those of you not willing to take this course without credit should be allowed to drop out today, while there is still time to substitute another. But once you leave, you cannot return."

A huge gasp arose, and students scrambled for the exits. When quiet returned, Rawlings calmly addressed the few who were left: "You just had your first lesson. Good writers must learn to look for the true meaning of words. You certainly will receive credit for this course. Who said you wouldn't? Not I."

Even if you use a tape recorder, you should write down the most important of a speaker's comments. Writing down key points helps you remember what a speaker has already said as you ask questions and work toward an understanding of his or her ideas. Note taking also helps you recognize and focus on central facts and ideas. Listening and keeping track of speakers' main points are central to your job. Words or phrases like "as a result," "nevertheless," and "in other words" usually signal that an important piece of information or a central idea is coming; speakers also often present important ideas by summarizing what they've said already.

Use silences to review the main points a speaker has made. Fight the temptation to jump in and fill up every period of silence; when a speaker suddenly lapses into silence, he or she is thinking, and the next comment he or she makes is likely to be significant.

When a source is silent, make sure you remain attentive and receptive. Do not, however, be afraid to let the silence continue until the speaker makes his or her next remark. Only when a speaker is silent because he or she has completed a response to a question should you be the one to interrupt the quiet.

Writers cannot let distractions like an incessantly ringing telephone or a word they don't recognize keep them from continuing to listen. Unless you overcome distractions, you'll lose your focus on what speakers are saying and end up concentrating on some peripheral matter instead. Giving in to distractions can lead you to miss vital information, misinterpret what a speaker says, or fail to ask questions that clarify a speaker's meaning. By realizing that distractions are your responsibility rather than the fault of someone else or of the environment, you can learn to ignore them. When you ignore distractions and keep listening, speakers will realize that they and what they have to say are your primary concern.

The most common distractions are environmental: ringing telephones or telephones answered within earshot; conversations nearby; other people cutting into your conversation; the sounds of car horns, people moving furniture, or barking dogs. Before you begin to listen to a source, close doors and windows to block out sound and interruptions if you can, and, when you can, move to an area where there are no telephones. You can also avoid telephone interruptions by meeting with a source during a time of day when phone calls are unlikely. When a speaker is interrupted by a phone call, use the time the source spends on the phone to review your notes and thoughts or, if you're in the speaker's office or house, to observe and take notes on the source's surroundings.

You might also be distracted by a speaker's use of vocabulary you don't know, by a regional or foreign accent, or by phrasing that has more than one possible meaning. Concentration is the key to dealing with unfamiliar words and with accents. Unless you can figure out an unfamiliar word's meaning from context, though, go ahead and ask what it means; you may need to understand its meaning to be able to understand what the speaker is trying to say. Careful questioning can eliminate the difficulty caused by phrasing that has more than one possible meaning. After the death of J. Edgar Hoover, former director of the FBI, the New York *Post* published a brief story telling how Hoover had become irritated while reading a long report because the writer had not observed the bureau's margin requirements. At the top of the first page, Hoover wrote, "Watch the borders." Because no one asked Hoover exactly what he meant, orders went out to FBI field offices to "watch the borders," and for weeks agents guarded our borders with Canada and Mexico. Your questions about what a speaker has said should clear up this sort of ambiguity.

The key to improving your listening ability is objectivity. No one has such good listening ability that he or she doesn't need to eliminate some bad habits. Be honest with yourself about which listening skills you're good at and which you need to enhance.

To become an effective listener, strive to bring your habitual listening up to the quality of your capacity to listen. Deal with your weaknesses in listening habits as if they must be corrected immediately to prevent serious problems, and practice continually the habits you want to be able to rely on as a writer. Daily practice—not just for a week or two but over months and years—will help you replace sloppy habits with the rare talents of a good listener.

To test your objectivity about your own feelings, here is an observation by a noted writer, Phyllis McGinley, that may apply to your own emotions and those of many in your class. She once wrote these words:

The flaw in the "child-parent relationship" (to quote the current jargon) is too often the amount of fussing about it that parents do. Children from 10 to 20 don't *want* to be understood. Their whole ambition is to feel strange, alien, misinterpreted, so that they can live austerely in some stone tower of adolescence, their privacies unviolated. They resent nothing more than elders' attempts to make friends. To them that's not comradeship, but prying. Authority they will accept; it's something to complain about and to rest against. Their confidences come only when they're not applied for.

Part of listening is watching. Note a speaker's tone of voice. Is his or her voice overbearingly loud, so soft it's difficult to hear, rushed, or breathy? Does the speaker's voice reflect his or her vitality? Is it flat and colorless? Do you hear any tension in the speaker's voice?

Expressions that a speaker uses over and over can also help you understand his or her attitude. When a speaker says, "I don't mean to change the subject," for example, he or she probably intends to do just that. A speaker's ending sentence after sentence with "You know what I mean?" or "Okay?" may mean that he or she doubts your ability to listen and understand.

Albert Mehrabian of the University of California at Los Angeles has reported research indicating that only 7 percent of what a speaker communicates when he or she talks is conveyed through words. Mehrabian concluded that 38 percent is conveyed by a speaker's manner of speaking and 55 percent is conveyed by facial expression, eye behavior, posture, and gesture. In another study, Ray Birdwhistell of the University of Pennsylvania found that in an average two-person conversation, words carry less than 35 percent of the interaction's social meaning; more than 65 percent is nonverbal. The differences in the two studies' percentages arose because the researchers investigated different speech situations. The conclusion of both studies is the same: most communication is nonverbal.

If research findings have failed to convince you, consider the true story of von Osten's horse, bought in Berlin in 1900. Von Osten's horse, Hans, became famous for counting; adding, subtracting, multiplying, and dividing; tellng time; using a calendar; and performing other feats—all by tapping his hoof. At public demonstrations, Hans counted the number of people in the crowd and the number wearing glasses.

A committee of psychology and physiology professors, cavalry officers, veterinarians, a circus director, and the director of the Berlin Zoological Garden examined Hans when von Osten was not present. The horse still counted correctly, and the committee concluded that Hans actually was able to perform as advertised.

When a second committee was formed, however, one of the examiners told von Osten to whisper a number in one of Hans's ears and another examiner to whisper a second number in Hans's other ear. Hans could not add the numbers. Similar tests revealed why Hans had failed: he couldn't see anyone who knew the answer. When Hans had been asked questions, anyone who knew the answer had unwittingly become expectant and assumed a tense posture. When Hans's hoof taps had reached the correct total, onlookers would relax and, unwittingly, make a slight head movement. Hans had learned to respond to this nonverbal signal by stopping the hoof tapping.

Hans's ability to observe hints at how much people say nonverbally.

LEARNING ABOUT OBSERVING

William Faulkner, when asked to describe his ideal woman, said:

"To see the world in
a grain of sand,
And a heaven in a
wild flower,
Hold infinity in the
palm of your hand
And eternity in an
hour."

WILLIAM BLAKE

> Well, I couldn't describe her by color of hair or color of eyes, because once she is described, then somehow she vanishes. The ideal woman which is in every man's mind is evoked by a word or phrase or the shape of her wrist, her hand. The most beautiful description of a woman is by understatement. Remember, all Tolstoy ever said to describe Anna Karenina was that she was beautiful and could see in the dark like a cat. Every man has a different idea of what's beautiful, and it's best to take the gesture, the shadow of the branch, and let the mind create the tree.

The kind of description praised by Faulkner is very difficult to achieve because it requires careful, diligent observation—a power that usually does not come naturally but is fundamental to good writing. Observation is vital to a truthful report. Like interviewing, direct observation yields liveliness, and the journalist who can't observe can't succeed. Early in his career, Bruce Bliven had the good fortune to work under Fremont Older, a demanding San Francisco editor with "a personality so vigorous that you could feel his presence through a brick wall." Deciding that one dull reporter could write compellingly only by immersing himself in his subject, Older assigned him to write about the Salvation Army and gave him all the time he needed to research and write captivatingly. But after three weeks with the "Army," the reporter turned in his usual flavorless stuff. "Didn't you observe *anything?*" Older bellowed. "At night, for instance, *where did they hang the bass drum?*" The reporter did not know. He was fired. Older repeated the story for decades to push young reporters into becoming sensitive observers. The lesson stuck so well with Bliven that, fifty years after his own experiences with Older, Bliven said, "After I meet someone, I ask myself questions about his personal appearance, to make sure I really *saw* him."

During John Steinbeck's college days, he thought that Professor Edith Mirrielees was the greatest writing teacher of all. She told him, "It will take a long time and it will never get easier," a truism Steinbeck acknowledged long after his student days at Stanford. By then, Steinbeck had become a wonderful observer.

Although Steinbeck's most detailed observations were of animals, he also observed people with a careful eye. On his way to North Africa to cover World War II as a correspondent for the *Herald Tribune* and the Hearst syndicate, Steinbeck wrote this account of the military ship he traveled on:

> The major impression on a troop ship is of feet. A man can get his head out of the way and his arms, but, lying or sitting, his feet are a problem. They sprawl in the aisles, they stick up at all angles. They are not protected because they are the part of a man least likely to be hurt. To move around you must step among feet, must trip over feet.
> There are big mishappen feet; neat, small feet; shoes that are pol-

ished; curled-toed shoes; shoestrings knotted and snarled, and careful little bows. You can read character by the feet and shoes. There are perpetually tired feet, and nervous, quick feet. . . .

At night on a blacked-out ship, you must creep and feel your way among acres of feet.

Dogs and shoes may seem too trivial to be the focus of good writing. By looking at a sequence of books Steinbeck wrote and some of the everyday observations they were based on, however, you can see how details that most people never notice can grow into substantial writing. As a boy, Steinbeck spent hours in the fields surrounding the agricultural community of Salinas, California; at the tide pools below his family's summer home near Monterey; and in the hills near his uncle's ranch outside of King City.

Steinbeck left the Salinas Valley to attend Stanford University, off and on, for six years. Interwoven with his stints at the university were periods of work as a salesman, ranch hand, chemist, and member of a dredging crew, and during these jobs Steinbeck wrote down ideas on various scraps of paper, stuffed the notes into his pockets, and eventually emptied the notes into a dresser drawer. Biographer Jackson Benson has written that Steinbeck "was liable to stop and scrawl a note or two at almost any time, even while making love to a girl in the back seat of a car."

When Steinbeck had dropped out of college permanently and become a published writer, he continued to explore and observe his surroundings. Hired by the *San Francisco News* in 1936 to write a series of articles on migrant farm workers, Steinbeck talked with his editors at the newspaper and with federal officials and then set off on a tour of California's huge San Joaquin Valley.

As he visited squatters' camps before moving on to see the camps provided by the federal government, Steinbeck noticed a family that, he would later write, had built its house by driving branches from a willow tree into the ground and then matting weeds, flattened tin cans, and paper together between the branches. A man, a woman, and three children slept on the ground under a soiled piece of carpet, Steinbeck noticed, and the youngest child, a three-year-old, sat in front of the hut in the sun, a gunnysack tied around his malnutrition-swelled belly for clothing, fruit flies crawling up his nose and into the corners of his eyes. The child, who had had no milk for two years, Steinbeck would write, was so slow in his reactions that he seldom and only weakly waved the flies away from his face.

From this and other observations of migrant families, Steinbeck wrote this composite description for the *News:*

He will die in a very short time. The older children may survive. Four nights ago the mother had a baby in the tent, on the dirty carpet. It was born dead, which was just as well because she could not have fed it at the breast; her own diet will not produce milk.

After it was born and she had seen that it was dead, the mother rolled over and lay still for two days. She is up today, tottering around.

The last baby, born less than a year ago, lived a week. This woman's eyes have the glazed, faraway look of a sleepwalker's eyes.

She does not wash clothes anymore. The drive that makes for cleanliness has been drained out of her and she hasn't the energy. The husband was a sharecropper once, but he couldn't make it go. Now he has lost even the desire to talk.

He will not look directly at you, for that requires will, and will needs strength. He is a bad field worker for the same reason. It takes him a long time to make up his mind, so he is always late in moving and late in arriving in the fields. His top wage, when he can find work now, which isn't often, is a dollar a day.

The children do not even go to the willow clump anymore. They squat where they are and kick a little dirt. The father is vaguely aware that there is a culture of hookworm in the mud along the river bank. He knows the children will get it on their bare feet.

But he hasn't the will or the energy to resist. Too many things have happened to him.

Steinbeck's trip through the valley eventually led also to his Pulitzer Prize–winning novel *The Grapes of Wrath* and to the script for a film, *The Forgotten Village.* His encounters with the public health nurses who struggled against the habits and superstitions of migrant farm workers led Steinbeck to suggest to the movie's producer that the film focus not on a poor Mexican family caught up in the turmoil of revolution, as the producer had suggested, but on the same kind of family caught in the conflict between modern medicine and their traditional culture.

By applying the skills explained in the rest of this chapter and habitually writing down what you've observed, you too can gather the raw material for vivid, convincing writing. The first thing you must do is learn to pay attention to the surroundings you live in. Attentiveness to your surroundings will show you the potential for writing that lies all around you.

The stimulus that good writing grows out of is usually the commonplace: a chance remark, an incident the writer observes, an experience someone else tells the writer about, or even a picture or article the writer notices in a magazine or newspaper. Writers and other artists maintain a sense of wonder at everyday details and events that most other people take for granted.

By talking with others, reading widely, and using your memory and your senses, you can mine the rich veins of experience that run through your life every day. Constant curiosity is the most valuable habit a writer can have, and there is no good writer who isn't attentive to and curious about his or her environment.

As much as they can, writers show instead of telling. Details are what gives writing authority. Only when readers encounter details infused with the strength of truth can they believe what a writer has to say. By showing the details of an experience, the writer makes the reader a participant in that experience. Once the reader has seen and experienced what the writer has, the reader is prepared to accept the writer's conclusions.

Even though writers seldom write description for its own sake, then, descriptive detail is the lifeblood of almost every kind of writing. Sensory detail—detail a reader can picture, hear, smell, taste, or touch in his or her imagination—is the kind of detail most successful at grasping readers at a gut level. Sensory detail pulls readers into a piece of writing, making them feel as if they are right where the writer was.

Read for detail these two paragraphs by Nancy Roberts:

Clad in jogging pants and a teal T-shirt that intensifies the blue of her eyes, Barbara Hultmann relaxes in a bentwood rocker in her home in the Minneapolis suburb of Edina. Her living room bears the stamp of someone who loves beauty, from the basket collection on the oyster walls and the antique oak washstand to the lavender chive blossoms and plum-colored irises in a graceful glass vase. Hultmann's sense of humor is evident in the sampler on her front door announcing that "A clean house is a sign of a misspent life" and in the papier-mâché pink flamingo that flanks the greenery by the picture window. From her adjacent studio Hultmann can gaze at her garden. Ruffled peach irises, lacy phlox, and bluebells share space with pink lupine, lilies of the valley, and yellow evening primrose. A fashionable loft studio downtown has never tempted her. "I love being able to paint right at home," she says, "where I can stop to pet the cat, ride my bike, or take a walk among my flowers."

Hultmann's flowers have found their way into numerous watercolors, acrylics, and pencil drawings. One series of watercolors portrays the tangerine-colored day lilies she delights in. In another series, she paints pink cyclamen against several backgrounds to emphasize the petals' delicate interlacing. The work Thistle depicts the solitary roadside weed, grand in its simplicity.

Here is a writer named Molly Brown who always carefully observes her subjects during interviews. Her profile follows her words.*

I never put a pen to paper until I have the whole article written in my mind. To get my creative juices flowing, I read over my interview notes four or five times. While I read, I try to find a thread that runs through the interview—an angle that can give my article some semblance of order. For example, I once interviewed the owner of a small winery in Memphis, and when I began to shape my article about him, what stood out most in my mind was his casual, laid-back attitude. During the interview he wore a T-shirt and jeans and recounted his life in a very frank, tell-all manner. My image of the Memphis winery owner took on a special significance since it was so different from the stuffy stereotypes that are normally associated with wine connoisseurs. As I wrote the article, I was careful to sprinkle in observations that would give the reader a clear picture of the down-to-earth winery owner. Once I had

---

*Reprinted by permission of Molly Brown.

developed this angle, my story started to come together and take its shape, and it finally became something more than just a string of disconnected observations.

READING BODY LANGUAGE

When listening to subjects during interviews, concentrate on observing them closely. Gestures and facial expressions make up an important part of what a speaker says. A single gesture may not mean anything; a speaker who rubs the back of her neck, for example, may simply be massaging a sore muscle pulled during a rough football game the day before. If she rubs the back of her neck repeatedly, however, combs her fingers through her hair, and uses fistlike or karate-chop motions repeatedly, she is probably feeling frustrated. Note speakers' facial expressions and clusters of two or three of the following gestures:

> **"Beware lest you lose the substance by grasping at the shadow."**
>
> AESOP

MOLLY BROWN

There is a gentle drawl underlying Molly Brown's pose, a lyric style that conveys a strong sense of southern life, its culture, and its people. Having grown up in Memphis, Tennessee, she is not an outsider peering through the window of the South, describing what is superficially visible. Rather, she seems to implicitly understand the region and, in particular, the unique southern character.

Her writing career began early, while she was attending high school at St. Mary's Episcopal School. In her sophomore and junior years, Brown was a first-place winner of the Memphis Law Day Essay Contest. During her senior year, she turned to journalism, working for the school newspaper as editor and head photographer. Under her direction, the paper received an "excellent" rating by the Tennessee High School Press Association; Brown herself won second place in the editorial category and first places in the news and sports feature categories.

College did not disrupt her flow of writing. Instead, she became involved in more than one publication at Stanford University. Beginning as a photographer and reporter for *The Stanford Daily*, Brown became its assistant night editor within the same year. Then she worked as a photographer and darkroom technician for *The Stanford Quad,* the school yearbook, and was editor of *The Stanford Photography Club Newsletter.*

Somehow Brown manages to apply the same energies toward her academic career. A coterminal student pursuing a bachelor's degree in English with a creative writing emphasis and a master's degree in English and American literature, she has a schedule that would intimidate the most ambitious scholar. Yet her writing reflects nothing of the flurry of classes, the hurried deadlines, and the pressure of examinations.

It is in this way that her prose is distinctively southern. Brown begins her articles leisurely, matching the unhurried pace of the South. One can almost imagine her sitting on her front porch in Memphis, inviting the reader to pull up a rocking chair and listen. Her subjects are described as "down-home" people, ordinary folk with humble origins. When she writes about an African-American street performer, his tap shoes flutter on the page; one sees his bony hands and hears the clink of change placed into his pocket. A wine maker, starting his first family enterprise, proudly displays pictures of his wife and children helping in the production process. It is through her patient beginnings, combined with a keen eye for detail, that Brown creates a portrait of the true Dixieland; she misses nothing. Most important, she manages to capture the vision held by her subjects, their own perceptions of life and personal philosophies. These she weaves together, reflecting not only a knowledge of history but also an understanding of the people who make up the magical region called the South.

Defensiveness   Crossing arms over the chest; crossing legs; placing hands on the hips; using fistlike gestures or karate chops; pointing an index finger at others while talking.

Suspicion   Crossing the arms; glancing sideways; drawing away; touching or rubbing the nose; rubbing the eyes; buttoning a jacket.

Cooperativeness   Sitting on the edge of a chair; using hand-to-face gestures; tilting the head; opening the hands.

Frustration   Rubbing the back of the neck; combing fingers through the hair; using fistlike gestures or karate chops; pointing an index finger while speaking; wringing the hands; breathing or speaking in short breaths.

Insecurity   Rubbing one thumb over another; keeping hands in pockets; biting fingernails; chewing a pen or pencil; pinching own flesh.

Nervousness   Covering mouth with hand while speaking; tugging at pants while seated; tugging at ear; fidgeting in chair or with some object; picking or pinching own flesh; not looking at listener; wringing hands; whistling; smoking; clearing throat.

Confidence   Steepling hands; placing hands behind back; sitting up straight, hands in pockets with thumbs out.

Evaluation   Stroking chin; tilting head; using hand-to-face gestures; putting hand to bridge of nose; peering over glasses; taking glasses off or cleaning them; using pipe-smoking gestures; biting on earpiece of glasses.

Rather than assuming that a subject's gestures reveal a particular state of mind, show the gestures themselves. When you show how a subject behaves, your audience can understand what a subject's gestures reveal as well as you do. Assuming that a subject feels a certain way is risky: you may be wrong. Reporting a subject's facial expressions and gestures, on the other hand, can only contribute to understanding. Nora Ephron used description of nonverbal communication to describe the first woman to umpire a professional baseball game:

> . . . But if you ask Bernice Gera a question about that suit—where she bought it, for example, or whether she ever takes it out and looks it over—her eyes widen and then blink, hard, and she explains, very slowly so that you will not fail to understand, that she prefers not to think about the suit, or the shoes, or the shirt and tie she wore with it one summer night last year, when she umpired what was her first and last professional baseball game. . . .

Ephron allows her readers to understand for themselves how Gera feels. As you can see from Ephron's writing, observation enlivens reports based on interviews. In addition to observing and reporting tone of voice, facial expressions, and gestures, you can also observe the following:

Body characteristics   Physique or body shape; features; skin color and tone; fragrance or odor; clothes; make-up; hairstyle.

Proxemics How a subject uses and perceives personal and social space—how he or she acts at a family gathering; in a small group of friends, colleagues, customers, or constituents; in a crowd; on stage.

Personal surroundings The environment a subject creates in his or her home or office—furniture; objects on walls and on tables or desks; lighting; temperature; smells; colors; noises and music.

NOTICING SENSORY DETAIL

Use the technique of paying attention to each of your senses as you observe, and let your readers see, hear, feel, taste, and smell what you have. Including too much sensory detail, or showing experiences that aren't central to what your writing is trying to say, can bog readers down and distract them from your point. Use sensory detail often, but use it primarily to add flavor to your main points.

In writing about a person, for example, first use your ability to see. Does the person arrange and rearrange paper clips in piles on a desktop? Brush hair back from his or her forehead whenever you bring up an upsetting topic? Also notice how the person speaks. Softly? Crisply? Or is the person's voice harshened by anxiety? Warmed by a kindness that also shows in the person's eyes? If you remember to notice and write down sensory details like habitual gestures and the sound of a subject's voice, your writing will show in the flesh the person you've chosen to introduce rather than just presenting him or her as a name followed by a string of statistics.

Along with sight and sound, be sure to use the less obvious senses: touch, smell, and taste. Because we rely on these senses almost subconsciously and rarely use them in verbal description, for a writer these senses are the most powerful of all. Think about what smells you remember vividly. The smell of a neighborhood in your city? Of the home of a grandmother or a childhood neighbor? What did you touch when you were in those places, and how did it feel? What did you reach out to explore with your fingertips, find yourself brushing against, or even get pushed into? How was your sense of taste involved when you were in those places? The tastes of foods will stand out first. And then there are other tastes, like those of exhaust, sweat, or oven cleaner in a stuffy kitchen.

Your five senses are almost always operating. Your task as a writer is to pay attention to those senses as you observe, write down what they have perceived, and then use the most striking of your perceptions to authenticate and highlight the experiences you write about.

The primary job writers have is to examine their surroundings to find and understand their subjects. Whether they write poems or sales reports, writers must search their environments for subjects and for details about those subjects.

Three habits acquired in the course of growing up can be particularly damaging to your ability to observe fully: ignoring what you are accusto, failing to concentrate on the significant details in the complex fabric of experience, and perceiving things as you expect them to be.

Ignoring what you are accustomed to   A series of studies showed that students usually can't describe the entrance hall of their college or university. Even though they've seen the entrance countless times, they've never really looked at it. This research illustrated the tendency all of us have to overlook what we see most often. To write well, you must continually work at perceiving the most repetitive and commonplace elements of your environment.

Failing to focus on the significant details in the complex fabric of experience   The saying "A picture is worth a thousand words" has special meaning for the writer. It would take many, many words to describe every single detail in a particular picture—and most of those words would bore and irritate readers. The writer has the difficult task of sifting through all the sensations bombarding him or her every moment and concentrating on the most significant ones. Here's how the essayist Carol Bly chose among all the sensations involved in a day spent plowing a field in an old, open tractor:

> Hour after hour I sat up there on the old Alice, as she was called (an Allis-Chalmers WC that looked rusted from the Flood). You have to sit twisted part way around, checking that the plowshares are scouring clean, turning over and dropping the dead crop and soil, not clogging . . . how unlike this all is to Keats's picture of autumn, a "season of mists and mellow fruitfulness."
>
> . . . But there is a more hidden psychology in the issue of enclosed combines versus the open tractors. It is this: one gets too many impressions on the open tractor. A thousand impressions enter as you work up and down the row: nature's stubbornness, politics, exhaustion, but mainly the feeling that all this repetition—last year's cornpicking—is taking up your lifetime. The more repetition reveals your eventual death.

Bly sifted out many more details than she included: the color of the tractor, how many years old it was, what the weather was like, and hundreds more. By focusing on the details that would help her achieve her purpose—simply the rust on the tractor, her having to twist around to look behind her as she worked, a line from Keats, and the reflections allowed by the repetitiveness of plowing—she shares her unique experience and understanding with her readers.

Perceiving things as you expect them to be   Psychologists have shown again and again that we perceive not what actually happens but what we expect will happen. In a 1983 experiment, for example, participants watched a videotape of a young girl taking an academic test. Before they were shown the tape, some of the participants were told that the girl's family was in a low socioeconomic group, and others were told that her family was in a high socioeconomic group. After the participants had seen the videotape, those who had been told that the child was in a high socioeconomic group rated her academic ability as being above average ability for her grade level and cited behaviors they had observed in the videotape to support their opinion. The participants who had been told that the child was in a low socioeconomic group rated the child's ability as being below the average for her grade level and also cited behaviors shown in the videotape to support their opinion. Both groups saw the same videotape, but each noticed the behaviors in the tape that corresponded to what it expected to see.

As you start working again to regain the desire and ability to observe that you had as a child—the capacity to see the routine, the significant, and the unexpected—consider this advice to beginning painters from artist Ben Shahn:

> Attend a university if you possibly can. There is no content of knowledge that is not pertinent to the work you will want to do. But before you attend a university work at something for a while. Do anything. Get a job in a potato field, or work as a grease-monkey in an auto repair shop. But if you do work in a field do not fail to observe the look and the feel of earth and of all things that you handle—yes even potatoes. Or, in the auto shop, the smell of oil and grease and burning rubber. . . .
> Listen well to all conversations and be instructed by them and take all seriousness seriously. Never look down upon anything or anyone as not worthy of notice. In college or out of college, read. Read Sophocles and Euripides and Dante and Proust. . . .

After reading Shahn's suggestions, you may feel as if you're just beginning the work of learning to observe. You will never master the task, but you must continue making progress—seeing, listening to, asking and reading about, and understanding your environment—more perceptively than you did yesterday or the day before.

If there were an easier method for writing well, it would be suggested here. There isn't one. The difficult task of perception, however, does give the writer an advantage most adults forfeit: life lived fully, rich in both wonder and understanding.

WEIGHING THE EVIDENCE

No matter how penetrating your eye is or how fresh your viewpoint, you still represent a single point of view, restricted to one physical place in the scene and surrounded by impressions particular to that position. Imagine two reporters at an antinuclear rally. One reporter stands near the platform, within feet of the various speakers, close enough to read their expressions and see the intensity they bring to their words; the surrounding supporters listen avidly, applaud, and break into the chant "No Nukes, No Nukes" at staggered intervals. Organizers bustle around with their clipboards, brushing past the reporter, who is pressed into the packed crowd.

The second reporter observes the rally at a distance from the stage—near enough to hear every word of the speeches, amplified from the microphone, but outside the knot of people chanting slogans against nuclear power and nuclear weapons. The crowd here is scattered and indifferent, most of them idle bystanders attracted by the noise and signs. Next to the reporter, a handful of utility workers on their lunch break shuffle their feet and mutter comments: "Bunch of dummies," "Communists," "What about the Russians . . . my job . . . the Arabs?"

Obviously, the two reporters' accounts of the rally are likely to differ in many important respects. Writers who let the constricted immediacy of an event serve as a reflection of the whole do a disservice to the truth. This danger of letting your subjective experience dominate what you report extends even to limited encounters, such as a conversation with one or two people in a quiet room. Some of the first unconscious assumptions people make ride on other people's looks. In an article on the feminist struggle with first impressions, Letty Cottin Pogrebin wrote:

> "The more attractive a woman is, the more feminine she seems, and the more feminine she seems, the less suited she is believed to be for decision-making or leadership," explains psychologist Madeline Heilman of New York University. The same "feminizing" phenomenon operates in politics, says Ann Bowman, a political scientist at the University of South Carolina. When all a voter knows about a candidate is how she or he looks, the attractive man wins votes, but the attractive woman loses. In women, attractiveness is equated with sex appeal, while in men, good looks are equated with kindness (believe it or not).

Not only must writers guard against being swayed by the insistent voices around them, they must also keep a wary eye on subtle inner voices as well.

THROUGH A GLASS DARKLY

Careful observation and accurate reporting of what we observe are daunting tasks. Beginning writers can best train themselves to see sharply by recognizing some common pitfalls.

The Unconscious Editor

Gordon Allport and Leo Postman explored the basic psychology of rumor by repeating a simple but imaginative test of observation. A series of subjects, one by one, entered a room where an audience sat viewing a slide projection of a mildly dramatic scene; the subjects stood in a position where they could not see the slide. The first subject heard a description of the scene—about twenty details. This subject then attempted to describe the scene as accurately as possible to the second subject, the second to the third, and so on.

The presence of an audience, the minimal lapse of time between hearing and reporting, and the absence of conflicting motives should have ensured a high degree of accuracy. The resemblance between the projected scene and the verbal reports, however, deteriorated rapidly in three ways: (1) the descriptions became shorter, easier to grasp and tell; (2) certain de-

"Millions saw the apple fall, but Newton was the one who asked why."

BERNARD BARUCH

tails gained unusual prominence as others fell away; and (3) challenging information was reinterpreted to mesh with the subject's personal view of reality.

The Process of Distortion

All writers attempting to be observers should remind themselves that human perception is fallible and that habits, interests, and sentiments are deeply embedded and likely to affect the way one takes on new information. We simplify and select—or distort—what we observe. Remembering this tendency should cause one to go slowly to guard against the effects of distortion.

Gut Reaction

Writer Mary Kay Blakely, as she began collecting clips on the gang rape that took place in New Bedford, Massachusetts, in March 1983, thought she could handle her shock. But the hard reality of the fact that other men in the bar not only failed to report the crime but actually cheered it on jerked her out of her detachment. She drew on her intense emotional reaction to write an enormously effective article on that rape, an article she directed, as the following shows, at a particular group of readers—men:

> Since I can think of nothing more to ask of women—except that we keep doing what we're doing—I am asking you to hand this section of the magazine to the man you love, perhaps the man sitting in the easy chair in the living room, reading the newspaper. If he is a man who shares your vision of equality, if he shares your horror over the tragedy in New Bedford, I need to talk to him.
>
> I will not try to lean over my typewriter and grab him by the lapels and pull him into my panic. But the probability that another generation of children will be sacrificed to the brutal violence of rape makes me wild with pain. I believe with every inch of my being that rape is preventable . . . but it can't be stopped without the help and commitment of good men.

Emotional, yes. But Blakely succeeded in firmly guiding her audience through a reasoned personal assessment not only of that rape but also of the issue of male violence in general.

When an event makes a writer react emotionally, his or her impressions are especially vulnerable to distortion. You can often resolve this problem by recording your impressions immediately after the event to capture its details and then later, at a more tranquil time, assessing your first account to find and correct distortion.

Tight Focus

You as observer must decide beforehand which forms, events, or details are worth your attention. Your task as an observer attending a political convention, for example, would be hopeless if you did not have in mind or on paper what you expected to focus on. You must train yourself to concentrate on

"A straight path never leads anywhere but to the objective."

ANDRÉ GIDE

what is significant for you. The ability, or the will, to concentrate varies, which is the reason that some football coaches are better than others at scouting upcoming opponents and picking out small, but crucial, details of interior line play while nearly everyone else in the stadium is watching the ball. But everyone with vision can learn to focus it.

Concentrating on the important visual details is a difficult job. However, if you manage to recognize the data that fit your focus, whole worlds will open up—even in a simple bowl of water, which Annie Dillard described in an article in *Harper's* magazine:

> Often I slop some creek water in a jar, and when I get home I dump it in a white china bowl. After the silt settles I return and see tracings of minute snails on the bottom, a planarian or two winding round the rim of water, roundworms shimmying frantically, and finally, when my eyes have adjusted to these dimensions, amoebae. At first the amoebae look like *muscae volitantes,* those curled moving spots you see in your eyes when you stare at a distant wall. Then I see the amoebae as drops of water congealed, bluish, translucent, like chips of sky in the bowl.

The Blinkered Point of View

The attitude you bring to your subject can color your interpretation of events. The more willing you are to suspend subjective opinion (which first requires a conscious awareness of exactly where your prejudices lie), the better able you are to observe with accuracy. Essayist Ellen Willis considers Tom Wolfe's book *The Electric Kool-Aid Acid Test* to be the best of his early work because he succeeded in maintaining a blend of identification and objectivity. She wrote:

> What makes the book so powerful—and so brave—is the way Wolfe allowed the Pranksters' vision to challenge and stretch his own. Ken Kesey and his friends created a wondrous new style, rooted in American history, myth, technology, and popular culture, but their aim was not only aesthetic—it was messianic. If Wolfe's pop sympathies were engaged by the style, his antiutopianism must have been equally offended by the aim. Yet the two could not be separated, for they were complementary aspects of a central unifying impulse—to live out and spread the psychedelic experience. If Wolfe was really to do his job—report accurately on what the Pranksters' trip was about—he could not take them seriously on one level, dismiss them as silly hippies on another. Like everyone else he had in some sense to choose: was he on the bus or off?

We can generalize this problem of constricted viewpoint to less personal circumstances: writers can cover only so much physical territory in pursuit of a story.

Distortions of Perspective

The most obvious method of avoiding this pitfall is to recognize that any single perspective is necessarily limited and must be supplemented with others. Careful researchers are usually quick to recognize that they must consider other perspectives when they are weighing another observer's report, but they may not be so quick to supplement their own observations. Nearly all observers are too ready to trust the evidence they have seen. Wilbur Schramm, a thorough investigator, says that whenever possible he arranges to have another researcher accompany him for observing and interviewing. He has learned that checking one impression against another often yields surprising and useful results.

The Undercover Observer

Undetected observation has obvious advantages. Some professionals argue that concealment is justified only if the people or gathering being observed is open to public inspection anyway. Others argue that unobtrusive observation is acceptable in most cases, as long as the subjects in the subsequent article remain anonymous.

If your investigations require that you actually participate in the events you are reporting, however, you risk distorting the behavior of the group you join, if only by increasing its numbers; you also risk losing your own detachment. This problem especially affects proponents of the New Journalism: the delicate balance between experienced reality and reportage.

One of the more widely known insider accounts is editor-writer Gloria Steinem's 1963 article "I Was a Playboy Bunny," in which she documented not only the economic exploitation of the women working as Bunnies but the sheer physical pain of the job. She wrote:

> Serving lunch for four hours wasn't quite enough to open up all my old foot wounds, but the piled-up plates of roast beef . . . make a tray even heavier than a full load of drinks. The customers are all men: the heavy sprinkling of dates and wives in the evening crowd disappears. One told me over and over again that he was vice president of an insurance company and that he would pay me to serve at a private party in his hotel. Another got up from his fourth martini to breathe heavily down my neck. When I pulled away, he was sincerely angry: "What do you think I come here for," he said, "roast beef?"

The risks, in this case, turned out to be great. The consequences of publication for Steinem included a long conciliatory letter from Hefner, an unsuccessful and harassing libel suit, several weeks of threatening phone calls, the temporary loss of serious journalistic assignments, *Playboy's* repeated publication of her employee photograph, and twenty years of sporadic phone calls from retired and working Bunnies with tales about working conditions and sexual demands—each caller amazed to find Steinem's name listed in the phone book.

Exercises

1. Divide the class into small groups of four to six students. Choose one person to interview another in the group. The interviewer should practice keeping eye contact, taking notes while listening to the speaker, and concentrating on the person's ac-

tions. Afterward, the group should discuss the interview. Was it conducted well? How were the interviewer's tone of voice, posture, eye contact, and physical signals? Can the group offer pointers and suggestions for improvement? Did the interviewer ask a sufficient number of questions to understand the subject's responses? After the discussion, choose a different interviewer and subject and repeat the exercise.

2. For this exercise, you should choose a person with whom you speak frequently (such as a roommate, parent, sibling, friend, boyfriend or girlfriend, teacher, etc.). Rather than interviewing the person, simply engage in normal conversation. To practice your listening skills, concentrate on the person's words and actions. Take notes during the conversation, but make sure you keep eye contact and seem interested in every sentence. After the conversation, think about how you used the skills presented in this chapter. Did you forget any of them? Did you find one of them more difficult than the others? Be prepared to evaluate your performance in class.

3. Invite a journalist from the local newspaper to your class. Discuss the importance of listening to sources. Ask him or her how to improve listening skills. How does he or she conduct interviews? After the discussion, the reporter can choose a student volunteer to interview. Then the student should interview the reporter. Analyze the interviews. Can you make recommendations?

4. To practice your listening and note-taking skills, choose someone to read the following paragraphs out loud. Without looking at this page, take notes while the person is reciting. Later, compare your notes with the written version.

These paragraphs were written by Philip Caputo for *Esquire* magazine:

> He wakes up late on what he knows will be the last day of his life. Late rising has been his pattern for the past three weeks. His neighbors at the El Rancho Motel have seen him only at night, coming or going on foot or in his car, a restless young man with an intense and heatless light in his blue eyes. Possibly he's been suffering from the insomnia that has plagued him for years. Possibly, by prowling around till all hours, he's been trying to avoid his recurrent nightmare. Possibly he has been going over his plans. Who can say? Dave Goodman, who lives in the room next door, thinks he acts like a·speed freak. He has been an alcoholic and addict since fourteen—plenty of pills, booze, and reefer—but he's stayed clean this time. He needs a clear head for what he is about to do.
>
> Let us try to imagine how he looks as he gets out of bed and stands in the curtained light of room 104: his unkempt dirty-blond hair, his 140 pounds stretched over a frame an inch under six feet, his moustached face possessed of what the newspapers will later describe as "scruffy good looks." He is twenty-four years old. He begins to dress. Combat boots, jeans, brown camouflage shirt. It looks like a uniform. Perhaps he takes a moment to admire his outfit in the shadowy mirror. He's not in a hurry.

5. Invite a group of teachers to your class for a panel discussion on the importance of listening. Because teachers have a great deal of experience in talking to students, they should be able to tell when students are pretending to listen. Ask the teachers how they know if someone is genuinely interested in what they're saying. Are there physical signals? Before the panel discussion, the class should write a list of questions to ask the teachers. Review this chapter for important points.

SEVEN

INTERVIEWING

INTERVIEWER: *Willie Sutton, why do you rob banks?*

SUTTON: *Because that's where the money is.*

There aren't any embarrassing questions—just embarrassing answers.

CARL ROWAN

Magazine writer Richard Meryman, who specializes in getting people to produce their own self-portraits for his *Life* articles, says, "The perfect interview is a perfect set of questions." For every hour spent interviewing his subject, Meryman spends an average of five hours on advance groundwork, interviewing people close to his subject, working out his questions. "I don't touch any alcohol for about three days before an interview," Meryman says. "I try to get a great deal of sleep. I don't eat starch or sugar. I spend half the day before in bed, then eat steak for breakfast. Basically, I'm clearing my mind, getting my reflexes and attention as high as I can so that, as the person is talking, I am supersensitive to those half-articulated hints which clue me in to the all-important follow-up questions—which eventually get you to the nub."

Writing articles requires research, and journalists use various methods, including interviewing. How you conduct an interview is crucial. Interviewing is a highly personal process, and your own curiosity, intelligence, and warmth are valuable assets. These qualities will often carry you through an interview with greater success than an exhaustive study of other professionals' techniques or experience. But even though development of an interviewing style depends on the individual, writers can benefit from learning some common pitfalls to avoid when conducting a question-and-answer session.

ALL THE WORLD'S A STAGE

> "My idea of an agreeable person is a person who agrees with me."
>
> BENJAMIN DISRAELI

As a journalist, you will play different roles in different interviewing situations. Usually you will find yourself wielding a certain amount of power because of the pleasure most people take in their own importance and in the prestige of your reporting what they say; you may be a vital conduit for getting someone's opinions into the public eye. You may, however, find yourself playing the role of adversary or pursuing an uncooperative official in the course of researching a politically volatile exposé. The role the writer plays has a considerable impact on the atmosphere of an interview and its results.

Looking the Part

Bernard Shaw once said, "People are always blaming their circumstances for what they are. I do not believe in circumstances. The people who get on in this world are the people who get up and look for the circumstances they want, and if they cannot find them, make them."

Keep Shaw's words in mind when interviewing, and stay in control of your surroundings. Watch your subject carefully at all times. You must be prepared to adjust your manner—and even your personal appearance—to develop a conversational rapport with the individual you are interviewing. This requires a recognition of the "social distance" between interviewer and interviewee, a division heightened by such factors as sex, race, fashion, and even age, as well as class distinction. Usually we attempt to reduce the social distance, although journalists such as Tom Wolfe, who affects an extreme flamboyance, have found a vast social distance to be useful.

If you have done your homework, you will know enough about the interviewee to modify your approach in the direction of more or less formality, respectful deference or cheerful camaraderie, carefully framed speech or streetwise jargon, and so on. Often the individual you interview will set the tone for you. Saul Pett, a veteran writer for the Associated Press, experienced two radically different meetings with two equally strong-willed subjects: Dr. Albert Kinsey, the sex researcher, and writer Dorothy Parker. Kinsey met Pett exactly at the appointed time, took a travel clock from his pocket, wound it, set the alarm, placed it on a table, checked the clock against his watch, and, looking up for the first time, said, "Yes." Dorothy Parker, on the other hand, greeted Pett at the door with the question, "Are you married, my dear?" When he said he was, she turned. "Well, in that case," she said, "you won't mind zipping me up."

Forming Questions

Although most professionals prepare a few questions, they do not compile long lists for lockstep delivery. Questions should grow naturally from the conversation, each answer suggesting the next question. This method allows the reporter to improvise during the interview—to pursue different perspectives or new facts that emerge from the responses. With practice, continuity and transitions become natural.

In free-flowing interviews, however, the interviewer is in danger of guiding responses by asking leading (or loaded) questions. Notice in the following sequence of questions how the interviewer elicits certain answers:

Q What kind of writers are left in television then?

A Those who are still around are trained in the taboos of the business . . .

Q Again, this stems from the commercial exigencies of television, doesn't it?

A It comes from the commercial nature. I don't want to be unfair to the businessman, but . . .

Q But all these purposes—artistic, commercial, etc.—are at war with each other.

A Continually at war. The thing I object to is that the world of commerce is using the resources of the theater, of all our culture, for sales purposes.

In general, you should frame questions that are responsive to the natural flow of conversation but open-ended, implying that no right or wrong answer exists. Whether you agree or disagree with your subject's position should not affect the interview.

Expressing Yourself

However detached and noncommittal they try to be, reporters cannot escape the fact that they do have opinions—and that the interview may run into difficulty if they are unable to express their views. In some cases, the easygoing conversational mode permits the person being interviewed to hide behind bland statements rather than risk betraying genuine emotion or conviction, particularly if such expression leaves him or her vulnerable to public or political backlash. Gloria Steinem faced this dilemma in her attempt to interview Pat Nixon in 1968. In a later article on that interview, Steinem described her frustration with Mrs. Nixon's evasiveness:

> Explaining my doubts about writing from clips, I asked if there were any persistent mistakes in the press that I should take care not to repeat. "No, no," she said, smoothing her skirt. "You ladies of the press do a fine job. I think the stories have been very fine." Did that mean she liked everything that had been written? "Well, actually, I haven't had time to read a lot of them lately." . . . We went round with that a few more times. Then she was, I told her, the only person I'd ever met, including myself, who liked everything written about them. There was a flicker of annoyance behind the hazel eyes—the first sign of life.

To get a meaningful interview, Steinem was forced to inject her own opinion into the conversation. Much later in the interview, exasperated by Mrs. Nixon's professed identification with Mamie Eisenhower, Steinem expressed herself again—and finally triggered from Mrs. Nixon a revealing flood of controlled resentment.

When you cannot avoid an argument or see no way to get an honest interview without taking a challenging stance, keep in mind Benjamin Franklin's advice about disagreeing with people diplomatically:

I made it a rule to forebear all direct contradiction to the sentiments of others, and all positive assertions of my own. . . . When another asserted something that I thought to be an error, I denied myself the pleasure of contradicting him abruptly, and of showing immediately some absurdity in his proposition; and in answering I began by observing that in certain cases or circumstances his opinion would be right, but in the present case there appeared or seemed to me some difference, etc. I soon found the advantage of this change in my manners; the conversations I engaged in went on more pleasantly.

This writer followed Franklin's advice:

. . . it was important in writing "Airports: Our Newest Billion-Dollar Business" to know the annual earnings of Kennedy International Airport. But the New York Port Authority, which runs the airports as well as the docks and bus terminals, did not want the earnings of any unit of its operations revealed. The authority juggles funds from one unit to another as the directors see fit. The figure for Kennedy International could not be drawn out of any official. But during the friendly, conversational interviews with many officials, enough manipulations were revealed to enable the writer to add two and two from annual reports and come up with a close estimate of Kennedy's earnings. After the story was published, the New York City Corporation Commissioner called to ask how the earnings figure was derived and admitted, "*We've been trying to get it for more than a year.*"

Also remember that although hard-boiled questions may emerge from the journalist's personal convictions, asking tough questions is, personal bias aside, his or her job. Former California governor Edmund B. ("Pat") Brown advised a relaxed attitude toward the news conference: "Harrowing as they are, news conferences do provide a chance for correspondents to bore in, a practice that philosophers find a healthy thing for the democratic process. Few governors take any comfort in that."

Nevertheless, the aggressive reporter who zeroes in with rifle-shot questions can sometimes cause the interviewee to bring up defenses and reveal as little as possible, even about matters that would have been open to discussion under more relaxed circumstances. Tough questions usually belong near the end of an interview.

In fact, sometimes an interviewer isn't at all sure that the interviewee will respond to *any* question. Kay Bartlett, a highly practiced interviewer with the Associated Press, has run into such people. The following words are Bartlett's. They will be followed by her profile.*

Setting up an interview with an author who has a new book coming out is usually akin to asking a panhandler if he would prefer $10 to the quarter he requested.

Book publicists have been known to volunteer to fly authors in to

---

*Reprinted by permission of Kay Bartlett.

meet you and suggest the interview be conducted in the most expensive French restaurant in town. They gush about what a pleasure it would be for you to meet their client.

Not so with the Rev. Andrew Greeley, the controversial novelist-priest who is coming out with his 13th book. Sure, he would be interviewed, but only in the form of Q and A — I would ask, he would answer. I would not be allowed to select, paraphrase, edit quotes, describe, etc., all the necessary tools of feature writing.

Those were his rules, the publicist explained, since he felt he had been burned a lot by the media. He would give real feature-type interviews only to reporters he knew, except for the contrived Q and A format.

We couldn't go for this lifeless format, which would hardly do justice to the story of a sociologist, author of more than 100 scholarly tomes as well as fiction, newspaper columnist, professor at the University of Arizona, Chicago Bears fan, soon-to-be screen writer, crack water skier, but as he says, "first, foremost and forever a priest."

Greeley will agree to interviews on television, because there he feels he has control. But those feature writers. . . .

It was time to call upon one of the AP's great strengths, the men and women who have covered a beat for many years and have established a reputation for fair and accurate reporting. One of those is long-time religion editor George Cornell.

What if Cornell were to vouch for me?

That, the publicist thought, would work.

It took only one telephone call from Cornell, who had not only Greeley's unlisted number but his trust, and Greeley agreed to the interview.

Greeley and I laughed a lot during our conversation, especially while the local publicist was figuring out where to buy a black clerical

KAY BARTLETT

There are characters and there are characters. Kay Bartlett, news features writer for the Associated Press, knows that fact. She has covered quite a few characters in her reporting; one she has interviewed was the antihero of Watergate, G. Gordon Liddy.

Surprisingly, Kay found Liddy to be a "courtly gentleman with a sharp sense of humor who would love to spend an entire interview boasting about his wife and children." This was the same man who held a cigarette lighter under his arm until the skin turned black to prove he could never be made to talk. Liddy was only one of the many candid personalities that she interviewed for the Associated Press.

Bartlett has traveled a long way from her beginnings in Cincinnati. She graduated from Our Lady of Cincinnati College in 1982 with a B.A. in English. She went to graduate school at Indiana University, half in English, half in journalism. Unfortunately, Kay says that she completed all the course work but became one of the statistical wonders who never wrote a thesis. Nonetheless, she worked at the *Worcester* (Massachusetts) *Telegram* for a year, then joined the Associated Press.

Bartlett has written a variety of pieces dealing with various issues, such as adoptees and whether they have a right to know their biological parents; sexual harassment; bulimia; and alcoholism. She has also written off-the-wall articles that range from those who make a career of pursuing Bigfoot to the Amazing Randi before he became rich and famous.

shirt. Greeley, it seems, forgot to pack one and although he wore a civilian shirt and windbreaker for our interview, he was going on television the next day and needed full regalia.

I even came to understand why Greeley is a little gun-shy about interviews.

And that brings me to a little confession I have to make. I really did have to use the word "steamy," you know, Father, the word that drives you crazy.

But I tried to explain why it gets your Irish up.

I think I can go in peace.

Besides, I have already done my penance. My cruel editor made me cut 500 words out of my story and if you're a journalist you know what that's like.

You're On

Patricia Lasher describes the wide range of situations she and her photographer encountered while interviewing the cross section of women in her book *Texas Woman—Interviews and Images*:

> The first interview and photography session for this book began on a sweltering day in 1978 at the Armstrong Ranch in south Texas. Our final meeting was at the Hyatt Regency Hotel in Houston during a thunderstorm and partial flooding in late 1979. In the eighteen intervening months, Beverly Bentley and I carried camera bags, tripods, and tape recorders around the state and, when necessary, to other states to meet with our interviewees in zoo carts and airplane hangars, judges' chambers and operating rooms, executive suites and private homes.

This variety of circumstances shows how impossible it is to formulate a single hard-and-fast interviewing technique.

SOME TECHNIQUES

The following suggestions are rules of thumb to follow when conducting interviews.

Prepare for the Interview

Make an effort to learn as much as you can about your subject before the actual interview. If you don't, even the most patient of people will find your ignorance if not infuriating, at least worrisome: the interviewee is relying on you to make an accurate and understandable report. Learning the basic facts about the people you interview compliments them and encourages their respect and response. Writer John Gunther advises, "One thing is never, never, never to ask a person about his or her own first name, job, or title. These the interviewer should know beforehand." These details, of course, are only the beginning.

Extensive preparation not only reassures the person you interview but also helps you develop a perceptive and casual line of questioning. You can

> "It's always easy to do the next step, and it's always impossible to do two steps at a time."
>
> SEYMOUR CRAY

often infuse an interview with an energy and organic strength it would otherwise lack by easily recognizing your subject's references and following his or her line of thought. Catharine Stimpson, a professor of English, in her interview with Gerda Lerner, a founder of the study of women's history, clearly demonstrates her interest in and familiarity with Lerner's field:

> **CS** No one has ever said that you are not strong and no one has ever said that you are not individualistic. But you write eloquently about the need for the collective work. How did you reconcile an individualistic core and collective action?
>
> **GL** In 1963, my position was necessarily individualistic. But I had been involved in organizing and working with women for twenty-five years before that—at the workplace, in the community. As a historian, I brought the questions I had experienced into my scholarship. The Women's Movement, in the late 1960s, made the scholarship collective.
>
> **CS** You often speak of the need to connect the female experience and academic theory.
>
> **GL** That's right. A feminist style of learning implies the fusion of theory and practice.

And so on. This particular example shows a sympathetic interview; the advantages of possessing a substantial array of relevant facts when faced with an evasive or hostile subject are obvious.

Doing your homework extends past studying your subject's life and writings to formulating the questions you wish to ask. Although flexibility and a conversational tone are sufficiently important to lead some journalists to do no more than jot down a few key words before an interview, beginners should write down a number of questions—and leave space to record answers. Until you gain experience in directing the course of an interview, you are in danger of floundering into silence and forgetting crucial questions.

Take Notes

Writers disagree on when and how to take notes. Some people become self-conscious when you start to record their answers; others freeze up entirely. Nevertheless, more and more professionals are turning to tape-recorded interviews. Taping often reassures interviewees who might worry that you will try later, without success, to remember exactly what they said.

A number of journalists follow this rule: take notes freely or tape the interview when talking with people accustomed to speaking for public consumption (politicians, business leaders, entertainers, and so on), but be careful around those who are not in public life. Such people usually have trouble relaxing in the presence of a notebook or tape recorder, and that can dilute the natural flavor of the interview. One reporter has made this suggestion:

> Flipping out the notebook the minute you flush the quarry has never worked too well for me. It scares some subjects. The best excuse I find for breaking out the pad is a bit of blue-eyed admiration for some happy observation they've just made. I may try, "Say, that's good. I want

to be sure I get that down just right." And write. The notebook now spells reassurance.

Most journalists eventually devise their own shorthand for writing down answers. One useful technique for getting down an important answer without allowing an awkward silence to fall is to immediately ask another, minor question—and fully record the first answer while the interviewee is responding.

Keep in mind, however, that machines (and interviewers) are not infallible. Even when the recorder operates perfectly, you still must interpret the results and select the telling detail from an often unwieldy mass of information that can become oddly obscure without the corresponding visual cues. One newspaperman advised a young reporter who was making voluminous notes as they talked to put away his notebook. "Why don't we just talk?" he said. "Then go off and write up your impression of it all. It's the difference between a sketch and a snapshot: a sketch—how you see me—is interesting because it's individual, but a snapshot will be more or less the same no matter who holds the camera."

In general, tape those interviews for which an exact record may be necessary later to resolve disputes, and tape everything while you are still developing your system of shorthand. Rely on written notes to take down salient direct quotations and subsequently to write the article.

Encourage Response

Only with obviously busy people—and those who are merely suffering the interview—should you start immediately asking questions. Small talk at the beginning will put the interviewee at ease and ensure an easy, conversational tone. Of course, direct your chitchat at the topic of concern in the interview, so you do not have to make an awkward leap from, say, the local baseball team's chance for the pennant to your subject's candidates for Congress.

The ideal interview strikes a balance between monologue and dialogue. If you let the people you interview monopolize the conversation, they are likely to miss (or evade) vital issues. On the other hand, if you do half of the talking, your subject is likely to retreat or even become annoyed. You somehow must produce appropriate comments and develop your next question without dominating the interview. Intelligent comments can help draw out a full response as the speaker gains confidence in the interviewer's ability to understand and report what he or she says. Do not hesitate, however, to ask questions that might betray your ignorance on certain points; if you already know it all, why conduct an interview in the first place? This cannot be emphasized enough. Otherwise, you are in danger of misunderstanding what is said and later of misrepresenting the facts.

Inevitably the awful occasion will arise when a bored interviewee answers only in monosyllables: "Yes." "No." "Who knows?" One way out of these deadly situations is to ask the simple question "Why?" Granted, people confronted in this way can always shrug, but if they have established a stance on an issue with a "Yes" or "No" answer, they usually will feel obliged to explain themselves, especially if the issue interests them. Gunther has said: "One thing I have found out is that almost any person will talk freely—such is human frailty—if you will ask him the measure of his own accomplishment."

Gunther's advice is sound and can be used to turn a poor interview around. On getting people to talk about themselves and their work, another veteran writer has said:

> I've found that as soon as I've discovered a man's obsession or enthusiasm and have got him started talking about it, I've opened the gate. All I have to do is nudge him now and then with a question to keep him talking. If I have any curves to throw at him, I save them until the end of the interview, when we're on pretty good terms; and then I don't throw spitballs, just curves.
>
> Once, a union boss hit me with a spitball before I could begin questioning him. He asked, "How much did Joe Sevier (an opponent of the boss) pay you for writing that story about him in *Nation's Business?*" I thought about it a minute, to keep from replying angrily, then told him, "Well, he paid me exactly what you're going to pay me for doing this story about you." He grinned, and then we had a long and congenial interview that ended with an invitation for me to attend a meeting of his union that night—an unheard-of invitation because reporters were usually excluded.

Although a laconic interviewee may tempt you to accept pat answers or to encourage greater expression by smiling, nodding, or leaning forward, you should be careful not to inadvertently lead the other person. Your own interest (or desperation) could cause you to pursue a line of comment irrelevant to the interviewee's actual position or force the person to state a particular attitude more strongly than would normally be the case.

This does not mean that you should not probe for a response if circumstances seem to warrant it. Strong probing is often essential, especially in political journalism. Reporters were known to scramble for even chance openings with President Ronald Reagan, who seldom held press conferences. Early in September 1984, eight weeks before the presidential election, the president concluded a briefing session with the Washington correspondents by announcing that he would meet with Soviet Foreign Minister Andrei Gromyko. Maureen Santini, the Associated Press White House correspondent, had just given the traditional question-ending "Thank you." President Reagan responded with "What?" These questions and his answers followed:

Q Could I . . .

A I was hoping to get beyond the second row.

Q Mr. President . . .

A I can't. Maureen is . . . Maureen said, no.

Q Yes, but you pointed out . . .

A No, but let me tell you . . .

Q The moving finger points and having pointed . . .

A   No, let me just say, we'll be back and there'll be more of . . . we'll be having more of these. So . . .

Q   Oh, when?

A   What?

Q   Before the election?

Q   We'd like to make a date.

Q   What about debates?

A   I'm just going to wait and surprise you again.

Q   Are we going to have a full-scale, half-hour news conference, sir, before the election?

A   I don't know, but I've been talking about that myself.

Q   When's the first debate?

A   What?

A   Can't take any more questions.

Q   How's the campaign going so far?

A   Save them for the next time. Save it for the next time.

Q   But we're not certain there's going to be a next time, sir.

Q   Thank you.

Play Fair with Sources and Readers

Newspaper reporters learn quite early that they must play fair with those they interview. If a reporter misconstrues ideas, garbles quotations, or identifies an interviewee who expected anonymity, his or her source may decide to be a source no longer. This problem is seldom so acute in magazine writing because few free-lancers or staff writers must return to a source again and again. Writers often obtain information from a different set of sources for each article.

Confidentiality

Journalists are often asked to keep certain information confidential. Sometimes interviewees, worried that they have been indiscreet or lured into revealing more than they should have, ask the reporter to refrain from publishing a large part of the interview. Although you have a right to refuse such a request, you can avoid these delicate situations by clearly establishing at the start of the interview how much of what kind of information you will be free to disclose.

Washington correspondents and government officials have fairly explicit ground rules for attributing information: "off the record," "background only," and "not for attribution." Obviously, reporters would have only limited access to sensitive information if they had to attribute everything they printed to a specific source. It is your job to decide whether the informant is attempting to serve the public interest or to use you for his or her own purposes. These motives naturally overlap to a large extent. Writers must learn to recognize when confidentiality begins to seriously damage or distort the truth.

Although some writers prefer to say to their subjects, "Don't tell me anything that can't be printed," the gray area of confidential information can be useful. Just be sure to establish clear ground rules before the interview and to follow them when you are writing the article later, respecting the confidences you've agreed to keep.

Ethical writers never take unfair advantage of their sources. Unethical writers soon develop a reputation for casual attitudes toward the truth; outraged sources complain to editors. Young writers, however, may get into trouble or fail to get information because they do not know that the conventions of interviewing enable them to protect a source who fears being quoted directly or being identified with the information he provides. The conventions include:

Indirect quotation   These are remarks that may be quoted only in substance (not verbatim). Usually, however, they are attributed to an identified source. A little-used convention, this is sometimes valuable for someone like the president, whose words will be studied for shades of meaning if he is quoted directly.

Off the record   Information that is to be held in complete confidence, off-the-record facts are not to be printed under any circumstances or in any form. For the most part, these are facts needed to grasp the significance of complicated events. Off-the-record information is usually given to writers to orient them to future events that will require special handling by those who are thoroughly informed.

Not for attribution   This is information that should not be attributed to a named source but to one who is identified generally: "a reliable source," "a longtime friend of the entertainer," "an authority on international law," or the like. In many instances, the source is not named because the fact that the individual disclosed the information might embarrass or injure him or her.

Background   Information that may be used by a writer entirely on his or her own responsibility, background may not be attributed even to "a reliable source." The writer presents the information as though it had been developed from original research. Ordinarily, the reason background may not be attributed in any way is that even a reference to a general source might lead to identification and cause embarrassment or injury.

These conventions are useful primarily because the writer can offer them as cloaks to someone who is reluctant to be quoted directly. On the other hand, they can be dangerous for two reasons. First, a writer may offer anonymity of one sort or another too freely and thus hide sources who should be identified. The writer may even discover that he or she has granted anonymity to so many sources that the article reads as though the writer had made it all up. Second, the conventions that allow anonymity tempt the source to grind an axe as he or she likes, unobserved. At bottom, anonymous interviews circulate information for which no one takes public responsibility. The writer may wake up to discover that he or she has held a cloak behind which a source was manipulating facts and fashioning his or her own version of truth.

The worst danger is that these interview conventions may serve to destroy the ultimate aim, which is to play fair with the reader. This danger creates a dilemma. Presenting the facts provided by only those who will be identified is not likely to add up to the truth. For example, the president of the United States will talk on the record to present his version of the truth about foreign policy. A civil servant in the State Department who has a firmer grasp of the facts is not likely to contradict the president publicly. Granting anonymity to the civil servant will best serve the reader. But the writer may inadvertently grant anonymity to a source who hopes to mislead. The writer must protect everyone by granting anonymity when it seems desirable or necessary but must also check carefully to try to make certain that he or she is not being used to mislead the public.

Direct Quotations

Playing fair with sources and readers is also at the center of problems with direct quotations. The most common question about quoting—How exact must quotations be?—can be answered simply: Never use quotation marks unless you are certain that the words are precisely what was said. If it ever made sense to quote *approximately* what was said and to improve the grammar of public figures—once fairly common, but a dubious practice in journalism—it no longer does.

Writers seem to agree almost unanimously that only in unusual cases—highly technical articles, for example—should sources be allowed to read before publication the articles in which their quotations appear. A source makes a contribution to an article, but the writer is responsible for the whole of it. A source views a completed article from a point of view distorted by his or her own self-interest. Most writers will agree to call or write to a source when an article is complete and give the person a chance to check his or her own words. These practices raise a question of ethics only when the writer has promised that a source may read all or part of an article before publication and fails to follow through. Professional writers rarely make such promises.

Quoting Out of Context

There is a real danger that a source who is allowed to read an article before publication will try to influence a revision selfishly, but another danger may arise if the source is not allowed to read it. One of the most acute problems in journalism is quoting out of context. This kind of distortion is never so blatant in article writing as it is in theatrical advertising, where a reviewer's "The play is a terrific bore" is quoted highly selectively in ads that attribute to the review this judgment: "Terrific!" The problem is much subtler in magazine writing. Quite often, well-intentioned writers are so intent on the point they want to make that they fix on (and write down) sentences that support a theme and ignore others that counter it. Or the writer quotes a part of an interview that fails to reflect the meaning of the whole of it.

Perhaps the best way for writers to avoid injuring a source and misleading readers is to remind themselves over and over that quoting out of context is a persistent danger. Seasoned magazine writers avoid it by a method no more complex than putting themselves on guard.

An Article's Publishability

Everyone who is approached for an interview deserves an honest judgment of the likelihood that an article will be published. Interviewees give time, energy, and information, and writers should repay them with honesty. Beginners should make it clear that they are speculating about the possibility of publication—if they are—even though many sources will probably give them less time and attention than they would give a well-known free-lancer or a staff writer on assignment. Honesty offers several compensations. If the writer has admitted that the article may not be published, the source is not as likely to call periodically to ask when the article will appear. Some public officials who are inclined to guard information are also more relaxed with beginning journalists (especially students) and tell them more than they would tell established writers. Finally, some sources try to help beginning writers by giving them much time and attention. These occasional benefits do not negate the fact that, in many cases, the established writer has a distinct advantage. But beginners who try to pass themselves off as experienced writers who are virtually certain of publication are virtually certain to fail.

Verify Dates and Numbers

Do you remember when you last heard Uncle Bob or Aunt Elizabeth speak of going to college? When was it? You may answer in this way: "It was last year. No, it was two years ago. I don't know what month it was, but I'm *sure* it was three years ago because I visited Uncle Bob's home on the other side of town three years ago . . . I *think.*"

The same kind of answer—disguised by the interviewee by not saying "I think"—will probably come from the interviewee. Very few people can accurately state when certain of their actions occurred. In many cases, interviewees will remember actions they have performed as being more recent than they are.

Moreover, when you ask a question that involves numbers, it is likely the interviewee will be wrong (often honestly) about money or almost any other answer that includes numbers. If you can check dates and numbers, do the research. Or, if you cannot use reference books and other publications to verify the answers you are given, search for another person who can answer the same questions. If these methods fail, make certain that you attribute the answer to the interviewee, not to yourself.

Leave an Opening at the End

Writers often find it pays to end an interview by saying something like "My hindsight is better than my foresight. When I check over my notes, I'll undoubtedly find that there are questions I'll wish I had asked. May I come back with another question or two?" This tactic keeps the door open for follow-up questioning. A single brief interview is seldom adequate for picturing a person or relating his or her policy; the true situation is almost always multifaceted; and your understanding is likely to deepen if you pursue longer or repeated interviews with your subject.

You may also get some interesting results if at the end you throw the ball into the interviewee's court. Peter Sandman described how he customarily closes his interviews:

> I make it a habit to ask the source a broad leading question toward the end of the interview—something like, "Is there anything I haven't asked you that you think I ought to ask or that you are anxious to answer?" It sometimes opens up whole new fields of exploration that I didn't even know existed.

One final note: be wary of basing an article on interviews with a single person. As Joseph and Stewart Alsop point out, "The reporter has to talk to enough people so that he can reduce the degree to which he is misled." Additional interviews and careful research enable the writer to triangulate: here is what he or she says, here is what others say, here is what the record shows. You are more likely to find the facts of a situation in this way than by relying on the words of a single interviewee.

CHECKLIST: CONDUCTING AN INTERVIEW

1. Call to schedule an interview with your subject. Tell the subject who you are and what the interview is for—such as for a specific article, a school magazine, or a class assignment.

2. Research your subject before the scheduled interview. Interview people who know the subject, and read any articles about him or her. Learn as much as possible before you meet your subject.

3. Bring a notepad and a tape recorder to the interview. Do not rely only on a tape recorder because it might not function properly; likewise, do not rely only on your ability to take notes accurately. Check batteries and test the tape recorder prior to the interview.

4. At the beginning of the interview, engage in casual conversation to relax your subject. Ask easier questions first; save tough questions for the end of the interview.

5. Adjust your manner to promote conversation between you and your subject.

6. Ask open-ended questions rather than leading or loaded questions. Do not allow your opinions to affect the interview or bias your reporting.

7. Do not be afraid to ask questions that betray your ignorance. If you already knew everything, you wouldn't need to conduct the interview.

8. Probe for a response when necessary.

9. Try to verify information (especially dates and numbers) revealed during the interview.

10. End an interview by saying that you may need to contact the subject for follow-up questioning.

11. In most cases, do not allow the subject to read the article before it is published; doing so may lead to unnecessary problems. Assure the subject that fact-checking procedures will promote accuracy.

Exercises

1. Because interviewing is central to almost any journalist's job, you must first prepare yourself to interview—and this is much more than knowing the interviewee's name and job. Practice your first interview by learning everything you can about the interviewee. For this exercise, choose an interviewee whose name is all you know. Before talking to him or her, see how much you can learn without speaking to the interviewee. Bring what you have learned to the next class session.

2. Tape-record an interview with someone you plan to write a story about. Then listen carefully to the tape in order to discuss which of your questions were most effective in eliciting the kind of information you wanted. Which questions were not, and why? Discuss how you might have improved the interview. Did you miss any opportunities for follow-up questions or phrase your questions so that the subject could easily respond with single-word answers and in the process subvert the interview?

3. To practice concentrating only on the interviewee and ignoring distractions, try interviewing someone in a noisy place, such as the school cafeteria or a dormitory. Even though there may be music playing, ringing telephones, or loud voices, conduct the interview as if no one else were in the room with you and your subject. Afterward, evaluate your performance.

EIGHT

LIBRARIES AND LEGWORK

The love of learning, the sequestered nooks,
And all the sweet serenity of books.

HENRY WADSWORTH LONGFELLOW

The works of P. G. Wodehouse, playwright and author of the famous Jeeves books, may seem to be bits of fluff borne on the vagrant breeze, but it is not so. Each was based on some four hundred pages of handwritten notes and forty or fifty pages about the characters, all boiled down to two or three pages of scenario, before the actual writing began. In *Author! Author!* Wodehouse wrote: "When, in due course, Charon ferries me across the Styx and everyone is telling everyone else what a rotten writer I was, I hope at least one voice will be heard piping up, 'But he did take trouble.'"

Research—a key to solid writing—usually means trouble for writers. Whether you choose to write in the style of traditional journalism or to use more flexible forms for feature and magazine writing, you need to develop strong research skills and know where to look for certain information. As newspapers and magazines become more sophisticated, writers are finding that they cannot survive without effective use of the library.

A RESEARCH GOLD MINE

Libraries of all kinds (public, university, newspaper, and even personal collections) offer an invaluable resource to the professional writer. One of the first volumes to consult on almost any assignment is *Readers' Guide to Periodical Literature*. The writer must know what else has been written on his or her subject or on related subjects, and *Readers' Guide* approaches being an exhaustive listing. Reading what has appeared on a subject may persuade a writer that it has already been covered too heavily to warrant another article—at least for a time. But the writer will usually discover that other articles have covered only some aspects of the subject. The writer will learn which angles have been explored and will turn up leads to sources of information for a different approach.

In some cases, much of the information for a story must be dug out of a public library or newspaper library, and in some instances serious research in

> "A dwarf standing on the shoulders of a giant may see farther than a giant himself."
>
> ROBERT BURTON

160

libraries can yield startling results. For example, during World War II a German spy in the United States shunned cloak and dagger in favor of libraries. Government officials learned after the war that by analyzing newspapers, magazines, and technical journals, he was able to predict American war production more accurately than the United States government did.

Many veteran writers build their own libraries as well as being familiar figures in the reference room of the public library and in that of the nearest metropolitan newspaper office. They keep on their own shelves the books they are likely to use again and again: *Readers' Guide,* a standard encyclopedia, an almanac, a desk dictionary and an unabridged dictionary, a thesaurus, and probably a dictionary of quotations. Personal libraries may contain thousands of books. Many writers also build extensive files of newspaper and magazine clippings. Because they cannot hope to collect all the reference books or clippings they may need to use someday, writers eventually establish close relationships with reference and newspaper librarians.

Some writers occasionally boast that they have written articles "from the clips," which means that they have used only newspaper and magazine clippings. But for every such article that succeeds, fifty fail. A common complaint among editors is that some writers simply rehash material that has already been printed. Magazines with large research staffs sometimes look carefully at articles that seem stale, and a writer who develops a reputation for rehashing is in trouble. The chief point to remember about library research is that it is only a supplement, if a valuable one, to the other kinds of research that enliven writing.

One word of warning: publication does not guarantee that information is error free. Unsubstantiated data find their way into print with alarming frequency. Even general reference works such as dictionaries and encyclopedias suffer from inherent limitations. Keeping up with new developments in the English language is a nearly impossible task for teams that compile dictionaries, and encyclopedia editors have been known to assign biographical and other articles to people with vested interest in their subjects.

Some writers have developed rituals to make their writing error free. Here is one writer whose habits should be considered. Organizing a first draft of an article is torture, but Nancy L. Roberts has accomplished it hundreds of times. Here she describes her routine:*

> All writers have their rituals, and I am no different. From long habit I prefer to write first drafts in my study, a sanctuary from the rustlings of my dachshund. E. B. White made hay out of his, a distraction. Morning is my favorite time to write, when I'm most rested and optimistic. It's easier, as I sip that first cup of coffee, to get the words to mesh.
>
> As a free-lance magazine writer, I enjoy the freedom to select my own assignments. Yet writing remains a bittersweet pleasure. The process of creating an article is stimulating and enjoyable, but it can

*Reprinted by permission of Nancy L. Roberts.

also be uncertain, arduous, and therefore, tempting to avoid. And so I always dread sitting down to write that first draft. It helps to recall Flannery O'Connor's working habits. As a daily discipline, the late fiction writer made herself sit at her desk, with paper at hand, for a certain number of hours. If inspiration struck, splendid; if it did not, she still sat for the required time. No trips to the kitchen for a little this or that, no strolling among the peacocks.

While some writers favor such diversions when they are "stuck," I have found inspiration in O'Connor's approach. Mindful staring into the computer screen in a quiet room eventually yields what I seek.

Yes, word processing is essential. I've written with the aid of a computer for the last four years, and can't imagine going back to a typewriter (on which I used to compose). The ease of making changes and corrections on a computer encourages you to try creative strategies that you might resist if each alteration could mean laborious retyping. As I try out different ideas on the screen, I vocalize them softly, testing

NANCY L. ROBERTS

Nancy L. Roberts once wrote an article for the 1985 issue of the *New York Alive* titled "Lasting Impressions." Here is the way she began her article: "She was barely five feet tall, with watery blue eyes and a face like a wrinkled prune, as I knew her in her eighties." It was a short biographical piece on her "granny," and it left the reader with a lasting impression. Roberts certainly knows how to write.

An associate professor of journalism at the University of Minnesota, Roberts has the power of the descriptive perfected to a science. Her works evoke feeling and warmth that go beyond sentimentality. After reading one of her articles, one has the impression that Roberts and her writing have heart.

Of English and Welsh stock, Roberts is completely without pretension as she describes her grandmother's youth: "Clad in the starched white pinafore of the Victorian maid, she was still in her teens when she served some of the grand old English country mansions of that era." It is this attention to the ordinary aspects of life that makes Roberts's writing so appealing. She favors subjects that have an everyday quality—something all her readers can relate to, in one facet or another.

A successful free-lancer, Roberts recently completed her book on the playwright Eugene O'Neill. *As Ever Gene: The Letters of Eugene O'Neill to George Jean Nathan* was published in 1987. Roberts also wrote an excellent article on the O'Neill family's summer home for *The Philadelphia Inquirer* (January 8, 1987). In the article, she has achieved the moodiness and haunting quality

that is generally associated with the playwright and his works. Roberts writes: "Elms and maples still shroud the house, much as they did in O'Neill's childhood. His mother often complained that the trees made the house seem gloomy. Morning sunlight streamed through the east-facing parlor windows, but by afternoon the trees closed in and all was somber." In fact, Roberts seems to have captured the essence of O'Neill's writing. She noted that in his play *Desire Under the Elms,* his own stage directions state: "[The elms] brood oppressively over the house. They are like exhausted women . . . and when it rains their tears trickle down monotonously and rot on the shingles."

An unerring attention to detail is inherent in her works. But, more important, there is a common thread of imagery that winds through her articles from start to finish. Regardless of whether she is explaining a complicated artistic technique or relating the trials and tribulations of a family-owned used book business, Roberts keeps her prose straightforward yet picturesque—she enables her readers to *see* the subject matter.

Between her free-lance commitments and her duties as a writer and editor for *Midwest Art,* Roberts has ample opportunity to continue to perfect her craft. She keeps busy as a professor, guest lecturer, and University of Minnesota Service Committee member. She is truly recognized for excellence in her field, having received the prestigious Who's Who Professional and Executive Woman distinction in 1986.

the rhythm and the syntax. If you walk by my study and hear lots of murmuring, you know hard work is going on.

If the story is long, I'll have made a one-page outline to chart the way. Sometimes I just jot down the main ideas that should be included, checking them off as they are used. Because my handwriting is not pretty, I often type my summary notes as a warm-up technique. This sets ideas to simmer that may mysteriously emerge later as pot liquor, while I'm writing.

Over the years, it's become easier to edit right on the screen, although I like to print out a paper copy on my letter-quality printer to ease reading. Editing is the part of writing that I relish, and unlike writing first drafts, I'm ready to edit at any time of the day or evening. I do like to sleep on everything I've written. The more time that elapses between the writing and the editing, the keener my eye.

Editing—the polishing and embellishing—are the parts of writing that give me the greatest reward. But to get there, you need a first draft. Whoever defined writing as the art of applying the seat of the pants to the seat of the chair was wise. No secrets, just that.

THE MOTHER LODE

The following sections provide annotated samplings of standard reference works that are frequently useful to professional writers. These lists are far from complete, and they ignore the innumerable references and scholarly journals that concentrate on specialized fields. Nevertheless, they should give you the basic underpinnings to good library research.

General Dictionaries

Lexicographers who compile dictionaries these days are more likely to regard their function as historical and descriptive than critical and prescriptive. They see the purpose of their work as that of recording the language in common use rather than culling the language for grammatically "pure" words.

This means that "ain't" appears in a number of dictionaries, as do many other colloquialisms, not to mention the earthy vulgarisms that pepper English speech. Colloquial and vulgar language is labeled as such or as "nonstandard." Much popular jargon enters and leaves the language so quickly that dictionaries never record it. As a rule, however, lexicographers attempt to include any word that appears in "standard speech and literature"—a standard that may be somewhat casual.

Most of the unabridged dictionaries that top the following list provide spelling, pronunciation, syllabification, definition, and grammatical usage. They usually supply an illustrative example for most entries and even some general descriptive material.

A Dictionary of American English on Historical Principles (University of Chicago Press, 1965). William Craigie's dictionary, known as the *D.A.E.*, is the American equivalent of the *Oxford English Dictionary*. Consult it for the complete history of words having American origins (identified by a plus sign): when, how, and in what form each word entered the language, as well as all changes in spelling, meaning, and usage that have occurred. Although it is an excellent resource, this four-volume set is somewhat dated.

Funk & Wagnalls New Standard Dictionary of the English Language (Funk & Wagnalls, 1963). Comparable to *Webster's,* this dictionary emphasizes contemporary usage, "*all the live words* of the English language," so much so that it even lists current meanings first.

Oxford English Dictionary on Historical Principles (Clarendon Press, 1973). The *O.E.D.* supplies "the meaning, origin, and history of English words" in general use from the thirteenth century to the present day. In addition to providing the same kinds of data as the *D.A.E.,* this twelve-volume dictionary lists a series of quotations for each word to illustrate its evolution from the first known occurrence in the literature to modern usage.

Webster's Third New International Dictionary of the English Language, Unabridged (Merriam-Webster, 1986). The oldest and best-known of American dictionaries, with the largest number of entries as well, *Webster's Third* dismayed purists by opting for a descriptive approach rather than prescribing proper—or even preferred—usage. All criticisms aside, the *Third* did add 100,000 new words or meanings to those of the second edition.

American Heritage Dictionary of the English Language (American Heritage and Houghton Mifflin, 1978). Applauded for its readability, this smaller dictionary arranges the definitions with the central meaning of the word first, takes care to explain shades of differences between synonyms, and includes many apt quotations from literature for illustration.

The Random House Dictionary of the English Language, Second Edition (Random House, 1987). An abridged dictionary, this volume limits both the number of entries and the length of definitions (sacrificing information on word origins) but makes an effort to include new words and current meanings; it is an easy dictionary to use.

Specialized Dictionaries

Although the field of informal English is narrowing as more and more lexicographers admit popular, if improper, usage into the standard dictionaries, scholars still find room to collect and describe unconventional words. Others compile volumes for purposes other than general reference (e.g., to index synonyms). The following list opens with a book that addresses the whole sticky issue of correct usage.

American Usage and Style: The Consensus (Van Nostrand Reinhold, 1980). Roy H. Copperud has collected and compared the opinions of experts from Theodore Bernstein (*The Careful Writer,* Atheneum, 1965) to the English scholar H. W. Fowler (*A Dictionary of Modern English Usage,* 2d ed., Oxford University Press, 1965) to provide a useful overview of the various judgments on proper usage. An example:

> **anyplace** Disapproved by Bernstein and Bryant as colloquial for *anywhere,* accepted by Fowler as a U.S. usage, and considered standard by Evans and Flesch. Among the dictionaries, Webster and American Heritage accept it as standard, but Random House calls it informal. Here, as in other instances when the authorities fall out, the writer may safely make his own decision.

New Dictionary of American Slang (Harper & Row, 1986). The compilers of this dictionary had as their objective a volume "that points out who uses slang and what flavor it conveys." They identify all slang used in the United States as American without regard to its origin or use in other countries.

Dictionary of Slang and Unconventional English, Eighth Edition (Macmillan, 1984). Originally published in 1937, with subsequent "addenda" collected in a second volume, this dictionary reflects Eric Partridge's scholarly interest in word origins, but this purpose could not quite succeed in avoiding the censure of school library committees. Asterisks mark objectionable words.

Roget's International Thesaurus (St. Martin's, 1977). The most recent editors of Peter Mark Roget's 1852 book of synonyms and antonyms had a better understanding than he did of the needs of both general readers and specialists. The volume's over 250,000 entries are organized in an easy-to-find and readable index.

Webster's New Dictionary of Synonyms (Merriam-Webster, 1978). This large volume includes both unusual and commonly used words with their identical or nearly identical meanings, making careful distinctions among the multiple meanings of single words.

Encyclopedias

Although any in-depth article requires research far beyond what encyclopedias offer, writers can get a general idea of their subject by consulting these compendiums of knowledge. Carefully selected authorities write most encyclopedia articles, and the major publishers attempt to keep their sets up to date by issuing yearbooks.

Collier's Encyclopedia (Collier-Macmillan, 1989). Determinedly modern, with its large print, pictures, and contemporary focus, this twenty-four-volume set is distrusted by scholars but is a favorite of reference librarians because it is so "fact conscious."

Encyclopedia Americana International Edition (Americana Corporation, 1980). This thirty-volume set gives particular attention to American places, organizations, and institutions and boasts an uncommon series of articles tracing human history.

Encyclopaedia Brittanica (Encyclopaedia Britannica, Inc., 1983). The fifteenth edition of this encyclopedia comprises three parts: a one-volume expanded table of contents and index; a ten-volume compendium of short articles, including digest versions of the articles in the remaining volumes; and a nineteen-volume "Macropaedia" containing articles of around five pages each, written by respected authorities for the intelligent layperson. This readable and innovative set may reshape the entire industry.

The Concise Columbia Encyclopedia (Columbia University Press, 1983). Despite the small print and constricted articles, this one-volume desk encyclopedia is the most convenient quick reference around.

Lincoln Library of Essential Information (Frontier Press, 1976). This little-known collection, although organized for self-education, is a useful source of concise information on literature, fine arts, music, education, and biography.

Biographical Resources

Dictionaries and indexes of biographical material can be overwhelming in scope. Some run to twenty or more volumes, and others grow by periodic issues that are often bound into annual volumes. Not listed here is a set of companion volumes published by R. R. Bowker citing the careers of many college and university professors.

Biography Index (Wilson, 1946–, quarterly). Similar to *Reader's Guide,* this index covers biographical articles in current books and 1,500 periodicals.

Contemporary Authors (Gale Research, 1962–, semiannual). Limited to living authors and continually updated, this collection includes many authors without published biographies and those who have written sparingly or in obscure fields.

Current Biography (Wilson, 1940–, monthly). Current news makers appear in informal word portraits, often with accompanying photographs.

Dictionary of American Biography (Scribner's, 1928–1973, with supplements). With a reputation as the greatest of American biographical dictionaries, the twenty-volume *D.A.B.* assesses scholars, politicians, scientists—all Americans who have made significant contributions and are no longer living.

Dictionary of National Biography (Smith, Elder, 1885–1901, with supplements). This monument of biographical scholarship, originally 63 volumes, focuses on over thirty thousand deceased citizens of Great Britain and its former colonies.

Index to Women of the World from Ancient to Modern Times (F. W. Faxon, 1970). This index contains nearly one thousand biographies touching on some chief contributions of women through recorded history.

National Cyclopedia of American Biography (White, 1898–1986, with a current series for living persons). This comprehensive series indexes not only biographical articles but also names, events, and other items cited in those biographies.

The New York Times Obituaries Index, 1868–1968 (New York Times, 1970). This useful resource is a cumulative index to obituaries that have been printed in the *Times.*

Webster's Biographical Dictionary (Merriam-Webster, 1976). Ranging from simple identifications to longer profiles, this volume is convenient for checking names, dates, and places of birth.

Who's Who (St. Martin's, 1849–, annual). The original model for *Who's Who,* this British edition provides short biographies of distinguished living citizens of Great Britain and a few other countries.

Who's Who in America (Marquis, 1899/1900–, biennial). This standard reference on notable living Americans presents concise, fact-filled biographies and current addresses; the same publisher also brings out a biennial edition of *Who's Who of American Women.*

Yearbooks and Almanacs

Canadian Almanac and Directory (Copp Clark, 1847–, annual). Adamantly Canadian, this almanac misses little of its targeted subject—from abbreviations to zoological gardens.

The Europa Year Book (Europa Publications, 1959–, annual). Issued in two tightly packed volumes, this reference opens with information on the United Nations and other international organizations, then arranges data about each country of the world alphabetically by country, ranging from an introductory survey to a list of universities.

Information Please Alamanc (Simon & Schuster, 1947–, annual). Featuring wide coverage of statistics in geography, U.S. government, and biography, this imaginatively edited almanac is a useful supplement to practically any book of facts.

Statistical Abstract of the United States (Government Printing Office, 1878–, annual). A digest of the findings of all statistical agencies, both public and some private, in the United States. Another publication, *Historical Statistics of the United States, Colonial Times to 1957* (Government Printing Office, 1960) documents early records; Fairfield Publishers came out with an updated version in 1965. Also, starting in 1967, the U.S. Bureau of the Census has issued a biennial summary of statistics on the United States titled *Pocket Data Book.*

Whitaker's Almanac (Whitaker, 1869–, annual). The British counterpart to the American *World Almanac,* this collection is an excellent source of statistics on Great Britain and the Commonwealth, although its focus on such items as orders of knighthood betrays its British origins.

World Almanac and Book of Facts (Newspaper Enterprise Association, 1868–, annual). Perhaps the most popular reference in the United States, this famous collection of miscellany is invaluable as a general quick-reference resource.

Books of Quotations

Bartlett's Familiar Quotations (Little, Brown, 1991). This famous list of sayings and writings ranges from ancient to modern times. Its chronological arrangement by author can be baffling, but the index helps.

Home Book of Quotations (Dodd, Mead, 1967). More comprehensive than *Bartlett's,* this collection of over 50,000 quotations is arranged alphabetically by subject. The author index, which also references all cited quotations, provides the name of the person quoted and birth and death dates.

Altases and Gazetteers

Columbia Lippincott Gazetteer of the World (Columbia University Press, 1979). This notable geographical dictionary provides an exhaustive list of place names and geographical features around the world, with pronunciations and variant spellings as well as general information on each location.

Encyclopaedia Britannica World Atlas International (Encyclopaedia Britannica, Inc., 1980). Scholarly, up-to-date, a convenient size, this is perhaps the best atlas for everyday use. It includes sketches of world political geography, comparative world distribution maps, and tables summarizing the geopolitico-economic makeup of each country.

Rand McNally Commercial Atlas and Marketing Guide (Rand McNally, 1972–, annual). This annually revised atlas offers large, detailed, easy-to-use maps, with excellent treatment of the states and outlying possessions of the United States.

Books of Miscellany

The American Book of Days, Third Edition (Wilson, 1978). This book-calendar of celebrations includes religious and historical holidays, famous American birthdays, local festivals, and odd facts; an index lists entries by topic.

Book of Days: A Miscellany of Popular Antiquities (Chambers, 1899). This two-volume calendar set covers customs and holidays and unusual information, primarily in Britain—good for browsing.

Famous First Facts (Wilson, 1981). This compilation (the original edition and its supplement) lists the first occurrence of practically everything: athletic feats, discoveries, and bizarre events.

The Guinness Book of Records (Guinness Superlatives, Ltd., 1990). Originally published as a Guinness promotion piece for pubs, this collection of the mosts, leasts, longests, shortests, and so on, has become a best-seller in both Britain and the United States (where it is titled *The Guinness Book of World Records*).

What Happened When (Washburn, 1966). This diverting volume lists by day a selection of historical and human interest events, primarily from the nineteenth and twentieth centuries.

Book Indexes and Lists

Book Review Digest (Wilson, 1905–, annual). Similar to *Reader's Guide,* this digest skillfully condenses critical opinion from reviews in a range of general American and British periodicals. It virtually ignores, however, avant-garde publications and literary magazines.

Book Review Index (Gale Research, 1965–, annual). More comprehensive than the *Book Review Digest,* this index lists reviews from nearly two hundred journals, without excerpts or condensations. Citations are indexed by the name of the author whose work is reviewed.

Books in Print (R. R. Bowker, 1948–, annual). A widely used reference, this two-volume set lists all the books in print in the United States by author and title, with a companion two-volume index arranged by subject.

An Index to Book Reviews in the Humanities (Phillip Thompson, 1960–, annual). This book is similar to *Book Review Index* but covers many more reviews from nearly seven hundred popular and scholarly journals.

Literary Market Place (R. R. Bowker, 1940–, annual). A business directory of American publishers that identifies not only the publisher's chief executives and editors but also its specialties. This book also lists almost any agency or service useful in placing or promoting literary property.

Paperbound Books in Print (R. R. Bowker, 1955–, three times annually). Composed of issues of *The Month Ahead, PBIP* indexes current paperbacks by author and title with a selective subject index.

Publisher's Weekly (R. R. Bowker, 1955–, weekly). A good source for information on recently published books; each issue announces as well the publication dates of forthcoming books. Alphabetical listings provide title, publisher, date of publication, and price.

Newspaper, Magazine, and Television Indexes and Lists

Ayer Directory of Newspapers and Periodicals (N. W. Ayer and Son, 1880–). No other reference carries as much data as *Ayer's,* which gives a geographical listing of all the daily and weekly newspapers and magazines in the United States, Canada, Bermuda, Panama, and the Philippines, plus a sketch to place each publication in its local context.

Editor and Publisher International Yearbook (Editor and Publisher, 1920–, annual). This reference does an excellent job of listing and supplying basic information on the daily newspapers of the United States and Canada, with less extensive coverage of newspapers in other countries. The same company issues *Editor and Publisher Syndicate Directory,* a useful source on syndicates that lists syndicates, features by subject, and authors as an annual supplement.

Facts on File (Facts on File, Inc., weekly). An encyclopedia of current events, this loose-leaf file culls and compiles news stories from a number of metropolitan dailies; the indexes are cumulative.

The New York Times Index (New York Times, 1851–, semimonthly). This subject guide to the *Times* has an uncertain index but is useful for dating events and locating reports in other newspapers. Similar indexes are published for the *London Times,* the *Christian Science Monitor,* and the *Wall Street Journal.*

Poole's Index to Periodical Literature, 1802–1906 (Houghton Mifflin, 1891). This pioneer index of periodicals from 1802 is virtually the only reference of its kind for the nineteenth century.

Public Affairs Information Service Bulletin (PAIS, Inc., 1915–, annual). Similar to *Readers' Guide, PAIS* is a selective index, arranged by subject, of articles in the loose category of "public affairs."

Readers' Guide to Periodical Literature (Wilson, 1900–, bimonthly). Although it is a valuable index of the contents of over one hundred general magazines, this guide does exclude some quality magazines. It appears in paperback cumulations and later in bound volumes.

Social Sciences and Humanities Index (Wilson, 1907–). Originally a *Reader's Guide* supplement, then an international index, this source now focuses on the more analytic publications.

Television News Index and Abstracts (Vanderbilt University, 1972–, monthly). Since August 1968, Vanderbilt has videotaped the evening news broadcasts of the three major networks. This Vanderbilt Television News Archive also includes related news documentaries. This index is a guide to that collection—indispensable for research into network news.

Ulrich's International Periodicals Directory (R. R. Bowker, 1932–). *Ulrich's* list of current periodicals, index to new periodicals, and cross-referenced list of titles and subjects are of particular value for their worldwide scope.

Willing's Press Guide (Willing, 1874–, annual). This publication, along with *Newspaper Press Directory and Advertisers' Guide* (Benn Bros., 1946–, annual), provides a good overview of the British press.

Government Publications

The United States government publishes a huge number of books and pamphlets, few of which find their way into lists of books in print or card catalogs. Several guides exist to these publications. Early publications can be tracked in the two-volume *Comprehensive Index to the Publications of the United States Government: 1881–1893* and the twenty-five-volume *Catalog of Public Documents,* both published by the Government Printing Office.

Monthly Catalog of United States Government Publications (Government Printing Office, 1895–). This is the most comprehensive catalog of current publications, with annual and cumulative indexes to provide a guide to publications.

Subject Guide to Major United States Government Publications (American Library Association, 1980). This volume lists hundreds of useful publications.

PUTTING IT ALL TOGETHER

Research is the raw material from which articles are made. Skimpy research leads to equally thin articles. Novelist John Cheever once claimed that he could detect a single glass of sherry in a writer's prose; insufficient research is as easy to spot.

In addition to library reference materials, you will need to interview subjects, write letters, and observe and record events. Every story benefits from information that comes from such research, but it is a rare writer who can produce a top-rate story based entirely on any one of these elements alone—library work or interviews or observation.

Professionals always wonder whether they have covered all the bases, whether there might still be some important element to the story that they have overlooked. Lesser writers look instead for only enough sources to provide sufficient information on which to base the story. Beginners often carry both these tendencies to the extreme. They either become so preoccupied with doing thorough research that they miss their deadlines or, even worse, never get to their typewriters at all, or they do so little research that writing their stories is like trying to fill a balloon with a hole in it. The best approach lies somewhere in between.

Many beginning writers who have written only compositions, essays, and term papers are likely to lean too heavily on library research and their own ideas as they begin a career in journalism. And the more seasoned writer who has worked for a small paper is accustomed to the usual hectic newspaper pace and is likely to clip an old story or two, conduct a one-hour review, and then try to stretch 2,000 or 3,000 words out of these scraps. Neither method alone will work very often.

Both beginning newspaper writers and newspaper staffers trying to switch from conventional newspaper style to the longer, more demanding feature or in-depth article must accustom themselves to a new pace. They must learn the background that goes into writing lengthy articles. Legwork adds to initial, thorough library research the extra dimension achieved from multiple or repeated interviews and enhanced whenever possible by direct personal observation.

The rule for writers, beginning or professional, is that they must gather at least twice as much information as they can use. Writers who have collected more information than they need are freed from the necessity of using everything they have. They can *select,* which is the key to all successful writing. Instead of recounting both a tasteless anecdote and one that actually reveals character, they can choose seven revealing anecdotes from a stock of twelve. Instead of attempting to describe a political convention that someone has described to them, probably ineptly, they can draw on the experience of hours of watching the maneuvering on the convention floor.

Consider how Maurice Zolotow, a veteran free-lancer, researched an article on Salvatore Baccaloni, a Metropolitan Opera tenor. Zolotow began by reading eight books on opera (from *Opera, Front and Back* to *Caruso's Method of Voice Production*). Not one of the books said anything about Baccaloni; Zolotow was merely educating himself on opera in general. Next, he went backstage at the Metropolitan to get the feel of the place. Only after completing this "atmospheric research" did he begin with Baccaloni—and he began by reading everything on the tenor in clipping files of the *New York Times.*

Finally, Zolotow got around to Baccaloni himself, interviewing him six times and traveling from New York to Boston to watch him perform. Then he interviewed ten people who knew Baccaloni. Still, Zolotow did not consider himself ready to write. As usual, he devoted several days to brooding about the article, then spent a week organizing it mentally. At last, he was ready. He wrote the twenty-page first draft in three days.

Such legwork is central in writing 99 percent of all articles, and it is fun. Writers open doors that are closed to others; they meet interesting people and learn interesting things. The late James Thurber viewed legwork this way:

> If an astonished botanist produced a black evening primrose, or thought he had produced one, I spent the morning prowling his gardens. When a lady sent in word that she was getting messages from the late Walter Savage Landor in heaven, I was sent up to see what the importunate poet had on his mind. On the occasion of the arrival in town of Major Monroe of Jacksonville, Florida, who claimed to be a hundred and seventeen years old, I walked up Broadway with him while he roundly cursed the Northern dogs who jostled him, bewailing the while the passing of Bob Lee and Tom Jackson and Joe Johnston. I studied gypsies in Canarsie and generals in the Waldorf, listened to a man talk backward, and watched a blindfolded boy play ping-pong. Put it all together and I don't know what it comes to, but it wasn't drudgery.

CORRESPONDENCE

Allen Barra, while growing up in Alabama, always said, "Thank God for Mississippi!"—meaning that no matter how low Alabama ranked nationally in education and per capita income, Mississippi would surely be just a little lower.

According to Barra:

> The irony is that so much of what shaped my youth—indeed, shaped American culture in this century—came from Mississippi. I had driven through the town of Meridian countless times without stopping at the museum built in honor of the "Father of Country Music," Jimmie Rodgers, and I had passed within miles of the birthplaces of Robert Johnson, Skip James, Muddy Waters and a dozen other legendary bluesmen. William Faulkner, Tennessee Williams and Eudora Welty all came from "the most illiterate" 47,689 square miles in America.

As the poet Michael Swindle has said, Mississippi is to America what Ireland was to the British Empire: "Woefully behind the norm in virtually everything held in value by civilized standards, and producing more genius per capita than Athens under Pericles."

This story reveals that it is possible for talented writers to come from rather impoverished backgrounds. Although many places lack valuable resources, innovative minds can compensate through various channels. On some occasions, much of an article may be researched through correspondence. In one instance, a writer was gathering information on an international scholarship program that brought highly placed officials and businesspersons in mid-career to the United States. The writer had an opportunity to interview the director of the program, who had large files of reports written by the foreign visitors, but the visitors themselves had returned to their homes. There was nothing easily at hand that would help bring the article to life.

The only solution short of traveling to many countries for interviews, which would have made the article prohibitively expensive, was correspondence. It worked. Most of the visitors described in detailed letters how study and travel in the United States had enhanced their skills and their opportunities back home. Interviews with the foreigners would have improved the article, but with the director's help, the writer was able to stitch together their correspondence and his notes on interviews into a readable report.

Perhaps writers should use correspondence more often than they do, but it is seldom central to research. Most writers have found that they can set up interview appointments and gather a few facts by letter, but the flavor and anecdotes that enliven writing are difficult to collect through correspondence. Most often, letters are valuable at the beginning and at the end of research. A writer who has developed the idea for an article can write letters to ask for interviews and, in some instances, ask for return letters that will help establish whether there is a sound basis for the piece. He or she can also write to ask for an opportunity to telephone, and this is usually wise; phoning out of the blue—without writing a letter first—often catches a source unprepared and busy, with thoughts on other matters. At the other end of the writing process, letters may be written to ask for facts that were not gathered during the interviewing and observing period. No matter how carefully a writer plans an article, he or she is likely to find an overlooked item or two. A letter and sometimes a phone call usually help. They may even bring a response that adds a dimension the subject failed to mention during interviews.

How library research, interviewing, observation, and correspondence fit together to produce an article is illustrated by the researching and writing of "What the World Owes to the Gardens at Kew." Much of the research went into determining whether Kew Gardens would actually make a story. The notion that it was more than a horticultural showplace came from a passage in a travel book that mentioned as an aside that King George III, who had provoked the American colonies to revolution, could at least be credited with having helped to establish the gardens. The king had supported British horticulturists who hoped to start a vast glass conservatory for acclimating and upgrading plants from Britain's tropical colonies. They had invented a miniature portable greenhouse that enabled them to keep plants and cuttings from dehydrating during long voyages. Thus, Kew became the incubator of great new industries: the rubber saplings transplanted from South America to Kew to Malaysia; the pineapple plantings of Ceylon; the "horticultural booty," as it was known, that launched sisal, cinchona for quinine, oil palms, ginger, allspice, and numerous trees prized for their beauty.

After the editors approved the idea, the writer studied Kew Gardens in encyclopedias, in horticultural books, and in botanical articles located through *Readers' Guide.* When he arrived at Kew Gardens, he was amused to discover that neither the director nor his staff could answer some of the key questions. They sent him to Kew's botanical library to rummage through scrapbooks and records going back more than a century. This yielded the gist of the story—Kew's great usefulness to mankind during its first half-century.

Then the writer toured the extensive greenhouses, some more than a century old, to observe how Kew created artificial climates suitable for cultivating plants from all over the world. He thought he had everything for his article when he left England to return home to the United States. But when the editors worked over the manuscript, a few more questions came up. Back the writer went to correspondence to wrap up the assignment.

All writers develop their own research methods, of course, and alter them with the varying demands of different pieces. But it is especially important to you as a beginner to practice all these research techniques so that you can call on any or all of them.

Exercises

1. Do research in the main library and write answers to the following questions:
   a. What is the meaning of "acupuncture"?
   b. How many syllables are there in "enthusiastic"?
   c. Which of the dictionaries in the library list the consultants who determine what the words mean?

2. Do research in the main library and find the answers to these questions, noting the name of the book and the page number(s):
   a. What is the difference between the atomic bomb and the hydrogen bomb?
   b. What scientist headed up the development of the atomic bomb at the Los Alamos Scientific Laboratory?

3. Using the *Readers' Guide to Periodical Literature,* research a topic of your choice. Use at least five sources listed in the *Readers' Guide* to write a brief report of no more than 1,000 words. Include full references of your sources.

SOME JOURNALISTIC FORMS

*I never desire to converse with a man who
has written more than he has read.*

SAMUEL JOHNSON

L ord Chesterfield said, "Learning is acquired by reading books, but the much more necessary learning, the knowledge of the world, is only to be acquired by reading men, and studying all the various editions of them."

These words of wisdom are heeded by the editors of many magazines, who try to learn as much as they can about the people who read them. Because of the specialized nature of most magazines, magazine writers usually know exactly what kinds of persons will read their articles. Readership surveys indicating the sex, age, education, income, and interests of the magazine's average reader enable writers to compose as though they are addressing particular individuals. In contrast, newspaper writers must usually aim their articles at the broadest possible audience.

The problem of trying to offer something for everyone, while making each reader feel that his or her particular interests are being covered, is one that is especially important for newspaper feature writers and editors. To a certain extent, the straight news content of a paper is dictated by its editorial policy of covering international, national, or local news. But there are no easy rules for creating feature coverage. Feature articles are often linked to news stories, but they may also exist independently on the basis of interesting subject matter. This is where writers and editors exercise their leeway to choose subjects that will interest the range of people in their audience.

Depending on the size of a newspaper, reporters may do much more than write articles. At a large metropolitan daily, their only task may be to cover a certain beat, but at a small weekly paper, reporters may have other roles to fill. Here is how Jeanette Germain, a reporter at the *Mountain Express* in Ketchum, Idaho, described her job:

> We marvel at the time everyone [on dailies] has to stand around and talk about the nuances of their work. They spend hours on ethics, days on stories, weeks on personalities. Can it really be like that on daily newspapers? we ask.

It's not like that here in Ketchum, Idaho. We don't have that kind of time. We've got too much to cover and too few people to spread around. The woman who takes classifieds also answers the phone. The photographer works on sports pages and does subscriptions. Everyone, from the office help to the editor, takes turns cleaning the bathrooms, driving the paper 100 miles to the printer, and collating for delivery at 6 A.M. on Thursday mornings. Collating is about the only time we have to chat with one another. Every other day of the week, we are running.

Deadline fever starts Monday mornings. I wake up before the alarm rings and immediately start setting priorities. Within the next two and a half days, I will have to gather the information, write and illustrate at least a dozen stories. I have to decide which stories deserve some time and which do not. I must produce a few hard news stories, a few pieces of fluff, some tidbit fillers, and visuals or photos to accompany them. I can't hesitate to dispatch a routine story. I have to know how to locate a source or information without delay. The editor won't give me assignments or babysit me through the upcoming edition. She has other things to do. I know I must fill, fill, fill.

By Wednesday afternoon, the writing is done. I pitch in to help with proofreading, layout and the opaquing of page negatives. A 64-page tabloid is complete by 4 or 5 P.M. We sweep up and go home for one short evening of rest before the weekly schedule starts all over again.

People ask me why I work like this, in a pokey little town where the pay is low and the winters long. They ask me if I'm hiding from the real world of competitive journalism. Am I afraid that I won't measure up? Am I wasting my training and talent?

I don't think so. The response to my work here is direct and immediate. The phone rings every Thursday morning as soon as the paper is on the streets. People call with compliments, complaints, additional information, or another question. When I've made a mistake, I hear about it. When I've touched someone's life, he stops me on the street to tell me. Petitions appear when the community as a whole responds to something I've written. I love the feedback. I don't think it would come as easily in a bigger community.

Feature writing is just one of many tasks Germain completes in her weekly schedule. She usually writes features on Thursday or Friday, because on those days she has more time to devote to them. Like Germain, most reporters must decide for themselves which stories are suitable for feature slants, then take enough time to both research and write the stories carefully.

In discussing how they do this, we should consider why newspaper feature articles exist in the first place. Without them, newspapers would be quite dull! Feature articles are published to liven up the papers and to provide relief from the somewhat dry tone of most news stories. They fill our need to know more about the world than the standard formula for news stories provides. This chapter discusses how feature articles differ from other types of newspaper stories and how they fill the information gap in news coverage.

JOURNALISTIC FORMS

Most newspaper staff writers are primarily reporters. Often, they must be facile at writing in many journalistic forms. First, let us review briefly the various types of news writing.

"The last thing that we find in writing is to know what we must put first."

BLAISE PASCAL

Straight News Reports

The straight news report—also known as the objective report—is a timely account of an event. A newspaper report of a speech is usually straight news. Because it covers only what happened during a brief period, straight news provides a valuable focus—valuable also because it makes such limited demands on reporters that they can come close to presenting an objective report of verifiable fact. Straight news is written by a formula that requires the first few sentences (in some cases, the first sentence alone) to report at least the who-what-when-where-why of an event, with the details strung out in descending order of importance. Because this formula gives reporters little leeway for self-expression, and especially because reporters are instructed neither to editorialize nor to use words that even hint at an opinion, the report usually lives up to its name—"straight." For example, here is the lead from a straight news report:

> The Washington Teachers' Union yesterday agreed not to strike the District of Columbia schools following an agreement worked out in a four-hour meeting in the office of Mayor Walter E. Washington.
> The union had threatened to begin its walkout Tuesday, but after yesterday's session, William Simons, president of the teachers' union, said, "School will be open Tuesday and every day. . . ."

But if writing according to the formula prevents reporters from editorializing, it also prevents them from helping readers understand events. Because straight news isolates a small slice of life at a particular time and reports none of the surrounding facts that might provide meaning, it is usually superficial. For that reason, many reporters argue that nothing like the full truth can emerge from such reports. They are aware, of course, that some events are not *worth* more time and attention than a straight news report offers, but their arguments for more complete reports on important events are the principal reason that other forms of news writing have emerged.

Depth Reports

The depth report takes a step beyond straight news. Instead of merely trying to mirror the highlights of an event, the reporter gathers additional information that is independent of the event but related to it. A reporter who covers a speech on medical practices in China may consult experts and reference sources, then present the speaker's words in a larger framework. In some cases, additional information is placed in the report on the speech; in others, it is reported separately. In either case, depth reporting calls for transmitting information, not the reporter's opinion. Verifiable fact is as basic to depth reporting as it is to straight news reporting.

Although a writer's opinions have no place in a depth report, the facts gathered may rebut or refute the speaker—in which case the speaker or his or her supporters may charge that a report is slanted. Perhaps it is. The crucial decision has been *which* of the many available facts a reporter uses to build the larger framework, and this decision may create bias.

This depth report was written by a student. Notice how he examines criticism of lawyers without voicing his own opinions about it:

> American ire is flaring up at lawyers. Across America lawyers increasingly find themselves the butt of jokes and the object of sneers. There is this notion that lawyers exist in overabundance and are overconfident, overbearing and, worst of all, overpaid. Americans are beginning to strike out.
>
> Lawyers often demonstrate characteristics that disturb the average, middle-class American. They earn well over the minimum/hourly wage—and make no secret about it. In some states lawyers' fees are so exorbitant their bill replaces the pleasure of winning a case with a considerable amount of financial pain and suffering.
>
> They have a jargon of their own. Black wording on a white page never looks so intimidating than when it is legal lingo. No matter how many Nobel Prizes a physicist may have won or how many Pulitzer Prizes a writer may have collected, both the physicist, the writer and everyone in between must call a lawyer to interpret anything with a legal tone. This makes most of us feel helpless and dependent . . . and the last 20 years has seen an increase of legal lingo in our lives.
>
> The bombastic lawyer, called a shyster even in polite company, who worked his way through law school selling cars is the contemporary villain. Even politicians, many of them former lawyers, are beginning to lawyer-bash. Lawyer jokes and jabs are common in political speeches. Lawyers are blamed for syphoning money away from more productive uses and the legal profession itself is berated for swiping our brightest students from science, manufacturing, and engineering.
>
> Three congressmen from California are going farther than humor and ridicule. They are sponsoring a California ballot initiative that responds to the people's outcry. Attempting to reform the tort system by cutting down the number of lawsuits that clog up the legal system, this ballot initiative would hold a plaintiff's lawyers financially responsible for pursuing a "malicious" or "frivolous" suit. The interesting twist is that two of the congressmen sponsoring the initiative are lawyers.

Interpretive Reports

Interpretive reports—also known as *news analyses*—are another step beyond straight news. These usually focus on an issue, a problem, or a controversy. Here, too, the substance is verifiable fact, not opinion. But instead of presenting facts as straight news or a depth report and hoping that the facts will speak for themselves, the interpretive reporter clarifies, explains, analyzes. The interpretive report usually focuses on *why:* Why did the president take that trip, appoint that person, make that statement? What is the real meaning of the event?

In this interpretive report, the writer explains why small investors are suffering:

> Negotiated commission rates, begun on Wall Street on May 1, have resulted in almost no savings whatsoever for the ordinary investor buying or selling stock.
>
> There are some special plans offered to the investor, such as Merrill Lynch's "Share-Builder Plan" or Paine Webber's "Alpha Account." But over all, the brokerage industry has preferred not to negotiate with small investors.
>
> There are several reasons for this reluctance. For one thing, small investors have little negotiating clout. . . .

Whatever their intentions, reporters who arc given the freedom to interpret events may inadvertently offer their opinion; they are always in danger of using words that steer their readers toward their particular impressions and beliefs. Because clarification, explanation, and analysis require that reporters weigh and filter facts, the interpreter approaches the reporting process much more personally than do other reporters. And because an interpretation is not written by formula, reporters have latitude that makes it easier for them to disguise personal opinions.

Investigative Reports

Investigative reporting, which some call "muckraking," is the practice of opening closed doors and closed mouths. As in interpretive reporting, the focus is on problems, issues, and controversies. In fact, interpretive and investigative reports are the same in cases in which the reporter must unearth hidden information in order to clarify, explain, and analyze. Normally, though, interpretive reporters have relatively little trouble finding facts because they are endeavoring to explain public events, and they can usually find many sources who are happy to help them. (In fact, the danger in all reporting is that a source may want to provide information that will serve its own private interests.) In contrast, the investigative reporter must try to discover facts that have been hidden for a purpose—often an illegal or unethical purpose.

In this excerpt from an investigative piece, the writer sifts many reports, talks to many government investigators, then writes:

> Federal agents, conducting a sweeping investigation here and in other ports, are piecing together a picture of corruption in the handling, grading, and weighing of grain that raises questions about the quality of grain shipments to foreign buyers.
>
> Seven privately employed inspectors who are licensed by the Department of Agriculture have been indicted thus far in an investigation with charges of bribery for certification of ships for fitness to carry grain. Five of the inspectors pleaded guilty to accepting bribes.
>
> Agents conducting a continuing investigation have been taking secret testimony. . . .

Features

Features differ from news primarily in their intent. Whereas a news report ordinarily presents information that is likely to concern readers, a feature is usually designed to entertain. The feature reporter casts a wide net in search for facts, sometimes pulling in and using things a news reporter would consider frivolous. The feature writer's report provides a reading experience that depends more'on style, grace, and humor than on the importance of the information. This difference is reflected in the fact that those who produce features exclusively are called "feature writers," not "reporters." Slowly, though, features are becoming less distinguishable from some of the other forms of news writing.

Here is the lead of a feature:

> Tens of thousands of black and Puerto Rican teenagers in New York City are "piling up at the bottom" of the recession. With no jobs and no prospect of jobs, they are abandoning their dreams of education, and the belief in the institutions of a civilized society, and are slipping back toward the drugs and hustling of "the street."
>
> "I'm up at 5:00, going places, getting rejected," said one South Bronx teenager who has a small daughter. "I'm not a moron, but it feels degrading."
>
> "Once they know I never worked and have no skills—no job," said Migdalia Colon, 20 years old, also of the South Bronx. "That's not right. We need a chance."
>
> "Best that you can do is hang out, get out," said a young black woman. "All that's out there is reefer. Either smoke it or sell it, or both."
>
> Anger, frustration, hopelessness. . . .

This story differs from the usual feature that appears in many small newspapers. In metropolitan newspapers, journalistic forms overlap. Traces of depth or investigative reporting may appear in a feature, sometimes quite strongly. An interpretive report may have both feature and investigative elements. Often, a feature may seem to be weighted as heavily with matters of concern as with matters of light interest.

Here is the lead of a feature that focuses on a woman's plight in a dangerous neighborhood:

> Dorelle Roddy, of East Palo Alto, California, is a woman whose personal crusade against drugs in her neighborhood has led drug dealers to attack her property and person. Despite the violence and threats, Mrs. Roddy has continued her work under the 24-hour supervision of the Guardian Angels organization.
>
> Roddy and her battle against drugs stand in stark contrast to the current crop of issue-hungry politicians, most of whom are far removed from the real problem. They are busy pontificating about theoretical solutions to the drug problem and offering such inane and irrelevant advice as "Just say no."
>
> But Roddy actually lives in a drug-infested neighborhood. She witnesses the effects of drug use daily. She has taken dramatic action in

her effort to battle her environment. She has put herself in danger and has continued her struggle after being victimized by drug dealers.

USING JOURNALISTIC FORMS

Consider this description of how the same subject could be approached for an article in a campus daily, using any of several different journalistic forms.

Imagine that university administrators, discovering that too little dormitory space is available for all the students who want to live on campus, have leased 100 trailer homes and have parked them on the edge of the dormitory area to house 400 students.

Assigned by the editor of the campus paper to write a straight news report, you as reporter would quote the speech or the press release in which the administration announced the establishment of "Trailer Dorm." If student leaders spoke for or against the conditions of trailer living, you would quote them as well. If students held a protest rally, you would report its highlights dispassionately.

Assigned to write a depth report, you might gather opinions by questioning students, compare home campus housing with that at a nearby university, interview housing officials, or report the results of library research. The limits of your resources are marked only by the imagination you bring to your research.

Assigned to write an interpretive report, you might interview administrators to determine why they decided to lease trailers rather than make other arrangements and interview student leaders to determine why they support or oppose the trailer park. Again, you as reporter can use many approaches to gathering information to help clarify, explain, and analyze.

Assigned to write an investigative report by an editor who suspects that the administration was lax in not planning for more dormitory space, or that an administrator's brother owns the trailers, you must interview widely and adroitly and check financial records. The most difficult kind of journalism, investigative reporting requires a researcher who is imaginative, industrious, patient, and aggressive. You must write a hard-fact report, not speculation.

Assigned to write a feature, you would look for the color and flavor of trailer life. Do trailer residents live differently from other students? How? Have they painted their homes in wild colors? Are they planting gardens? Who does the cooking—and with what results?

Read this article, written by a student, and consider which journalistic forms he used. Did he combine many of them? Can you find examples of color? Is there evidence of investigative or interpretive work? Would you categorize this article as a feature?

First dates, blind dates, singles bars, and double dates are Greek to a Taiwanese, who rarely dates at all. Several [other] non-Westerners don't date either. And if they do, it's dating with a difference. This article looks at what dating and sex mean to college students from different countries and cultures.

When Deng Xiaoping opened China's doors to the West five years back, he certainly had no intention of putting sex on the import list. But once the reins are loosened, who's to say what the horse will bring home, and before you can say gee whiz, it's 1987 and Chinese authorities are spending sleepless nights over the same question *Ladies' Home Journal* asked readers in July 1949: Has "going steady" become a national problem?

It's fast becoming one, says Li Lubo, a Knight Journalism fellow at Stanford University. Although dating is prohibited in high schools, all of which are coeducational, the influence of popular culture (a euphemism for sitcoms, soaps, movies, and junk romances) and the spread of knowledge about birth control are fast eroding traditional values, sexual mores, and lifestyles.

"Kids of 14 and 15 years sit in front of the TV watching love stories; it's natural for them to learn about dating," says Lubo, allowing a teeny-weeny note of bewilderment into his voice. The bewilderment is natural, because dating is not a homespun concept in China, much like in other parts of the world.

But dating is taking hold in Chinese soil, and more youth, says *Newsweek,* now "cruise the streets looking for heat." And what is more, says Lubo, they're dating "for fun," not to shop for a spouse, a concept that is as alien to the Chinese as drinking Kamikaze shots. So why are they doing it? Perhaps as a reaction to the austerity of Chinese universities, says Lubo. "Girls with high hopes and romantic ideas find [university] boring."

The dating game, if it begins in high school, is littered with obstacles. Students caught indulging in the "immoral" pleasures of the flesh may be expelled or sent to juvenile delinquent schools, or even to labor reform schools, says Lubo. And those who indulge in the lesser sin of falling in love incur peer and parent pressure. "They make you feel uneasy," Lubo explains.

It doesn't become much easier in the universities. Although Lubo cites poll figures which show that 80 percent of college women are all for dating, hurdles loom large. One of the biggest: lack of one's own living space. Living with one's family curbs premarital sex as effectively as thinking Victorian. "You cannot do it on the streets," says a pragmatic Lubo.

But what can be done on the streets is done. For instance, Shanghai couples squeeze into park benches along the river at night. "Each couple sits at the end of a bench talking quietly and secretly, and ignoring the other end," says Lubo, who doesn't say if they do anything else.

Lubo's reticence to talk about the sexual lives of singles is echoed by Lie-Yea Cheng, an electrical engineering major who comes from a country that was one with China fifty years back—Taiwan. Cheng says she never talked about sex with her friends when she was an undergraduate in Taipei, Taiwan's capital city.

Cheng, a petite five-feet-two, tells how Taiwanese films avoid showing sex or nudity.

THE FEATURE SLANT

There is one rule for all features: the story must be endlessly interesting. The feature is as important in the middle as it was at the beginning, as important at the end as it was in the middle. You must tell your story clearly and simply. It must be readable. The following guidelines for feature writing should help make all of your writing clear and readable.

Sentence structure   This is the basis of readability in nearly all sentences. Usually, sentences should be constructed as follows: subject, verb, object. That may sound simple, but many sentences begin with clauses or adjectives. Beginning writers often like to twist their sentences. They should do this rarely, for effect. The overarching rule is that most but not all sentences should be as simple and direct as possible.

Sentence length   Generally, the shorter sentences are, the more readable they will be. It is true, of course, that if you write for *Harper's,* for example, you can write in a more complicated form—as long as you can control it. But if you write for newspapers or for widely circulated magazines, as a rule you must keep your sentences reasonably short.

Concreteness   Wherever possible, you should use concrete words instead of abstract words. The following excerpt of the abstractions of James M. Landis, who was an assistant to President Franklin Roosevelt, and the revision made by the president is a good illustration. Landis wrote:

> Such preparations shall be made as will completely obscure all Federal buildings and non-Federal buildings occupied by the Federal Government during an air raid for any period of time from visibility by reason of internal or external illumination. Such obscuration may be obtained either by blackout construction or by termination of the illumination. This will, of course, require that in building areas in which production must continue during the blackout, construction must be provided that internal illumination may continue.

President Roosevelt said to rewrite it this way:

> Tell them that in buildings where they have to keep the work going to put something across the window. In buildings where they can afford to let the work stop for a while, turn out the lights.

Verbs   Making the verb do the work of adjectives is always preferable. A verb expresses action, and if it is carefully chosen, it can even describe personality. For example, all the reader learns from "The four men were on hand in the office" is the number and location of the men. But if you say, "The four men sprawled in the office," you have conveyed a great deal more about the men's personalities.

Adjectives   The fewer adjectives a writer uses, the more readable the style. For example, "The sharp-eyed, gray-haired general's sharp eyes flashed as he got up and shook his head" could be better put this way: "The general's sharp eyes flashed as he rose and shook his gray head."

Story structure All beginning writers are told that a lead must catch and hold their readers. If possible, the lead should be a startling, witty, or pithy statement. It is usually a mistake to devote the beginning to summing up a story, much as a straight news story often does. That is the death of the feature.

Transitions Learning to link the paragraphs in a way that pulls the reader on is a skill that distinguishes the professional from the amateur. After the first paragraph, what comes next? A beginning writer can learn much by studying *Time* and *Newsweek*, both of which require smooth transitions. This subject will be discussed in detail in the next chapter.

Notice how this writer used simple sentences in this interesting feature about a local event:

> This year, and for the past three years, a group of spirited students have staged a race known to them as Bay Area Road Fun, in which clues hidden in locations ranging from Santa Cruz to Vallejo direct the groups to the next clue.
>
> First held by a small clique of friends in the freshman dorm, the game has expanded to include eight teams of eight people each. All members ride in the same car and help solve the clues, which are in the form of puzzles, riddles, or tasks to complete. Each year a new person has created the course, though his identity remains a mystery until the race is over.
>
> Just to get clues in the past, participants have had to reach over the railing of the Golden Gate Bridge, imitate street singers in Berkeley and actually get a donation, and climb the large metal windmills found along the side of Highway 580 in Oakland.
>
> Perhaps the most challenging clue received was a key to a locker in the San Francisco airport. Inside the locker was a blank piece of paper. The participants had to figure out that the ink on the paper was written in an invisible metallic material that could be read only by running the paper through the airport metal detectors.
>
> There is no prize for being the first to complete the race, aside from being able to gloat about the victory for the rest of the year. Simply completing the race is a victory in itself.

THE NEW JOURNALISM

Tom Wolfe has written resignedly of the New Journalism: "Any movement, group, party, program, philosophy or theory that goes under a name with 'new' in it is just begging for trouble, of course. But it is the term that eventually caught on." It *is* the term that caught on. Much of the criticism of the New Journalism springs from adverse reactions to many who practice it. It has its unobtrusive personalities—Lillian Ross, who writes for the *New Yorker,* and Gay Talese, for example—but it has more than its share of practitioners who range from the irritating to the insufferable. Norman Mailer seems to ask to be disliked, in person and in print. Some of the young who model themselves after him—and think they model their writing on his—

blend bad manners and bad prose. But it may be that Wolfe, who is personally engaging and has done more than any other writer of the New Journalism to promote that form, is responsible for more adverse reaction than any other New Journalist.

Like the blind men examining the elephant, writers inspecting the New Journalism find it easier to describe its distinguishing characteristics than to comprehend the whole beast. This difficulty occurs partly because the work of writers who have been called New Journalists is so diverse. The group includes Tom Wolfe, Jimmy Breslin, Gloria Steinem, Norman Mailer, Joan Didion, Rex Reed, and many others with equally divergent styles. Some writers whose work has been classified as New Journalism by other practitioners adamantly refuse the label because they do not believe that their writing should be lumped together with that of others whose styles differ from their own.

One of the most vocal advocates of the New Journalism is Tom Wolfe. He has defined it as the use in "nonfiction of techniques which had been thought of as confined to the novel or the short story, to create in one form both the kind of objective reality of journalism and the subjective reality that people have always gone to the novel for."

It may be misleading to speak of the New Journalism as a "form"; it certainly is misleading if that is taken to mean a formula like the who-what-when-where-why of the news story. Rather, the New Journalism can appear

GAY TALESE

The beach in winter was dank and desolate, and the island dampened by the frigid spray of the ocean waves pounding relentlessly against the beach-front bulkheads, and the seaweed-covered beams beneath the white houses on the dunes creaked as quietly as the crabs crawling nearby.

This sentence might seem more appropriate opening a novel than introducing an autobiographical work in progress, but Gay Talese is not a novelist. Instead, his colorful imagery, powerful description, and detailed observation distinguish him as a pioneer of the New Journalism, associating him with such distinctive personages as Tom Wolfe and Lillian Ross and earning him a place among today's chief innovators.

He is a man for whom risk taking is part of the job. Not content to subject himself to the physical danger of the Mafia world while researching for his 1971 book *Honor Thy Father*, Gay Talese in 1980 voluntarily opened the secrets of his own private life to public scrutiny by including personal examples in a reveal-ing best-seller on the sexual life of Americans. To Talese, the explanation is simple:

> In everything I write I'm trying to get as close as I can to a fuller truth, using real names, real situations, not falsifying or fabricating. And I believe that if I want that from other people, I have to do the same thing myself. . . .

It is this kind of honesty and straightforwardness that characterize the majority of Talese's work and that have brought him success and critical acclaim time and time again. He has made a career of observing, describing, and revealing aspects of life that, he feels, give a clearer view of humanity than that conveyed by much journalistic writing. Using techniques generally associated with fiction, Talese endows his nonfiction with the emotional appeal of the human perspective, of life seen through the eyes of its participants.

Growing up in Ocean City, New Jersey, Gay (born Gaetano) Talese spent his childhood developing this observational

in many forms. Tom Wolfe developed his particular form by accident. Assigned to write an article for *Esquire* on custom cars, he did the research but then developed a writer's block and found that he was unable to complete the article. One of the editors of *Esquire,* Byron Dobell, told Wolfe to type his notes and hand them in so another writer could turn them into an article. Wolfe obliged him, but he wrote the notes in the form of a memo to the editor. Dobell was so pleased with it that he simply removed the "Dear Byron" salutation and published the memo as an article.

There is more to Wolfe's method, of course, than writing articles as memos, but this incident suggests the kind of subjective involvement and the kind of form that he often favors. It is informal writing that owes part of its appeal to the simple fact that it is different from the relatively formal, relatively detached writing of the past.

Here is a writer who taught Wolfe the new method. Gay Talese is one of the few journalists who have far transcended the matter-of-fact reporting that marks nearly all who pursue facts. Talese's words that follow are a reminiscence about four people whom he made subjects of profiles:*

I try to follow my subjects unobtrusively while observing them in revealing situations, noting their reactions and the reactions of others to

---

*Reprinted by permission of Gay Talese.

---

skill. Catholic and Italian in a predominately Irish Protestant neighborhood, he spent his time on the outside, watching and listening to the world around him. Autobiographical sketches published in *Esquire,* for which he is a contributing editor, show both the strength of his observational skill and the descriptive grace of his style:

Each night I went to bed dreading the next morning's ride on the bus, a rusting vehicle of a purplish-black shade that precisely matched the colors of the robes worn by the nuns who dominated the classrooms. The school's bus driver, Mr. Fitzgerald, was a crusty Dublin-born janitor who wore a tweed cap and whose breath exuded a sour blend of oatmeal and whiskey.

It is vivid description characterized by a sense of imagery and an appreciation of the full range of stimuli offered by the world. But the power of Talese's observation is not confined to what he himself has experienced; he displays similar deftness in reconstructing the lives of others, as in this description of the betrothal of his grandparents:

. . . there was a redeeming stubbornness and strength about this man that Angelina found comforting, and it was also true that gentility, sensitivity, and a flair for romance were not quintessential requisites among Italian courting couples in America at the turn of the century. Life to them was a very practical matter—and it certainly was to this widow and widower who were getting no younger in Brooklyn in 1902 . . . Angelina married Russo, and thus began a lengthy relationship during which Angelina resigned herself, with the help of prayers and her own perseverence, to the burden of being Russo's wife.

By depicting human events from the *inside,* Gay Talese manages to convey to his readers a broader conception of his subject, evoking a real world that lives and breathes all over again. More than a journalist, he is truly a *writer.*

—Alicia M. Barber

them. I attempt to absorb the whole scene, the dialogue and mood, the tension, drama, conflict, and then I try to write it all from the point of view of the persons I am writing about, even revealing whenever possible what these individuals are *thinking* during those moments that I am describing. This latter insight is not obtainable, of course, without the full cooperation of the subject, but if the writer enjoys the confidence and trust of his subjects it is possible, through interviews, by asking the right question at the right time, to learn and to report what goes on within other people's minds.

. . . My first attempt at what would be called the "new journalism" began with some of the profiles that I did for *Esquire*. In the Joe Louis piece, for example, the article begins with Louis, fatigued after three frolicsome days and nights in New York City, arriving at the Los Angeles airport and being met by his wife, a lawyer—a scene that could have led into a short story situation; later in the article, the writing style falls back on straight reportage, indicating my own uncertainty with the form at that point, but still later the approach is again scene-setting and dialogue and away from rigid reporting.

A more successful attempt at using fictional techniques for factual situations is the profile of Joshua Logan, the theatrical director. I happened to be in the theater one afternoon watching Logan rehearse his play when, suddenly, he and his star, Claudia McNeil, got into an argument that not only was more dramatic than the play itself, but revealed something of the character of Logan and Miss McNeil in ways that I could never have done had I approached the subject from the more conventional form of reporting.

While researching the Frank Sinatra piece, I also happened to be in the right place at the right time: On the night Sinatra objected to the attire of the young man playing pool in the game room of the Daisy Discotheque on Rodeo Drive in Beverly Hills, I had been standing near the bar in the other room. While I missed the opening exchange between Sinatra and the young man, I did arrive in time to hear most of what transpired; later, with the cooperation of witnesses who had heard it all, I was able to reconstruct the scene.

Sinatra was not very cooperative during my stay in Beverly Hills. I had arrived at a bad time for him, he being upset by a head cold among other irritants, and I was unable to get the interview that I had expected. Nevertheless, I did observe him periodically during the six weeks that I spent on research, watching him at recording sessions, on a movie set, at the gaming tables in Las Vegas, and I was able to perceive his changing moods, his irritation and suspicion when he thought that I was getting too close, his pleasure and charm when he was able to relax among those he trusted. I gained more by watching him, overhearing him, and watching the reactions of those around him than if I had actually been able to sit down and talk to him.

Joe DiMaggio was an even more reluctant subject when I began the research on him in San Francisco. I had met DiMaggio six months before in New York, at which time he indicated that he would cooperate on the article; but his attitude was radically different after I had appeared outside his restaurant on Fisherman's Wharf. And yet the tense and chilly reception that I received, initially, provided me with an interesting opening scene in which I was not only a witness but a participant being ejected from the premises by DiMaggio himself. The fact that I was able to become reacquainted with DiMaggio a few days later was the result of a request that I had made through one of DiMaggio's friends and golfing partners that I be allowed to follow their foursome through one eighteen-hole round. During the golfing session, DiMaggio, who hates to lose golf balls, lost three of them. I found them. After that, DiMaggio's attitude toward me improved noticeably; I was invited to other golf matches and to join him in the evening with his other friends at Reno's bar, where much of my work was done.

Some Techniques

New Journalists use many conventional reporting and writing techniques. Beyond these, there are four central devices:

1. Scenic construction, moving from scene to scene and resorting as little as possible to sheer historical narrative.

2. Recording dialogue in full.

3. Presenting scenes through the eyes of a character by interviewing the subject about his or her thoughts and emotions at the time of the event the writer describes (also known as *interior monologue*).

4. Recording everyday gestures, habits, manners, customs, styles of clothing, decorations, styles of traveling, eating, keeping house—everything, Wolfe says, "symbolic, generally, of people's *status life.*"

New Journalism's reliance on interior monologue is one of its most controversial aspects—the journalist cannot possibly have observed or listened to the inner thoughts of another person. Yet many writers can and do write very effectively about what an individual was thinking at a certain time.

Some Practitioners

Gay Talese is regarded as one of the more adept New Journalists—especially with interior monologue. Consider this excerpt from an article he wrote about Joshua Logan and Claudia McNeil, the star of one of Logan's plays. In it he records dialogue, a perfectly acceptable old-style journalistic technique, but at the end he switches to interior monologue:*

> "Don't raise your voice, Claudia," Logan repeated.
>
> She again ignored him.
>
> "CLAUDIA!" Logan yelled, "don't you give me that actor's vengeance, Claudia!"
>
> "Yes, Mr. Logan."
>
> "And stop yes-Mr.-Logan-ing me."
>
> "Yes, Mr. Logan."
>
> "You're a shockingly rude woman!"

> *"Writing is an adventure. To begin with, it is a toy and an amusement. Then it becomes a mistress, then it becomes a master, then it becomes a tyrant."*
>
> WINSTON CHURCHILL

---

*Quotations from Gay Talese's works are reprinted with his permission.

"Yes, Mr. Logan."

"You're being a beast."

"Yes, Mr. Logan."

"Yes, Miss Beast."

"Yes, Mr. Logan."

"Yes, Miss Beast."

Suddenly Claudia McNeil stopped. It dawned on her that he was calling her a beast; now her face was grey and her eyes were cold, and her voice almost solemn as she said, "You . . . called . . . me . . . out . . . of . . . my . . . name."

"Oh, God." Logan smacked his forehead with his hand.

"You . . . called . . . me . . . out . . . of . . . my . . . name."

She stood there, rocklike, big and angry, waiting for him to do something.

"Oliver!" Logan said, turning toward his coproducer, who had lowered his wiry, long body into his chair as if he were in a foxhole. He did not want to be cornered into saying something that might offend Logan, his old friend, but neither did he want Claudia McNeil to come barreling down the aisle and possibly snap his thin form in half. . . .

Recalling his work on this article, Talese said, "They got into an argument that not only was more dramatic than the play itself, but revealed something of the character of Logan and Miss McNeil in a way that I could never have done had I approached the subject from the more conventional form of reporting." Talese was simply an observer at the time the confrontation took place, so he was able to record the dialogue in full. But by talking to Oliver, and by observing him, Talese was also able to write about what Oliver was thinking when Logan turned to him.

Despite criticism of his techniques, Talese continued to use them when the situation seemed appropriate. Whether an obscure old bridge tender was being left jobless by the construction of a modern bridge in Brooklyn or the uncommunicative Joe DiMaggio was refusing to grant an interview, Talese tried to report what each was thinking. Talese explained that in interviewing a subject, he would "ask him what he thought in every situation where I might have asked him in the past what he said. I'm not so interested in what he did and said . . . as in what he thought. And I would quote him in the way I was writing that he thought something."

In *The Kingdom and the Power,* the human history of the *New York Times,* Talese made effective use of the interior monologue. This and a rich descriptive narrative based on his perceptions during his years as a *Times* reporter enabled him to capture the interpersonal drama of the great liberal establishment newspaper. Instead of the usual dull press history approach, Talese wrote about the pettiness, bickering, and self-doubts of *Times* executives. He showed how management wielded power and controlled the lives of some of America's most talented journalists. The book offended some of his subjects, but his frequent use of interior monologues has brought the most intense criticism. Here, for instance, Talese probes the mind of Frank Sinatra in a piece that was published in *Fame and Obscurity:*

Sinatra had been working in a film that he now disliked, could not wait to finish; he was tired of all the publicity attached to his dating the twenty-one-year-old Mia Farrow, who was not in sight tonight; he was angry that a CBS television documentary of his life, to be shown in two weeks, was reportedly prying into his privacy, even speculating on his possible friendship with Mafia leaders; he was worried about his starring role in an hour-long NBC show entitled *Sinatra—A Man and His Music,* which would require that he sing eighteen songs with a voice that at this particular moment, just a few nights before the taping was to begin, was weak and sore and uncertain. Sinatra was ill. He was the victim of an ailment so common that most people would consider it trivial. But when it gets to Sinatra it can plunge him into a state of anguish, deep depression, panic, even rage. Frank Sinatra had a cold.

Talese keyed his entire article on Sinatra's cold, which he explained later: "Frank Sinatra was not feeling well and everyone was very nervous— "everyone" meaning those people who worked for Sinatra, like the publicity man and a dozen other people who have various roles. And Sinatra had a cold. Because he had a cold, he was very irritable. . . . He was not able to sing with the ease and perfection that he might otherwise be able to do. That was interesting. The cold afflicted not only him—it affected his whole group, his whole organization."

Both Wolfe and Talese have said that they admire the journalism of Norman Mailer, who is generally considered the most skilled of the New Journalists. The form of Mailer's work is deceptively simple: he uses himself as a character in his own journalism. In *The Armies of the Night,* Mailer wrote interior monologue—his own:

> "You know, Norman," said Lowell in his fondest voice, "Elizabeth and I really think you're the finest journalist in America."
>
> Mailer knew Lowell thought this—Lowell had even sent him a postcard once to state the enthusiasm. But the novelist had been shrewd enough to judge that Lowell sent many postcards to many people—it did not matter that Lowell was by overwhelming consensus judged to be the best, most talented, and most distinguished poet in America—it was still necessary to keep the defense lines in good working order. A good word on a card could keep many a dangerous recalcitrant in the ranks. Therefore, this practice annoyed Mailer.

Some Imitators

The legions of young writers who try to imitate Mailer soon find that his method is not nearly as easy as it looks. This is largely because they are not as talented as Mailer, but their failures also spring from the fact that they write about themselves rather than about events. In opposition to this trend, Herbert Gold wrote, "The first-person arias of the Wolfettes and Mailerlings center the whole world in the self of the writer. They don't do their job of telling and sharing experience. Instead, they sacrifice knowledge for a parading of personality. . . ." There is a subtle difference in Mailer's work; the reader gets not only a view of how events affect Mailer but also a sense of how Mailer viewed events. The reader may learn much about the writer, but the primary message is about the events in which the writer participated.

Beginners often mistakenly believe that writing in the style of New Journalism requires less discipline than writing conventional articles. They do not realize that New Journalists have mastered the techniques of basic news and feature writing before experimenting with innovative forms. Tennis players need to learn basic ground strokes before trying to put spin on the ball. If they don't, it's unlikely that they'll be able to control their shots. The same applies to naive writers who want to use the techniques of New Journalism.

Despite the emphasis many New Journalists place on truth as opposed to facts, New Journalism does not relieve the writer of responsibility for accurate reporting. Dan Wakefield explained in his article "The Personal Voice and the Impersonal Eye" that "*Esquire*'s editorial attitude seems to be anything goes as long as it is interesting and true. The magazine has a research department, and every fact in every nonfiction piece is checked and verified. The license they offer writers is not for distortion of facts but experimentation in style."

Employing the New Techniques

Beginners who want to try to use New Journalism techniques can start right away, but slowly. Writers may try it first by putting themselves in the place of the person they are presenting. Here is a short example from *Time* magazine of the writer's putting himself in the shoes of Lawrence O'Brien, chairman of the 1972 Democratic National Convention:*

> . . . O'Brien picked up the huge gavel. Too heavy, he thought. Why not get an electric buzzer next time? He whacked it down, and the great spectacle of Miami Beach was on. He made an early decision. The noisy mass below him had to be managed, somehow led through four days of business, but more important were the millions and millions of Americans who were watching through those blinking red eyes directly in front of him. Talk to them, he told himself, wondering what the man in San Clemente would be seeing in a few hours.
>
> The convention was already behind time when O'Brien started his speech. That was deliberate. Don't harass or push. Stay loose, he kept telling himself. The noise on the floor hardly subsided as he talked—the old Irish rasp, the square sentences full of platitudes, annoyingly interspersed with film clips. Yet here and there people began to listen. It was not the familiar polemic against Richard Nixon. It was not the extravagant praise of the Democratic past. He talked about "the crisis of truth," of the Democrats being "on trial." He did not avoid blame for problems, and he tried to warn his youthful audience that the world is not remade by "a stroke of the pen."

---

*Reprinted by permission from *Time, the Weekly Magazine,* copyright Time Inc.

Saturation Research

Another aspect of the work of the New Journalists that beginners can adopt immediately might be called saturation research. This requires that researchers do much more than ask a few people a few questions. It requires that they become involved in their subjects the way Mailer became involved in the march on Washington so that he could write *The Armies of the Night* or the way Wolfe and Talese became involved with subjects by staying with them for long periods. Wolfe pointed out, "You start following somebody or a group around, and you really have to end up staying with them for a day, sometimes weeks, sometimes months, even. And you are waiting for things to happen in front of your eyes, because it's really the scene that brings the whole thing to life."

This kind of research is essential in producing the New Journalism, but it is also important in producing imaginative articles of any kind. Some successful articles are written without this whole-souled approach to research, of course. But it must be obvious that this kind of exploration enables writers to understand their subjects fully and thus enables them to help their readers understand. Whether you are a free-lancer or a staff writer, promoting understanding should be your goal.

The Controversy: Objectivity Versus Involvement

Even though leading practitioners like Tom Wolfe and Gay Talese began as newspaper writers, a strong controversy rages over the propriety of the New Journalism. This argument is largely between the old and the young, many of the older journalists holding that established standards of objectivity and verifiable fact must be observed. Many young journalists argue that since everyone agrees that absolute objectivity is impossible and since the established standards rarely enable one to report more than mere facts, ignoring the *truth about facts,* freer forms are essential. This controversy is not the old argument over objectivity versus interpretation—certainly not if one defines interpretation as no more than clarifying, explaining, or analyzing problems, issues, or controversies. The New Journalism goes far beyond interpretation because it calls for the direct involvement of the writer in his or her article.

Sometimes this involvement creates the impression that the writer of an article is more important than the subject he or she is writing about. The temptation to insert the writer's presence into the story is very strong. Such stories often begin with sentences like "When I first decided to interview _____, I thought . . ." or "When I walked into _____'s house, I felt . . ." This autobiographical approach can be successful when the subject of the story is an intriguing situation in which readers would like to find themselves, or a person they would like to meet. In those cases, the writer can share his or her firsthand experience with readers by writing about his or her own thoughts and feelings. The same technique applied to an article about an unknown subject is often less effective. When no inherent interest in a subject exists among readers, their need to share the writer's experience is not as great as their need to learn about the subject itself and why it is being discussed in an article. Tom Wolfe has suggested that autobiographical journalism is most appropriate when the author is a leading character in the event being written about. When this is not the case, personal point of view merely distracts the readers from the story.

Yet it is this personal aspect of the New Journalism that appeals to many writers and readers. Ronald Weber explained its popularity by writing that New Journalism is " 'I' writing for an 'I' time, personal writing for an age of personalism. All about us ego seems loosed into the cultural air as never before. Notions of detachment, objectivity, and neutrality conflict in every sphere with a passion for uninhibited individual expression. Both one's first and last duty now belong to oneself." Whether or not one agrees that New Journalism is a reflection of the times it grew out of, this style of news writing is certainly much more subjective than its predecessor.

Exercises

1. Because you may want to be convinced of the difference between features and news stories, you should do the following: clip five features and five news stories from a newspaper. Are the features more interesting at the end than the news stories are at the end? In the aggregate, which are more interesting, the features or the news stories? Why?

2. Interview a veteran reporter or editor at the nearest daily newspaper. Ask him or her whether the mission of any reporter is different from what it was ten years ago. Ask whether the term "reporter" applies to everyone or whether "feature writer" describes some of the employees. Are the reporters also feature writers? Ask him or her which three staff members are considered best at writing (not at reporting). Are they reporters, feature writers, or both?

3. Go through an edition of a daily newspaper in your area and determine how much space the paper devotes to straight news stories and how much it devotes to feature articles. Do the same for another newspaper, then compare the two. How does the use of feature articles affect the overall tone of the newspaper?

4. Find someone who has recently had an unusual experience (a fight, a job interview, an odd conversation with a stranger, an athletic contest, a stressful encounter, or something similar) and interview the person about it. Then write two one-page stories—the first in conventional third-person reporting style and the second using the first-person interior monologue style of New Journalism. Which is more effective? Which was easier to write, and why?

5. Discuss which kinds of stories you think are most suitable to the techniques of New Journalism. Which kinds of stories are not suitable, and why?

TEN

LEADS, TRANSITIONS, AND ENDINGS

Build me straight, O worthy Master!
Staunch and strong, a goodly vessel.

H. W. LONGFELLOW

G ene Shalit of NBC-TV "Today" commented: "When school ends, millions of children will head for the beach or will climb into the family station wagon for a trip to Grandmother's. But none will travel farther than the child with a book who goes only to his own room or to the shade beneath a backyard tree.

"The books of childhood are always with us. Lost in their pages, a child may swim in the bluest sea, rise on the highest swing, engage in the grandest adventure."

Many novice writers probably share Shalit's opinion about the wonder of childhood books. Yet readers enjoying a fascinating story may fail to realize that the pages in which they are absorbed were once blank sheets of paper. Few objects are quite as intimidating to novice writers as a pile of blank paper. A symbol of the writers' unwritten stories, blank paper is a reminder that they must solve one very important problem before completing their articles—how to begin. Yet waiting for them at the other end of their journey is another certainty; they must write a good last sentence or closing paragraph. And along the way they must travel smoothly and easily from idea to idea and from paragraph to paragraph, with transitions as inconspicuous as editing splices in a movie.

WRITING LEADS

Journalists writing straight news stories generally rely on a formula to produce their leads. The ingredients are familiar—who, what, when, where, and why. Once the writer has composed the lead, the rest of the story follows naturally from an elaboration of each of these elements, in order of importance.

There is no formula for writing feature stories or magazine articles, nor is there a rule for how to write their leads. The possibilities are infinite, and this is what confounds many beginners. If ten journalists were writing from the same material, perhaps no two would choose the same lead. However, if all ten were professionals, each different lead would accomplish the same objectives:

1. To attract the reader.
2. To give the reader the central idea.
3. To lead the reader into the story.

If you are writing a newspaper feature, you must try to establish your central idea from the beginning. You do not have as much freedom to establish your lead as the magazine writer, who may sometimes take up to 500 words. You need not, however, jump into the central idea in the first sentence, as is done in most straight news stories. For example, you might introduce your piece this way:

> In Florida, they tell it this way: A new arrival in heaven was well pleased with the place. He found everything to his liking, deciding that it was all it had been cracked up to be.
>
> Then one day he came upon another who had been admitted to the heavenly portals; this man sat in the corner with a ball and chain attached to his ankle. The new citizen, puzzled, went to St. Peter and asked: "How come this man has to wear a ball and chain?"
>
> "Well," St. Peter replied, "that man's from Florida and every time we turn him loose he tries to go back."
>
> The people who live along the 100-mile stretch of that curve along the Gulf of Mexico from Pensacola to Panama City vow that the man was from Northwest Florida. . . .

This lead is entertaining, a natural beginning for this story—informal, amusing, and boastful. It does not matter that the lead runs five sentences. The reader who begins this story is hooked. Although he or she may not finish the story, the reader must at least go to the end of the lead. Remember, however, that if you have used a lead like this as a means of getting the reader into a story, you must see to it that the tone of the rest of the story matches the lighthearted flavor you have established.

A grim story would not, of course, lend itself to a cheerful beginning. For example, consider this lead:

> February 12, 1974: "Mom, dad, I'm okay . . . I'm not being starved or beaten or unnecessarily frightened . . . I know that Steve is okay . . . I heard that mom is really upset and that everybody is at home . . . I hope this puts you a little bit at ease . . . I just hope I can get back to everybody real soon."
>
> April 24, 1974: "To the pig Hearsts . . . I am a soldier in the people's army . . . I have chosen to stay and fight . . . as for my ex-fiancé I don't care if I ever see him again. . . ."
>
> After Patricia Hearst was kidnapped February 4 from an apartment in

Berkeley a few blocks from the University of California campus, the gossip of San Francisco was that she was in on it from the start.

This story was published June 3, 1974, months after the kidnapping of Patricia Hearst. The writer, Jack Fox of United Press International, had been mulling over what would be the appropriate lead for a story that had broken months before. It suddenly came to him to use two direct quotations pointing up the dramatic change in the kidnapped young woman's attitude.

Of course, magazine writers have much more freedom than newspaper reporters when writing leads. Leads in magazines are of all different lengths and styles. Here is the way the writer Don Shewey began his magazine article on Wallace Shawn:

> It was a steamy summer evening, and Wally Shawn was calling from a pay phone on the street. I had asked him for a copy of a play he had written years ago, and we were arranging to rendezvous somewhere between my place and his phone booth. This was before we had ever met and a couple of months before *My Dinner with Andre* opened at the New York Film Festival, so his question wasn't completely ridiculous. He was probably best known at that time for playing Diane Keaton's ex-husband in *Manhattan,* so when he said, "Do you know what I look like?" I almost blurted out, "Oh, yes, you're the one that Woody Allen referred to as 'that homunculus.'"

Developing Leads

Clay Schoenfeld, a veteran writer, has outlined these suggestions for those who have trouble writing leads:

1. *Link.* This lead is an integral part of the feature and supports a natural flow of thought from the beginning to the development.
2. *Exposition.* Before writing a single word, it's always helpful to spell out your article in a few sentences. What is the heart of the article? Its central idea?
3. *Appeal.* Explore anecdotes, try for narrative hooks, or use a striking statement.
4. *Direct connection.* You must try to establish a direct connection with your readers.
5. *Slant.* Try always to slant your writing to the interests of the readers of a particular newspaper or magazine.

Kinds of Leads

There are many different kinds of leads from which to choose. Consider the following and their appropriateness for various types of stories:

Summary

This is the standard straight news lead that literally summarizes all the key elements of the story in a single sentence. Because it conveys the tone of a breaking news story, the summary lead is usually unsuitable for a feature article. Columnist Herb Caen of the *San Francisco Chronicle* once called this example of a summary lead "The all-time All-Timer":

> Communist-led terrorists on a hashish-crazed rampage through Kwilu province shot down a United Nations helicopter with a bow and arrow yesterday as it was flying eight Congolese nuns to safety.

Description

Writing a descriptive lead is often difficult for a beginner because the language must be vivid and colorful. Even the comic strip character Snoopy of "Peanuts" finds it challenging. He sits atop his dog house writing again and again, "It was a dark and stormy night." Writers searching for strong descriptive phrases often go astray, as Herb Caen pointed out in another example involving a young reporter sent to cover a flood. The reporter, wiring in his article, began this way: GOD SITS ON THE HILLS OVERLOOKING JOHNSTOWN TONIGHT. According to Caen, the editor wired right back, TO HELL WITH THE FLOOD; INTERVIEW GOD.

A good descriptive lead can sometimes create dramatic impact, as does this lead from a sports story:

> Running a marathon in 95-degree heat is like walking into a death trap, and that's how hot it was in Hopkinton, Massachusetts, the Monday of the Boston Marathon.

But a descriptive lead need not be dramatic to be effective, as this lead illustrates:

> Louisiana has been the moon-dipped, myth-draped strange sister among Southern states since its Arcadian beginnings, but its political upheavals during the past three decades have been unusual even by Louisiana standards.

Descriptive leads are often useful in profiles of interesting or colorful characters. The description can be of the subject's appearance or personality, but it can also focus on his or her accomplishments, as in this lead by George Dobbins, former managing editor of *Peninsula* magazine:

> He stands at the pinnacle of American culinary success. The more than 20 worldwide restaurants bearing his name gross over 36 million dollars annually. And if you have never eaten at one of those, it is still likely he has influenced your eating habits. For he is not only a restaurateur but an innovator. He created the Mai Tai. Professionals consider his bartending guides classic. He has fostered dishes so unique that his cookbooks are sought by the kitchen dilettante as well as the discerning chef. This is Hillsborough resident Victor Bergeron, better known as the internationally famous Trader Vic.

Here is another descriptive lead, but this one stresses the subject's actions and appearance. Notice how much detail is included in this fairly long lead:

Hands knotted in her lap, head thrust forward like a hawk assessing its prey, Sheila Weber is concentrating on the two students before her. Behind thick, round glasses, her eyes are small, intent, and focused. Her petite, wiry frame is motionless. As the students finish their scene and turn toward her expectantly, the room is hushed, but Weber will not be hurried. She gazes at them for a few silent seconds, and then nods her head and pronounces their fate with a single, golden word: "Good." The budding actors glance at each other in relief and the others look on enviously, as Weber brushes a hand through thick, gray hair and, continuing the motion, turns slowly toward the class. "They were *doing,* that time, hmm?" She handles her words like precious jewels, chosen carefully from the treasures accumulated through decades of the theatre, and delivers them in an accent that lies somewhere between Brooklynese and British. "Acting," she pronounces slowly, emphasizing each syllable, "is doing the real," she pauses again, "in *imaginary* circumstances." This said, she directs her gaze from face to face, challenging each student in turn, with eyebrows raised, demanding agreement. As they nod sagely together, Weber turns back to the two in front, and claps her hands once, victoriously. She is pleased. "Very good," she says to them alone, and smiles.

Direct Address

This kind of lead can be used to involve the reader in the story immediately. It is often written in the form of a question, such as "Where were you when . . ." The following lead from an article titled "Fear of Figuring" shows how it works:

Do numbers make you uneasy? Would you prefer to do almost anything rather than solve a math problem? Do you consider the hand calculator a menace? If your answer to any of these questions is "yes," you may have a handicap that afflicts thousands of Americans—women especially: math anxiety. It can keep you out of a job you want, or from progressing in the job you have.

Travel writers often use direct address to entice their readers into the setting they are writing about. Such leads can combine descriptive elements as well, as illustrated in this example:

Imagine yourself on a mountaintop in the morning, sailing in the afternoon and at the theater that night. Imagine a day of rafting through white water, followed by an evening at a four-star restaurant. Imagine that snowcapped mountains are only an hour's drive from your hotel, and that from your room you can see their peaks silhouetted against the evening sky. Now picture yourself in Seattle, one of the few cities in the United States where this fantasy can be a reality.

Striking Statement

This kind of lead makes the reader ask, "Is that true?" It may refute some commonly held belief, as in "Drinking alcohol is good for you." Or it may represent a startling statistic, such as "Seven million women in this country have had their jobs canceled and find themselves without financial support." It may even make a surprising assertion, such as "If a basketball game is ever held on the moon, Geese Ausbie will surely play it." But regardless of the form, the intent is the same—to get the reader's attention quickly by making a statement that is so striking that he or she will feel compelled to read on in order to discover why the statement is true.

Narrative

The narrative lead is often like a short story. It may be an anecdote or a description of a scene that creates the setting for the article. Consider this example from a profile of skier Katie Morning:

> The sky was clear at the Mammoth Mountain ski area in California that winter day. Spectators watching the giant slalom race from the bottom of the snow-covered slope could just about discern a brightly colored shape at the top of the mountain. As the spot of color zigzagged down the course, onlookers anticipated a good run. The unrecognizable dot had just taken human form when suddenly the figure slipped, transformed from a speeding skier into a tangled mass of flailing arms, legs, and skis; careened downhill with horrifying velocity; and finally landed in a motionless, crumpled mass. For a frightening moment, no one moved. Then, as though by some invisible cue, there was a rush toward the still body.
>
> "Cut!" screamed the director.
>
> Katie Morning picked herself up from the snow, brushed off her parka, and inquired, "How'd I do?"
>
> It was the final day of filming "The Other Side of the Mountain," the story of champion 18-year-old Jill Kinmont who was paralyzed from the shoulders down in a tragic fall on the slopes.

Here is another narrative lead. A writer, David Hellerstein, began his article this way:

> One evening not long ago, I ran into a friend of mine—let's call him Alex Weber—on Manhattan's Columbus Avenue. I was waving for a cab when he grabbed me; he was standing with his arm around his latest candidate for the perfect woman. Tall, blond, dazzlingly dressed, she was, Alex told me in one breath, an investment banker with a Harvard M.B.A., a Brearley education, and a father in the University Club. Her name was Nicki. They'd met three weeks ago and were madly in love. (They dragged me into a bar.)
>
> We chatted for a few minutes, and then Alex went into a long, amusing anecdote about his latest antitrust case. Nicki was enthralled.
>
> That's the effect Alex has on women, and to tell the truth, I've never completely understood it. Physically he's attractive enough, with fair curly hair, intelligent eyes, a tennis player's wiry build. He's extremely bright and he *is* amusing in a cynical way—but so are other men. What sets him apart is a certain boyishness, a Peter Pan quality, an elusiveness that can be both seductive and maddening. Nobody can quite capture him. Why women like that so much is another question;

but they do, and Nicki was no exception. She was gazing at Alex with an expression not much short of rapture.

In a few minutes Nicki went to make a phone call; as soon as she left the table, Alex turned sour.

"She is fine, but she's not *right,*" Alex said. . . .

As shown in these examples, leads come in many lengths. And just as obviously, writers of magazine articles and feature stories are not bound by the same restrictions that guide the work of straight news reporters. Nor must they listen to newspaper editors complain like the one in this story recalled by Herb Caen:

And then there was the city editor who roared that his reporters' leads were too long. "Short, keep 'em SHORT!" he hollered, and one of his heroes promptly turned in a story that began:
Dead.
That's what John Doe was yesterday after an auto accident at—."

WRITING TRANSITIONS

A film editor makes transitions from one shot in a movie to another by deftly splicing together hundreds of separate pieces of film. When a splice is poorly made, so that people or objects seem to leap from one position to another, the jarring result is called a "jump cut." A writer avoids jump cuts and tries to join the units of a story (sentences and paragraphs) so smoothly that the reader is unaware of the progression from beginning to end. This smooth progress is what is meant by "flow."

Beginners sometimes err on the side of too much transition in their efforts to create a cohesive story. It is important not only to use transitions but also to use them inconspicuously. Consider these examples of too much transition:

. . . labels are pinned to cognitive cues. Cognitive cues in this case could be. . . .

. . . he would eventually like to go into some form of education. But before education, Terry's first goal is the pros. His coach. . . .

. . . increased ability to score has added a new dimension of respect from opposing guards. "I guess I improved most during the summer," he said.

During the summer months he worked on his quickness and driving ability while playing basketball in Australia and New Zealand for a . . .

. . . played a guard, although he was 6′ 4″ by his senior year. Surprisingly, John's first goal upon entering high school was to play baseball.

"Before I went to high school my dream was to become a pro baseball player." Davis was a pitcher, with excellent control, more . . .

In each case, the writer has been much too obvious in making a transition: "cognitive cues. Cognitive cues . . . ," "some form of education. But before education . . . ," and so on. Now consider some closely knit excerpts about Margaux Hemingway. Note that the end of each paragraph is tied strongly to the beginning of the next paragraph by an echo, but the writer does not obviously repeat words, as in the examples above:*

Says Designer Halston: "She has all the components to become a modern young superstar—openness, infectiousness, beauty, and the ambition to follow through."

Openness and a boggling spontaneity have made Margaux something more than a model, a pop personality. . . .

Says Scavullo: "She talks a mile a minute. She chews gum until she gets in front of the camera; then we carry a silver spoon and platter to her and take the gum."

Margaux did pine for the great outdoors. "I saw *The Four Musketeers* and I wanted to fence," she said wistfully. . . .

"I felt so energized," she beamed.

"That's how I like to feel—healthy and energized."

That is how Margaux grew up in Idaho's spectacular Sun Valley, where her father, Jack, Ernest's eldest son, settled down in 1967 after throwing over a career as a stockbroker. . . .

"Margaux never did like competition," says Jack, "and I think that's why she wasn't too interested in school."

Her parents encouraged her to try art school, but Margaux was too energized to buckle down and took off after a year for Europe. . . .

Her younger sister, Mariel, is not so sure: "I don't know—Margaux is kinda crazy."

Crazy like Napoleon. Margaux has. . . .

Not many writers are so attentive to their transitions, although they should be. An article should flow from beginning to end. For example, here is one that is disjointed in several places and limps to a close:

. . . In a recent class, Marti remarked, "Music today is written for you— if you can't listen to it, the music shouldn't be written." Emphasis is on construction of the musical idea, no matter what historical period it is from. Marti's intent is that any well-structured part is capable of being a legitimate esthetic whole, without judgments of "good and bad" music.

Students' enthusiasm for this thoroughness was reflected by awarding him the Gores award for excellence in teaching, which cited him for "elegance in both lectures and performance" and his "multifarious contributions" to education as Faculty Resident of Twain House. Marti's comment, "It's nice to know they felt as warmly about me as I feel about them," carries because of his sincerity.

His family? It's pending any day now. For at least a month, Barbara and he have considered names—Igor, Percy, and Bliss are definitely out. "I really don't care what the baby is," he admitted somewhat

---

*Reprinted by permission from *Time, the Weekly Newsmagazine,* copyright Time Inc.

abashedly. "Just nervous." They are currently Faculty Residents at Lagunita.

A fascination with the state of the world has long honed Marti's political intellect, but he also confesses a fascination with the state of the sandlots. "If I had more time, I'd be a jock," he laughed. "I'm a New York City boy; it'd be fun to play ball." It's the kid that makes him fun as a professor.

When one begins a paragraph with a question ("His family?"), that's usually a sign that the unity is breaking down. In effect, the writer is saying, "Now, how do I work his family into this?" Such a transition weakens the cohesion. But the writer has an unusual opportunity to make all this cohesive by considering the preceding paragraph. The teacher in question is a "Faculty Resident." In such cases, the family is usually almost as involved as the teacher, which would have made it easy to talk about the family without having to leap to make the transition.

To have made the transition neatly, the writer should have had information that she didn't think she needed when she began the article, since she probably didn't realize that she would have trouble working the teacher's family into this. The writer should have asked questions about the subject's residency at Twain and his residency at Lagunita well before beginning to write, on the chance that any notes taken would turn out to be useful later. Then, when the time came to tie the family into the article, the writer would not have had to stumble from Twain to Lagunita by disjointedly saying that he was once at Twain and is now at Lagunita with his family. Instead, the writer would have had the information to enable her to move pleasingly from other matters to the subject's family by talking about the family in the context of their house residency.

The larger point, and one that has been made earlier, is that a writer should have much more information than can possibly be used. The essence of good writing is being selective. You must have a range of alternatives so that you can choose the best material. You need to ask yourself what has gone before. In the article cited, the last paragraph is about politics and athletics. What does that have to do with the subject's family and his work as a resident? Perhaps he talks politics with the students at Lagunita (perhaps with his wife included in the group), and perhaps he plays volleyball or other games with the students. You need to use connections like these to make all your writing neatly transitional.

Tying One Paragraph to the Next

David Cannadine, a British historian, may not lure many readers who do not share his interests, but those who know about the sheer beauty of prose might well read Cannadine's writing just to appreciate its rhythm. In fact, he is usually praised for his flowing style—but those who analyze his writing find that Cannadine does much more than choose the right words; he is a marvelous maker of transitions between paragraphs.

In the following quotations from Cannadine's "The State of British History," published in the British *Times Literary Supplement* (October 10, 1986), Cannadine illustrates transitions. Each quotation is from the end of a paragraph, followed by the first sentence (some only in part) of the next paragraph:

> . . . "The present seems thoroughly satisfactory," observed one commentator in 1969, "the future rosier still."
>
> It was in such an atmosphere, and for such an audience, that a new generation of post-war professional scholars produced an array of seminal books on British history. . . .

> . . . even if the events of 1688 no longer seemed glorious, they still seemed revolutionary.
>
> Likewise, the most modern period of British history appeared equally eventful.

> . . . the Great Reform Act was itself a "revolution in government" carried out by zealous Benthamite bureaucrats.
>
> Thus did the new professional scholars of the 1950s and 60s retell the story of Britain's recent history. . . .

> . . . They boldly sketched out arresting and wide-ranging arguments, and they propounded interpretations which often ran ahead of the evidence they cited in support.
>
> As such, this version of modern British history was not only intrinsically exciting and attractive: it also embodied a vision of the national past. . . .

> . . . the industrial revolution was the crucial pre-condition for the "affluent society"; and the nineteenth century was viewed, in essence, as a prelude to modern times.
>
> Yet at the same time, our national past was also of a much broader interest, to a global audience anxious to understand how the contemporary world, and in particular the Western world, had come into being.

> . . . And, since Britain's past was always anticipating the present in this way, this version of its history naturally appealed to almost anyone who wished to understand modern times.
>
> But, in addition, there were many people abroad who wished to know about Britain's past for its own sake.

It is not necessary to appreciate, or even like, British history to be grateful to Cannadine. Anyone who studies his writing will soon be thankful that Cannadine took the trouble to link each paragraph to the preceding paragraph. His writing deserves serious study.

This beginning writer has already learned how to use transitions to tie paragraphs together. Her article began as follows:

> Glancing at my watch, I remembered how late I thought I was, but, still, there were only students in the studio. Suddenly, the door opened and a man of small stature, but obvious presence, planted one Reebok

in the doorway while he faced outside, finishing a conversation with a graduate student. Turning to face the room, Nathan Oliveira let go of the door, sauntered inside, and sweeping the air with a curved hand, announced, "We'll start with four five-minute sittings, and then have a short crit . . ." As soon as he gave the signal, we set our hands to work. As I madly scratched black strokes across a white page, I could feel him weaving in and out of the drawing tables, evaluating each drawing as he passed. Soon he was at my left shoulder. Trying not to slow down, I kept drawing until a TAP TAP TAP of his fingers on my paper startled me out of my concentration . . . "Good drawing, good drawing . . . keep going."

Finally the sittings were over, and we all gathered around Oliveira to discuss our work. Despite his dulcet tone, his words seemed to command the attention of every student. As he spoke, his chocolate brown eyes would rest on one person at a time; but they stared very intently, as if he were having a private conversation with each one of us. At last, we had critiqued every drawing that was pinned up on the wall behind us; yet, Nathan Oliveira kept talking. He stepped up from the models' platform where he was sitting, put his right hand on the top of his thick grey hair, and said, "I won't be in a week from tomorrow. I have to get a minor operation." He paused for a brief second and, cracking a tiny grin, qualified his statement: ". . . just a brain transplant."

And as I looked up I saw Oliveira stroll out of the studio, passing by the model, who broke his pose for a moment, to smile.

WRITING ENDINGS

"If I didn't know the ending of a story, I wouldn't begin. I always write my last line, my last paragraphs, my last page first."

KATHERINE ANNE PORTER

A writer who has been a straight news reporter may often have problems with endings since news stories gradually taper down to almost nothing. They begin with the most important elements and then let the story run out. The style of straight news writing may become habitual. Such reporters need to remember that the form of the magazine article or feature is different; its ending is as important as its beginning.

For example, consider this ending to the earlier-quoted story about the Patricia Hearst kidnapping (first, the lead again):

February 12, 1974: "Mom, dad, I'm okay . . . I just hope I can get back to everybody real soon."

April 24, 1974: "To the pig Hearsts . . . I am a soldier in the people's army . . . as for my ex-fiancé I don't care if I ever see him again. . . ."

After Patricia Hearst was kidnapped February 4 . . . the gossip of San Francisco was that she was in on it from the start. . . .

And now the ending:

Randolph Hearst said he had not given up hope but he now felt Patricia believes in what she is doing.

"I think it happened as a result of duress," he said. "This apparently can happen when a victim has no hope, when the only salvation for the victim is the oppressor."

Using the direct quotation from Randolph Hearst is highly appropriate. A thousand words later, it raises the point made in the lead, knitting the story together nicely.

Some writers, especially beginners, have great difficulty trying to tie the story together with an appropriate ending. For example, read this lead:

> 8:30 a.m. Robin swings her legs over the edge of the bed—thirty minutes to shower and get out the door. The to-do list is long today: deposit checks; pick up cleaning; drop off box at printer's; lunch with a friend; grocery shopping. Sound like the chores of a homemaker? Perhaps. Oh, add one more item to that list: Executive Writers' meeting at NBC.

Although the writer continued by giving details about her subject, she was unable to end the profile with a strong statement. Instead, the final sentence is weak and does not tell the reader anything that wasn't obvious from reading the article. Here is the ending:

> Robin is anything but unfocused now, however. She created Remington Steele out of desperation at the sexist job market, and her career took off from there. She now has over thirty television serials, three feature films to her credit. Robin's come a long way since her indecisive college days.

Other writers are better with endings. This student wrote the following lead:

> "I once lived in a house where I could look out a window as I worked at my desk and observe a small herd of cattle browsing in a neighboring field. And I was struck with a thought . . . You never get the impression that a cow is about to have a nervous breakdown."
> Although John Gardner looks nothing like a cow (he is a tall, lean man who sits and stands naturally erect), he, like a cow, gives the impression that he will never have a nervous breakdown.

After describing Gardner and his tremendous speaking ability, the writer ends the article with a very simple, effective sentence. Notice how this ending adds emphasis and ties the final paragraph to the lead:

> No cow, dead or alive, could ever communicate like John Gardner.

Completing an Analogy

Sometimes a writer can use an analogy in the lead, carry it through in the development of the story, and go back to it for the ending. In the following excerpt from an article on racquetball, the writer used a combination descriptive-narrative lead to begin the article, set up an analogy using the "family" theme, then returned to it to tie the piece together at the end:

> **Lead:** Two players enter a white handball court carrying rackets that

look like the broken remnants of a tennis tantrum, strings intact but handles only a few inches long. They warm up, whacking a black rubber ball that rebounds off two, even three walls before hitting the floor. A spectator assessing the scene through a Plexiglass window notes the knee pads of one player and predicts knowingly, "She's a diver." Bruises the size of coffee cups cover the arms and legs of the other player, and as the ball streaks like a riotous comet through this small galaxy, it's not hard to guess where they came from.

The game is racquetball, stepchild to squash and cousin to handball, tennis, and paddleball. The racquet sports family doesn't quite know what to think of its new relative, but racquetball's popularity quiets any objections to the game's pedigree.

Ending: New courts are designed with spectators in mind, and an all-plexiglass portable court that can be erected in auditoriums or gymnasiums is available. Television coverage is the goal, but no sponsor has yet appeared to make racquetball a media star. Tennis needn't worry yet about losing its backers to racquetball; the sport has a long way to go before that happens. But the racquet sports family had better start setting another place at the table—its new relative has come to stay.

A Summary Ending

The ending need not always refer to the lead, of course. It may be a summarizing statement, a revealing or insightful quotation, or a striking statement that stands on its own as a kind of culmination to the buildup of the article. It may even be an anecdote, as in this illustration from Rex Reed's "Ava: Life in the Afternoon," a profile of a fading star:

Outside, Ava is inside the taxi flanked by the N.Y.U. student and Larry, blowing kisses to the new chum, who will never grow to be an old one. They are already turning the corner into Fifty-seventh Street, fading into the kind of night, the color of tomato juice in the headlights, that only exists in New York when it rains.

"Who was it?" asks a woman walking a poodle.

"Jackie Kennedy," answers a man from his bus window.

Experienced writers can often spot the ending to an article among the interviews, notes, and other material they have gathered before they even write the lead. A good ending can even suggest a lead, or give the writer a sense of the direction in which the article is heading. There is a pitfall, however, in saving an item that appears to be a good ending—sometimes a good ending is really a good beginning in disguise. Writers must learn to tell the difference.

A REMARKABLE STYLE

Here is a writer whose style is evident even in a few brief paragraphs of type. Following is an excerpt from Tracy Kidder's *The Soul of a New Machine:* *

---

*Reprinted by permission of Tracy Kidder.

One holiday morning in 1978, Tom West traveled to a city that was situated, he would later say guardedly, "somewhere in America." He entered a building as though he belonged there, strolled down a hallway, and let himself quietly into a windowless room. Just inside the door, he stopped.

The floor was torn up; a shallow trench filled with fat power cables traversed it. Along the far wall, at the end of the trench, enclosed in three large, cream-colored steel cabinets, stood a VAX 11/780, the most important of a new class of computers called "32-bit superminis." To West's surprise, one of the cabinets was open and a man with tools was standing in front of it. A technician, still installing the machine, West figured.

Although West's designs weren't illegal, they werc sly, and he had no intention of embarrassing the friend who had told him he could visit this room. If the technician had asked West to identify himself, West wouldn't have lied and he wouldn't have answered the question, either. But the moment went by. The technician didn't inquire. West stood around and watched him work, and in a little while the technician packed up his tools and left.

Then West closed the door and walked back across the room to the computer, which was now all but fully assembled. He began to take it apart.

West was the leader of a team of computer engineers at a company called Data General. The machine that he was disassembling was

TRACY KIDDER

Tracy Kidder's Pulitzer Prize–winning *The Soul of a New Machine* poetically traces the development of a supercomputer within the human boundaries of a corporate hierarchy. The book, receiving its impetus from the computer generation of American culture, sparked journalist Tracy Kidder's creativity and propelled him to the forefront of the literary world.

Critics applauded Kidder's skillful handling of his technical subject. Kidder exposed the raw power behind the industry that created the computer. His book focused on the heightened moments of drama, compelling the reader to become engrossed in a tale of technical adventure. With genuine sentiment, Kidder approached *The Soul of a New Machine* trying to uncover the human aspects of a technical institution. Samuel C. Florman, in *Contemporary Authors,* claimed that Kidder's characters "are portrayed as eccentric knights errant, clad in blue jeans and open collars, seeking with awesome intensity the grail of technological achievement."

A key factor in the success of *The Soul of a New Machine* proved to be Kidder's own journalistic ideology. Due to his extensive training in the world of journalism, Kidder developed an acute sense that research provides the drive in producing narrative. In *The Soul of a New Machine,* Kidder was able to detail the extensive inner workings of the computer, deriving his technological thrust from the months he spent in the basement of the laboratory observing the engineering teams. The technological tidbits Kidder collected in his research aided the validity of the book and revealed the creative genius of the computer experts.

The Soul of a New Machine remains compelling for Kidder's innovative presentation of a technical subject. His thorough research and dynamic characterization combine into narrative art. His book produces both illustrative adventure and complex entertainment. Thus, readers and critics close the final pages surprised at their new degree of understanding of, and delight in, the computer phenomenon.

produced by a rival firm, Digital Equipment Corporation, or DEC. A VAX and a modest amount of adjunctive equipment sold for something like $200,000, and as West liked to say, DEC was beginning to sell VAXes "like jellybeans." West had traveled to this room to find out for himself just how good this computer was, compared with the one that his team was building.

West spent the morning removing the VAX's twenty-seven printed circuit boards. He'd take one out, study it, make a few notes, and then put it back. These boards were flat plates, each about the size of a shirt cardboard. In regular columns across their surfaces lay small rectangular boxes. Each of these boxes enclosed an integrated circuit, or "chip"; if bared and examined under a microscope, the chips would look like mazes—imagine the wiring diagram of an office building inscribed on a fingernail. It's possible to get inside the chips, inside the littlest boxes inside the boxes that constitute the central works of a modern computer, and, bringing back the details, to create a functionally equivalent copy of a machine. "Reverse engineering" is the name for that art, and it takes time and equipment. West called such engineering "knock-off copy work." He had a simpler purpose. He was not going to imitate VAX; he just wanted to size it up.

Looking into the VAX, West felt that he saw a diagram of DEC's corporate organization. He found the VAX "too complicated." He did not like, for instance, the system by which various parts of the machine communicated with each other; for his taste, there was too much protocol involved. The machine expressed DEC's cautious, bureaucratic style. West was pleased with this idea.

His hands in the machine, West was also studying and counting parts; many of the chips had numbers on their housings that were like names familiar to him. When he was all done, he added everything up and decided that it probaby cost $22,500 to manufacture the essential hardware of a VAX. He left the machine exactly as he had found it.

"I'd been living in fear of VAX for a year," West said one evening afterward, while driving along Route 495 in central Massachusetts. "I wasn't really into G-2. VAX was in the public domain, and I wanted to see how bad the damage was. I think I got a high when I looked at it and saw how complex and expensive it was. It made me feel good about some of the decisions we've made."

West was forty but looked younger. He was thin and had a long narrow face and a mane of brown hair that spilled over the back of his collar. These days he went to work in freshly laundered blue jeans or pressed khakis, in leather moccasins, and in solid-colored long-sleeved shirts, with the sleeves rolled up in precise folds, like the pages of a letter, well above his bony elbows. He expostulated with his hands. When dismissing someone or some idea or both, he made a fist and then exploded it, fingers splaying wide. The gesture was well known to those engineers who worked for him. Long index fingers inserted under either side of the bridge of his glasses signified thought, and when accompanied by a long "*Ummmmmmmmmh*" warned that some emphatic statement was near. Indeed, West made few statements that were not emphatic. Seen at the wheel of his shiny red Saab, he made a picture of impatience. His jaw was set; he had a forward lean. Sometimes he briefly wore a mysterious smile. He was a man on a mission.

"With VAX, DEC was trying to minimize the risk," West said, as he swerved around another car. "We're trying to maximize the win. . . ."

Exercises

1. You are writing an article about the rate of heart disease among working women and have assembled the facts listed below. Write three different leads for the story based on your reading in this chapter.

Dr. Suzanne Haynes at the National Heart, Lung and Blood Institute conducted a study in which she found that working women did not have a significantly higher rate of heart disease than did housewives.

American women live an average of almost eight years longer than American men do.

Type A women (those who are hard-driving, aggressive, and competitive) have a much greater chance of developing heart disease than do more relaxed, Type B women.

Scientists have identified a number of coronary risk factors, individual characteristics of health and behavior, that when taken together predict the likelihood that a person will develop heart disease. Among them are cigarette smoking, excess body weight, salt intake, saturated fat and cholesterol intake, level of physical activity, and level of stress and tension.

The rate of smoking among young women has nearly doubled in the past 14 years. It has declined slightly among women over 30.

2. Choose a magazine article that you think is particularly well written. Identify the transitions in the article and discuss how the writer used them to change topics or to change ideas. Then choose an article that you think is poorly written and do the same thing. To what extent do you think the transitions in the poorly written article contribute to its low quality?

3. Read several articles in the same magazine, giving particular attention to the leads and endings. Compare those that you like with those you consider ineffective and explain why. Can you detect any similarities in style that may have come from the magazine's editors instead of from the article writers?

ELEVEN

VOICE AND FLOW

*Every writer, by the way he uses the
language, reveals something of his spirit,
his habits, his capacities, his bias.*

E. B. WHITE

Producer Jules Dassin once submitted a play to Katharine Hepburn. She read it, then went to her desk and wrote: "My dear Mr. Dassin: Thank you so much for sending me this fascinating play. I found it most interesting, but unfortunately. . . ."

She stopped, offended by her false tone, and began again: "Dear Jules Dassin: Try as I will, I cannot make head or tail of this confusing manuscript. . . ." She stopped again and tried once more: "Mr. Dassin: This is the most idiotic and *depressing* piece of claptrap I have ever. . . ."

No, she had gone too far, she thought. Finally: "Dear Mr. Dassin: I am grateful to you for thinking of me, but I am not available. . . ." No, again. Why lie?

Later, she told friends of her struggle to find the proper response. Asked what she had finally decided, she said, "Oh, I just put all four of them into an envelope and sent it off to him!"

Hepburn is not the only person who has trouble deciding exactly how to say or write something. Although most readers have some idea about what they don't like in a passage, they are unsure how to improve it. Using precise words in concise, informal sentences is essential, but there is much more to style. This chapter focuses on three techniques for using your voice in writing.

CHOOSING A VOICE

The late Harold Ross of the *New Yorker* was a great editor primarily because he read everything submitted to his magazine as though he were a subscriber. He sometimes carried the reader's point of view almost to absurdity. At one weekly staff meeting, he looked with bewilderment at a cartoon other editors were chuckling over and asked, "Where am *I* in this?" That was his blunt way of saying, "Imagine that this is a real scene the reader is watching. Exactly where is he standing?"

Writers must ask themselves: Where do I want the reader to focus? On me? On his or her own involvement in my topic? On something or someone distant from both of us? Answering such questions helps determine which voice to use.

Although it requires exact language used in tight, informal sentences, plain style entails much more. Such writing may be plain, but it is not prosaic. A number of techniques can help give writing spark and vibrancy. Lively writing relies on a genuine voice that suits its subject.

Which Voice to Use

Virginia Woolf in her essay "A Room of One's Own" uses voice adroitly to define her audience and its relationship to her *I*. She begins: "But, you may ask, we asked you to speak about women and fiction—what has that got to do with a room of one's own? I will try to explain." And she proceeds to draw the reader gently through a range of attitudes, from a listening *you* to an observer who accompanies her through the retrospective examination of her thoughts to a partner in mock complicity, as in the following self-interruption: "I turned the page and read . . . I am sorry to break off so abruptly. Are there no men present? Do you promise me that behind that red curtain over there the figure of Sir Charles Biron is not concealed? We are all women, you assure me?"

Woolf's pointed presentation of her reader reflects the question writers must ask: What focus do I want to establish? Should my readers observe me, observe themselves involved within my topic, or stand with me to observe a distant subject? Determining this focus helps the writer choose a voice.

Authors seldom use the first-person *I* in a textbook, because texts focus more on students and subject matter than on their writers. More appropriate to written instruction is *you*, although *we* is almost as prevalent, representing those of us who comprise the community of writers. (Writers also use the so-called editorial *we* in reference to themselves alone.) This book usually addresses "the writer" because that is its natural audience. Although *one* appears on occasion, it is formal and, when used too often, can sound awkward: "If one assumes one can succeed, one can."

Some general advice is helpful when selecting a voice.

The Hazards of *I*

When your subject is yourself, using *I* comes naturally. You need only check to make sure that *I* does not crop up repeatedly in each sentence. When you write about someone other than yourself, however, you run the risk of succumbing to an unconscious egoism that inserts *I* into practically every sentence. A student who proposes to write about an unlikely friend may begin:

> I dislike sports. Uncompetitive and basically lazy, I start a slow retreat when someone suggests a game of touch football or maybe a little soccer.

> You can imagine my dismay when I was invited to meet Alex at the local gym.
>
> Get the picture: a noisy basketball court at the gym. Almost everybody is running up and down dribbling a ball. Others are practicing shots at a free basket. I am standing in the doorway shivering in my shorts. I had promised myself. . . .

This student is uncompetitive, lazy—and self-centered. We have more than seventy-five words about the writer's predicament and are still a long way from meeting the ostensible subject of the piece, Alex.

You do not have to efface yourself totally to describe another person. A skillful writer can show us a character by reflection. Annie Dillard begins a piece: "The island where I live is peopled with cranks like myself. In a cedar-shake shack on a cliff is a man in his thirties who lives alone with a stone he is trying to teach to talk." She continues: "No one knows what goes on at these sessions, least of all myself, for I know Larry but slightly, and that owing to a mix-up in our mail. I assume that, like any other meaningful effort, the ritual involves sacrifice, the suppression of self-consciousness, and a certain precise tilt of the will, so that the will becomes transparent and hollow, a channel for the work. I wish him well." Dillard concentrates on her assumptions about Larry (although she does use *I* often), and her focus is always on the man and his task. She reports her reflections to illuminate Larry.

Many of us naturally gravitate to using *I* in our writing. We need not avoid it entirely. Personal accounts become awkward if the writer tries to get around using the first person. In an attempt to appear detached and impartial, some journalists refer to themselves by another name or as "this reporter"—a practice that can sound absurd. Including yourself in a piece can individualize and deepen the writing, but self-indulgence is a continual danger. To avoid this, ask yourself these questions before using first person:

Why am I putting myself here?

Does the piece need me?

Can it work as well without me?

Can it work *better* without me?

Whether you use *I* usually depends on your topic: is it a concept or a personal experience? Writers who present topics they have studied or heard about or seen probably should maintain some distance from the topic—as they did in life. But writing based on experience requires a demonstration of the writer's own involvement, as this excerpt from Anaïs Nin's first diary illustrates:

> When I look at the large green iron gate from my window it takes on the air of a prison gate. An unjust feeling, since I know I can leave the place whenever I want to, and since I know that human beings place upon an object, or a person, this responsibility of being the obstacle when the obstacle lies always within one's self.
>
> In spite of this knowledge I often stand at the window staring at

the large closed iron gate, as if hoping to obtain from this contempla-
tion a reflection of my inner obstacles to a full, open life.

No amount of oil can subdue its rheumatic creaks, for it takes a
historical pride in its two-hundred-year-old rust.

But the little gate, with its overhanging ivy like disordered hair
over a running child's forehead, has a sleepy and sly air, an air of being
always half open.

I chose the house for many reasons.

Nin is using her own psychological state to describe the gate she sees
from her window; she is not present in the scene merely to indulge herself.
Her attendance clarifies the gate for her readers rather than obscuring it.

Here is how a writer began an article about a personal experience:

I was almost beside myself in frustration until the fourth night of the
session, as I sat in the center of the cabin after all the boys had finally
settled down for the night. Suddenly, I heard a noise unlike anything I'd
heard before—a kind of quiet whining alternating with short squeaks
and puffs. Following the sound to a bed against the far wall, I found
Terel with his pillow over his head, sobbing uncontrollably. As I
touched his shoulder, he looked up at me with big tear-filled brown
eyes and said, "Momma, I miss Momma." I sat with him for over an
hour, rubbing his back until he fell asleep, and tried to imagine a life
without sound, without even being able to hear yourself cry. From my
position there, I could hear the tiniest things—the cabin shifting on its
foundation, wind blowing through the trees—and Terel's sobs getting
softer and softer until he began to breathe peacefully. There was so
much love kept inside of him that people might not ever try to see.

Obviously, this paragraph would have been awkward without the use
of *I.* However, the article did not focus entirely on the writer. The next paragraph described children with diabetes, mentioning the writer only when
appropriate:

From that day on, I became determined to learn what was going on
inside our campers' heads, to try to understand how life appeared to
them. A camper with cerebral palsy, named Nancy, taught me more
basic sign language until I could hold a pretty decent conversation. But
Diabetes Week proved the biggest challenge for me, as I attempted to
find that camper perspective. Three times a day, and sometimes more
often, the girls in our cabin would take their insulin shots, preparing
their syringes under the care of a medic staff member and shooting
themselves in the leg or arm with the long, thin needle. One evening,
our medic turned to the counselors and asked, "Do you guys want
to try?"

Speaking to *You*

Italo Calvino pulls the reader into his fictional worlds by using second person
to create an overwhelming immediacy. In his book *Invisible Cities,* he uses
the narrator Marco Polo to describe the city of Phyllis:

But it so happens that, instead, you must stay in Phyllis and spend the rest of your days there. Soon the city fades before your eyes, the rose windows are expunged, the statues on the corbels, the domes. Like all Phyllis inhabitants, you follow zigzag lines from one street to another, you distinguish the patches of sunlight from the patches of shade, a door here, a stairway there, a bench where you can put down your basket, a hole where your foot stumbles if you are not careful.

The reader is captive of both Phyllis and Calvino's imagination.

If we could always write to one reader, we would have no difficulty seizing our audience's attention—but we cannot. Writers of great talent can appear to speak directly to all readers: a journalist can portray events so that they seem to touch everyone's lives, or a novelist can offer such insight into human nature that all who read the book can feel themselves a part of it. These, however, are not the rule.

Writers who wish to tap their readers' natural self-interest may use second person in an attempt to create an imagined intimacy. Calling the reader *you* has advantages long recognized by those in advertising. "How-to" books and articles and direct-mail appeals use an implied *you* to attract the reader. *You* comes naturally to writers of instructional material. Travel writers also use second person to good effect ("To your left, after you leave the darkness of the corridor, is the sand and rock composition of Mirei Shigemore . . .").

Although effective, *you* often proves bothersome. The insistence of the repeated *you* can make readers self-conscious, too aware of the writer's technique. We usually find it difficult to use *you* for long in a conversation: "You will like this restaurant because you do so much Northern Italian cooking yourself, and you can appreciate. . . ." Continual use of *you* eventually makes both writer and reader uncomfortable and tired; it is the hardest of the three voices to sustain. A writer who starts out in second person, finds it unwieldy, and moves to first or third person can leave a bewildered reader behind, wondering, "What happened to me?"

This writer began in second person and quickly changed to third person:

Meet Jeff Blazy: stand-up comedian, rising media star, and one-half of the "Blazy and Bob" morning drive team at San Jose's KOME (98.5 FM), the most popular and highest-rated rock station in the Bay Area. Blazy plays comedian to his partner Bob Lilley's straight man, and listeners are often treated to Blazy's antics over the air, like the time he tried a live telephone hookup with Fidel Castro. Blazy also creates his skits using original characters and material from his stand-up acts.

The Serviceable Third Person
That the more intimate voices *I* and *you* should be impractical under so many circumstances in writing may seem odd. Our only recourse seems to be a remote third person, which sets reader and writer at some distance from each other. But is this voice really so detached?

A good writer can actually use third person to accomplish much the same results of using *I* and *you*—without the dangers of those more inflexible forms of address. In the following passage, Nora Ephron describes Julie Nixon Eisenhower on the platform at a Right to Read conference:

> . . . her face is perfect, not smiling, mind you—this is too serious an event for that—but bright, intent, as if she is absolutely fascinated by what he is saying. Perhaps she actually is. . . . Throughout she listens raptly, smiles on cue, laughs a split second after the audience laughs. Perhaps she is actually amused. On the way out, she says she hopes she will be able to obtain a copy of the speech she has just sat through. Perhaps she actually thought it was interesting. There is no way to know. No way to break through. She has it all down perfectly. She was raised for this, raised to cut ribbons, and now that it has all gone sour, it turns out that she has been raised to deal with that, too.

Ephron might have opened the scene with "I watch her take a seat near the lectern and can see that her face is perfect. . . ." Or Ephron might have written: "From the audience you can see that her face is perfect. . . ." The use of *I* or *you* serves no real purpose, however. The reader knows Ephron undoubtedly sat in the conference audience taking notes, so why intrude with *I?* And many readers may find the heavy irony of Ephron's observations incompatible with their own habits of thought, so *you* becomes an awkward fit. Instead, Ephron's careful description of Julie Eisenhower deftly positions the reader at the conference, simultaneously "seeing" the speaker and sharing the writer's wry observations about her.

Using this focused third person, the writer can concentrate on the particulars that compose a person or scene. Another option is the more omniscient third person that opens up a panoramic view, reaching beyond the limited vision of a single observer. A skilled writer with careful organization can learn to move smoothly back and forth between the sharp focus and panorama.

Here is another example of an article, written in the third person, that focuses closely on the subject:

> She sits there peacefully, feet firmly placed on the floor, back straight, head held high, and with an obliviousness to the world around her. Not once in the last fifteen minutes has this graceful figure looked away from the object of her attention—her canvas. She remains expressionless, and, ostensibly, without a care in the world.
>
> Though surrounded by penciled drawings and self-portraits, colorful abstract paintings, and uncanny reproductions of Picasso and Matisse masterpieces, her latest work, a landscape painting of Billings, Montana, seems to be a drastic departure for this budding young artist.
>
> An artist who quietly wears the name, she may be said to typify her profession with pronounced features, a nuance of mystery, and a plethora of talent. Though only 24 years old, this dark-haired beauty wears a rugged countenance far sooner than its time, leading one to wonder whether this young woman's difficult life finds true release through her art.

If you have reservations about the adaptability and power of third-person address, remember that *I* and *you* in some cases can serve as well or better. Whatever voice you choose, its effectiveness depends on its imaginative use in concert with other techniques.

MAKING IT FLOW

"Not chaos-like,
together crushed
and bruised . . ."

ALEXANDER POPE

Some of the techniques used to make writing flow smoothly from point to point are so subtle and so important that few readers are aware that they enjoy the work of some writers at least partly because it is coherent. Readers usually praise writers for other qualities: "She puts things so well." "He says exactly what I've been thinking but didn't know how to say." "Her writing is so colorful." "The phrases are so clever." "He really knows what he's talking about." And so on.

Failing to think of the orderly flow of facts and ideas is understandable. Readers expect coherence. If a piece is wildly disorganized, they will almost surely dislike it and probably throw it aside after reading a few paragraphs. Readers interested in a topic may suffer their way through some disorder. But when they discover a piece that moves so logically from point to point that it is seamless, they are pleased without knowing why.

Coherence in writing comes from sequential thought, which attaches one frame of fact and idea to another so that they fit together without rattling or falling apart. Thinking in sequence is difficult even when we are not writing. Norman Cousins, former editor of *Saturday Review,* points out that it calls for a staggering number of mental operations:

> The route must be anticipated between the present location of an idea and where it is supposed to go. Memory must be raked for relevant material. Facts or notions must be sorted out, put in their proper places, then supplied with connective tissue. Then come the problems of weighting and emphasis.

Writing sequentially requires another complex operation: anticipating how readers' thoughts will move. The following passage shows how easy it is to forget readers:

> "Astrology, palmistry, phrenology, life reading, fortune telling, cartomancy, clairvoyance, clairaudience, crystal gazing, hypnotism, mediumship, prophecy, augury, divination, magic or necromancy" for money are illegal activities in Palo Alto and licensed businesses in Menlo Park. Both laws have been on the books for forty years and read as though they came from a Model Government Game, with blanks to fill in, permitted or not permitted.

"Both laws"? When readers come upon those words, their minds say that no law has been mentioned. The long series of unusual words in the first sentence is difficult to digest (while puzzling over a quotation attributed to no one); they haven't thought of "illegal activities" and "licensed businesses" in terms of law. An activity is illegal as a result of a law, a business is licensed because of a law; neither is a law. Moreover, the analogy of the "Model Government Game" in the second sentence makes readers use their imaginations, which they can't do while puzzling over "Both laws." To understand "Both laws," readers must look back at the first sentence to trace the meaning, which halts their reading and irritates them.

This error could be corrected by treating "illegal activities" and "licensed businesses" in terms of laws in the first sentence: ". . . illegal in Palo Alto and permitted by law in Menlo Park." The ease of correcting may make the principle seem unimportant, but if we do not think sequentially in small matters, we may be powerless with larger ones.

The largest problem in writing coherently grows out of the infinite number of ways we can combine the two basic kinds of order, chronological and subtopical. We can arrange the parts of a topic according to the time certain events occurred. We can arrange them according to the way subtopics fit together. In most cases, the topic itself helps us decide which kind of order should dominate. For example, the need for more opportunities for women to participate in campus athletics is likely to require arrangement by subtopic; it is focused on the present. A section of the piece could be chronological—perhaps recent actions by the administration to help satisfy the need—but arrangement by subtopic would dominate. If the topic, though, is the growing need, the piece would lend itself to a chronological account, probably with the first few sentences focused on the present, then a flashback.

This article is organized by using both methods:

The democratic dream that Americans hold today has existed since 1620, when the Pilgrims first settled in America. America's first constitution, the Mayflower Compact, with its emphasis on liberty and resistance to elite control, served as a foundation for the democratic dream. This "dream" is for individuals to live in an ideal society of equality, independence, freedom, and prosperity. The question is, "Does democracy truly allow for complete independence and freedom?" In a society divided between rich and poor, educated and uneducated, can everyone achieve the "American Dream"?

A few months ago an event took place in New York that made me rethink the meaning of democracy and of the "American Dream." In a black community where Korean Americans have immigrated to consist of almost half the population, the pursuit of the dream has led to fighting and extreme cultural tension. The blacks have boycotted a small grocery market owned by two Korean American brothers who immigrated to the States only 5 years ago. Many believe that this is a sign of racial tension resulting from the blacks' resentment toward a "new minority" coming in and taking away their opportunities for economic and social advancement (in other words, inhibiting their acquisition of the "American Dream").

The Korean Americans claim that they will not "Go back!" as the blacks chant from the sidewalk, because they came to America to pursue the American dream and desire the freedom to pursue capitalist ventures. As a result, blacks claim that they will continue to boycott the over 14 markets owned by Korean American immigrants in the area.

First, the writer put his information into chronological order. By including historical facts, he placed the article's main topic in context. However, he soon abandoned the chronological organization to focus on the present problems faced by Korean Americans. The rest of his article was organized subtopically.

Writing about a person usually calls for arrangement by subtopic, with a section devoted to the person's past related chronologically. If the topic idea is to show what a person has become, though—perhaps a profile of success that grew out of small beginnings—time elements should dominate.

In addition, profiles may be organized chronologically if the writer is tracing the subject's activities over a period of time. For example, read this profile written by a student:

> Steve Buddie looked at the clock nervously. It read 6:58. With one hand holding the agenda from the Lagunita resident assistant staff meeting and the other clutching the worn straps to his gym bag, he rushed toward his rusty ten-speed. Balancing the bulging bag of sweats and wrestling head gear over his shoulder, he raced toward the Old Pavilion, where his teammates awaited his arrival. Coach Chris Horpel shouted while laughing, "Here comes King Lag, 'Dumb Jock R.A.!'"
>
> By 7:15, Buddie had shed his tortoise-rimmed glasses and baggy shorts. Buddie's eyes no longer carried the warmth and humor they did while at the resident assistant staff meeting. Buddie now stood with hands extended as if ready to pounce and legs bent in preparation to lunge toward the number one Falcon wrestler from the Air Force Academy.
>
> With the drop of the referee's hand, the 177-pound Freshman All-American sprung with the force of a panther and grace of a hawk upon his opponent. He entangled his limbs around the torso of the writhing figure beneath him. The mass of flesh, tumbling and rolling upon the mat, left streaks of sweat upon the Stanford Cardinal emblem where they fell again and again.

Choosing the Right Words

Jennifer Koch, a practiced writer, goes through a routine with her roommate in search of *the* correct words:*

> "What's another word for compassion?"
>
> My roommate, long accustomed to this routine, sets down her book and performs her human thesaurus imitation for me. "Consideration . . . understanding . . . sympathy. . . ."
>
> "No, no. Those aren't right at all," I say, only slightly agitated.

---

*Reprinted by permission of Jennifer L. Koch.

"The one I want begins with an 'm,' I think . . . uh . . . sensitivity, that's it! Thanks."

With an almost imperceptible shake of her head, my friend returns to her book.

I continue to mumble aloud, searching for an appropriate descriptive word for a tan. Dramatic terms such as "incredible" or "flawless" are finally discarded in favor of "deep." Reading through the Stanford water polo story I am freelancing for the *San Francisco Sports Review,* I pause at all the words or phrases I have underlined in the revised revision of the first draft. An underline signifies a problem, often an entire paragraph that needs to be replaced or rewritten.

Descriptions that don't achieve their intended effect are immediately emphasized with a dark line, as are complicated explanations that need to be split into several simpler sentences. Reading each sentence aloud, both when it is originally written and several more times when parts of the "final" story are scribbled out and deserted in disgust, tends to activate that black pen.

During this process, the contrived adjectives—most of them, anyway—are simplified or eliminated. The words that combine awkwardly are smoothed over. The phrases that sound as if they are trying too hard to create an image are rewritten. And invariably, there is a long, uneasy struggle to allow the transitions to flow with ease. . . .

After much anguish, I abandon the phrase "impeccable rows" for the word "neat" and decide that "bleachers" and "shivering" can stand alone without the aid of trite descriptive words. A confusing, overly long sentence about the team devoting exclusive attention to the coach is replaced by "focusing its collective stare." The final underline in the paragraph refers to an attempt to convey how the attitude of the coach conflicts with his tough-guy appearance. Running my hands re-

JENNIFER KOCH

When a professor faced his students for the first time in 1985, he saw a lovely blonde, Jennifer Koch, in the class. He thought, "Here's another beautiful girl who'll make, at best, a C. Oh well, what can I do to teach her about writing? Probably nothing." When Koch turned in her first paper, the professor was so startled by her concise, wonderfully chosen words that rather than award Koch an A+, because he would surely regret that grade, he marked it "A," thinking that her fine paper was probably an accident. Minutes later, he revised her grade from A to A+. Every other paper she wrote that term deserved and received an A+. Two years later, when she had been in the professor's classes three times, he gave her three grades of A+.

Koch's determination to revise her writing almost endlessly began in high school in her hometown, Buffalo, New York. She sailed through college, impressing everyone who read her writing. In addition, she proved she was a woman who apparently had a steel-trap mind.

In fact, one of Koch's friends mailed her story of revising words—which appears immediately before this profile—to William F. Buckley, Jr., editor of *National Review.* After reading Koch's writing, Buckley gave it to his staff with a recommendation that it be published.

peatedly through my hair doesn't seem to improve my creative powers, but after a pizza break I manage to achieve the image I want with a
sentence about the coach's sunglasses.

> Dettamanti demonstrates this sensitivity by leading his team
> meetings with an extraordinary blend of friendship and leader-
> ship. The team, deeply tanned, sits in neat rows on the bleachers
> by the pool, shivering in red Speedos on the windy October af-
> ternoon, focusing its collective stare directly at the coach. Team
> members follow Dettamanti's example, whether joking or se-
> rious, but offer him their complete attention at all times. And
> Dettamanti speaks to, and about, his players with a sincerity un-
> masked by his dark, mirrored glasses.

> Satisfied with this effort, I turn to the conclusion, in which I had
> simply and cleanly attempted to tie the entire story together by refer-
> ring back to an image in the opening paragraph. The final paragraph has
> been underlined.

Sequence of Time

The simplest chronological order is obvious: one thing happens, then another. But when you are writing a piece based on subtopical order that contains time sequences, you sometimes focus so strongly on arranging the
subtopics and on reasoning from cause to effect and evidence to conclusion
that you confuse the sequence of time. In the middle of a piece on a controversy involving African-American filmmakers, a student wrote:

> Prior to this turn of events, a group of black artists who work in the film
> industry decided to enter the controversy. Previously, groups such as
> Blackploitation and the Beverly Hills chapter of the NAACP Rating
> Committee for Black Films had approached the problem from the
> standpoint of censorship. They believe that only the positive aspects of
> blackness are acceptable. The negative side must not be seen at all. The
> Black Artists Alliance was created to challenge institutional racism in
> the film industry and other media.

"Prior to this," then "previously"—twice readers are pushed backward in time. They first absorb the information about the group of African-
American artists and fix in their minds that the group began its work before
the events just described. They can do that fairly easily. But then they must
place themselves in an even earlier time, take on information about two
other groups, and learn the purposes of those groups. At the end of the paragraph, they must return to the first group to learn its purpose. Even if readers
are not confused, they must work to follow the sense.

Here is a better arrangement:

> Groups such as Blackploitation and the Beverly Hills chapter of the
> NAACP Rating Committee had long before approached the problem as
> censors. They believe that only the positive aspects of blackness are

acceptable. Then a group of black artists who work in the film industry entered the controversy, challenging institutional racism in films and other media.

When one action follows another in time like this, readers can easily follow chronological order. Sometimes whole paragraphs must be rearranged, as in this case:

> Friday has finally arrived. Midterm week is history. But before the week turns into recorded grades, the weekend is before you, and it's time to get away. The beaches of the Pacific Coast provide an escape from the hassles and pressures of college life.
>
> Thoughts of differential equations, iambic pentameter, and amino acids drift from your mind as you bask in the sun and listen to the waves. The wind may chap your skin and whip through your hair like a savage current, but a relaxing day at the seashore brings inner peace.
>
> The only requisites for this excursion are a free day and a car or bike to take you to the water. But you should also take with you. . . .

Smooth as this may seem, it mixes time elements. In the first paragraph, readers think about the beach. In the second, they are on it. In the third, they are back in the dormitory getting ready for the trip. It is not essential to arrange the paragraphs in chronological order—readers need not work to understand the passage, as they must work to understand the passage about the African-American groups—but writers should be aware of such minor faults. They should write sequences of time that are logical, and, in addition, they should try to arrange them for the positive effects that grow out of passages that move smoothly from one moment to the next.

Sequence of Space

Sequences of space can also be written to produce subtle effects. At the beginning of one of his best short stories, Joseph Conrad shows a man at the bow of a boat that is making its way upriver. The passage is narrow, the shore thick with trees. The man's vision is constricted. So is the vision of the reader. Then the river widens, the man can see more, and, suddenly, so can the reader. It does not matter that readers do not analyze the technique. They are affected by it.

Readers are affected negatively by faulty use of space, as in the following:

> Wave after wave of organ-launched tones charge the vaulted cavern of the church, crowding and jostling and invading every recess, resounding to assault each person from all sides. The congregation at the church's depths populates rows of parallel pews in a multicolored array, arranged in mysteriously random groups of different sizes.
>
> The people had gathered for the Sunday 11 o'clock service to hear John Hamerton-Kelley preach. Three domed sections of the church joined a fourth elongated section to form a hollow crucifix. The junction, bordered by four cement-cylinder arches connecting corner

pillars, draws sunlight through a cloudy skylight capping the central dome. Far below, in the twilight of the filtered sunlight, stands a figure robed in black satin and velvet, a brilliant red stole over his shoulders. The music evaporates. With a sweep of his hand, the congregation shuffles to its collective feet. His voice. . . .

This passage contains far too many forceful adjectives and adverbs, but a worse flaw is the zigzag effect. The writer describes the church in the first sentence, the congregation in the second. The second paragraph starts smoothly: the congregation is mentioned, which provides a link to the preceding sentence, and the focus narrows to the preacher. Then, unaccountably, the writer describes the church again, then the preacher again. The writing leaps about and readers must try to follow it.

As a writer, you should look carefully for flaws in what you have written; beyond that, you can improve your writing by thinking positively about sequences of time and space. Ask yourself: How can I arrange time and space so that readers can move smoothly?

Speeding the Pace of Sentences and Paragraphs

Writing each sentence so that the reader moves easily from one point to another speeds the pace of each paragraph. The second paragraph from this description of students in a beginning tennis course needs a bit of editing to give readers a sense of movement:

> They relax arms and shoulders with broad, slow arcs in the air. Each scrambles for a ball and consciously adjusts his psyche. They serve in threes. "Weight back—push your racquets down, toss, come up, and hit," the instructor intones. Three balls wobble up and are knocked from their paths. Three more, three more, and three more fly up together, separate on contact with the racquets, and go up, over, down, or nowhere, according to the server's skill. The drill is repeated with little more success.
>
> The instructor demonstrates. He steps in front of the class and executes the exercise. The ball performs admirably, sizzling a quarter-inch over the net. The next serve easily floats away, accurate again.

Note that each sentence in the first paragraph carries the reader forward. The beginning of the second paragraph, however, is halting: "The instructor demonstrates. He steps in front of the class and executes the exercise." Although different words are used, the second sentence says little more than the first. (If the writer were describing complex action, the classic device of restatement in different words might be useful.) In effect, the reader is marking time instead of marching. The writer can speed the pace by combining sentences like this: "The instructor steps in front of the class and demonstrates." This enables the reader to move into the sentence beginning "The ball performs" with a sense of fast pace.

Except when the writer is trying to produce a special staccato effect, most short sentences should be combined to help speed the pace. Here is an example of a paragraph that seems a bit halting because all of its six sentences are short and of approximately the same length:

> To Texas students, a football game is many things. To some, it is an all-day party. To others, it is an opportunity to socialize. To still others, it is a great place to get a tan. Some come primarily to watch the band perform. A few even come to watch the game.

Each sentence moves a bit because each offers new information. But the pace is slow between the first sentence and the last. Perhaps the paragraph should read:

> To Texas students, a football game is many things: an all-day party, an opportunity to socialize, or a great place to get a tan. Some come primarily to watch the band perform. A few even come to watch the game.

The first four sentences were combined to speed the pace. The fifth was not changed because a different rhythm prevents monotony.

If the Texas students had been in action in the stands, that paragraph might have been written at greater length to include action and might also have been written as one or two sentences to make the prose move as fast as the action. Hemingway, who usually wrote short sentences, sometimes wrote long ones to give a sense of action, as in the sentence at the end of his story "The Short Happy Life of Francis Macomber":

> "He's dead in there," Wilson said. "Good work," and he turned to grip Macomber's hand and as they shook hands, grinning at each other, the gunbearer shouted wildly and they saw him coming out of the bush sideways, fast as a crab, and the bull coming, nose out, mouth tight and closed, blood dripping, massive head straight out, coming in a charge, his little pig eyes blood-shot as he looked at them. Wilson, who was ahead, was kneeling shooting, and Macomber, as he fired, unhearing his shot in the roaring of Wilson's gun, saw fragments like slate burst from the huge boss of the horns, and the head jerked, he shot again at the wide nostrils and saw the horns jolt again and fragments fly, and he did not see Wilson now and, aiming carefully, shot again with the buffalo's huge bulk almost on him and his rifle almost level with the oncoming head, nose out, and he could see the little wicked eyes and the head started to lower and he felt a sudden whitehot, blinding flash explode inside his head and that was all he ever felt.

This is hurry-up language that carries the reader along as it runs to keep pace with the bull. Structuring fast-paced sentences usually requires revision; Hemingway was known for repeatedly revising his sentences.

If you start nearly every sentence with subject, then verb, you can be certain that the pace of reading will be slow. This paragraph was preceded and followed by many sentences beginning in that conventional form:

> I first saw Huahine in 1968 from a DC-3 enroute from Tahiti to Bora Bora. I was visiting the islands for a three-week period. The island

looked startlingly pristine. The vegetation looked unbelievably thick. The island, divided into two parts by an inland bay, was surrounded by one common barrier reef, which was spectacular in its colorful variations of blues and greens.

The paragraph could be revised in many ways to speed the pace. Consider this revision:

I first saw Huahine during a three-week trip in 1968 from a DC-3 enroute from Tahiti to Bora Bora. The island looked startlingly pristine, the vegetation unbelievably thick. Divided by an inland bay, it was surrounded by a common barrier reef, which was spectacular in its colorful variations of blues and greens.

To summarize the principles that help in speeding the pace of paragraphs:

1. If short sentences are not written for a particular effect and reading them is monotonous, combine a few sentences.
2. You can make language keep pace with action by writing long sentences, usually during revision.
3. For variety in sentence structure, invert some sentences and begin some with prepositional phrases and dependent clauses.

Read this paragraph and notice how the writer used a variety of sentence structures to achieve a quick pace:

When Kay Tittle was called into her tennis coach's office after practice, she prepared herself to receive a lecture. There had been tension between her and the coach for the past week. Kay, furious with Frank, had ceased to acknowledge his presence, except to complete the assigned drills with the enthusiasm of a machine. When Kay reached Frank's office, what she saw made her do a double take. Her coach, an intimidating, six-foot, 200-pound man, had tears in his eyes. "Kay, I can't stand to have you hate me. I really care about you." These were the last words Kay expected to hear, but it is this sensitivity and caring, combined with a strong determination, that make Frank Brennan the man and the successful tennis coach he is today.

Coherence enables readers to go faster, but the actual time readers spend reading is not as important as their sense of speed. You can understand that sense if you have ever become so absorbed in reading that you wondered later where the time went. The pace may have seemed fast because you were caught up in the story or topic, but reading also seems swift when one sentence grows out of another and one paragraph out of another in a tight structure that could be represented graphically by a line running straight from the first word to the last. Carefully written sequences and transitions both draw that line and lead readers along it. A writer can keep readers moving through a story effortlessly by making certain that each sentence has momentum.

Exercises

1. Part of this chapter argues that one should consider carefully whether to use *I* in writing pieces that do not report on the writer's own experiences. The May/June 1971 issue of *Columbia Journalism Review* carries a long article about the underground press, heavily dotted with *I*. Read the first four paragraphs of the article, which follow, and rewrite it without using *I*. Compare the two versions, then decide which you prefer and why.

> Anyone who is guilty of being forty-five years old, as I am, is probably so afflicted with the tunnel vision of his generation that he can judge other generations only by his standards rather than theirs. Thus, for a long time I dismissed the underground press because it seemed to have all the stability of a floating crap game. My opinion began to change because of these events:
>
> The Los Angeles *Free Press* installed a time clock. I didn't like time clocks when I had to punch one twenty years ago, and I wouldn't like to punch one now. But an underground paper that begins to check on the comings and goings of its staff members takes on a businesslike aura that might lure a smile from William Randolph Hearst.
>
> The owner of the Berkeley *Barb,* Max Scherr, and his staff began to fight over money. The staff wanted to buy out Scherr and cited evidence that he had been making $5,000 a week from the paper. Although reading the *Barb* fairly regularly persuades me that I do not share many values of Scherr and his staff members, this financial wrangle suggests that they share at least one of mine.
>
> Citizen Zenger Company, publishers, of Fairfax, Calif., has issued a prospectus for a kind of *Reader's Digest* of the underground press. In keeping with the casual underground spirit, some of the pages are numbered and some are not. But the prospectus is thick, it seems to cover all the factors that might bear on the success of the venture, and it reflects a serious effort to raise $100,000 to start the *Underground Digest.* Reading these plans sets me to wondering whether, like these entrepreneurs, DeWitt Wallace was foresighted enough to copyright *his* prospectus.

2. The following paragraphs are taken from the middle of an article about a student. Rewrite them in a different order that places like paragraphs together, then write a paragraph explaining why you changed the order as you did.

> She is very active during dinner, especially when there is an extra spoon on the table. She uses it as leverage. After calculating the right momentum, she places a pack of sugar on the end and Wham! the sugar lands in someone's lap. She has almost reached the point of starting a food fight with the adjoining table.
>
> When she doesn't feel like answering a question, she says, "I didn't come here to be insulted," or, "Aw, shucks." Such responses startle those who are not accustomed to her.
>
> She has started a campaign against dirty plates. Every night at dinner, she insists that everyone who sees a speck of dust, dirt or dinginess on his plate take it to the kitchen and complain.

3. One of the passages quoted in this chapter shows how Hemingway used a long sentence to give readers a feeling of action. In the following passage he wrote a long sentence, but the action description is different; Hemingway is *talking about* an action, not describing one. Compare the two passages and decide which is more effective and why.

If the spectators know the matador is capable of executing a complete, consecutive series of passes with the muleta in which there will be valor, art, understanding and, above all, beauty and great emotion, they will put up with mediocre work, cowardly work, disastrous work because they have the hope sooner or later of seeing the complete faena; the faena that takes a man out of himself and makes him feel immortal while it is proceeding, that gives him an ecstasy, that is, while momentary, as profound as any religious ecstasy; moving all the people in the ring together and increasing in emotional intensity as it proceeds, carrying the bullfighter with it, he playing on the crowd through the bull and being moved as it responds in a growing ecstasy of ordered, formal, passionate, increasing disregard for death that leaves you, when it is over, and the death administered to the animal that has made it possible, as empty, as changed, and as sad as any major emotion will leave you.

TWELVE

HUMAN INTEREST

Our most important sights are those which contradict our emotions.

PAUL VALÉRY

P oet Jesse Stuart described returning to the Kentucky hills:

> "Chickens come home to roost," my mother told me. I did, too, and that country never looked as good to me as then. The dogwood blossoms were a little whiter, the redbud a little pinker, the streams a little bluer. I was away from college, away from town, back to the life I knew. I was home—and the poems came to me. I wrote 42 in a half day and never revised them.

Stuart's revelation when arriving home led to the creation of dozens of poems. Similar experiences can lead to excellent writing because they create genuine, human feelings—which are transmitted to the readers. A human interest story has a definite aim. It should engage its readers emotionally, stimulating or depressing, angering or amusing them, awakening sympathy or distaste. Several decades ago, the human interest story was the worst variety of writing. Often it was called a "sob story," an obvious appeal for sympathy. A few elements of the newspaper industry still produce human interest writing whose only design is to wring tears. Generally, however, these stories are now much more restrained. It would be difficult to find stories today like this one of three decades ago:

> Dry your eyes, Mother Hubner. Choke back the tears, Father Hubner. Little Alice of the golden smile. . . .

A STORY FROM THE HEART

Today's feature writer is more sophisticated. In this long story, Jerry Flemmons of the *Fort Worth Star-Telegram* knows well the line he must take, even though his story is close to wringing tears.

"The human heart has hidden treasures. In secret kept, in silence sealed."

CHARLOTTE BRONTË

COMMENT

Consider the easy way Flemmons decided to knit the story together. He starts with Roy, the drunkard, then fills in the background, paragraph after paragraph.

Note especially that Flemmons does not try to make bright phrases. Instead, he has a story that he tells simply.

Consider how easily the transitions come, even those that come after subheads. The preceding paragraph ended, in part: "Townspeople, in fact, rarely complained about Roy's stealing. Roy was just an irritating cross they bore." That sentence led him to the sentence that begins, "Somewhere in Roy's background was a prison sentence, probably endured for theft. . . ." A neat transition.

HUMAN INTEREST STORY*

Roy has been dead almost a dozen winters now and no one remembers him. He had no friends and Roy was not the type of man to cause those who knew him to reminisce.

People in the small East Texas town said only of Roy that he was "the most useless man in the county" and I guess he was. Roy—his complete name was Roy William Simpson—never held a job or did anything that could be considered steady work.

Roy's only pastime was drinking. He consumed whiskey and cheap wine in awesome amounts if he could obtain either but usually he could not. More often he drank after-shave lotion, hair oil, various cooking extracts and other everyday, ordinary liquids no one but Roy considered alcoholic.

Roy existed by stealing. He stole vegetables from gardens and nearby farms. Regularly he stole from old man Otis Williams' egg farm. He never swiped chickens, which would have made Otis angry enough to call the sheriff.

He took only eggs and Old Man Williams would tell about Roy's thievery to the men at the filling station and laugh. "Roy can steal an egg before it's laid," Otis claimed.

Once, between vegetable seasons and when Otis' chickens stopped laying for some reason, Roy was forced to steal Mrs. Truax's registered poodle. He apparently intended selling the dog for funds with which to buy his distilled liquors or vanilla extract. The sheriff caught him and returned the poodle. He did not arrest Roy. Roy never was arrested for his thefts. Townspeople, in fact, rarely complained about Roy's stealing. Roy was just an irritating cross they bore, like mosquitoes in the spring or a faulty sewer system.

No Alcohol in Prison

Somewhere in Roy's background was a prison sentence, probably endured for theft of something more costly than vegetables, eggs or poodles. He rarely spoke of his jail days but once told me prison for him was not oppressive except that he suffered from lack of alcohol. He had worked for a time in the penitentiary in the license plate shop and, later, transferred to the laundry where he washed sheets and stitched up rips in mattress ticking.

In addition to stealing, Roy's source of income was curious. He was an object of ridicule to the local teenagers and station loafers.

The kids would say to Roy, "Bet you a quarter you can't run to the cafe and back in 30 seconds." Roy knew he could not but he always tried. He also knew the quarter was for his trying, and he would start off in a sort of shuffling trot, pumping his arms in an awkward rhythm, like a man going nowhere. Or one of the loafers would call, "Roy, can you dance a jig? Betcha four bits you can't." He attempted that, too. Or he would pat his head and rub his stomach for a dime.

*Reprinted by permission of Jerry Flemmons.

The loafers and teenagers never tired of the cruel game and it may have been their unconscious way of supporting a frail, liquor-ruined old man.

No Variety in Wardrobe

Note that this is not a first-person story. "I" appears infrequently. As this is written, it is as though the narrator calls on many who knew of Roy and pieces out the story from the information he gathered.

I never saw him when he was not wearing the same clothes. His wardrobe did not change, winter or summer. Roy wore dark green, dirty corduroy pants, once-brown shoes with thin heels, a bluish work shirt and the Eisenhower jacket. The scarf given him by Mr. Ferris, red and green scotch plaid, either hung straight under his jacket or was crossed over in the Continental style.

The jacket's regular buttons had been lost or removed and Roy had replaced them with bright, yellow plastic buttons. The yellow buttons only made Roy seem more of a clown.

Roy slept for years on a dirty old rug in the tool shed behind the cotton gin. When the area's cotton crop declined and the gin was torn down he moved to an ancient sharecropper's shack, a couple of miles south of town, on land owned by the bank. He boarded up windows and stuffed wadded newspaper into cracks. For a stove he used a rickety ice box lined with asbestos shingles. Roy took the rug, his only possession, and continued sleeping on it.

This is an important bridging paragraph. Flemmons must bring into the story another leading character, Margaret Lee, and still seem not to desert Roy. He begins the paragraph by linking Roy's death with the tragedy, Margaret.

See how honestly Flemmons writes "Margaret Lee was not a pretty child." And, "The mother was plain, too." Many writers would somehow see these as beautiful people. But Flemmons tells it starkly.

The September before the winter in which Roy died the community suffered a tragedy. Tragedy is the soul of small communities because one man's misfortune becomes public property. Tragedy assumes a collective face and the sorrow is borne by all.

Margaret Lee was not a pretty child. She was 5, perhaps 6, with straight blonde hair, the color of cobwebs, and watery blue, almost icy, eyes. She was thin and her skin was sickly white.

The only time I saw her she wore a print little-girl's dress and carried a battered rag doll, lying across the crook of her left arm. She and her mother lived a block south of the filling station in a three-room frame house. The mother was plain, too, and big-boned. She came from Austria and spoke English with a lowkeyed accent.

Policy, Baking Only Income

Margaret's father had met and married the woman while stationed in Europe as an Army corporal. Margaret was 4 when her father was burned to death in a gasoline truck accident on a lonely Kansas road. Mother and daughter lived on the little insurance money left by the father's death. For additional income, the mother baked and sold pies and cakes.

Flemmons tells of the gradual death very plainly. He does not attempt to wring tears from his readers. He tells the story matter-of-factly.

In September doctors confirmed Margaret had leukemia. Unable to save Margaret's life, they set about the tedious work of prolonging it. The mother almost was insane with grief and cried hysterically when neighbors came to visit.

Margaret was weaker and sicker. Her mother argued with doctors who wanted to hospitalize the child. The mother asked to keep Margaret home until the grandfather arrived. So the Methodist women continued their weekly drives to the county seat hospital for Margaret's treatments. More than a week before

Christmas the letter containing air fare and expense money was sent to the small Austrian village.

The next day Margaret lost her rag doll.

The Methodist lady whose turn it was to drive Margaret to the hospital thought the doll had been left in the waiting room. Perhaps it was, but the doll could not be found when they returned. There began another round of contributions by the church women. Dozens of rag dolls were delivered to Margaret, some store-bought, some homemade, but the child rejected all. None, she cried, was her rag doll.

Her father had given her the doll. That was the difference, explained the mother. Margaret, pale and nervous and weak, announced that Santa Claus would return her doll.

Christmas approached and the town prepared to make the holiday the happiest ever for the little girl. They bought most of the smaller toys in Mr. Ferris' store and made trips to the county seat for larger games and mechanical contraptions to please the little girl.

Last Journey across Fields

To appreciate this transition, consider the preceding paragraph. Note that the first sentence begins, "Christmas approached and the town prepared. . . ." This shows how the writer mentions others, then deals with Roy: "On the 23rd Roy. . . ." Then Flemmons goes back to Margaret in the next paragraph. This is a neat device to have the readers consider Roy again.

On the 23rd Roy received one of his $10 envelopes and immediately purchased the extract and bottle of whiskey. He struck out across the blackland fields and no one saw him alive again.

That Christmas for Margaret, although she was cranky and whiney about the loss of the doll, brought the town together as nothing before. There was a moment of concern, the day before Christmas, when Margaret was rushed to the hospital for more blood, but she returned and was put to bed.

A Lions Club member volunteered his pickup truck and toys were collected from homes and delivered to Margaret's house about 10 P.M. Christmas Eve.

Before she slept that night she talked about the doll Santa would return and her grandfather who was expected on the 28th. Christmas morning there were rag dolls but not her ragged doll, the one she missed and cried over. She opened each package and hoped, and when it was not there she wept. Later she played listlessly with her toys as she lay in bed.

Christmas Day the snow began, huge uncommon flakes for that season in East Texas. Margaret and her mother watched the snow from a front window and they talked about the grandfather.

Snow continued to fall as darkness arrived.

Here, Roy comes back into the picture.

Her grandfather came. I never saw him but people said he was a small man with a gray mustache and that he spoke no English. The grandfather and Margaret visited for a day. Then an ambulance came and took the child to the hospital.

Snow stayed on the ground for two days before melting but the weather remained unseasonably cold early in January and snow came again, not as heavily, but the ground disappeared again under the layer of white. Late in January two rabbit hunters found Roy's body.

Empty Bottle as Monument

He was stretched out under a small oak tree, in the center of a field midway between the town and his shack. An empty whiskey bottle was beside Roy. Roy had not worn his Army jacket or scarf but the corduroy pants were his, so the sheriff identified the body that way. Roy, the sheriff reasoned, had wandered into the field with his whiskey and passed out. The snow had covered him.

Roy was buried in the cemetery behind the Methodist Church, off in a corner, with the county paying funeral expenses for its most useless citizen. Sober folk saw Roy's death as retribution for a wasted whiskey-filled life and no one seemed to care very much that he was gone.

Margaret died in early March with her grandfather at the bedside. The funeral brought out most of the town's population. Mr. Ferris closed his store and even the loafers left the station long enough to watch Margaret buried on a bright spring day beneath a cordial blue sky. The mother sold the frame house and she and the grandfather left the little town and returned to Austria.

Almost a month passed before I heard about Margaret's rag doll.

Mr. Ferris said she had the doll when the ambulance came to take her to the hospital and he thought it was the doll she had lost. Later when he noticed it closely he knew and he asked the mother. Margaret thought Santa had brought it to her, she said.

Christmas Day, an hour after dark when the snow had stopped, the mother heard a noise on the porch and opened the door. The rag doll lay in the snow, next to the steps. She saw no one.

Margaret loved the doll on sight. It was a pitiful thing, ugly and poorly made, but Margaret said if Santa could not find her doll he knew the kind of doll she wanted. She loved the doll and she was happy.

Mr. Ferris recalled that the doll was much like the old one, ragged and worn and lumpy. But it had, he said, red and green scotch plaid skin and, for eyes, two bright yellow plastic buttons.

> With the mention of Roy's death, Margaret again comes into the story, as she dies. Thus, the reader makes the connection between Roy and Margaret at the end.

> Flemmons is subtly leading the readers to ask, "Was that Roy?" If that is your question, the answer can be read in the last paragraph. Recall how Flemmons gave the stress of an entire paragraph to describing "regular buttons," "bright yellow plastic buttons," and finally "yellow buttons."

This story is the epitome of simplicity. Flemmons has not tried for phrases. He does not try to coax tears for the dead Margaret Lee or even for dead Roy Simpson. He tells the story straightforwardly—first describing the old alcoholic, then weaving in the story of Margaret, then blending Roy into that story. At the end, Roy and Margaret are brought together through the rag doll episode. Flemmons's method is highly effective.

But it is also the story itself that makes this article a good one. Finding equally effective material can be a difficult task for writers. There is no simple solution to the problem of where to look for human interest stories because they can be found everywhere. The best approach is to become a keen observer of humanity and a good listener. As you learn to think in terms of article ideas, your skill in both these areas will improve.

Offhand comments made by people you encounter are often a productive source of ideas. For instance, a woman conducting a tour of a children's hospital said, "Often the person most in touch with a dying patient's feelings is the cleaning lady who comes at night. She's often the only one with the time and inclination to listen." Any writer who fails to hear the human interest story behind that remark had better change careers.

One former reporter recalled that his best source of ideas was the evening edition of the previous day's paper. He scanned the articles looking for the angle that was overlooked or the story behind the story that was already written. It was a rare day when the search did not prove fruitful. Whether you choose to look in the newspaper or to explore your own environment, the important thing is that you do look, and that you practice ferreting out the human interest stories in the world around you.

Effective human interest writing must be true; otherwise, the writing may sound false or tinny. Here is a true story written by Richard S. Davis of the *Milwaukee Journal:* *

> Last night in the Auditorium, one of the great artists of the day, a tall, handsome woman with sorrow in her face, sang for an audience of thousands, who whispered to themselves: "There simply couldn't be a lovelier voice than that one. Nor could there be a greater gift for singing."
> And that was right.
> Last night in the Auditorium, the tall woman with the almost tragic face—yes, of course, she was Marian Anderson—stood as she sang beneath a huge American flag. People commented: "There's meaning in that, her singing there against the background of the flag."
> And that was right.
> Last night in the Auditorium, when the woman sang the "Ave Maria" of the tender Schubert and the hall was as hushed as a house of prayer, there were tears on hundreds of white cheeks, and tears on scores of black cheeks, and when the last golden note had floated away, the listeners said: "No song by any singer was ever more beautiful."
> And that was right.
> Last night from the Auditorium, the people poured into the crisp night and every face was lighted. The great majority hurried every which way to their cheerful homes, but those who belonged to the race of the incomparable singer had to carry their soaring pride into the ramshackle, tumbledown district where neither pride nor hope can long survive.
> And what was right about that?

---

*Reprinted by permission of *The Milwaukee Journal.*

A WAR WITH A WORD

Here is another human interest story:

The beginning of the end of a war with a word was signalled in April 1981 when this letter was received by the editor of the *Star* at Carville, Louisiana:

As you will recall, I promised to personally support your efforts to persuade people throughout the world to use the term "Hansen's Disease" rather than "leprosy." Carville is now known as the National Hansen's Disease Center. I am pleased to send you the first letter to be written under our new letterhead with my very best wishes for your continued success.

The writer of this letter was Dr. John Trautman, the director of the National Hansen's Disease Center. His letter went to one of his patients, Louis Boudreaux, the blind editor of the magazine published at the Center.

That letter was the end of a forty-year struggle to rid the hospital of the word "leprosy." The war was begun by Stanley Stein, the first editor of the *Star,* who began the magazine in 1941. He was a short, balding man, who had a misshapen nose—and was also blind. Until he died in 1967, he had what was known as "leprosy."

During Stein's life, I once counted all the letters he wrote that appeared in five daily newspapers for a year. I counted twenty letters—all worded differently—for Stein didn't write form letters. Blinded by the disease that the world calls "leprosy," Stein had been at war with a word for more than twenty-five years. From his little, ramshackle home at the U.S. Public Health Service Hospital in Carville, Louisiana, Stein had been sending letters by the thousands to writers, editors, and doctors pleading for the replacement of the term "leprosy" by "Hansen's Disease."

Nonetheless, Stein had undertaken a near-impossible crusade, which is shown by a letter he received from John Popham of the *New York Times:* "Ever since I visited Carville and talked to you I have been so much more alert to the numerous instances every day in which public print carries some item about something showing the 'leprosy' of this, or the 'leprosy' of that, always making it impossible for anyone ever to think of the word in any sense at all except as a horror-inducing term. The worst aspect of anything, from politics to knitting, is always called a 'leprosy,' or likened to a 'leper.'"

Like Popham, I became one of the ardent supporters of Stein's crusade and wrote editorials in the Baton Rouge, Louisiana, *State-Times* asking for new thinking about "leprosy" and the "leper." But I had no illusions of ultimate success in the war with a word. I had heard of the woman who thought she had leprosy, learned that she had actually had cancer, and cried, "Thank God, it's only cancer." And I knew of many Americans who had committed suicide on learning that they had "leprosy," in spite of the fact that it is one of the most feebly communicable of all contagious diseases and many a "leper" could sit unnoticed in almost any gathering.

It was only after the publication of "The Name Leprosy" in *The American Journal of Tropical Medicine and Hygiene* by Dr. Frederick C. Lendrum that our spirit for this crusade, and our hopes for its success, began to approach Stein's. Before Stein had been basing his war with a word on bits and pieces from biochemists, doctors, patients, and scholars of the Talmud, all of which were helpful, but none of which made up a definitive and authoritative whole.

Lendrum, who had seen "the terror aroused by the word 'leprosy'" when he was a physician at the Mayo Foundation, brought to his study the necessary combination of learning. Not only did he hold M.D. and Ph.D. degrees, he was the son of an "active Methodist clergyman, from whom," he said, "I learned to regard the study of Latin, Greek, and Hebrew as a means of illumination rather than as a means of torture."

He found that the paper that was always referred to as the link between the leprosy of Biblical times and the disease we now call "leprosy" was in the Ebers Papyrus. "During the past twenty years," Lendrum said, "a discussion of 'leprosy' has usually included the remark that 'leprosy was described in the Ebers Papyrus in 1500 B.C.'" The source for this dogmatic statement is not given. Yet it is made with the air of final authority that the same physician does not use even when he describes the observations which he has made in his own laboratory."

Lendrum flatly labeled this reference as "fraudulent erudition." He said, "The names of diseases and forms of medication are, even now, little more than a pyramid of hypotheses."

Comparing the languages, Dr. Lendrum discovered that "the phrase 'leprous as snow' would be highly appropriate for psoriasis, and equally inappropriate for the disease which is now called 'leprosy.'" He also learned that at least one traditional text has the word "lepra" as a reference to diseases including psoriasis, dry eczema, dry ringworm, and "probably even dandruff." He concluded that there should be a change in the official nomenclature. In short, Lendrum concluded that Stein was right in pleading that the more than 20,000,000 people known over the world as "lepers" (and hence carrying a biblical stigma of uncleanness) have Hansen's Disease, not biblical leprosy.

Naturally, Stein was ecstatic when he heard of Lendrum's findings—but he expected too much. Letter after letter arrived from his little international network of correspondents reporting new uses of the word "leprosy," and its more-hated offspring, "leper." One of the most disheartening items was a comic book showing a shipwrecked group landing on "Leper Isle," which was peopled by grotesques, horribly mutilated.

When I discovered at Carville the strong resentment among some of the patients against Stein, I began to understand that his war with a word was only part of his struggle. Among the 350 patients at that time were many who were shunned by relatives and friends and left to die. Crushed, they thought the less said about their disease—whatever it's called—the better. For in spite of remarkable recent successes with sulfone treatment, these patients knew that to the uninformed world, a "leper" was untouchable. Few patients feared the disease itself any longer; all of them feared the *word.* But they thought Stein's battle was hopeless.

Most of them fought Stein's open-gate policy bitterly, not wanting curious visitors roaming the hospital grounds. But Stein won. Now anyone 16 or older can visit Carville. Many now do, for as Stein told me: "They're learning we're not monsters."

Today, some of the patients whose disease has been arrested are free to leave the hospital, but they will not leave. They shudder with fear at the thought of the outside world.

But one of Stein's friends, the magazine's photographer, left the hospital when his disease was arrested. He settled down in a small community, afraid that he would be discovered, half-convinced by Stein's courage that he should tell his story. He opened a photography shop under his real name, then told the story to a newspaper. The night before the article appeared, he was convinced that he had made a mistake, that there was no understanding of "leprosy," that there wouldn't be understanding for centuries.

The day after the story appeared, everyone who saw the photographer stopped him and shook his hand.

That is what Stein has accomplished—the impossible.

A STUDENT'S EFFORTS

Students often have wonderful ideas for human interest stories, and most enjoy writing them. Read this article, written by a student who shares her experience working at a summer camp. Although this piece is touching and sincere, it is not a sob story:

Memories of my first summer of camp are incredibly vivid. In a single afternoon of recreational swim time, I am alternately splashed, dunked, dragged across the pool, and plunged into fierce games of keep-away, basketball, and Marco Polo for two straight hours. My buddy is Alan, a seven-year-old with a taste for the daring, and with his dexterity, my speed, and a plastic squirt gun he calls Smiley, we are an intimidating team; he'll shoot water at some unsuspecting drifter, and we'll be off, across the pool, charging to safe territory, until with a crack, he sends a wave crashing down on the head of someone else, and we charge away again, laughing. Suddenly, with a shrill blast, the lifeguards spring to their feet. "Cayuga and Oneida cabins, out!" one of them yells, and Alan complains in my ear, "We're always first!"

Releasing my firm grip on his body, I shift him around so he lies in my arms, legs scooped up with my left hand, and steer us over to the shallow end. As he cries, "Ready, setty, go!" I swing his light body up the steps and over to the long, blue bench, picking out one leg brace from the sprawling pile of worn sneakers mingled with socks, shirts, and various arm and leg supports tossed haphazardly by their owners in the mad dash for the water. As I rub Alan dry with his huge G.I. Joe beach towel, he pulls on his socks and fastens the Velcro straps of his plastic brace over the top. Heading back to help the other counselors, I pass five or six wheelchairs of various sizes that stand attentively at the shallow end of the Olympic-sized pool, their bright metal reflecting blinding rays of sunshine. It is the begining of July, and I am one of the new counselors at the Rotary Club's Sunshine Camp for Handicapped Children, in upstate New York. Like many of his friends here, Alan has cerebral palsy, a disease that requires him to wear a brace in order to walk.

Just two weeks earlier, during orientation, I sprawled with the other counselors on the floor of our dining hall and wondered what I had gotten myself into. At the front of the room, our director, Frank, was describing the various types of cerebral palsy, muscular dystrophy, and spinal injuries we would be seeing, and I was seized by fear and doubt. What did I know about working with handicapped children? I'd never even met one before. How would I treat them? The technical terms sailed past me as I sat there wide-eyed, when another counselor leaned over and whispered, "Don't worry about it. Just listen to what the kids tell you they need, and have fun." I nodded, but the words did little to calm me. I hoped that I could just stand back and watch for a while until I learned the proper way to handle the kids.

No such luck. Assigned with six other counselors to a cabin of eighteen little boys, I had to pull my weight from the very start. Swim time found me standing in the center of the cabin, looking around in confusion, until Mary, the head counselor, saw me and pointed to one corner of the room.

"I think Hrant needs some help with his shirt over there."

Taking in his wheelchair, I whispered, "What does he have?" and she answered, in a normal tone of voice, "Muscular dystrophy. He'll tell you what to do. And don't let him push you around!" She laughed, and I approached Hrant gingerly. He'd evidently been watching me, through thick, owl-like glasses that made him look extremely intellectual.

"Hi. Looks like you're new at this," he said, peering up at me.

I smiled anxiously, taking in his lifeless arms and legs. "I guess you can spot the newcomers a mile away, can't you?" He made some noise of agreement, and I motioned to his shirt. "Should I just . . . ?"

"Yep, just take it off," he said, and looked up at me, as if to see how I would handle this one. I took a deep breath and grabbed the bottom of his shirt, pulling upwards lightly and trying not to hurt him, but was suddenly confronted by two pudgy arms. Carefully lifting one of them up and bending it slightly, I tried to slip the sleeve off, but it wouldn't stretch far enough, and I must have looked exasperated because Hrant took pity on me.

"You can bend my arm a lot further, you know." He looked amused.

"Right," I said, and pushed a little harder when his head suddenly fell to one side. I cringed, and tilted it back to center. "Sorry!"

"No problem," he said. At this point, I finally had the shirt up to his neck, and was pulling it slowly over his head when a muffled voice came from inside the shirt, mumbling, "If you don't hurry up, I'm going to suffocate." Immediately, I whipped the thing off, and there Hrant was, shirtless at last. I let my breath out quickly, as his owl eyes looked me up and down.

"I give you a 4.5. Practice up and maybe I'll give you another chance." Then he smiled, and I laughed in relief. This was a new concept; handicapped didn't mean fragile. Hrant wasn't about to break into a million pieces; in fact, far from it—he looked like he could endure just about anything. But maybe he was just a special case, an anomaly among the disabled. I'd probably have to be more gentle with the others.

The arrival of Terel proved me wrong.

Exercises

1. Find a human interest story from your daily environment. Don't go anywhere you don't usually go or do anything you don't normally do. Your task is to discover a human interest story that has been right in front of you all along.

2. Using a copy of your local newspaper, find three potential human interest stories. Whom would you interview and what places would you visit to research each of these three stories?

3. Find an article from a daily or weekly newspaper and analyze it according to the following criteria: (1) sources of information, (2) organization, (3) clarity, and (4) completeness. How do you think the article could have been improved?

THIRTEEN

DESCRIPTIVES, NEWS FEATURES, AND COLOR STORIES

I was eyes to the blind. . . .

JOB 29:15

Pearl Buck stated:

> The truly creative mind in any field is no more than this: a human crea-ture born abnormally, inhumanly sensitive. To him a touch is a blow, a sound is a noise, a misfortune is a tragedy, a joy is an ecstasy, a friend is a lover, a lover is a god, and failure is death. Add to this cruelly delicate organism the overpowering necessity to create, create, create—so that without the creating of music or poetry or books or buildings or some-thing of meaning, his very breath is cut off from him. He must create, must pour out creation. By some strange, unknown, inward urgency he is not really alive unless he is creating.

Magazines need creative minds to write imaginative, vivid stories. Magazine descriptives rely on visual writing to make readers see subjects in their minds. Once, such articles comprised at least half the content of popular magazines, but competition from television has reduced that percentage sig-nificantly. It has also changed the way magazines handle these stories. Some depend heavily on full-cover photographs to supplement the text, while others use illustrations, but nearly all insist that descriptives be tailored spe-cifically to the interests of their audiences.

One of the staples of descriptive writing in both magazines and news-papers is the travel story. This kind of article takes readers somewhere through descriptions of the sights, sounds, tastes, smells, and other sensations they would experience there. Yet despite the popularity of travel articles, magazine editors still demand that such stories appeal to the particular pref-erences, interests, and incomes of their readers. You won't find an article on New York budget hotels in a magazine like *Carte Blanche*. Its readers are upper middle class and affluent; they're more likely to be interested in four-star hotels and restaurants. Likewise, a magazine like *Working Woman* that has an even narrower audience wouldn't run an article on travel in San Francisco simply because it's an interesting place to visit. The story would need to have an angle of interest to women with careers, such as how a woman can combine a business trip to the Bay Area with a special vacation deal at one of the city's best hotels.

Descriptives benefit from a "news peg"—a newsworthy justification for running a particular story at a particular time. A travel story on a city or part of a city might run the month before a convention or some other event is scheduled to take place there. A news peg isn't necessary, but it's a handy tool for selling a story idea.

DESCRIPTIVES

The following two excerpts are descriptive passages from descriptive stories titled "New 'Old' Homes" and "Freestyle Camps." As you read the two, try to determine how they help readers "see" their subjects. Is one passage more effective than the other? Why?

> "Nouns and verbs are almost pure metal; adjectives are cheaper ore."
>
> MARIE GILCHRIST

In beautiful old New Orleans homes, the complaint that "they don't build 'em like they used to" no longer applies. Not only has a local real estate lawyer found a way to build houses like the ones built here a century ago, she's done it by replicating the best aspects of the old in combination with the convenience and practicality of the new. The result is a row of charming Creole Porte-Cochère townhouse reproductions located on the street whose name best characterizes these new "old" homes—Harmony.

At first glance, the coral- and beige-colored buildings could easily be mistaken for well-restored uptown homes. That is the effect lawyer Jacqueline McPherson wanted to achieve when she first hit upon the notion to build reproductions two years ago. A preservationist with 10 years experience, she was working on her 19th Century home on Exposition Boulevard near Audubon Park, when a stream of admiring and envious friends and neighbors convinced her that many New Orleanians were looking for a combination of classic design and modern comfort that was nearly impossible to find uptown. The answer, decided Ms. McPherson, was to build new houses from old designs, using modern building materials.

Arnold Palmer wouldn't recognize his old golf course in Stratton, Vermont. Wet-suited people with dripping hair and sun screened noses slosh from the pond at one end to the trampoline at the other, toting skis and poles instead of irons and drivers. Formerly the peril of the fairway, the pond is presently the most popular place on the course, only now it's bodies instead of balls that land in the drink. Across the green, skiers dig their edges into artificial turf as they maneuver down a wooden ramp.

These grass-bound skiers may appear somewhat confused, but as participants at a summer freestyle skiing training camp, they're well aware that snow is four months away. Skier Mike Shea's Stratton camp is one of half a dozen sites run by professional freestylers, ski equipment manufacturers and ski resorts around the country. For fees of about $300 for a ten-day session, campers learn how to perform the aerial, ballet and mogul routines that have given freestyle skiing its reputation as a good sport for the incurably insane.

The broken bones and bruised limbs of early freestylers are past history to today's hotdoggers, who are coached not only by their predecessors but by experts in tumbling and gymnastics as well. Unlike freestyle's pioneers, they don't just trudge out to the snow and hope for the best. Instead, they go to summer training camps where trampolines, carpeted ski decks and water jumps cushion the blows so frequent to beginners. Fellow campers may include professional freestylers, many of whom travel the training site circuit during the summer in preparation for winter competition.

The most obvious difference in the language of these two excerpts is that the first relies heavily on adjectives while the second depends more on verbs and nouns in helping the reader "see." A comparison of phrases from the two shows this clearly:

New "Old" Homes	Freestyle Camps
beautiful old New Orleans homes	people . . . slosh from the pond at one end to the trampoline at the other, toting skis and poles instead of irons and drivers
the best aspects of the old in combination with the convenience and practicality of the new	
	bodies instead of balls that land in the drink
a row of charming Creole Porte-Cochère townhouse reproductions	skiers dig their edges into artificial turf as they maneuver down a wooden ramp
the coral- and beige-colored buildings	
	they don't just trudge out to the snow and hope for the best
a stream of admiring and envious friends	
a combination of classic design and modern comfort	

While no editor would advise a writer to discard adjectives altogether, most would agree that it is best to use them sparingly, even in a descriptive story. Vivid verbs are usually more effective than adjectives.

This beginning writer overuses adjectives. By including too many visual words, she subtracts power from the ones that would be effective when standing alone:

One usually hears, rather than sees, Frank Quaratiello busily typing, his long, agile fingers moving nimbly over the keyboard in front of him. The clickety-clack of his computer is the only audible sound coming from the small, poorly lit room in which he works. Frank thinks quietly, speaks quietly, and, when he is working diligently—as he most often is—even breathes quietly. As he hunches his lean, longer-than-six-foot body in the too short, too narrow, and too uncomfortable wooden chair, an eerie green glow from the terminal masks Frank's face, making him seem, at best, far thinner than he already is, and at worst, grotesquely distorted. For a well-financed paper at a high-priced private university, *The Stanford Daily,* Frank's place of employment—and sometimes, it seems, his home away from home—is far from making the list of the "Top Ten Most Pleasant Places to Work." Yet Frank, with his fire-red hair and his warm, infectious smile, is always able to make it a friendly and inviting place to be.

Notice how the last sentence included five adjectives: fire-red, warm, infectious, friendly, and inviting. The sentence would be better with only one adjective and a vivid verb.

Now read these words by Joyce Carol Oates. She is a writer with an uncommon ability to choose the colorful, correct words:*

One of the strangest experiences in my life came to me by way of my writing. It was mysterious at the time, and remains mysterious, still.

In 1977 I wrote a short story, very short, deliberately spare and uninflected, I decided to call "November Morning." It was about a boy

---

*Reprinted by permission of Joyce Carol Oates, copyright The Ontario Review, Inc.

JOYCE CAROL OATES

The author of nearly forty books, Joyce Carol Oates is distinguished not only for the quantity of her works but also for her wide range of literary genres and nonfiction subjects. Born June 16, 1938, in Lockport, New York, Oates is the daughter of a tool and die designer. In 1961, she married an English professor and received her M.A. from the University of Wisconsin.

At the age of twenty-five, Oates published *By the North Gate,* her first collection of stories. The *Wilson Library Bulletin* reviewer wrote that Oates revealed "an interesting combination of storyteller's address with a sense of language that is refined without self-consciousness, imaginative without ostentation. But what is extraordinary beyond these assets is her ability—rare in a new writer, rarer still in a young woman—to treat large-scale emotions with a control that conveys them rather than diminishes them."

One year later, Oates's first novel, *With Shuddering Fall,* was published; M. L. Barrett called it "an extraordinary first novel, sustained at a strong emotional level, rich, poetic, hard and tender . . . perfect in form and probably . . . a small

masterpiece." Many of her stories are set in Eden County, a mythical place she has filled with characters.

Oates's teaching career began in 1961 at the University of Detroit, where she taught English; today she is a professor at Princeton University, where she continues to write novels. A recent novel, *Marya,* has been called "an exceptionally forceful piece of fiction" by Patricia Craig, who wrote, "Joyce Carol Oates' vigorous, impatient approach, her eagerness to jot down the essential detail, makes her plunge straight into the centre of some crucial incident, before going on to indicate the circumstances surrounding it."

Although Oates has written numerous books, she does not find the art of writing easy, or even easily understandable. In "A Terrible Beauty Is Born. How?," an article in the *New York Times Book Review,* Oates examines the difficulties in writing, calling the beginnings of works of art "utterly mysterious."

Oates explains that much deliberation and strategy go into any work of prose fiction. For this reason, an author often needs to revise what he or she has written. A good example,

of eight whose father has been killed, though the boy himself doesn't quite understand what has happened. He is taken to see his father's corpse, in a county morgue; but his father has been so badly beaten or mutilated (it isn't clear which, to the reader) that the boy doesn't seem to recognize him. The story is told not by the child but by way of his limited consciousness and his reluctance to understand what has happened in his family. The setting of the story was rural, naturalistic but dream-like. The time was several decades ago.

I finished "November Morning" in a few days, and sent it to my agent. Though I went on to other projects I found that I was still thinking about the story, haunted by it, as if I hadn't really finished it. My practice as a writer might be defined as an active pursuit of "hauntedness": I can't write unless I am preoccupied with something, sometimes to the point of distraction, or obsession. But rarely am I haunted by a piece of writing, after I have finished it. . . . Though the story was accepted by a magazine, I decided I didn't want it published in that form; but when I tried to withdraw it from publication I learned that I had waited too long. So the story, incomplete, teasingly "wrong," was published.

The test of a work's integrity is its appearance in print: you know then, if you didn't know beforehand, if it is honest or not.

(Cocteau said that writing is a force of memory which is not understood. Certainly there are times when the prospect of writing

---

Oates believes, is D. H. Lawrence, who "was the most intuitive of writers, yet he was willing to write numerous drafts of a work and even to throw away as many as one thousand pages. . . ." Oates adds: "His deep faith in himself allowed him the energy to experiment in following his voice and his characters where they would lead."

Virginia Woolf, whom Oates believes to have analyzed the complexities of a writer's life better than anyone, wrote in a letter: "But a novel . . . to be good should seem, before one writes it, something unwriteable; but only visible; so that for nine months one lives in despair, and only when one has forgotten what one meant, does the book seem tolerable."

Again, Oates uses D. H. Lawrence to illustrate her point: "I am doing a novel which I have never grasped. . . . There I am at p. 145, and I've no notion what it's about. I hate it."

Oates explains that Lawrence "made several false starts in its [The Sisters'] composition before realizing that he must give his heroine some background. This background rapidly evolves into the germ of a new, separate novel. . . ."

Emphasizing the need to rewrite, Oates writes about Ernest Hemingway, who had to "grope his way into what would be his first book of fiction, In Our Time: Writing at first with extreme slowness and difficulty until he set down his 'one true sentence'—usually a brief, declarative sentence—and could throw the earlier work away and begin his story."

Oates's latest book, On Boxing, was published in the spring of 1987 and is considered part prose poem, part history lesson. Oates thinks that male aggression is a combination of hormones and social conditioning. She has become sympathetic with masculine violence and views it as "really inevitable and quite natural."

Trying to communicate the "imprecision of the creative enterprise" of writing, Oates uses the quotation "The sand takes lines unknown." She thinks this is the "conjunction of inner and outer forces we try in vain to understand and must hope in the end only to embody."

—Christine Mergen

leaves me virtually faint with longing; a yearning, a desire so palpable it's almost physical, bound up in some complex, undefinable way with memory. This yearning can't be satisfied except by the head-on plunge into work, in which, somehow, God knows how, raw instinct and critical acuity come into some sort of equilibrium. People who don't write might think it is easy. Or, considering me, as a writer labelled "prolific," that it is easy for *me:* but nothing is farther from the truth. Writing is not easy for most writers nor is it easy for me.)

So I rewrote the story another time. At some point it struck me that the protagonist should have been a girl, and not, as I'd thought, a boy. And that would make all the difference.

Except for the bare outline of the plot everything was recast entirely: tone, texture, rhythm, the silences and spaces between words. Immediately I had my "real" character; I knew her thoroughly; Marya, Marya Knauer, eight years old as the story opens but already in my imagination an adult woman—the thirty-six-year-old woman she would be when the novel ends. (I seemed to know too that Marya's story could not be eight pages long but would be novel-length. Many pages, many years, many experiences would be necessary to bring her into focus and to the culminating point of her life.) I had the ending, now; the final image; I had a number of scenes, "dramatic interludes," in the middle; I saw, or seemed to see, the ghostly outlines of characters whom Marya would encounter, who would act upon her in crucial ways, if not radically alter her life. Most of all I "saw" Marya—a girl, and then a woman, with a face not unlike my own yet not my own: kin of some kind, perhaps sisterly, but unknown to me.

It wasn't until I had finished a first draft of the novel that I learned, by chance, that the story I believed I had invented recapitulated an incident in my mother's early life. Not my father, of course, but her father had been murdered; not I, but my mother, had been "given away" after her father's death, to be brought up by relatives. Marya is eight years old at the time of the event that changes her family's life; my mother was an infant of six months. Somehow, without knowing what I did, without knowing, in fact, that I was doing anything extraordinary at all, I had written my mother's story by way of a work of prose fiction I had "invented". . . .

The Essentials of the Descriptive

Here are three essentials of a descriptive:

Focus on distinctive characteristics. By carefully selecting minutiae, a writer can sketch a picture that sets forth the unique quality of a place.

Use careful phrasing. Descriptives depend largely on the way words are put together to achieve their effect. The substance of the descriptive is, of course, important also.

Provide a reading and viewing experience. The success of a descriptive is not determined by whether readers *learn,* in the sense that they learn facts or ideas from other kinds of articles. Success pivots almost entirely on whether readers finish a descriptive with the feeling that they have been through a satisfying reading experience. The most evocative descriptives—those fashioned by writers who have developed and refined a talent for using visual words—are also *viewing* experiences.

Read this descriptive and notice how the writer chose words for their visual effect:

> The crowd suddenly turns its collective attention to the pitching mound, where the pitcher appears to be faltering slightly. The crowd rallies to his defense with shouts of "Work the socks"—a reference to a stalling mechanism which appears to improve his concentration. The support is apparently not enough to dissuade the coach from a slow, measured walk onto the field. The students count each footfall—step, step—until he establishes eye contact with the pitcher, signifying that he will allow his starter to remain in the game.

You can almost see the anxious pitcher "faltering slightly" and the coach's measured steps. Such careful phrasing promotes a reading *and* viewing experience. When written exceptionally well, descriptives can be emotional experiences, too.

NEWS FEATURES AND COLOR STORIES

If a dozen reporters were assigned to cover the same event and write a straight news story about it, they would probably produce articles that were quite similar. But if the same reporters were assigned to write a news feature or color story, it is likely that no two would choose exactly the same angle.

Just as witnesses to an accident rarely remember the same details, feature writers select different elements of a scene to report. One might discover an interesting individual; another might observe a revealing exchange between several people; a third might focus on the overall scene without choosing any particular element in it. Such choices are largely subjective, but a reporter learns how to make them with an eye toward the best story material.

News features and color stories are often, but not always, keyed to news events. When they are, the writer must assume the roles of both factual reporter and keen observer. Then he or she must write the article as a smooth blend of news and description.

News Features

Beginning feature writers are often captivated by their own graceful writing, letting their skill overshadow the fact that they are linked closely to the news. They must learn to recognize that their proper position is halfway between the news story and the feature. In the following excerpts, a student has written the article that appears at the left. A professional writer, whose story appears at the right, has struck the proper balance between news story and feature.

> "The man who cannot believe his senses and the man who cannot believe anything else are both insane."
>
> G. K. CHESTERTON

Article

The sky is falling. Or so say the international mélange of soothsayers who met this month to deliberate the destiny of 1975. Crystal balls in hand, they emerged from their traditional meeting spot—a devilish Druid cave—to decree a significant upswing in air crashes for the coming fiscal year. But one need not be a Merlin or Mephistopheles to notice the trend towards tragedies in the heavens. As the price tags on aircraft soared to $25 million with the advent of the 747, one is led to wonder who picks up the tab for such aerial disasters. These risks royale must be underwritten, and the princely premiums must be paid. But how?

Article

In oil-rich Saudi Arabia, an absolute monarchy where royalty payments are more than just a figure of speech, King Faisal has argued for years that his nation should own part of the production facilities and operations of the Western-owned oil company that has a concession in his realm. This week Saudi Arabia agreed to pay an amount estimated to top $500 million for a one-fourth interest in the oil and gas producing operations of Arabian-American Oil Co. in Saudi Arabia.

The lead at the left was written by a talented writer, but he is trying too hard, making it difficult for a casual reader to grasp the point of his article. The professional writer, in contrast, is quick to recognize that his first responsibility is to the news.

This student writer uses a catchy lead to introduce the topic of his news feature. After first providing information about his subject, he uses more description in later paragraphs:

> We all know that "what goes up must come down," but how about "what goes away must come back"? Though it's not an official saying—yet—it may soon become one, thanks to a new toy invented by Alan Adler, a lecturer in mechanical engineering at Stanford University. The Aerobie Orbiter is a flying object that, with a relatively soft throw, will travel around the thrower in a circle with a diameter of 90 to 100 feet and then return to him or her.
>   The Orbiter is a modification of the Australian boomerang; it's lighter, easier to throw, less dangerous, and aerodynamically designed to fly better than the original model. And, it's shaped like a triangle. So far, The Orbiter has been a commercial success, selling out faster than store buyers expected.
>   Adler's first contribution to the flying game industry, The Aerobie Flying Ring (The Aerobie) has also been a tremendous success. Even more so when you consider that Adler has no formal background in toy marketing, aerodynamics, or even mechanical engineering; he never even completed high school.

We turn now to part of an article written by a student who is following up a controversy at the Hoover Institution. He begins with a reference to the controversy, neatly dips into the beginning of the institution, then brings it up to date. Note that the aim here is *not* to try to imitate the kind of scholarly writing common to many universities. There are no footnotes and no weighty tone, as should be the case even when a news feature is lengthy and serious. The feature writer's goal is to produce a clear, logical story—neither primly formal nor chatty. The foundation of the story, however, must often be formal: What is the significance of this institution? How can I present the story to make it widely readable? The resulting news feature is interesting to anyone concerned with the subject. Note that many stylistic matters are given attention in the comments to the left of the story.

COMMENT

This news-peg lead is an excellent entry into the subject.

If you don't call something by its right name (Hoover Institu*tion*), readers who know its name will be distracted from what you're saying by the oddity. It's also likely that a reader who is irritated by what you're saying may dismiss the entire article with, "He doesn't even know the name of the thing he's writing about." Little mechanical elements of a story *are* important, and not merely because you want to be correct for the sake of being correct.

Since the preceding sentence put a focus on the conference, the next need not include "of the conference." Look for opportunities to be concise.

This is a wise development of the subject. The author is weaving interview material and written material into a coherent picture of the current controversy.

NEWS FEATURE

"The Iranian conference is our latest excursion in controversy," said Jim Hobson, public relations officer for the Hoover Institute. "We don't knowingly get into these situations; they just occur."

Hobson was speaking of the conference "Iran: 25 Centuries of Achievement," sponsored by the Hoover Institute to celebrate the 2,500th anniversary of the Persian monarchy. Speakers at the conference were heckled by a small group of Iranian students.

The students charged the Institute with providing a one-sided view of the monarchy's achievements. The charges reopened a dispute about the role of the Institute and led a student to write in the business school paper, *The Reporter*, "It is untenable for the Institute, a renowned symbol of reaction, to remain on the University campus."

Although there are relatively few deletions and substitutions on this page, if you read the page aloud in both original and revised versions, you'll agree that the deleted words aren't needed and that the substitutions help relieve the institute-institute-institute (which began in the last sentence).

It might have been valuable here to indicate *when* these quotations appeared in the *Wall Street Journal* and *Washington Monthly*. Note that the preceding page is all about a recent event. Some readers may assume that these quotations are current.

This is a nice transition. Note especially that the author is moving back into history neatly, tying history to recent events.

Changing the sentence makes for smoother reading. Note that the preceding sentences run subject-verb, subject-verb, subject-verb. Varying sentence beginnings is often effective.

Considering that the Hoover quotation refers to the war, it seems doubtful that "from the war period" has any value here.

"Supplied" suggests that an order was filled.

It may be overinforming the reader with "to include documents on," but the reader *could* think that the original phrasing means that the collection itself expanded into these areas physically.

Such criticism is not new, to the Institute. The *Wall Street Journal* called it "a haven for Goldwater men," and the *Washington Monthly* described it as "a cold-war college think tank." A demonstrator said at a rally that the Institution is "one of the world's main centers of counterinsurgency research."

The Institute's role has not always been so controversial. It was founded in 1919 when Herbert Hoover gave university President Ray Wilbur $50,000 "for an historical collection on the Great War." It grew rapidly as young scholars searched Europe for books, documents, and newspapers from the war period.

In 1927 the Rockefeller Foundation provided a grant to support research projects on Russia and Germany. After the second World War II, the scope of the collection expanded to include documents on Asia, Latin America, Africa, and the Middle East. . . .

Color Stories

The color story is a feature that plays up the descriptive elements of a news event. Color stories must occasionally strike a serious tone: the report of a disaster that must be accompanied by a color sidebar, or the death of a prominent figure that calls for a color story that sounds a sad note. In this case, the writer is tracing a danger that hounds a young woman:

> It has the elements of a chilling Hitchcock thriller: A young woman believes she is being stalked by a stranger. The police don't take it seriously. Her boyfriend is trying to protect her.
>
> Except it isn't a movie. It appears to be real, and it's happening in Chicago. . . .

The writer then narrates the events that have taken place very simply and starkly. First, the writer describes the many calls the stranger has made to the woman's apartment, the night he threw the switch in the building's fuse box and turned out the lights in the apartment house, the calls increasing in number, and, finally, a young man's knocking at the door—only to be confronted by the boyfriend. The man says that he is a repairman looking for an address, gets the information, then leaves. When the woman calls the repairman's alleged employer, she finds that a much older man works as their repairman. The writer closes his story simply:

> She has locked up her apartment and is living somewhere else for a while, with a friend.
>
> So far, the friend's phone hasn't rung.

Much more commonly, though, the feature writer is assigned to cover the color, flavor, and excitement of large crowds. Assigned a sports color story, instead of focusing attention on the players, the writer is likely to make the spectators, the cheering sections, the yell leaders, the half-time performance, and the mascots the focal points of the story.

Covering a college baseball game, this student wrote about the scene surrounding the event. After reading this color story, you could close your eyes and practically see the spectators:

> With a brief nod at the fraternity members perched on the railing, the three girls balance against the incline of the hill, careful to avoid scattered towels, flip-flops, and coolers of beer. After a moment's hesitation in the California sunshine, they remove their tank tops, revealing brightly colored bikinis. This ritual complete, the girls lean their elbows against the grass, adjust their sunglasses and slowly survey the baseball stadium. Spectators to the game on the field, each member of the crowd is an active participant in the games played in the stands.
>
> Although the action on the diamond is unquestionably the focus of the afternoon, it is rivaled by subtle social interactions skillfully executed by the spectators at Stanford's Sunken Diamond. Reporters from campus and Bay Area publications loosen their collars in the sun-proof press box. Not-so-inconspicuous professional scouts flash speed guns

at major league hopefuls. Alumni—ham and cheese sandwiches in hand—discuss the great plays of years past. And on a grassy embankment off the third base line, the students cheer for their classmates.

The score is 0–0 in the top of the third inning, and the lanky, blonde Stanford pitcher delivers a fastball for his third strikeout in a row. Far above the manicured grounds, the crowd applauds wildly, alternately yelling clever nicknames at the pitcher and comments such as "You're brutal, 8," to the opposing batter.

As the teams switch positions, members of the crowd turn to each other to discuss the previous play. Etiquette at the Stanford field traditionally demands that conversation be restricted to discussions of the current game, past games, or the personal lives of any of the players.

The three girls replace their tank tops and boldly join the men by the splintered wooden railing, flashing bright smiles and blue plastic cups in the vicinity of the fraternity's beer keg. These girls, characteristic of most students in the crowd, are wearing their own personal uniforms, not unlike those used to label the players on the field. In this particular game, the girls compete with one another, modeling very expensive outfits that look expensive only to those with similar clothes, and carefully styled faces and hair that achieve a carelessly casual look. They have made a great effort to appear as if they have made no effort at all. Back on the field, the first Stanford batter steps up to the plate, and the students dutifully turn their attention back to the game on the diamond.

The banter changes sides as effortlessly as the teams, with some of the more creative and biting taunts emanating from just above the home dugout. Amid a fleet of multicolored mopeds, the alumni gather to watch the new players each season, eager to remain part of a Cardinal program that consistently ranks among the nation's best. Some of these former students have missed relatively few home games, returning each year in the hopes of seeing a national championship team. Collectively wearing maroon and white attire and only slightly mangled baseball caps with a large white "S" emblazoned on the rim, this group yells stinging comments at the players in opposing colors. While overwhelmingly exaggerated and only occasionally deserved, the teasing remains confined to sarcasm concerning the athletic abilities of the players.

Back at the student-dominated "bank," the comments go beyond athletic prowess and usually involve assessments of personal characteristics such as weight or attractiveness. Often these include the dubious intelligence of students from opposing schools, particularly those from institutions in southern California. Elitist remarks such as "What was your SAT score, anyway?" and "Your number is higher than your IQ" are not uncommon.

The feature writer covers the election sidebar in much the same way. While the election reporter is concentrating on results, the color story writer describes the manner and the mood of the voters as they enter the election booths. He or she looks for quotable signs that herald the voters, listens to the sound trucks making last-minute appeals, and records the candidates' reactions on the last day.

Sometimes a color story focuses on individual reactions to an event, as illustrated by this excerpt from a story written by Jeanette Germain (reprinted with permission of the *Ketchum* [Idaho] *Mountain Express*):

> Passersby were scandalized. They were delighted. They couldn't believe their eyes.
>
> The setting was a Hotel Grande motel room, with static flickering across a television screen and red satin sheets on the bed. A bondage book and sexual fantasies magazines were strewn across the covers with an empty box of amyl nitrate tablets and silk pajamas. The cardboard mannequin wore black lace corset, bra, and garter belt.
>
> Avventura clothing store, known for provocative, innovative display windows, had gone borderline this time. The response at the Sun Valley mall was immediate and emotional.
>
> Salespeople were plagued by questions, compliments, and criticism. More men started browsing through the store.
>
> An anonymous critic wrote across the window in red lipstick. "This window is disgusting. I hope you do something about it soon." A similar comment was slipped under the door on a frayed cocktail napkin.
>
> Window designer Sherl Seggerman thought the lipstick comment, scrawled across the top of the window, added to the overall design. But store owners Connie Maricich and Millie Wiggins decided it should probably be washed off. The cocktail napkin could more discreetly be incorporated in the display. It was laid on the satin sheets with the other props.
>
> By the time the window was changed last week, the good comments had actually outnumbered the bad, Seggerman said. Shoppers loved the detail. They stood and looked and pointed things out to one another as they rounded the corner of the mall. The television set, dating from the 1930's, was especially popular.

Note how the writer uses adjectives sparingly and tellingly in describing the window scene and people's reactions to it. She simply presents a picture of what the scene looked like and records what various people wrote and said about it. The material itself tells the story, but it is the writer's selection and ordering of it that make the story effective.

Writing Good Color Stories

Although writing can be improved by editing, the editor, after all, hasn't covered the story. He or she is at the mercy of the writer. Here are a few suggestions for writing good color stories:

Make the story continuously interesting One sentence should grow out of another; one paragraph should grow out of another. The middle and end should be as interesting as the beginning. Although a color story has no standard structure, the "hard news" should usually be somewhere near the beginning.

Use imaginative description   Although you may be covering an event, try to avoid the dryness of straight news writing by creating vivid images.

One of the challenges in writing color stories is to use vivid, visual descriptions without relying on clichés to do the job for you. Successful writers do this by creating fresh, new images such as these:

a woman who could have danced cheek-to-cheek with Wilt Chamberlain	searching for another fix of fast food
a game that gives everyone a chance to read all the ads in the program	arguing beard to beard

Do not editorialize   Your goal in writing a color story is to create the flavor and feeling of a scene, not to judge it.

Provide sufficient information   Don't become so preoccupied with description that you neglect the essential details of the story necessary for the reader to understand what you are writing about.

Use dialogue to augment or replace description   Occasionally, reproducing dialogue relieves the writer of the burden of description (and of the hunt for fresh images), as in the following excerpt from an article by Paul Butler:

Leon Bacon had just finished a set of pulldowns when the phone rang. Letting the weight drop with a thud, he walked over and picked up the receiver.

"Barry's Musclehouse."

"Uh . . . hello," said a whiny voice. "What are your rates?"

"Cheap," said Leon, reaching up to reduce the volume on the wall-mounted stereo.

"I was thinking about joining your health club. Do you have a sauna?"

"This place is into serious weightlifting; we don't play around." There was a pause.

"I see. Well, can I talk to Barry?"

Leon began to get impatient. Barry wasn't within sight and he didn't want to interrupt his workout for some Pillsbury Doughboy.

"We buried Barry yesterday."

"Oh, I . . . uh . . . I'm sorry."

"Barry left everything in his will to the new manager."

"Who's he?"

"Wino."

"Wino?"

"His dog."

There was a short moment of silence, then a click. Leon broke into a broad grin as he realized the whole gym had stopped to listen in. He put down the receiver.

"Do you have a sauna?" he mimicked, in a high feminine voice. His training partner laughed.

"You're rude, man." Leon turned up the stereo again.

"Why should I waste my time with him. He'd never benefit from this place. He doesn't know what it's all about." He grabbed the pull-down bar to assist his partner.

"C'mon, last set. We're gonna make your back so wide your lats are gonna flap in the wind."

In this example, the dialogue tells more about the characters than any description could. The writer knew that and realized that he should let the two speak for themselves.

The Seasonal Color Story

Color stories are often linked to holidays and other seasonal events. Though some reporters dread writing these articles, others use them as opportunities to exercise their imaginations and descriptive abilities. Here is a story that shows how both can be used to create a fresh approach to an old subject:

COMMENT

The anecdotal beginning is useful in many kinds of writing (especially profiles). This lead seems to pull the reader into this story effectively.

Note that the writer uses adjectives and adverbs here and there, but the writing is not so obviously visual that it calls attention to itself. There is no piling up of adjectives and adverbs, no reaching for similes.

The worst flaw in most seasonal stories is that the writer tries too hard to be overpoweringly descriptive. Instead, the writer should be content with touches of description: a few visual verbs, an unpredictable adjective or two, an adverb that is allowed to do its work because it's in a crisp sentence rather than in a sentence burdened with other adverbs.

SEASONAL STORY

Count Dracula removed his fangs and leaned over the table toward a green martian with blinking antennae. "Frankly," the count said, "those lights are beginning to annoy me."

The martian reached for a switch somewhere under the table and—surprise!—his nose lit up. The count drew back, startled. He quickly installed his fangs, got up and hunkered over to the bar where he spent the rest of the evening nursing Bloody Marys.

"Some party," the martian said, his nose and antennae blinking in happy harmony.

It was a one-of-a-kind party. Radio station KNEW had hired Oakland's Goodman Hall and provided an incessant background of "golden-oldies" music, and 800 of the Bay Area's most bizarre citizens were at KNEW's Night-Before-Halloween Party.

On the dance floor, jitterbugging to Bill Haley's "Rock around the Clock," were a Playboy Bunny with lumps where they shouldn't have been and a young woman swaddled in just a diaper. Two chocolate M&M's covered the floor in a snappy tango to the same tune. And a young man in a brown nylon jump suit performed a solo, prancing unpredictably with his hands in the air.

This went on for some time, perhaps an hour, until the thrill of seeing the Hunchback of Notre Dame dance arm-in-arm with a girl in a fliptop Marlboro box wore off.

This seems an effective use of a fragment.

The writer resisted the temptation to strain for effects. He's quite content to describe the bizarre scene simply.

Then the entertainment.

Four men stepped from a time warp and took their places behind various musical instruments on the stage. They stood there for a moment waiting for the visual impact to register.

At the organ stood a man with long, silver hair slicked straight back to the nape of his neck, where a black, leather motorcycle jacket started. At the drums, in shades, was a greasy-looking character with a black Sam-the-Sham goatee. Behind the lead guitar was another leather jacket, Sam-the-Sham goatee and a stocking cap. And shouldering the bass! He swaggered to the edge of the stage, resplendent in his foot-high, pomaded D.A., shifted his gum and spoke into the microphone. "Hi," he said, "We're Big Art and the Trashmasters."

Here, the fragments intrude. First, the writer's use of fragments makes the reader too conscious of the device. Second, the fragments would be more effective as one sentence.

And with that they broke into the Ventures' version of "Walk, Don't Run." Proceeded to "Teen Angel," "Hound Dog." Then lit into "The Swim."

At the break Art paused before the microphone and said, "We have a dedication. From Laurie to Ed. Who used to be around." They played "Chicken Guts."

The writer obviously intends this to be an attention-compelling (ironic?) conclusion. "It was a . . . gas" is intended to mean much more than the trite expression imparts. The phrase is in keeping with Big Art's campy announcement in the preceding paragraph, although the connection is tenuous.

Then Big Art stepped forth for another announcement. "We have some fine machines outside, I'm told," he said, "A '55 Buick and a '51 Cadillac." He held up his hands as if to still the crowd. "Pearl-dust white," he said.

It was a . . . gas.

Exercises

1. Rewrite the following trite phrases using fresh imagery:

at a tender age   in no uncertain terms

too numerous to mention   clear as crystal

green with envy

2. Fill in the blanks:

His face was like _____.   Walking into class, I felt _____.

Talking to her was like _____.   He was so tall _____.

3. You have been assigned to write a news feature for each of the following events. Suggest two news feature angles for each:

a rock concert

a conference of student body presidents

a debate between two candidates running for governor of your state

opening night of a new play at the local theater

a ceremony in honor of the one-hundredth anniversary of the founding of your school

4. Read again "The Essentials of the Descriptive" from t.... chapter, then write a descriptive article of about 1,000 words on any place you have observed. Analyze the devices you have used in your article to make readers see the subject. Do you rely on verbs or adjectives, words or phrases? What senses besides sight have you used?

FOURTEEN

PERSONALITY SKETCHES AND PROFILES

There is only one thing in the world worse than being talked about, and that is not being talked about.

OSCAR WILDE

N o one would argue that personality sketches constitute "hard news," but newspaper audiences like to read them as much as reporters like to write them. There are no formulas for writing these articles; they offer reporters considerable freedom of style and content. Though newspapers are running longer stories, a feature writer usually has less space available than a magazine writer would for a similar piece. The challenge for the feature writer is to create a complete characterization or tell the entire story in the space allotted. Every word, every sentence, must contribute to development of the article.

PERSONALITY SKETCHES

Some personality sketches have grown to the size of magazine profiles. A sketch must be long enough to spell out the significance of its subject. How does the subject talk, move, walk, think, look? How does he or she relate to others and to the surroundings? Most important, how do others relate to the subject? What do they say about him or her?

One cannot gather all this information in an hour-long interview. It may take several interviews, hours of observation, and numerous phone calls to compile details of this nature. Yet newspaper feature writers often don't have the time to study their profile subjects in depth. Often their territory is the realm of what can be accomplished in half a day's work, sometimes less. Given this constraint, it is especially important for the writer to become a keen observer and recorder of significant details.

"Live to be the show and the gaze o' the time."

WILLIAM SHAKESPEARE

In this opening paragraph from his article "Ava: Life in the Afternoon," writer Rex Reed shows how a good eye for images and a flair for descriptive writing can combine to create a stunning picture of a personality:*

She stands there, without benefit of a filter lens against a room melting under the heat of lemony sofas and lavender walls and cream-and-peppermint-striped movie-star chairs, lost in the middle of that gilt-edge birthday-cake hotel of cupids and cupolas called the Regency. There is no script. No Minnelli to adjust the CinemaScope lens. Ice-blue rain beats against the windows and peppers Park Avenue below as Ava Gardner stalks her pink malted-milk cage like an elegant cheetah. She wears a baby-blue cashmere turtleneck sweater pushed up to her Ava elbows and a little plaid mini-skirt and enormous black horn-rimmed glasses and she is gloriously, divinely barefoot.

Few beginning writers could create lavish imagery as effectively as Reed does, but all should practice the kind of observation that enabled him to record these details.

The following article written by a beginner illustrates some common problems in writing personality sketches, as well as some effective techniques others should emulate:

COMMENT

Perhaps the subject's full name should have come a bit earlier than the end of the third paragraph, because readers may confuse "he," not knowing at some points whether "he" refers to the subject or the speaker. But this is certainly an engaging beginning, especially because a trait is mentioned, then illustrated. The deleted words seem unnecessary.

So much is made of Smither's wit that another example of it somewhere in the fourth or fifth paragraph would make the point that he is *consistently* witty.

PERSONALITY SKETCH

"Linus is a pleasure to be around because he amuses you," commented a young instructor who has been his straight man more than once.

He picked up a miniature green flag. Musing over it, he recalled that he had worn it in his lapel last St. Patrick's Day. ~~Upon noting the occasion, he continued,~~ Linus had eyed the decoration and punned, "I dreamed I was St. Patrick in my Eringobragh."

Some associates credit this humor to instinctive dry wit; others claim it is a cleverly acquired coverup for more revealing emotion. Whichever it is, it delineates Professor Linus Smither's personality and delimits his relationships with others.

Those who maintain that Smither's wit is a natural gift readily admit he lacks the normal kaleidoscope of moods. "He doesn't seem to show excitement or boredom," his roommate, Allen Ginsberg, noted.

---

*Tom Wolfe, *The New Journalism* (New York: Harper & Row, 1973), p. 56.

An important bit of editing. The colon after "disagreed" pulls the reader and allows a deletion.

This is a deft transition. The writer *uses* the preceding paragraph to dip into history.

Note especially that the historical tracing is *not* grafted on in a series of dull facts. The history is made an integral part of a thematic story.

Again, history is tied into the running story.

The basic difficulty is that the first sentence here doesn't seem to follow from the preceding graph. It follows from the graph above the preceding. Perhaps a better sentence: "Ginsberg, too, must speculate."

All this seems extraordinarily valuable, giving the reader a rounded view of the subject. Note especially that this kind of description is not negated by accompanying photographs. *Never* assume that pictures will describe. Few do. Only a long picture story, for example, could show how a subject walks, talks, and moves, the sound of his voice, his mannerisms, and so on.

Ginsberg did venture, however, that Smither has the potential for warmth and anger, whereas another contemporary disagreed "Basically, he's kind of antiseptic," Smither's friend explained. Theorizing that his dearth of moods stems from intense emotional control, he lamented that Smither "doesn't like you, but he'll laugh with you. Humor is his only emotion."

Smither's background could lend support to either claim. Born in 1940, he is the youngest in a Midwest dairy farmer's family of four daughters and two sons. The older children may have stifled outbursts from the "baby" of the family. On the other hand, a large family is rarely subdued: parental discipline may favor even-temperedness, but there is usually an undercurrent of warmth and excitement.

His former office-mate, another Midwesterner, expressed puzzlement about Smither's "closeness," which is alien to the Midwest. Having shared an office with Smither, acquainted him with the area, associated with him socially, and travelled with him, he was surprised at how little he knew about Smither.

He suggested that the transition from a small farming community to the urbanity of Cornell, where Smither earned both Master of Science and Doctor of Philosophy degrees in industrial engineering, may have effected his inwardness. Fellow students can have an "intimidating" effect upon someone unaccustomed to their sophistication, he commented.

Ginsberg knew remarkably little, too. He was unaware of Smither's Midwest upbringing or of his academic performance, although both majored in industrial engineering at Cornell. "Linus doesn't volunteer information," Ginsberg explained, "but he seems willing to be prodded."

Equally puzzling are Smither's immediately apparent inconsistencies. The quiet, young teacher owns a white Sting Ray and, according to Ginsberg, he "drives it in character—hard, fast, and very surely." Neither a smoker nor a drinker, he enjoys stag poker parties and has been spotted in Nero's Nook, the dimly lit nightclub in the gaudy Cabana Motor Hotel.

Tall (about 5′ 11″) and slender, his tan has only lately begun to fade. The blond streak in his light brown, slightly thinning hair attests to his daily afternoon swims and extensive outdoor activity. As a young bachelor, Smither enjoys a pleasantly varied social life. Girls will call him often, bachelor Ginsberg noted ruefully, and he will talk to them at length. He seems to be at ease among women, noted Ginsberg.

Pictures are barely supplementary. And one picture is almost useless except to offer a general impression. The *writer* must describe.

The description of the room seems strained: "nausea green" and "linoleum like grey amoebae" try too hard. Would the *room* smell musty rather than its wooden chairs?

English teachers once snorted at "enthused." And the writer should make the case with an example. *Show* Smither being enthused.

By the time the reader finishes this, he feels that he has been given views from a number of perspectives. And the ending, which ties back to the beginning, unifies the whole deftly.

Missing: quotations from Smither himself. The two puns are effective, but the reader never really *confronts* Smither in conversation.

However, Smither teaches mostly male engineers. Does his personality hinder his effectiveness? Apparently not.

He is faced with depressing odds—numbed, upperclass engineers; a room with carved, musty wooden chairs, nausea green walls, linoleum like grey amoebae, and half-hearted fluorescent lights. Yet he is enthused about the class, and the class is enthused about him.

Smither firmly believes in the values of humor and receptivity in teaching. These qualities pay off, for his students perk up at his witticisms and then ponder what he teaches. They agree that Smither is demanding but helpful. One who had difficulty keeping up at first despaired, "He takes off like a race horse out of the stocks." Yet among others word is spreading that Smither is attuned to the program and its problems.

Smither's personality may be an enigma, but his facility for punning is clearly irresistible. Everyone has his favorite Smither pun. The department secretary recalled a conversation between a professor and another secretary, a young mother. Questioning the desirability of being a working wife, they commented to Smither that his bachelorhood precluded such conflicts. Smither shot back: "You mean I'd have to live by the sweat of my frau?"

This personality sketch is basically well written. Note especially that this writer is showing rather than telling. For example, if she had said that Smither is very funny—a person who causes those near him to dissolve in laughter—the reader might or might not have believed her, depending on whether he trusts her judgment. And merely telling the reader that Smither is funny won't make him remember this trait for more than a few minutes. Since the writer has given examples of Smither's jokes, the likelihood that the reader will be impressed and will remember is great.

The writer could have improved this story by observing Smither at work. Moreover, the subject should have been interviewed again after the observation. It is very important for the writer to observe Smither. Sharp descriptions require observation reporting that would almost surely pose other questions.

Anecdotes as Small Stories

Arthur Koestler, a British writer, once stopped an overenthusiastic fan in her tracks by saying, "Liking a writer and then meeting the writer is like liking goose liver and then meeting the goose."

Properly used, anecdotes illustrate, sharpening a point that the writer wants to make. An anecdote brings a picture from black and white to color in the reader's mind.

Anecdotes are actually examples of behavior. There are other kinds of examples, of course. You could write that some evangelists are demagogues and yet not be particularly convincing. But citing Jim and Tammy Faye Bakker shows the reader what you mean. It is one thing to say that the subject of your writing is a comedian; it is another thing to tell one of her jokes.

Consider this passage from a long feature about Joseph Papp, who controls the stages at his fabulously successful Public Theater. This article appeared in the *New York Times*. The writer has introduced him, then observes him at length:

COMMENTS

Note especially how much detail this writer gives: "read over the phone (which has been equipped with a loud-speaker)," "he reads without feeling," and so on. The writer almost takes the readers to this scene.

Instead of merely telling the readers that Papp was outraged, the writer quotes him, which helps make this scene vivid. Note again how much the writer shows his readers: "Debuskey gives it to him and Papp charges across the room to the phone."

PERSONALITY SKETCH*

ABC's Kevin Sander's reaction is mixed. Then comes Clive Barnes's critique in the *Times*, read over the phone (which has been equipped with a loudspeaker so everyone can hear). The words are read by a man in the *Times*'s composing room. He reads without feeling: "*Boom Boom Room* is full of chic filth and a desperate Archie Bunker style of racism . . . an empty and poorly crafted play . . . It is said to be directed by Mr. Papp himself . . . Mr. Papp must take the rap . . . let us hope the Shakespeare Festival will have better luck next time. There is nowhere to go but up."

As soon as the review is finished, Papp leaps to his feet, enraged, and lets loose a torrent of four-letter words. "That s.o.b.! That —! What's Clive's number?"

Debuskey gives it to him and Papp charges across the room to the phone. Although it is 11:30 P.M., he dials Barnes at home. Everyone is deathly silent.

"Hello, Clive? This is Joe Papp. I just heard your review. And you are a ———. You think you're going to get me? Well, I'm going to get you. I am going to get you." He slams down the receiver and glares at us. Nobody speaks.

"You know why Clive did this?" he demands. "It's his personal vendetta. Because he doesn't think new American plays should be done at the Lincoln Center. He's mad because I wouldn't listen to him." He pauses. "If the *Daily News* pans *Boom Boom Room*, I'll know I've gone crazy."

Minutes later the *News* review is phoned in. Doug Watt calls *Boom Boom Room* "long, tedious and bleak."

*Reprinted by permission of the author, Patricia Bosworth.

As Papp grows calmer after Watt's review is quoted, the readers can see it. Only after the writer has established Papp's mood does she go on quoting Papp.

Here, the writer quotes Papp at length, which gives the readers a full view of the subject of this piece.

But after listening to this review, Papp grows strangely calmer. "Doug was objective about the play," he says. "Clive was not. Somebody must be crazy but I don't think it's me. I've been involved with a helluva lot of plays in my time and I happen to think *Boom Boom Room* is the most American play, the best, most significant play around. It was the only play I wanted to open Lincoln Center with. I feel very close to this play. This play is about sexual identity and resolving one's sexual identity and it's a raw emotional examination.

"You gotta see beyond the artifice, the bad jokes. Everything is there for a purpose, for Christ's sake. But the play either turns you on or turns you off. If Clive totally rejects the play on personal grounds, he should say so."

This excerpt is typical of the kind of anecdotal writing that is appearing frequently in large newspapers.

The following sketch was written by Alix Mitchell and published in the Sunday *Syracuse Herald-Journal.* Observe how well Mitchell knows her subject, which is essential to producing good stories:

Freshmen women tend to develop crushes on him. Artists are inspired by him.

Students who aren't enrolled in his courses attend them for the pure joy of listening to him teach.

But point it all out to him, and Professor David Miller, lecturer, author and scholar of theology and culture, will shyly say he's not aware that students are drawn to him.

Miller has an odd air about him of being both warm and reserved, and one can imagine that he does touch people without realizing it.

At 47, his looks are classic, clean. But in recent years a hint of tiredness, or sadness, seems to have crept in and replaced what was once an air of youthful confidence.

When his smile breaks, it seems to catch him by surprise, but is full of warmth. . . .

A beginner can learn a great deal about crafting personality sketches by studying magazine sketches and by becoming a good observer of people.

Here is Bonnie Remsberg, a writer of nearly one thousand magazine articles. She writes of finding anecdotes:*

Being asked to describe how you find anecdotes is a little like being asked how you walk. You can tell about it, but you get so self-conscious as you describe the process that, pretty soon, you fall down.

Anecdotes are everywhere, all around, in the air like radio waves.

Anecdotes are brief glimpses, little peeks, inside of a person or a situation. Anecdotes are tiny stories.

Anecdotes are useful. Anecdotes are spice. You can season with them, or you can overuse them and overwhelm your story. Judicious application is the rule. And that's the only rule. All other aspects of the use of anecdotes are up for grabs.

*Reprinted by permission of Bonnie Remsberg.

Some people make up anecdotes. Should you? Even in this age of journalistic self-examination, this ethical question is beyond the scope of our present task. Suffice to say that many magazine and newspaper articles you read which begin with the seemingly requisite three anecdotes have been, how-shall-we-say-this, enhanced by the writer's imagination. In defense, it should be stated that most of those anecdotes *could* have happened to someone, and that the people they are written about *could* have existed. It's just that they *didn't,* necessarily.

Anecdotes are the things that happen that cause you to catch, to stop, to notice. You somehow stumble on them. You catch with the irony, with the pathos. They are, somehow, intense. Something happens, when you hear them, so that your instinct says, "Wait a minute. That means something. That's an illustration of something." They may be brief. They may appear inconsequential. But they are, in some way, significant.

Anecdotes, by their nature, are not great big world-shaping events. They are human looks, at something. They have small cores, but radiate ramifications.

When you hear them, when you learn to recognize them, you must collect them and file them away. You can use, as a filing system, an actual filing system, a card catalogue, a Rolodex, a computer disk, or your own head. I find the latter most efficient. (In general, that is. When walking around the world. When you're on a particular story and you hear an anecdote, you'd better write it down that very instant or you will probably lose it. Keep good notes. When you review them, the anecdotes will pop out at you screaming for attention.)

Being a writer is being a storyteller, and since anecdotes are

BONNIE REMSBERG

Bonnie Remsberg, in her twenty-five-year career as a journalist, has written more than nine hundred nonfiction articles and dramatic narratives for most of America's leading magazines. Her writing has appeared in *Family Circle, Ladies' Home Journal, Woman's Day, Redbook, Good Housekeeping, Reader's Digest, Seventeen, Playboy, Esquire, Saturday Review,* the *New York Times Magazine, Success, Consumer Reports,* and many others. She has written frequently on a variety of topics for the *World Book Encyclopedia Yearbook.*

Remsberg is a modern writer who keeps the public informed "in the tradition of Samuel Adams, Tom Paine, Ida M. Tarbell and Woodward and Bernstein," according to *The Art of Writing Non-Fiction,* which was published by Syracuse University Press in 1987.

She is coauthor of *The Stress-Proof Child, A Loving Parent's Guide,* published by Holt, Rinehart and Winston in January

1985, by the New American Library in May 1986, and by Nightingale-Conant Audio Tapes in May 1987. Her book *Radio and TV Spot Announcements for Family Planning* is distributed by the United Nations and the Ford Foundation to developing countries around the world. Scripts from the book have been translated into more than twenty languages and are in production in dozens of countries. She has also contributed to numerous anthologies, including the acclaimed *Smiling Through the Apocalypse, Esquire's History of the '60s* (reissued in 1987) and *The Complete Guide to Writing Non-Fiction* by the American Society of Journalists and Authors (1983).

Showing remarkable versatility, Remsberg has written award-winning films, television documentaries, and speeches for the presidents and chief executive officers of major American and international corporations. From 1965 to 1983, she lived in Chicago, where she hosted a weekly television talk program on

simply little stories, they become your stock in trade. I love to tell stories; I think most writers do. We have, most of us, become writers not because we know a lot of words, but because of a compelling need to tell stories to other people.

How, then, to gather good anecdotes. A few rules, to follow or ignore. First, pay very little attention to yourself. When you are focused on yourself, on your looks, your clothes, your brilliant questions or clever repartee, you are just not tuned in to other people, and they won't tell you what's really on their minds. You become too insular, too self-involved.

Pay infinite amounts of attention, on the other hand, as much as you can muster, to the world, particularly the people, around you. When you do this, when you become genuinely interested in and open to other people, you will find anecdotes drop on you like rain.

You may occasionally have to prime the pump by telling a pertinent story or two about yourself.

Look, when hunting anecdotes, for the uncommon. Don't look for trendy; look for human. Look for something that taps in to something, some experience, some feeling, that's in everybody.

When you write up your anecdotes, don't overburden them with adjectives. Adjectives, in story telling, are accessories. Too many kill the effect. They get in the way. Too many adjectives and you can't see what's there. The bones, the good structure, of the little story get obliterated.

Here, then, from my own work, is an example of how the foregoing lessons apply. The article was "The Agonizing Decision of Debra Sorensen" (*Family Circle*, April 6, 1982), about a young couple who

---

NBC. Since then, she has hosted television programs and has appeared in interviews on ABC, CBS, and PBS. For Westinghouse Broadcasting Company, she wrote the docudrama, *Karen Ann,* about the historic Karen Ann Quinlan case.

Remberg's list of honors is lengthy, including many journalism awards, such as the prestigious American Society of Journalists and Authors Weisinger Award for Outstanding Magazine. This was given to her for her article examining the effects of atomic radiation on the citizens in a small Utah town. She has won the Sidney Hillman Prize Award for her outstanding articles on social issues, and twice she has received the Penney-Missouri Award for women's interest journalism.

In addition, Remsberg has been honored with seven Emmy Awards for television documentaries; three medical journalism awards; the Gabriel Award from the Association of Catholic Broadcasters; the Voice of Freedom Award from the Zionist Organization; and the Pioneer Women's "Celebration of Women" award. Cleveland Heights High School has inducted her into its Distinguished Alumni Hall of Fame.

As a journalism teacher, Remsberg has worked at the University of Chicago's graduate school, Northwestern University's Medill School of Journalism, Columbia University, and the University of Indiana.

A graduate of Northwestern and a mother of two, Remsberg is listed in *Who's Who in America, Who's Who of American Women, Who's Who in the Midwest, Who's Who of American Jewry, Working Press of the Nation, The World's Who's Who of Authors, The World's Who's Who of Women, Contemporary Journalists,* and *Contemporary Authors.*

had had a dearly wanted baby born so severely defective that they had to make a decision as to whether he should be operated on, and allowed to live, or not operated on and allowed to die. The mother was a lovely, gentle girl who was, understandably, nervous about baring her horrendous experiences to a stranger. She invited a girlfriend to the first interview because she was so afraid of what the experience was going to do to her. Gradually, over time, she became comfortable with me. She trusted me enough to be alone with me. We shared pizza and a bottle of wine. By the end of the last interview, after many, many tears had been shed by both of us, she was quite relaxed. "I have something to show you," she said, and disappeared into the bedroom. She came out with a plastic bag in her hand. The incident that happened then, when she was baring the bottom of her mother-soul, became the ending of my article. It reads like this: "Debbie keeps a plastic bag of Nicky's toys and clothes, just as it was given to her by the ambulance driver who dropped it off on the way to the autopsy. In there is the mirrored rattle, and the card and the first thing Debbie ever embroidered, a bib with Big Bird on it. Every so often, she takes the bag out of the closet and opens it. A sweet baby smell still rises from Nicky's things, and makes her cry."

I couldn't have made that up.

Description

Like anecdotes, descriptions lend authenticity to writing. Describing people gives the reader a far better sense of real people than does merely giving their names. Here is a description of a professor:

She breezes to the department on a yellow ten-speed bicycle and nods curt greetings to those she passes as she strides vigorously to her office. Floor-to-ceiling, wall-to-wall stacks of files, magazines, books, and papers await her there—solid piles that frighten the timid away. Piles of facts. Reality. Practicality. The phone rings all day; rarely is she there to answer it, and only on the twelfth ring does she answer with an abrupt, distracted "Yes?"

She is more masculine than feminine, and strong above all. Perhaps the epitome of androgyny, she would only confuse Virginia Woolf. Her life is fact. No visible emotion, no frills, very little humor. All day long, she is pursued for knowledge. She is a giver and receiver of facts.

One fact is that she is a beautiful woman. She is tan and healthy despite middle age. Her large, dangling earrings and scarlet lipstick would ridicule a complexion less dark, a face less forceful. She is easily pictured as a striking 18-year-old, grinding her way through a cutthroat world, successful because fear would never have occurred to her, and unhampered by her classic beauty that could have led her astray had she noticed it was there.

To describe fully a person in his or her story, a good writer will point up one facet on one page, another on a different page, and still another on still another page. When the writer has completed the story, readers will be certain that the subject is a human being, not just a person with a name who has never come into focus because of lack of description. Consider this description of a woman named Sharman Haley:

Page 2:

. . . she said, readjusting her wire frame glasses.

Page 3:

As Haley began describing the ordeal, her face softened, she removed her granny-like glasses, her lips began to quiver as the logical gave way to the emotional side of Sharman. Fighting the tears with the same gusto as she fights political battles was not enough this time; the walled-up emotions and unexpressed words began to flow.

Page 4:

. . . Haley has style and presence: She dresses in old-fashioned clothes and touts new, radical ideas. At five feet tall, her 100-pound body is often clad in long skirts, hiking boots and Salvation Army shirts. And, of course, she doesn't shave her legs (an important trademark, she says, to her beliefs). She is a product of the 1960s and 1970s.

Pages 4 and 5:

The lanky lady with high ideals has decided to turn her attention—for the time being—to life in Berkeley and academics. Her voice slows down, indicating the end of the interview; she begins to sound southern, with a drawl unlike her native Washington rapid-fire speech. Maybe that is part of the puzzle—a rich-kid-turned-socialist-turned-economics-student.

Notice especially that these descriptions approach the power of anecdotes. Without descriptions, readers would probably have trouble remembering the woman described in the passage, but they would remember Sharman Haley as she is described above.

Because descriptions are such a strong writing technique, they should be used abundantly. Excellent descriptions give writing the color and flavor of experience. All these facets of Haley are mixed with facts, examples, and quotations. These observations, which the writer worked hard at expressing well, are not the center of the essay. Instead, they freckle this profile so memorably that it is captivating.

Quotations Lend Authenticity

Like descriptions, direct quotations lend authenticity to writing. Quoting a person gives your readers a better sense of your subject than paraphrasing would. When you quote directly—provided you choose judiciously from what your subject says—your readers have the experience you had: they hear exactly what you heard.

A good quotation can reveal more about a topic and speaker than can several paragraphs by the writer. Direct quotations also relieve you of the responsibility of using opinion or arguable judgments about someone else. Instead, your subject speaks for himself or herself.

These quotations illustrate the value of well-chosen words:

Gore Vidal, the famous author, said, "Whenever a friend succeeds, a little something in me dies."

Clifton Fadiman, a critic of writing and a judge of the Book of the Month Club, said, "The author is a past master in making nothing happen very slowly."

Lillian Hellman, a famous playwright, once said, "If I had to give young writers advice, I'd say don't listen to writers about writing."

Often, such quotes are not spontaneous but are phrases that their creators thought of long ago and rephrased over time. You can hardly do better than to quote others who state succinctly the very idea you wish to convey.

Words as Words

Centuries ago, Philip of Macedon, a powerful king, threatened Laconia with this message: "If I enter Laconia, you shall be exterminated."

The Laconians replied with this message: "If." They used the power of the common word.

Studying a single language, your own, can be a delightful adventure or hated drudgery, depending on your attitude toward discovering new meanings of simple words. First, think of Abraham Lincoln's Gettysburg Address, in which he did *not* say "a people's government," nor "government of, by, and for the people." Instead, he said "of the people, by the people, and for the people." You have undoubtedly been warned against repetition, but observe why repeating "people" three times worked wonderfully well for him. Although a word was repeated in Lincoln's passage, each use of the word is preceded by a different one-syllable word: "of," "by," and "for." Moreover, note especially how he achieves rhythm here by using only "of the," "by the," and "for the," all followed by "people." Such is the power of common words if you think of them as Lincoln did.

Note especially, though, that Lincoln did not use repetition again in his speech. Reading the following passage aloud will convince you that he used repetition selectively. The verbs are italicized: ". . . our fathers *brought* forth on this continent a new nation, *conceived* in liberty, and *dedicated* to the proposition that all men *are created* equal." Lincoln knew that verbs are like hinges on a sentence, so he took special care about selecting them. Observe how his verbs beat a regular time and marked the cadence of the sentence; the rhythm is repeated, but not the sounds of the words or the words themselves.

Alliteration is a powerful tool as well, and a special kind of repetition. Alliteration is the repetition of specific sounds in a sentence, the technique Spiro Agnew used when he called the press "nattering nabobs of negativism." The phrase was memorable.

Captivating writing begins with careful phrases, not overpowering words. Here, for example, is not an attractive but an exhausting sentence: "Today, the monstrosity which sunders the City of Berlin exemplifies the incarnated East-West standoff in the heart of Europe while at the same time adding stimulus to the already electrified emotions of a severed nation." True, there is visual language here, along with a self-conscious vocabulary, but this sentence is inconsiderate to its subject. There is just too much nonsense about it.

Another example: "The Americans cannot plant the seeds of social unrest, nourish and fertilize them, and then leave them to pursue their own course." Note the mixed metaphor, which begins with agricultural images and ends with nautical navigation. It would have been far better had the student written "The Americans cannot plant the seeds of social unrest, nourish them, then leave them to grow untended." The difference in the second example may seem minor, but it shows that a mixed sentence can be fixed, much to the better.

It is all a matter of being alert to wording. Look at the following passage:

> Her pale, white skin, untouched by the intensity of the sun's rays, wrinkled in patterned lines at the corners of her mouth as she attempted to comprehend the mutterings of her student. Her right arm grew strength and touched the limp hand of the student in a simple gesture of compassion.

What does it mean, "her right arm grew strength"? And did the woman touch the student's hand with her *arm?* Don't let your enthusiasm tangle the images you use in your writing.

Visual Writing

To practice making visual phrases, make your own observation of, say, games—football, basketball, baseball—or parties, or any event where many people gather. You will see, just by making a point of watching, what many people fail to observe. Then you can summarize what you see in phrases such as these, written by students:

> *Football Game*
> The home crowd grumbled out of the stadium.
> The visiting band lined up in neo-Nazi formation.
> The crowd began to seep out of the stadium.
> Crowds jammed each gate, squirting files of fans.
> She hugged someone who looked unexciting enough to be her husband.
> The high school bands looked like children playing dress-up.
> . . . so hot that everyone is getting runny around the edges
> . . . examines the crowd through beer-bleared eyes
> A shirt comes off as one rooter surrenders to the sun.
> jeer leaders

Gambling
Dealers pause only to reshuffle the cards as marksmen at a mass execution reload.
. . . $100 bills as common as confetti
. . . signs that discourage financial flyweights

Parks
. . . the foul breath of suburbia's early-morning yawn
The dawn had grown too old.
Redwood trees stretched their limbs and fanned away into the clouds. The campground had already transformed itself into the setting for the daily rape of Yosemite's majestic calm.

Hospital
. . . contrary-to-nature colors, too perfect, too manufactured
. . . worn body and clothes slouched crowlike and defeated
. . . birdlike limbs exposed, legs hanging from her chair ironically

When you become accustomed to writing visually, you will find fashioning such phrases to be one of the chief pleasures of writing. But then you face another danger: becoming enamored of your own prose. The result is a purple profusion of cute phrases that will tire almost any reader—or a repetition of the same image until the image itself becomes tiresome.

One student fell into this trap when she decided that a certain professor looked something like a teddy bear. She fell in love with this sentence: "He looks like a teddy bear stuffed into a smaller doll's clothing." That image appeared on page 2. One page 5, she wrote, "His large, teddy bear–like body . . ." and, six lines later, "his looming, overstuffed teddy-bear physique . . ." Teddy bears are cute, but the repetition of this image is tedious. Many readers probably became irritated as a once memorable phrase became overmuch.

When you have created an original phrase, never repeat it in the same paper. Isolate your creation; it will draw more positive attention that way. What will you do when you are tempted to use it again? Make up a new one. It may not be pleasure to do so; it may be agony. But it is worth it; nothing can be compared to creating still another original phrase. Another inventive set of words will bring you only joy.

For example, when you use the phrase "as smooth as," don't settle for that tired cliché "as smooth as glass." Try again. The next may be this: "as smooth as borrowing your prospective mother-in-law's knife at dinner to pick your teeth with." You will not end up with such a phrase, because it is too long, but the idea may spark another one. Perhaps, after much thinking, you may think of "as smooth as a con man's manner" or "as smooth as an innuendo." When you do, you will be pleased with your work. Similarly, "as fast as" may yield "as fast as an antelope," which is a phrase much more old and tired than any antelope alive today. Try again. Like many college students, you may think of a negative phrase: "As fast as five-o'clock traffic." That is a tired phrase too. Eventually, though, you will think of a better one: "As fast as a keg gets tapped at a frat party." Or: "As fast as a greased rumor."

When you have exercised your creativity to find such visual phrases, you will have discovered as well the pleasure (and the pain) of writing. Your readers will be glad you worked as hard as you did.

HOW TO WRITE A PROFILE

The axiom that "people are interested in people" holds doubly true when applied to magazine articles. It is a safe estimate that nearly half of the articles now appearing in popular magazines are woven around interesting characters; their hopes; their problems, foibles, and adversities; and how they finally got around or over the hurdles in their paths.

> "I grow daily to honor facts more and more, and theory even less."
>
> THOMAS CARLYLE

In editorial parlance, these articles are "profiles." The first profiles were definitive character sketches written for the *New Yorker* in the early 1930s. Gradually, the term was tacked on to almost any personality piece. Many were articles about crusades, institutions, companies, sports events, political episodes, and the like, told in terms of a lead character involved in a struggle. This method gained popularity because editors and writers discovered that the surest and easiest way to make an otherwise heavy topic come alive was to cover it from the viewpoint of a person involved. Readers could easily put themselves in his or her shoes, whereas they had a hard time pulling on the boots of a corporation or an institution.

Profiles have since become even broader. It is now fairly customary in many magazine offices to speak of "profiles" of places and events. In such cases, the profile is much like the descriptive.

A profile is a written sketch of a person designed to show the reader *who that person is.* This is a weighty responsibility for any writer, especially a beginner, who may wonder: How can I show someone else who a person is? What if I get it wrong? How can I capture a personality accurately when I'm only one person, with one perspective?

Let's take a look at what your responsibility is as the writer of a profile. Like virtually all other pieces of writing, a profile is crafted with a reader in mind. The writing style, the length of the profile, and the subject of the profile are all subject to this one overarching rule: a profile is written for a reader.

The profile must still be accurate, however. You may be tempted to lionize your subject—to make a hero out of a person who is, after all, only human. You may be tempted to repeat the favorite stereotypes about a subject. You are not a cartoonist; you cannot create a personality, simplify it, and slap it onto a subject simply to make life easier for yourself and your readers. That is the world of television fiction; real people are much too complex for that.

As a sketch of a person, a profile has got to have more than color. It must have structure and shape. A profile must include the following information about the subject:

Basic information Full name, age, professional title, marital status, and number and ages of children (if any).

Physical description How the person looks and acts—and what his or her surroundings look like.

Profession or hobby There is a reason why a profile subject is chosen, and it is usually a profession or hobby. Describe what the person does that will be of interest to the readers.

These are the bare bones of a profile. What you need to do is present the basic facts deftly while you focus on presenting to the reader the subject *as a person.*

Although she is only a beginning writer, Megyn Price excels at writing profiles. She digs beneath the surface to explore her subject's personality, then she reveals it to readers. Here's an excellent profile of a Los Angeles attorney:

(To be read at thirty times normal rate of speech) "Hey, hey, hey, hey! That was an old gold from the prince with the pounds of sounds. Now, don't anybody sit down! Get your party shoes on, cause we've got a tune that's shakin' to get this house quakin', to rock your socks and make your feet dance sweet. Everybody out on the floor for the one, the ONLY, The Moooooooooooody Bubububububublues!!!!!!!!!"

The crowd of sweaty teenagers screamed as the opening drum-beats exploded through the gymnasium. The eight-foot speakers, strategically placed atop each of the basketball goals, pounded the rhythm directly into every dancer's soul. Bodies collided like supernovas in a mass hysteria of swinging arms and legs. One smaller boy came flying out of the mob, falling flat on the hardwood floor with a thud. Undaunted, he jumped to his feet and dove headfirst into the crazed riot.

One unheard foot taps in time with the beat. Behind the microphone, a perspiring, yet serene, face sits with a calm smile. The clear blue eyes are laughing as they watch the amazing energy emanating from the crowd. People are happy. They're having a great time.

Tom Price is an extremely conservative man in his mid-thirties. A graduate of Stanford Law School, Tom drives a black Mercedes-Benz, lives in Beverly Hills, and works as a corporate attorney for one of the largest companies in southern California. He is divorced, lives with a cat, and goes to church on Sundays.

This is probably how most people see Tom Price the yuppie. If you were to follow him around quietly after 5:00 P.M., however, you might be surprised. Driving home in rush hour traffic, with the latest remix of Jimi Hendrix's "Deep Purple" on the CD player, Tom reaches into the back seat and grabs his gym bag. As traffic slows to a stop, he begins the transformation. Tom quickly exchanges his coat, tie, and dress shirt for a beat-up Bruce Springsteen tour shirt and a black stonewashed-denim jacket. He'll have to change into the jeans at home. From the glove compartment, he gets his portable tube of hair gel and molds the blow-dried-lawyer hairdo into the spiky, nouveau-chic club look. Then he finishes with the pièce de résistance . . . one tiny gold hoop earring with a very cool rhinestone.

By the time Tom turns into the driveway, he's got thirty minutes to grab a bite to eat and be at Huntington Beach for his gig tonight. You see, if you haven't guessed by now, our Dr. Jekyll of the yuppie world by day becomes quite the Mr. Hyde by night. Yes, our conservative attorney is a disc jockey. "I prefer to think of myself as a scientist in the art of rock," Tom says with a laugh. "It just sounds more . . . I don't know . . . more respectable!"

When Tom Price graduated from Stanford in 1975, he had absolutely no idea what he wanted to do. He had already been accepted at Stanford Law School, but he suddenly found himself in a slump. "I don't really know what happened, but I felt like there was no point to anything. I guess it's just the senior blahs, but I definitely had a clinical case of it."

Tom had graduated with honors in psychology and economics, but his personality certainly didn't reflect what a brain he was. "I lived in a fraternity, went to every party ever thrown ANYWHERE—no lie." One of Tom's best friends in college, Pete Masumaki, confirmed Tom's unbelievable love for having a good time. "Oh, man, Tuna never spent more than maybe an hour and a half at a time studying. Every time he heard about a party—I mean, the damn thing could be in South Sacramento, and he'd get a bunch of us to blow off all our work and go out with him. Great friend, huh?"

The name "Tuna," we should all be hoping, was not given at birth. "Well, I probably *did* look a little like a tuna when I was born. I mean, don't we all?" Tom laughed. "No, actually, I got the name when I was d.j.-ing at the Zoo. I decided my own name wasn't memorable enough, so I started brainstorming about myself. I decided if I really am what I eat, then I should really be a tuna. Love the stuff—I eat it on everything. Gross, huh? Anyway, the Zoo is where it all started."

No, not the zoo with lions and tigers and bears, oh my. "The Zoo," as it is affectionately called by its followers, is KZSU, the student-run radio station at Stanford.

Researching a Profile

There are three ways, at least, to research a profile.

Interviews

First and most important of your researching will be your interviews with the subject. Two interviews is not enough for an excellent profile; three or more is better. Make a point of spending time with your subject, watching him or her at work and off work, if possible.

You are seeking a personality here. Within each person is a core, a nugget, a central question that you as a researcher can seek out during your interviews and present to the readers. That point may be a drive to succeed, a rage at injustice, a plaintive search for acceptance.

You will find such things only from firsthand interviews; your outside reading, your talking with acquaintances, and so on, will provide you with clues and with much of the raw data that you will use in your profile. But your perception of that person's central point will also be the central point of your essay.

Second, interview friends and acquaintances of the subject. They will have tales to tell and perspectives to add that you may never otherwise hear. One writer, researching a tale on a paraplegic who designs sports equipment, heard all about the man's various projects from the man himself; tales of how he put together the apparatus to sail a Laser sailboat, and so on. But his long-time friend tells how much he relies on other people. "I finally had to tell him, 'You know, your friends are not your slaves,'" the friend said. Another friend commented on how popular his paraplegic buddy was with women. "I kept hoping I could snatch one of them away from him," he said. "But I had no success."

Observation

Observe the subject. What does his or her office look like? Are there bizarre knicknacks on the shelves? Is the desk piled high with papers? Does the subject smoke a pipe? What about the clothes the subject is wearing? You will have leisure to notice such details if you spend some time with the subject; you may also be lucky enough to have to wait a minute or two while the subject makes some phone calls, giving you the opportunity to scribble down a few notes. The details you pick up will be invaluable when you write the profile.

Reading

If you choose a subject that has already been written about, you may find that reading what others have written is a mixed blessing. You can prejudice yourself by approaching the subject from another's perspective. On the other hand, you need information about the subject, so usually there is little alternative but to read such articles. Try not to take that author's opinion as your own, however. Try to keep a fresh eye.

What Belongs in a Profile?

Writing a profile is, in fact, difficult; it is even more difficult because the piece must capture the reader. Fortunately, there are ways to overcome both sides of the profile challenge at once. Is it hard to discern and show a personality? Is it hard to keep a reader's attention? Use anecdotes; use quotations; use the insights of other people who know the subject of your profile. Then, readers not only are beguiled by the tale but can also discern the personality, as it were, firsthand.

Here is the kind of information that belongs in a profile.

Anecdotes

Almost nothing is more valuable to a writer than anecdotes. Why? Few people are able to stop reading an anecdote until it is over. Can you reasonably put down an article when you are in the middle of a short, succinct tale that promises to have a punch line at the end?

Consider also how much an anecdote tells about a person. When he was a young man, the mustachioed Winston Churchill once attended a formal dinner party. In those days, mustaches were unpopular, and Churchill was rather outspoken about his political views as well. A dowager announced to him that she was offended by both his politics and his mustache. Churchill replied, "Madam, you are not likely to come in contact with either."

What does this tell you about Churchill? That he was outspoken and overconfident as a young man, very witty, perhaps even obnoxious. You also know that Churchill was at home in the toniest of parlors. The anecdote would be an excellent one to quote in a profile of Churchill.

Some anecdotes are funny, others simply revealing. While Oliver Wendell Holmes, Jr., was at Harvard, he wrote a fifteen-page essay criticizing Plato and showed it to Ralph Waldo Emerson for comments. Emerson returned it with the observation, "When you shoot at a king, you must kill him." Holmes destroyed his essay. This anecdote tells you that Holmes was an original thinker, a bright and brash student. It also shows that he was canny enough to listen to advice. This anecdote, though it will not produce a chuckle on the part of your readers, will nonetheless entertain them as it tells them about Holmes.

Such anecdotes are history, available to the reader of biographies in any reasonably sized library. You may have to work a little harder to find excellent anecdotes about your own living, breathing subject, but you will find some when you spend time with the subject and with friends and colleagues of the subject. You may even observe some incidents worth telling about.

Quotations from the Subject

Keep your ear tuned for what the subject says during interviews. Writers cannot interview subjects in an hour or two and be satisfied with what they hear, incidentally; to get excellent quotes, you may have to interview your subject over and over—at least twice and preferably three or more times. Important revelations will emerge when interviewers and subjects become accustomed to one another.

Megyn Price, whose profile of Tom Price was quoted earlier in this chapter, uses many quotations to help reveal her subject's personality. For example, read these paragraphs and notice how her subject almost writes the article for her by providing good quotes during the interview:

> After much deliberation, Tom finally decided law school might be, as he put it, "a blast." He really wanted to stay on at KZSU, and there was no way to do that unless he remained in school. After law school, the same dilemma arose again. Now, however, the stakes were greater. He had to choose what to do with a $150,000 education. "I couldn't exactly run off and d.j. somewhere. I had a hundred thousand dollars in loans, for pete's sake. I knew I had to live like a normal, boring human for at least a while."
>
> Leave it to Tuna to find an unboring way to be a boring human. He worked his way up, through a string of promotions and extremely

hard work, to the top position in a major corporation. "While I was groveling, scraping my way up, I really didn't have time for anything. It was probably the hardest I've ever worked in my life. But, oh, wow, it was so worth it."

Tom's higher position enabled him to work 9 to 5, period. No take-home files from the office cluttered his home, and his free time was finally his. He started making contacts with old friends in the Los Angeles area, and accidentally stumbled upon the answer to his prayers.

When I asked Tom to tell the story, he sat up in his chair and got the giggles. "It was the most amazing thing ever. I walked into this station down here and asked if they were looking for any moonlighting help. I told them what experience I had, and that I was really just looking for a good place to spin records. You know, I didn't want to be paid Fort Knox. Well, before the station manager could even say a word, this woman who had been sitting in the waiting room came running up to me. She asked where I went to college. When I told her Stanford, she starts yapping out my Tom Tuna introduction that I always gave when I was at KZSU. Then, she tells me she's the head of the city school board and she was at the station waiting to talk to one of the d.j.'s about doing private parties for public high schools. She begged me to take the job right there on the spot . . . and the rest is music history, sports fans!"

Would these paragraphs have been as effective without Price's words? Probably not. Powerful, direct quotations can be a story's backbone.

Quotations from Others

Writers should interview detractors as well as friends of the subject; no profile will be adequate until it incorporates the views of others. Following are the comments of Lou Cannon of the *Washington Post* speaking about his colleague, columnist David Broder:

David Broder is a great man. A wonderful colleague and a very good friend. I think that Dave is a strong columnist because he does do the reporting. But Dave has been extremely influential on that newspaper. The thing that he never really gets any outside credit for either is, unlike a lot of political stars of the newspaper, Dave tries to get everybody who is working on that paper in his area into the offense. I've really been able to come in there and do all kinds of important and political stories, which I know I wouldn't have been able to do on the other newspapers.

Dave is particularly good with young reporters. You know in every campaign we have reporters that are assigned to us from cityside who work on campaigns. Dave goes out of his way to make people who are part of a reporting team feel at home and see that they have an important role to contribute. I think that he is really kind of the renaissance man of political reporting. . . .

Such an encomium on any subject really should be balanced by some critical comments, which will obviously not be forthcoming from a colleague and admirer.

What would one use from such an interview? Depending on the unifying theme that you use to pull together your information on David Broder, you might say:

Colleagues agree that Broder's talents are rare. "I think that he is really kind of the renaissance man of political reporting," says Lou Cannon, a colleague at the *Washington Post*.

Or:

As a columnist, Broder goes for the kill. "Dave tries to get everybody who is working on that paper in his area into the offense," says Lou Cannon. "I've really been able to come in there and do all kinds of important and political stories, which I know I wouldn't have been able to do on the other newspapers."

As this example illustrates, you will use parts of long quotations to fit into what you perceive your subject to be—part of a picture that you see, a picture you have been able to paint because of your extensive research on the subject.

You have a responsibility to be sure you use a quotation "in context"—that is, you must represent a positive comment about a subject as positive and a critical one as critical. You would never say, for example:

Lou Cannon agrees that Broder is ruthless. "Dave tries to get everybody . . . into the offense."

You must accurately represent the comments of those you interview; however, you must never take another person's perceptions for your own. See for yourself and think for yourself.

Description

Writers should not confine their description of a subject to routine facts such as height, weight, and color of eyes and hair; special care should be taken to note the more vivid details of how the individual walks, talks, and gestures.

Here is how a *New Yorker* writer described Nicolas Slonimsky, a composer:

Slonimsky is clean-shaven—a short man of odd shape. He has written of "the unfortunate lack of Grecian golden mean" between the parts of his body. He has the legs, shoulders, and arms of a slight man, and then, he says, "where other people have abdominal cavities, I have convexity." His belly balloons—the buttons on his shirts strain to contain their unexpected bounty (any shirt that fits him at the shoulders will at best barely suffice to encompass his midriff). But then everything tapers precipitously from the waist down. . . . He resembles a skinny tenor trussed up in vast pillows for a stint as Falstaff. Walking, he pads along like a fat man, gingerly, carefully; talking, his arms and hands dart all over; seated, listening, he crosses his arms and rests them atop his belly as if on a bar counter. . . .

His face is smooth, virtually without wrinkles, like a turtle's; it rests on a neck that is jowly. He has a turtly beak nose, which swerves abruptly, halfway down, to his left, like a freeway on-ramp. . . .

But the contour of the voice is remarkable: he punches the words out, as distinct entities, in extraordinarily complex rhythms. . . .

Truth—And Consequences

One journalist said of interview subjects, "*I* want the truth; *they* want to be beautiful." As has been pointed out, when you write an interview, you will need to tell the truth as you see it. This may be somewhat at odds with the picture the subject wants to convey.

How can you reconcile the problem? Remember this: the profile will have your name on it. Represent your subject (and the comments of the subject's acquaintances) as accurately as you can, but do not, ever, let someone else tell you what to say.

One reporter found himself stymied when he gave away the right to choose his own focus. When Louisiana held statewide elections years ago, the reporter was assigned to write a profile of the successful candidate for attorney general. He conducted a highly successful interview. The new attorney general was expansive, talking at length about how he had long been an "almost man": almost elected president of the student council in high school, almost elected president of the student body, graduated second in his class in law school. He was overjoyed by the election results: at last, he had finished first. At the end of the interview, he said, "Of course, you'll let me read that story before it's published." Ignorant of common practice in journalism, the young writer said, "Of course."

The writer was proud of the story he showed to the attorney general. It was built around a theme tracing the career of the "almost man" through his many defeats to his eventual triumph. The attorney general admitted that nothing in the story was inaccurate, but he disliked the theme. "If the voters see this kind of emphasis in your story," he said, "they'll think they elected a second-rater."

Although the reporter had not agreed to change what he had written, the alternatives were clear. He changed it. The result was a routine story, not nearly as interesting or as unified—or, for that matter, as true—as the original version.

So: be true to yourself, and to your subject as well. If you use the techniques described in this section, not only will you have done that, but you will have pleased readers as well.

A Short Profile

In *Choice of Pearls*, Solomon Ibn Gabirol wrote:

There are four mental types among human beings:
The man who knows, and is aware that he knows: he is wise, so inquire of him.
The man who knows, but is unaware that he knows: remind him and help him that he forget not.

"When a majority pushes a minority up against the wall, it foolishly forgets Gracián's worldly wisdom expressed three centuries ago: "Never contend with a man who has nothing to lose."

SYDNEY J. HARRIS

The man who is ignorant, and knows that he is ignorant: teach him.

The man who is ignorant, but pretends to know: he is a fool, so keep away from him.

Consider the short profile of actor Peter Falk that appeared in the November 13, 1972, *Newsweek:*

The Real Columbo

COMMENT

Note that the writer begins immediately to describe the character, Columbo. The writer has been allotted only two columns, one of which will carry a small picture of Columbo. As a result, he hasn't the space for leisurely writing that he would have had if, for example, the *Newsweek* executives had decided that Falk would be the cover story.

The writer works consciously for descriptive phrases: "the wardrobe of a flood victim," "would seem hopelessly out of place in a Rolls-Royce or a pair of Gucci shoes," "like an off-duty janitor." No doubt the writer worked for hours—perhaps days— through many rewrites to get just the right tone.

The readers are induced to read on by the careful structure and phrasing of the profile.

PROFILE*

He has the face of a broken-down pug, the diction of a poolroom hustler and the wardrobe of a flood victim. He never flashes a gun, throws a punch or nestles against a voluptuous bosom. When tracking down a killer, his manner is so apologetic and stumbling that his quarry invariably regards him with bemusement rather than fear. In short, "Columbo" is the absolute antithesis of the typical television detective, a misbegotten dropout from the Rock Hudson-Gene Barry School of Sophisticated Sleuthmanship. Top marks from Nielsen, however, have made the "Columbo" segment of "The NBC Sunday Mystery Movie" series one of the five highest-rated shows on TV this season. The reason, of course, is Peter Falk.

Like the detective lieutenant he portrays, Falk comes across as a lovable, low-keyed Everyman who would seem hopelessly out of place in a Rolls-Royce or a pair of Gucci shoes. Clad in a graying white shirt and crumpled trousers, he shambled into Universal Picture's executive dining room last week, looking more like an off-duty janitor than an affluent actor who has won two Academy Award nominations and two Emmies. When the waitress informed him that the booth he had taken was reserved for a Universal VIP, Falk obligingly picked up his gnawed, 10-cent cigar and slouched to another table. But when he began analyzing his TV role for *Newsweek*'s Malcolm MacPherson, it quickly became evident that Falk's unpretentious pose—like that of Columbo—disguises a shrewd, sensitive intelligence.

"Columbo says things that children say and adults only think," rasped Falk, twisting his head upward in order to see through his one good eye (the right eye is glass, the legacy of a childhood tumor). "He asks naïve questions not because he wants to look like a farmer, but because he is genuinely inquisitive. He knows they're going to write him off as a rube, but he's not offended by it. It works to his advantage if he's taken for a farmer."

You don't have to be a buffoon to enjoy identifying with Columbo. He is the eternal doormat who always trips up high-and-mighty villains. The show's very

*From *Newsweek,* November 13, 1972. Copyright © 1972, Newsweek, Inc. Reprinted by permission.

predictability is part of the fun. Columbo may make a fool of himself, but the audience knows full well that in the end, his simple, unaffected virtue will triumph over such polished murderers as the smug symphony conductor (John Cassavetes) or the super-sophisticated private eye (Robert Culp).

Peter Falk has been living the life of Columbo for most of his forty-five years. Not long after graduating from high school in Ossining, N.Y., he signed on with the merchant marine, then embarked on a carousing tour of Yugoslavia with a girl friend. Returning to the U.S., he graduated from Syracuse University and served an unlikely tour of duty as an efficiency expert in the Connecticut Revenue Department before drifting into the theater. ("You mean," asked his father, the owner of a dry-goods store, "that you're going to paint your face and make an ass of yourself all your life?") In 1956, Falk had his first success in an off-Broadway production of *The Iceman Cometh*. Four years later, his portrayal of a hoodlum in the movie *Murder, Inc.* won him his first Oscar nomination. More recently, he has been acclaimed for his performances in Cassavetes's film *Husbands* and Neil Simon's play *The Prisoner of Second Avenue*.

Incredibly enough, NBC originally wanted Bing Crosby for the part of Columbo—but Crosby was too much of a golf freak to spare the time. Falk liked the role immediately, and within a short time made the character almost indistinguishable from himself. Columbo's ratty raincoat, brown suit and 1950s tie, for example, came out of the actor's own closet. Nor do the similarities between the two end off-camera. Recently, Falk's battered, 1959 Jaguar lost its forward gears as he was driving along Beverly Hills's Wilshire Boulevard. Undaunted, Falk found the one operable gear and happily drove along in reverse for several blocks. "Right now," he says with a one-eyed twinkle, "there isn't a car anywhere that goes better backward. I go backward everywhere." Columbo would understand that perfectly.

The piece on Falk is a skillful profile. The writer had only about 700 words in little more than a column and a half. He wrote the essential factors tightly. Obviously, he didn't have the leisure that permitted another writer to spell out one particular aspect of another profile, shown in this anecdote:

One day before the Big Game several years ago, Professor Gurley ambled up onto the stage in Economics I class as he had done for several years in a row: slowly, meditatively. As the students filed in, he charted several graphs on the four blackboards. When the boards were strangled with odd lines, letters, and jottings, he turned around and rapidly began to go through an incredible explanation far above the level of Economics I. As he wandered through several highly abstract concepts, he added new lines to his blackboard maze.

The amazed students scribbled everything down as fast as they could, understanding nothing. "Now, are there any questions?" he asked, suddenly turning. Four hundred hands blossomed. He stood silently, scrutinizing the faces with his sincere look, not moving an inch.

Within a second the auditorium blew up in a mixture of hissing, clapping, whistling, and screams. The graphs on the boards spelled quite clearly: "BEAT CAL."

Notice the link between this paragraph and the preceding one, which began: "You don't have to be a buffoon to enjoy identifying with Columbo." Then, to go all the way back to describe his childhood, the writer makes the transition with: "Peter Falk has been living the life of Columbo for most of his forty-five years." He adroitly writes himself up to the present by the time he reaches the end of the story.

Give close attention to the way the writer saved possibly his best story for the end. This gives the reader the pleasure of finishing the story on a high note.

For contrast, here is another description of the same teacher by another writer, who tries to portray the professor's humor using only a simple sentence:

> His dry wit is scattered throughout the lecture to keep everyone watching.

The least important error here is the use of the phrase "to keep everyone watching," which, because it is not *precisely* the phrase you want, is irritating. The most important error is to make a point, then just let it sit there. If you want to say he has dry wit, prove it. Cite some of his witticisms.

The Essentials of the Profile

What the subject says   In direct quotations and in paraphrase.

What the subject does   His or her actions, including anecdotes that illuminate the subject.

Description of the subject   Including not only such routine facts as height, weight, and color of eyes and hair but also the details that make a subject come to life—how he or she walks, talks, gestures, and makes small movements.

History of the subject   Although what the subject is like *now* is the important aspect, failing to color the person's background in at least a few paragraphs may suggest that the subject was always this way—that he or she was never in the process of *becoming*. Ideally, historical tracing helps to show how the subject became what he or she is. (But it is usually a mistake to begin an article with history. At least a few paragraphs should be devoted first to the subject at present, so that the reader will *want* to go back into history.)

What others—friends and detractors—**think and say** about the subject.

Like descriptives, good profiles make the readers *see* their subjects. Consider the following excerpt from a story about an African-American general, written by William Greider when he worked for the *Washington Post:*

> The general is a man of heavy presence, tall and broad-shouldered, with a deep and serious voice, a natural "command voice" that subtly extracts deference from those around him.
>
> So it was a rare moment, listening to this man after hours over drinks, in the standard red-brick general's house assigned to the base's vice commander. His voice turned soft and rheumy as he stretched out in the lounge chair and sketched word pictures from his past.
>
> "When I was going to school with my mother, we always did shows," he said. "We'd have an Easter operetta, a Fourth of July patriotic blast and I'd have the largest speaking parts."
>
> Lt. Gen. Daniel James, Jr., 55, talked about a small boy nicknamed "Chappie" standing on a stage, dressed in a pink tuxedo with white lapels while his cousin Mabel sang to him a song written by his older sister.

The general's voice shifted to a falsetto imitation of his cousin Mabel and he began to sing:

"Handsome is as handsome does, so the wise men say. Feathers fine may make fine birds, but folks are not that way.

"It's what is in your heart that counts, deny it if you can. I'm not impressed with how you dress, cause clothes don't make the man."

The general laughed at his own singing. Why, he wondered, do those words stick in his memory after all these years? He was growing up poor in Pensacola, Fla., only he didn't know it. His mother never told him. . . .

In this profile, Greider creates both General James and the South in which he lived as an African-American officer. We see. Good profiles create clear, vivid pictures—sometimes with sound, scent, and even taste—in readers' minds.

Exercises

1. Choose an interesting person who would make a good subject for a profile, then discuss how you would tailor the article to suit three or four different magazines. Which aspects of the person's career or personality would you emphasize for each, and why?

2. Find a magazine profile and a newspaper personality sketch that were written about the same person. (Use the *Reader's Guide, New York Times Index,* and other reference books to help you.) Compare the two stories and discuss how they are alike and how they are different. Does the fact that one is in a magazine and one in a newspaper affect the content or style of the articles?

3. Read again the description of Nicolas Slonimsky earlier in this chapter, then attempt to write something similar about another man or woman (a real person). Do not let your description be influenced by the description of Slonimsky. Instead, make your description as close as possible to the way your subject actually looks.

FIFTEEN

PERSONAL EXPERIENCES AND NARRATIVES

I could a tale unfold whose lightest word

Would harrow up thy soul, freeze

thy young blood,

Make thy two eyes, like stars, start from

their spheres,

Thy knotted and combined locks to part,

And each particular hair to stand an end,

Like quills upon the fretful porpentine.

HAMLET, ACT I

WILLIAM SHAKESPEARE

Not all stories promise as much as the one from the ghost of Hamlet's father, but that does not diminish the pleasure of telling them. Personal experiences and narratives bring out the storyteller in most writers. The role is one they relish because it offers considerable freedom. The only absolute requirement is that the story be a good one.

Another example of a good story comes from *Johnny, We Hardly Knew Ye* by Kenneth P. O'Donnell, which illustrates John F. Kennedy's campaign philosophy:

> One day, when he was running for the Senate, we were driving through South Boston. Kennedy spotted an old woman about to cross the street alone. He called to the driver to stop the car. He got out,

introduced himself to the woman, took her arm and escorted her across the street. When he came back to the car, one of us said, "You really want *all* the votes, don't you?"

He replied, "How would *you* feel if you lost South Boston by one vote and then remembered that you didn't bother to help this lady across the street?"

PERSONAL EXPERIENCES

"Humor is emotional chaos remembered in tranquility."

JAMES THURBER

The temptation to write articles in the first person is particularly strong now that the New Journalism has given its blessing to participation by the writer in his or her story. Yet most subjects are not suited to the first-person approach. When the subject is more important than the writer's reaction to it, his or her presence often becomes obtrusive.

How can you decide whether or not you have a first-person story? Did you actually experience what you are writing about, or were you there only as an observer? If you were a participant in the events you describe, that is an argument in favor of using the pronoun "I."

Answer these questions: Would the readers of my article want to have been in my place? Would they have wanted to meet the person I met, see the place I visited, do what I did? If the answers are yes, you may be able to share your firsthand experiences most effectively by using the first-person approach. If you interviewed Jackie Kennedy Onassis, your readers might want to know how you felt and what you thought on meeting her, but if you interviewed Jackie Doe from the local theater group, you'd need to concentrate instead on interesting your audience in your subject.

Publishable articles on personal experiences are rare. While they are prized by some editors, selling a personal experience to even the most receptive editor is difficult. The reason is probably obvious. Before the writer can do a readable personal experience story, she must have a thrilling adventure or an experience that is highly amusing or one that strikes home intimately with a million readers. The thrillers happen once in a lifetime—if then. Amusing incidents that can be woven into a tale that will draw chuckles are more frequent. But the writer must see the funny side of the experience and be able to tell it entertainingly—usually with himself as the fall guy.

The light approach can even be used when the subject is a serious one, as in this excerpt from an article on how the writer overcame a phobia:

Some people cross the street to avoid a black cat. I used to cross at the sight of a bird. It wasn't superstition that sent me zigzagging from one sidewalk to the other; it was fear. The mere mention of birds made me cringe. Their presence terrified me. I had a bird phobia—and a bad one.

Phobias are severe, irrational fears that compel people to avoid the things that make them afraid. Phobias actually interfere with people's lives. An aquaphobe will not go swimming; a person with fear of heights will not travel by plane. For me, a pet store was a chamber of horrors. Parakeets, even fluffy little chicks, filled me with terror.

The robins who visited my yard in the spring were as welcome as a flock of vultures. I once served leftover spaghetti to dinner guests rather than go through the ordeal of taking a chicken out of the refrigerator.

The rest of the story describes the writer's treatment by a clinical psychologist and how it helped her overcome the fear. Note how in describing her problem, she also provides the reader with information about phobias, such as what they are and how they affect people. This is obviously a first-person story, but it isn't one the writer will be able to repeat unless she develops other phobias. Even for a hungry free-lancer, that is asking too much.

Personal experiences needn't always be dramatic or humorous to be effective pieces of writing. This is particularly true when the writer has some expertise in a subject. Consider this excerpt from a nostalgic article about classic American cars:

Howard Carter could have had no greater sense of discovery entering Tutankhamen's tomb than Bobby Paine and I had, stumbling out of the warehouse lift into a fairyland of cars, caissons, machine guns and artillery pieces. The sight was so unexpected that we were momentarily dumbstruck. Once the shock was over, we raced past the merely fine cars toward the five great ones, parked together in a separate enclosure. The closest was a Duesenberg SJ Towncar. In back, almost obscured by the massive Duesenberg, were two Auburn sedans and a Packard phaeton. All the way over by the wall was an equally massive canvas-covered shape with huge red wire wheels.

We climbed into the Duesenberg. Her sleek black hood was a block long, or seemed so. Despite signs of superficial neglect, she looked like she was doing 80 miles an hour standing still. Lifting the hood with reverence, we found the biggest eight-cylinder engine we'd ever seen. It had dual overhead camshafts, four valves per cylinder, dual ignition, and, of course, a supercharger.

Even in these two short paragraphs, the writer communicates his love of old cars and knowledge about them. He is entitled to write in the first person because his point of view is essential to the article.

The Essentials of the Personal Experience Article

In writing about personal experiences, remember to do two things:

Share your experience   You must work to enable the reader to participate in your story. This can be accomplished only by graphically describing actions and emotions. It is very difficult to write about experiences that occurred in the distant past because you probably won't be able to recall significant details. Inventing them often results in strained and artificial-sounding sentences.

Maintain an unrelenting focus   Avoid digressions that are unrelated to the experiences you are describing. Occasionally an article succeeds even though the writer rambles through a long introductory passage that attempts to explain entertainingly who the writer is and how he or she was equipped for the experience, but it doesn't happen often. Keep the experience the center of attention, but be sure to give enough information about yourself and others in the story to create human characters. Do this without letting people overwhelm events. This balance is a delicate one to achieve.

NARRATIVES

> "An honest tale speeds best being plainly told."
>
> WILLIAM SHAKESPEARE

Narrative-style articles are essentially factual short stories. Like fiction, they rely on the unfolding of episodes for their compelling interest (this episodic structure makes many personal experience articles narratives also). The narrative is so easily the simplest form that a beginner may wonder, "Why don't I write all my articles this way?" There are good reasons. The most important is that many stories never become airborne when told chronologically from start to finish. Many articles require a carefully contrived lead to capture the reader's interest and hold the reader until he or she is absorbed in the story. Furthermore, editors consider pure narration an old-fashioned style of writing. Years ago, almost all articles were narratives. Today, to capture readers, a writer often has to jump into the middle of a tale for an exciting or significant sequence for the lead, and he or she may not get around to the narrative part until the middle or near the end. However, when the events that make up an article lend themselves to the narrative treatment, no other form provides such satisfying reading.

Here is a writer who was described by students at Harvard as the best anywhere. Famed for his fiction, in this case he has turned to nonfiction. When Stephen King writes for the august *New York Times*—as he is doing here—he can entertain almost anyone. The following words are King's: *

> It seems to me that, in the minds of readers, writers actually exist to serve two purposes, and the more important may not be the writing of books and stories. The primary function of writers, it seems, is to answer readers' questions. These fall into three categories. The third is the one that fascinates me most, but I'll identify the other two first.
>
> The *One-of-a-Kind* Questions: Each day's mail brings a few of these. Often they reflect the writer's field of interest—history, horror, romance, the American West, outer space, big business. The only thing they have in common is their uniqueness. Novelists are frequently asked where they get their ideas (see category No. 2), but writers must wonder where this relentless curiosity, these really strange questions, come from.
>
> There was, for instance, the young woman who wrote to me from a penal institution in Minnesota. She informed me she was a kleptomaniac. She further informed me that I was her favorite writer, and she had stolen every one of my books she could get her hands on. "But after I stole 'Different Seasons' from the library and read it, I felt moved

---

*Copyright © 1987 by the New York Times Company. Reprinted by permission.

to send it back," she wrote. "Do you think this means you wrote this one the best?" After due consideration, I decided that reform on the part of the reader has nothing to do with artistic merit. I came close to writing back to find out if she had stolen "Misery" yet but decided I ought to just keep my mouth shut.

From Bill V. in North Carolina: "I see you have a beard. Are you morbid of razors?"

From Carol K. in Hawaii: "Will you soon write of pimples or some other facial blemish?"

From Don G., no address (and a blurry postmark): "Why do you keep up this disgusting mother worship when anyone with any sense knows a MAN has no use to his mother once he is weaned?"

From Raymond R. in Mississippi: "Ever et raw meat?" (It's the laconic ones like this that really get me.)

I have been asked if I beat my children and/or my wife. I have been asked to parties and places I have never been and hope never to go. I was once asked to give away the bride at a wedding, and one young woman sent me an ounce of pot, with the attached question:

STEPHEN KING

"Don't write your novel with best-seller lists or movie companies or rich paperback houses in mind. Don't, in fact, write with publication in mind. Write for yourself."

So advises one of America's most popular novelists—Stephen King, whose proliferation spans well over twenty novels and into the movies. His success continually expands as the public demands to be terrified. While King admittedly does not write with specific themes but rather just to entertain, somehow his natural style captures the complexities of the human soul and everyday life.

One writer clearly captured the essence of King's writing: "He can (intermittently) write scenes about the terrible emotions of common life as powerful, if not as stylish, as any in contemporary American fiction; at such times, it is possible to see King flirting with seriousness, but a combination of sentimentality of thought, vulgarity of expression and a populist ethic which embraces these as positive goods will always keep him from consumption."

King made an unspectacular climb to his position as the king of horror. He grew up in a trailer, started off as a janitor, spent some time as a laundry worker, and then became a high school English teacher. After several of King's unsuccessful attempts at writing novels, Doubleday paid him a $2,500 advance against royalties for *Carrie*. Certainly the amount was not a hefty sum, but it paid the bills. When Doubleday called King about the sale of the paperback rights, *Carrie*'s success became strikingly apparent. The advance was $400,000. "The only thing I could think to do was go out and buy my wife a hair dryer. I stumbled across the street to get it and thought I would probably get greased by some car."

But King survived the ordeal to help his wife, Tabitha, look better, and soon his six-figure income became seven and the books rolled out, to be devoured by the public. And while he likens his work to a Big Mac and fries at McDonald's, he has strong opinions about how to become a good writer. Like exercising, writing is something that must be done every day. "If you write for an hour and a half a day for ten years, you're gonna turn into a good writer."

To those who aspire to be "The Next Stephen King," remember his words of advice:

"Start by believing in yourself. If you still think the novel is good, but you can't get it published as it stands, you must rewrite. And if you decide the novel is beyond repair, you must put it away in the drawer. Even a dead novel can provide a writer with valuable experience to take on to the next one. If nothing else, he's not a beginner anymore when he sits down to write that second book."

—Roger Feigelson

"This is where I get my inspiration—where do you get yours?" Actually, mine usually comes in envelopes—the kind through which you can view your name and address printed by a computer—that arrive at the end of every month.

My favorite question of this type, from Anchorage, asked simply: "How could you write such a why?" Unsigned. If E. E. Cummings were still alive, I'd try to find out if he'd moved to the Big North.

The Old Standards: These are the questions writers dream of answering when they are collecting rejection slips, and the ones they tire of quickest once they start to publish. In other words, they are the questions that come up without fail in every dull interview the writer has ever given or will ever give. I'll enumerate a few of them.

Where do you get your ideas? (I get mine in Utica.)

How do you get an agent? (Sell your soul to the Devil.)

Do you have to know somebody to get published? (Yes; in fact, it helps to grovel, toady and be willing to perform twisted acts of sexual depravity at a moment's notice, and in public if necessary.)

How do you start a novel? (I usually start by writing the number 1 in the upper right-hand corner of a clean sheet of paper.)

How do you write best-sellers? (Same way you get an agent.)

How do you sell your book to the movies? (Tell them they don't want it.)

What time of day do you write? (It doesn't matter, if I don't keep busy enough, the time inevitably comes.)

Who is your favorite writer? (Anyone who writes stories I would have written had I thought of them first.)

There are others, but they're pretty boring so let us march on.

The Real Weirdies: Here I am, bopping down the street, on my morning walk, when some guy pulls over in his pickup truck or just happens to walk by and says, "Hi, Steve! Writing any good books lately?" I have an answer for this; I've developed it over the years out of pure necessity. I say, "I'm taking some time off." I say that even if I'm working like mad, thundering down homestretch on a book. The reason *why* I say this is because no other answer seems to fit. Believe me, I know. In the course of trial and error that has finally resulted in "I'm taking some time off," I have discarded about 500 other answers.

Having an answer for "You writing any good books lately?" is a good thing, but I'd be lying if I said it solves the problem of *what the question means.* It is this inability on my part to make sense of this odd query, which reminds me of that Zen riddle—"Why is a mouse when it runs?"—that leaves me feeling mentally shaken and impotent. You see, it isn't just *one* question, it is a *bundle* of questions, cunningly wrapped up in one package.

The Essentials of the Narrative

Bernard Malamud said: "With me, it's story, story, story. Writers who can't invent stories substitute style for narrative. They remind me of the painter who couldn't paint people, so he painted chairs.

"The story will be with us as long as man is. You know that, in part, because of its effect on children. It's through story they realize that mystery won't kill them. Through story they learn they have a future."

The essential elements of the narrative are largely those of the personal experience. The difference is that the writer is not a factor in the narrative. Rather than relating an experience *she* had, she is reporting someone else's experience. The narrative is less a sharing of experience than is found in personal experience writing. It is nonetheless possible to present a story so graphically that the reader becomes involved in it. One must focus ceaselessly on the crux of the story in writing a narrative to hold the reader's attention.

In preparing to write the narrative that appears below, Rusty Todd of Austin, Texas, took copious notes on the campaign trail of Lieutenant Governor Ben Barnes. From these notes, he fashioned a revealing series of episodes. When he had finished this story, he called one source to verify a quotation. He used two books—*Texas Under a Cloud* by Sam Kinch and Ben Proctor, and *Money, Marbles & Chalk* by Jimmy Banks—to cross-check factual information. This report comes almost entirely from his notes. Pay particular attention to the comments on the narrative; they should give you some ideas on how to fashion your own narratives.

COMMENT	NARRATIVE
This begins boldly—"which has no middle"—making the reader expect a fast pace.	This story, which has no middle, begins in Amarillo, where Lt. Gov. Ben Barnes started his campaign for governor by boarding a rented train and storming across Texas in the grandest Woodrow Wilson style. It ends in the Capitol on election night.
This paragraph establishes a setting the reader can picture.	Amarillo has been called less than a dream city. It lies smack in the middle of the flat, treeless Panhandle, and its most glorious aspects include an old zinc smelter that gives the city the state's highest respiratory disease rate and the Helium Monument, a stainless steel atrocity whose plaque modestly informs one that Amarillo is the "Helium Capitol of the World."
	On Feb. 22, 1972, a bitter northwest wind was smashing through Amarillo from across the prairie, and thick rain clouds obscured the approaching dawn. At this hour the Barnes campaign staff, the press corps, and more than 400 local residents were awake and getting ready for the 7:30 A.M. departure celebration.
It is important to help readers see Barnes. Give him a sentence or even a paragraph that will enable readers to see him in the flesh.	None of them wanted to miss the beginning of another campaign for the biggest political *prima donna* Texas had ever seen, the man who in 1960 got tired of selling vacuum cleaners and in less than a year became a twenty-one-year-old state representative. Four years later he acquired the House speakership and the political support of Lyndon Johnson and John Connally. In 1968 he waltzed into the lieutenant governor's office to the tune of the largest majority in recent Texas history, and now it was time for Ben Barnes to tick off the next rung of the political ladder.

A "rung"? He "waltzes" in "to the tune"? Move the readers swiftly to the next point with precisely the image you want them to see. "With this rung, though, there were problems" gives the readers nothing precise or visual. In addition, the images are confused.

This section uses transitions well. Each paragraph is tied to its predecessor, even though the writer covers a great deal of Barnes's history: the reference to a stock fraud attempt, divorce and sexual escapades, a new marriage, and finally a reception, which enables the writer to return to the reporters.

With this rung, though, there were problems, substantial problems. First, the Capitol was being racked by a scandal of enormous proportion. The present governor, the speaker of the House, and various legislators had been implicated by the Securities and Exchange Commission in a stock fraud attempt. No evidence pointed to Barnes, but his three opponents were trying hard to associate him with the outrage.

Second, Barnes had in 1970 committed what can be a fatal error in Texas politics: divorce. Grandiose rumors of his sexual escapades (all unsubstantiated) had surrounded the split, and the odious image of "Bedroom Ben," had slowly crept across Texas. A popular bumper sticker read: "It's 10:30. Do you know where Ben Barnes is?"

A year later he married a deceased lobbyist's widow, who was eleven years his elder; writers wondered in print if the marriage had been arranged as a political expedient. At last night's press reception, Barnes acted like Nancy had been his wife for as long as he could remember.

The reception, incidentally, had been a wet one, and most of the reporters in the motel coffee shop this morning were nursing hangovers. The headaches were doubly intense since yesterday's Barnes-furnished aircraft from Austin had been amply stocked with liquor.

Two men who were not reporters (though they both had been) and who were not hung over (they had been that, too) also sat in the shop, talking about the train ride and their plans for it.

This is a skillful touch that gives good visual imagery of Read. That's just enough, since he isn't the central figure.

The one who looked like a king-sized Kennedy in a dated blue suit and narrow tie was Julian Read, who plotted the strategy of every one of John Connally's campaigns. He and George Christian, the same Christian who had been LBJ's White House press secretary, were running this campaign. Read was ravenously consuming a steaming plate of fried eggs and country sausage.

Across the table sat Terry Young, a heavier man than Read, of early rather than late middle-age, the number two man in Read's public relations organization. Young is normally unflutterable but tends to grow hypertense and lose weight during a campaign. His breakfast this morning consisted of black coffee and black coffee.

"By God," Read said to him. "This sausage hits the spot. We ought to have some Jimmy Dean sausage put aboard the train when it stops in Plainview."

"A fellow from the factory is bringing boxes of cooked sausage and bread to the depot there," said Young, who had thought of it himself.

A reporter and a Barnes cameraman joined the two publicists. The reporter had worked for Read and Young until last November and had known about the train even then. He had not seen Read since Christmas, but then Read was seldom seen outside an office. He and Young were good friends, though, and met often.

Here, the writer begins a nice passage that runs several paragraphs, providing the readers with information swiftly and also a highly readable short sketch of the scene. The natural question is: What does this contribute? Its primary purpose is to show readers the kind of reporter who is covering the story and the casual informality of such meetings. Such words as "Faaantastic" add to the informal tone.

"Good morning, Mister Read. Hi, Terry," the reporter said. He always called Read "mister" and always noticed the unconscious tendency to do so.

"Good morning. I'm glad you're getting to make the trip with us," Read said.

A waitress came for the orders, coffees for the newcomers and another coffee for Young. The reporter asked how the trip was looking.

"Faaantastic," said Young, characteristically stretching his favorite word. "You won't believe the train."

"Yeah," Read said. "But it's too bad that damned Nixon had to go to Peking this week and steal part of our thunder."

"Do you expect much of a crowd in this weather?"

Read was busy chewing eggs, and Young tried to look nondescript as he shrugged.

"We'll see. I think it'll be alright," he said.

The cameraman, Pickle, had not been saying much because of his headache, but Read roused him with a question about filming plans.

"It's gonna be tough to stay within the budget Wayne has us on," Pickle said.

By Wayne he meant Ralph Wayne, state representative, Barnes's best friend and nominal head of the campaign.

"Shoot what you need and we'll work out the budget," Read said. "The depot will be good this morning. It's cold and the crowd will be trying to jam inside."

"Yes, sir," Pickle said.

Everybody at the table but Read had another coffee before boarding the big Greyhound out front. During the drive Young talked with other reporters, trading wisecracks and helping out where he could.

Here, the writer describes the station in a quick sentence. It's far better to do the description in a single sentence because he can continue the reporter's action without interruption.

Santa Fe Station's old depot looked like a decrepit red brick castle in the dim light of a muted dawn. The reporter was startled when he saw the size of the crowd trying to squeeze its way inside.

The writer in the seat beside him said, "They really did some advance work on this one. You'd have to pay me to come out on a morning like this."

They threw sidelong glances at each other and laughed as the bus emptied. The fifty-two member press corps trudged around to the back of the building to stash their typewriters and get a look at the train.

With "Its six silver cars," the writer abandons his attention to the reporter. He has prepared us for this shift in emphasis by showing the press corps giving their attention to his next focus: the train.

Its six silver cars had been rented through Amtrak for a flat $16,000. Besides the engine and generator car, there was a dome car where reporters and dignitaries could view the passing country, a big lounge car to serve as the press room, a pullman where the candidate could rest, and a caboose with a special speaking platform.

These are excellent paragraphs, drawing in the atmosphere swiftly. Note especially that he does not make every sentence carry adjective after adjective. It's often a temptation for a writer to add heavily to his description. Yet you cannot find a sentence in which he has used adjectives and adverbs too strongly.

Here, the reporter introduces himself into the story with "the reporter." Nowhere does he use "I," even though he is on the train throughout this campaign tour.

Although the writer of this article is "the reporter" in the next paragraph, notice that the reporter never stresses himself. He is suitably not at center stage; he is never "I."

Cocktail bars had been installed in the dome and press cars, and big signs on the doors said "Refreshments Must Be Left on Board." Horn speakers on the rear platform were blaring "Wabash Cannonball" by the Nashville Brass, the same background music used on the University of Texas Longhorn football show, which Read produces.

Around the platform milled a riding club on horseback. A couple of the steeds had the audacity to defile the yard with piles of pungent, steaming excrement.

A belly-to-back crush inside the depot was thwarting the police efforts of thirty or so Jaycees in matching gold vests, and the local television crew was having a time keeping its equipment intact for the morning's live broadcast. The nasal, amplified wail of two high schoolers, one of them playing organ, subjugated any conversation attempts. They were performing a ditty called "Ben Barnes for Texas."

Many in the crowd were no older than the singers, and the reporter wondered if perhaps they had come to see the professional football players making the trip instead of the candidate.

He now heard the rumor spreading: They are here, they will be on stage any minute now. Ralph Wayne leaped onto the makeshift platform and commandeered a microphone.

"Okay! Okay now!" he screamed. "They're coming! They're at the back door! Everybody help us sing for the television! Come on now, real loud!"

He had the nasal singers burst back into "Ben Barnes for Texas," and half the audience sang lustily along, familiar with a song that had been "premiered" last night at the press reception.

Suddenly the celebrities stepped into sight: Dallas Cowboys Dan Reeves, Bob Lilly, and Walt Garrison; Baltimore Colt Bubba Smith; Cleveland Brown Bob McKay; and gubernatorial contender Ben Barnes. They were all from small Texas towns.

Ralph Wayne thrust his arms into the air, a tumultuous cheer erupted, and the television commentator began speaking quietly into his own microphone. Pickle, resembling a six-foot-four-inch mustachioed cyclops with a protruding metal eye, plowed through the crush, getting close-action footage.

Julian Read had climbed onto a sort of scaffold back in a corner to view the execution of his plans. Below him, Young zipped about, taking care of correspondents, speaking to supporters, happily tending whatever needed attention. That is the way Young works: Tell him to take care of one or two things, but he ends up taking care of everything.

He stopped by the reporter, his face flushed red, his eyes flashing exuberance.

"Don't worry about taking notes if you like," he said. "We've got secretaries taking down quotes and a mimeograph machine in the press car."

He vanished swiftly into the herd of people.

Reeves's quotation is revealing: it shows for the first time that Barnes is a fighter.

The "verbal fumble" is in keeping with the football players who are speaking.

Here, the writer gives a quick flash of description—"freckled face and sandy red hair"—but at no point does he *show* Barnes. That seems a mistake. Barnes is the primary actor in this drama. He should be given a full description.

Note especially how the writer goes into a transition that will enable him to move smoothly into the next paragraph: "where Barnes already held great support" merges into the next quotation.

On stage, Reeves had taken over the microphone to get the program underway. His first remarks drew girlish screams from the audience.

"I'm for Ben Barnes because he's got guts," Reeves growled. "He'll fight for you all the way."

Nancy Barnes now joined the group on stage, and Reeves decided to extemporize: "Nancy is a gracious and charming lady, a real pro in a professional role."

The press wrote that one down, knowing very well it would not make the mimeo sheet. That was the only verbal fumble the players made in three days of touring, but then it was the only time any of them attempted an extemporaneous remark.

As the football stars descended into the autograph hunters, Barnes began his address. His freckled face and sandy red hair made him look younger than his thirty-four years. He thanked the crowd for "a warm welcome on such a cold morning," something he did at every stop until the weather warmed up.

"I want to tell you that Amarillo's future is important to me," he was saying. "And I'll not let the state arbitrarily close an important industry like your smelter. . . ."

High on his perch, Julian Read intently watched his candidate, now and then allowing his gaze to sweep across the crowd. Young had left the press to its business and was talking with a Barnes worker.

"If I am elected governor," Barnes was saying, "we are going to have a state water plan to supply West Texas the water it needs. . . ."

In West Texas it was the water plan; in Central Texas it would be revitalizing agriculture; along the Gulf it would be hurricane insurance revision. The stock speech called for tougher welfare qualifications, better education, and so forth, but one well-researched segment of every address was keyed to the locality. The campaign strategists had decided to avoid the morals issue completely and would mention the stock scandal only in Houston and Galveston, where Barnes already held great support.

". . . and I think more and more people realize the man to beat in the governor's race is the peanut farmer from DeLeon."

With that Barnes, who had indeed come from a peanut farm in DeLeon, Texas, plunged into the crowd while the ubiquitous theme song clattered about the room. The audience was ecstatic. The commentator busily spoke into his microphone, telling his viewers what they had just heard Ben Barnes say.

Young was again circulating some information.

"The governor will speak from the caboose platform in a few minutes," he said. "When the train whistle blows, you have two minutes to get aboard."

The back door of the depot swung open, and Barnes led the throng to the train. Several of the horses started and reared, their nostrils spouting streams of steam into the frigid air. Somebody suddenly released several hundred helium balloons.

Note that the writer manages to sustain his theme. He is switching from one episode to another, but he nearly always controls his theme by giving close attention to transitions. Note that the beginning of each paragraph is tied to the preceding paragraph: "sudden barrage of sharp explosions" is tied to "a moment of confusion"; "a tiny parachute was ejected" is tied to the end of the first sentence in the next paragraph "attached to each chute," and so on.

As the "Wabash Cannonball" faded, Barnes climbed onto the caboose to thank the crowd and predict "a victory for everyone." The big engine whistle blew its warning only to be nearly overwhelmed by a sudden barrage of sharp explosions.

A moment of confusion seized the celebration, but the salvo turned out to be only fireworks, a large display of fireworks flashing those three American colors against the dead gray sky. When a rocket exploded, a tiny parachute was ejected to carry some cargo earthward.

The reporter trotted across the yard to discover a small American flag attached to each chute. Smaller children in the court began fighting over the mementoes.

Once again the whistle sounded, and the reporter jumped on board. A few of the crowd jogged along behind the train but were left behind as it gathered speed. Young and the reporter met in the press car.

"Terry, those flags. That was too much."

"Yeah, bad scene. I didn't know about that," Young said. He was grinning and bouncing from one foot to the other, barely jogging in place. "But wasn't that a fantastic beginning?"

Drinks were already being served at the back of the car, and the reporter took a Bloody Mary from the elderly black bartender. He walked up into the dome to consider a thought he had not been able to shake. . . .

[After the reporter explores his thoughts, he closes with this note that sums up his story:]

More and more articles are using this kind of ending, which does not attempt to sum up what has been said in the article. Instead, the writer decides that Pickle's comment is the apt quotation: "Maybe to them it did." (They lost.)

Pickle and the reporter walked back through the granite halls and left their empty glasses in the rotunda. They dashed through the mist to the car.

"It's too bad," the reporter said as they drove away. "I don't feel too bad about Barnes, but Julian and Terry did what they could, and it didn't matter."

"Maybe to them it did," Pickle said.

Exercises

1. Find a personal-experience article that has recently been published in a magazine. After reading it, answer the following questions:

   Why do you think the editor of the magazine accepted this article?

   Could this article have been published in other magazines? Which ones?

   What formula did the writer use to tell the story? (Example: statement of problem, development of problem, change, solution.)

2. Write a 1,000-word article about a personal experience you have had. Explain why you think the subject is a publishable one and which magazines might use the story.

3. To practice presenting a good narrative, choose a familiar story (such as a fable or a fairy tale), then think of three different ways to tell the story by changing such things as the order of presentation, the style of writing, the point of view, and so forth.

SIXTEEN

INFORMATIVES AND HOW-TO-DO-ITS

Have something to say, and say it as clearly as you can. That is the secret of style.

MATTHEW ARNOLD

A magazine publisher once told an editor: "Any issue with a how-to on its cover sells better than an issue without one." As a result, the editor struggled to write at least one how-to cover line each month, regardless of whether the article inside warranted cover treatment.

The popularity of how-to articles, guides, and informatives is most evident in the rise of city magazines like *New York* that feature page after page of material telling readers how to shop, eat, decorate, and even sleep. There was a time when such articles were the exclusive territory of women's magazines (also called service magazines in the publishing industry), but now these stories are the standard fare of even such "literary" magazines as *Esquire.*

Consequently, informatives and how-to-do-its have acquired a new respectability among magazine writers. Beginning staff writers will almost certainly be asked to write many of each, and free-lancers can count on a steady market for both.

INFORMATIVES

Columnist L. M. Boyd discussed the power of the news media: "On October 8, 1871, Chicago caught fire and about 300 people died. That same night, the town of Peshtigo, Wis., also caught fire, and more than 1,300 died—but because the telegraph lines burned down, the news was late in getting out.

"When the Peshtigo fire news finally came through, the papers were so absorbed in the Chicago fire there was little room for the holocaust which had taken more than four times as many lives. Few people today have ever heard of the Peshtigo fire."

> "No, I'm no enemy to learning, it hurts not me."
>
> WILLIAM CONGREVE

As Boyd's comments illustrate, newspapers are not always as informative as they should be. Yet all good magazines should strive to carry a sufficient amount of information to their readers.

All magazine articles should be informative, but those that take the readers behind the scenes of a process or service are given this particular name. Usually the subject is one of general interest, such as how the Internal Revenue Service uses computers to keep track of your income. But if the magazine has a particular focus, such as sports, the subject might be as specialized as how athletes train for the decathlon.

The cardinal rule in preparing an informative is that the writer cannot stint on research. Moreover, the writer must be selective with information, remembering that the aim is to capture the reader's interest. For example, Tim Ord noted that before he began writing an article on superports, he had first done the following research:

1. Read all or parts of the reports mentioned in the article.

2. Got information on petroleum refineries, demand, and imports from such sources as *Petroleum Encyclopedia,* the Bureau of Mines, and the California Department of Conservation's recent energy report.

3. Interviewed Col. Wm. E. Vandenberg, who's running the study for the U.S. Army Corps of Engineers; and Richard Eng, who's the coordinator of the study for the Corps.

4. Went to two public workshops given by the Corps to get public input.

5. Read three books on tankers and tanker terms, as well as much background information on the oil industry.

Then Ord wrote this fine piece.

COMMENT

Although the writer's subject is serious, he realizes that he must attract the reader. Note that he addresses the reader *directly.* This is an effective beginning.

At this point, the writer recognizes that continuing "you-you-you" would become monotonous. Although he has now dropped the direct address he has established that he is still speaking directly to "you," even though he doesn't use the word.

ARTICLE

Do you remember the two Standard Oil Company of California tankers which crashed in San Francisco Bay in January 1971, spilling 800,000 gallons of bunker fuel? Those were 16,000-ton tankers.

Do you remember the *Torrey Canyon* which went aground in the English Channel, fouling miles of beaches in Britain? That was a 119,000-ton tanker.

If you were among those cleaning fouled beaches or trying to save scum-covered birds, you might have thought those were pretty big tankers. After all, if the *Torrey Canyon* were afloat today it could dock fully loaded into only two ports on the whole west coast of the United States: Puget Sound and Long Beach. It could squeeze into San Francisco Bay if it were partially unloaded and came in at high tide.

But as far as the oil companies are concerned, such tankers are just not big enough, because the bigger the tanker, the lower the cost of transporting oil. In fact, the U.S. Corps of Engineers estimates that quadrupling the size of a tanker cuts the per-ton transport cost in half.

So now the oil companies are in a race to see who can build the biggest tankers the fastest. By 1975, Standard Oil of California (SOCAL) will have thirty-two "supertankers" of 250,000 tons or more. Each of these tankers will be over fifteen times the size of the SOCAL tankers which crashed in the Bay, and double the size of the *Torrey Canyon.*

Not to be outdone, Shell Oil Company recently ordered two tankers of 533,000 tons each. If one of these tankers were stood on its end, it would be taller than the Empire State Building. These quarter-mile-long ships will have a draft of 92 feet—two and one-half times that of the biggest aircraft carrier. If a tanker this size emptied its cargo at the rate of one SOCAL Bay oil spill per week, it would be four years before she were dry.

The Federal government seems to be going along with the oil companies' switch-over to larger ships: the Commerce Department is subsidizing the construction of at least eighteen supertankers in this country at a government cost of $286 million.

Safety Factor

The oil companies claim that carrying oil in big tankers will actually be safer than carrying it in small ones because there will be fewer tankers to get in each other's way.

However, this overlooks the fact that the bigger the tanker, the harder it is to control. A 1972 Maritime Administration report stated:

Because of their somewhat limited maneuverability and the distance required for them to stop, the use of large tankers in existing port channels would be extremely unsafe. The most important factor in connection with collisions and groundings is the "crash-stop" ability. Unfortunately, the ability of the mammoth tankers to come to a "crash-stop" as compared with smaller tankers has decreased as their size increases. . . . For example, a T-2 tanker of 16,000 tons can come to "crash-stop" within a half mile in five minutes while the straight-line stopping distance for a 200,000-ton tanker is about 2½ miles requiring about 21 minutes.

The *Wall Street Journal* recently reported that the propeller shaft on a 250,000-ton tanker "cannot even be stopped, much less reversed, inside of seven minutes."

And oil tanker collisions are by no means rare occurrences. The Maritime Administration reports that, "Within the last 10 years, there have been over 500 tanker collisions worldwide with 80 percent occurring while these vessels were entering or leaving ports. . . . Oil spills from tanker collisions average at least a million tons annually causing some $40 million in damage."

It is possible that supertankers have other inherent dangers not shared by smaller ones. . . .

[The article goes on for several pages. It ends:]

To hear some people tell it, superports are about the greatest things around. In the words of the Nathan study, "The United States has an historic opportunity

---

Consider how difficult it is to maintain the direct tone when the writer finds it necessary to report so many numbers. Yet Ord manages marvelously—making the numbers interesting by comparing the length and capacity of the ships to things the reader can visualize.

The writer often leans on the words of higher authorities rather than declaring his own bias against the supertankers. This technique is worth keeping in mind.

Even though Ord's article is opposed to the supertankers, consider how carefully he writes this strong ending. It is thought-provoking—not the kind of ending that seems to bludgeon the supertankers.

to achieve a bulk commodity port delivery system which *optimizes* economic benefit and benefit distribution and which provides *acceptable levels* of protection of environmental and ecological values." But if one of those behemoth tankers goes down in either our Bay or in Monterey Bay, San Franciscans may well have reason to wish that statement had been made the other way around.

The Essentials of the Informative

When she visited Stanford's Overseas Campus in England, Mary Sharp Liebersbach was as intrigued as her companions with the country pubs. She saw in them an unusual quality that led to the following article, which we can use to point up the essential elements of informatives:

Unearthing facts   Most informatives cover subjects that could be explored by anyone. Few are so esoteric that only the specialist can investigate and understand them. The writer of an informative customarily unearths the facts that undergird ordinary phenomena.

Dressing up the facts   The facts you use must be interesting, which means that the writer must select them carefully and present them pleasingly. This is true of all magazine writing, of course, but it is especially important in an informative because the unadorned presentation of facts about everyday phenomena and institutions is likely to bore readers. One way to dress them up is to be aware that readers are usually more interested in people than in things. When facts about things can be presented in relation to people—the people who use the things, the people who produce them, and so on—interest heightens.

Pub-Hopping in Britain

COMMENT

It's important, especially in a light piece, to make points as deftly as possible. Thus, specifying the subject (pub-crawling) in the first part of the sentence and repeating it again in the last part belabors the point.

The repetition of "miss" is awkward; "bypass" is a bit more precise.

"Not so with the British" is not parallel structure.

ARTICLE

Tours of England ~~would~~ *are* never ~~be~~ complete without at least a night or two of local pub-crawling, but caution—*it is not like* bar-hopping in the United States, ~~cannot be thought of as parallel to pub-hopping in Great Britain.~~ One can ~~miss~~ *bypass* Joe's Local *to bypass the Blue Man is to miss* Bar without missing a vital part of American culture, but ~~this is not so with the~~ British. The pub is an institution *ranking with teatime,* ~~as is tea.~~ No town, whether *of* 25,000 to 25, is complete without its church and local pub.

"As is" is less direct and forceful than "ranking with."

"Results in one acquiring" seems a bit awkward. In fact, "frequenting" and "frequents" are probably stilted in *this* article. (Whether a word choice is right depends largely on the tone of the article.)

This passage could be made more flavorful with a sentence or so of the local chat. The skill of the dart throwers, many of whom are excellent, might also be covered in a couple of sentences.

There's no real objection to using "quite" twice, but the repetition doesn't add anything.

Here, "pubs" has been used so often as to become monotonous.

"On the main road to Nottingham" has been moved up to the beginning of the sentence to bring the two verbs ("visit" and "meet") closer together. A small matter, but read both versions of this sentence aloud before judging.

Again, something specific would help. That is, two or three sentences from one of the "interesting conversations" would allow the reader to *confront*, rather than merely be *told* about, what goes on in a pub.

Social life in many small towns and villages consists of nightly excursions to the Arms, the George, or the Pig to play darts, have a pint of bitter, and chat with cohorts. ~~Frequenting~~ *One who frequents* the same pub nightly usually ~~results in one~~ acquiring *es* his own stool, yet the British countryman seems only too pleased to share his corner with a foreigner who wishes to engage in some of the local chat or join in a friendly game of darts.

A note to the woman traveler—for the most part, men make up the clientele of these country pubs, though women are welcome if escorted. British wives usually stay home while the men go for their nightly dart game and pint of beer.

The higher-class pubs, though without the consistent clientele and the ~~quite so~~ *in* formal surroundings, can prove to be quite jolly and entertaining (and women frequent ~~these~~ *them* more often). *On the main road to Nottingham,* ~~Y~~ou can visit a popular local pub like the Wheatshed Mouston Gap—"The Gap" to regular customers—~~on the main road to Nottingham~~ and meet any class of people from the tweed-jacket-wearing, pipe-smoking country gentleman to the rough-hewn shopkeeper. After a performance many of the Nottingham theater crowd race ten miles along twisting roadway (partially "dual carriageway"—four-lane road) to The Gap to enjoy a quick pint of bitter and hash over the latest plays in the warm, friendly atmosphere. There is always a fire going and many interesting conversations brewing in each of the three quaintly furnished rooms. If you go there more than three times the bartender may even remember your drink.

Such odd attractions as a duck that drinks a couple of pints of beer per day are always popping up in some of these out-of-the-way pubs. To experience British culture one need merely ~~to get out of~~ *leave* the big cities and spend a week or so touring the countryside and stopping by the endless variety of pubs that seem to pop out of every hedgerow. Within the limits of one English town, called Grantham, ~~consisting of about 20,000 people~~ *of about 20,000* there are *sixty-six* different pubs

Be convincing; name another such attraction. (Don't list *all* the oddities you know—certainly not if you know eight or nine. Be selective—but be convincing first.)

The different placement seems to make the sentence more graceful.

This is just the right number of names to cite. It gives the flavor without being boring.

bearing such titles as The Blue Man, the Angel and Royal, The Blue Pig, the Sir Isaac Newton, the Knipton, the Gregory Arms, and The Fox and Hounds. Local people ~~usually find one pub they prefer as their~~ *consider one their* second home, but they frequently drop by others as well. . . .

An Odd Choice

Those who know of John McPhee—a great observer, a marvelous interviewer—will wonder, "Why is McPhee in a section on informatives?" Read the following words from McPhee:*

> I wish I could help, but I just can't break my concentration to do it. For me, even two pages on something else causes a hiatus of a number of days before again picking up the threads of what I was doing—i.e., a long piece of writing that takes months to complete and has to be kept in the air all the while.
>
> The working day begins at 8 a.m. with nothing. By noon, it's still nothing. I go out and exercise. I eat a sandwich. I go back to work. Nothing. By 4 p.m., nothing. By 4:30, I'm beginning to panic. If I get nothing for the whole day, I'll go home miserable and sulk all night. Fear drives some mechanism that opens a hatch and some words come out. They relate to my project. I keep that up until 8 p.m., when I quit and go home. I have maybe fifty or a hundred words to show for the day. They are unprintable, but they are somewhere near the topic and the structure. This routine goes on every day except Sunday. By the end of the year, the collected droplets fill a small bowl. People look at it and call me prolific. I look at them with a glazed stare.

HOW-TO-DO-ITS

One can consider how-to-do-it articles as informative or classify them separately. Because how-to articles seldom depend on the conventional techniques used to excite readers' interest, we will treat them as a separate type. How-tos are durable—one of the oldest article types—and continue to be

---

*Reprinted by permission of John McPhee.

popular among the readers of a great many magazines. *Sunset,* for example, is packed with information on how to garden, build additions to homes, cook more appetizing meals, and plan trips. The "shelter" magazines (those that deal with the home)—among them *American Home* and *Better Homes and Gardens*—offer similar fare. *Popular Mechanics* is fat with information for hobby shop buffs.

One distinctive kind of how-to article is the list—"Ten Ways to Save Your Marriage," "Seven Steps to Better Grades," and so on. Not all lists are how-to articles, but many contain the basic elements of the how-to.

The Essentials of the How-to-Do-It

Information and advice   The how-to is usually loaded with information, but its major reason for being is to offer advice.

JOHN MCPHEE

McPhee is a journalist with nearly unbelievable powers of observation. Read how he chooses perfect details to bring this Alaskan trapper to life in his book *Coming Into the Country:*

> Cook is somewhat below the threshold of slender. He is fatless. His figure is a little stooped, unprepossessing, but his legs and arms are strong beyond the mere requirements of the athlete. He looks like a scarecrow made of cables. All his features are feral—his chin, his nose, his dark eyes. His hair, which is nearly black, has gone far from his forehead. His scalp is bare all the way back to, more or less, his north pole. The growth beyond—dense, streaked with gray—cantilevers to the sides in unbarbered profusion, so that his own hair appears to be a parka ruff. His voice is soft, gentle—his words polite. When he is being pedagogical, the voice goes up several registers, and becomes hortative and sharp. He is not infrequently pedagogical.

McPhee began his writing career penning television scripts and was a *Time* associate editor, but he has written for the *New Yorker* for twenty-five years. In the meantime, he has written a number of books, including books on birchbark canoes, New York produce farmers, and oranges, as well as his bestseller *Coming Into the Country* and almost a dozen others. Wrote Richard Horwich of the *New Republic:* "Sometimes it seems that

McPhee deliberately chooses unpromising subjects, just to show what he can do with them."

McPhee's skill with interviews may be as strong as his skills of observation. In another section of *Coming Into the Country,* McPhee interviews Alaska senator Bill Ray, who boosts Juneau over its rival city, Anchorage:

> ". . . There are more accidents in Anchorage—more air traffic and more danger. And how many people get killed in Anchorage in car wrecks? What are the chances of getting *shot* in Anchorage—by some drug-crazed son of a bitch? Or getting acid thrown in your face? Compare *that* with Juneau. I wonder if *anybody* remembers a murder here."
>
> He got up, stuck his head out the door, and asked if anyone out there remembered a murder. Zero.
>
> "I can tell you when the last one in Anchorage was," he went on, sitting down again. "It was last weekend."

Wrote Horwich: "McPhee's powers of description are such that we often feel the shock of recognition even when what is being described is totally outside our experience. He penetrates the surface of things and makes his way toward what is essential and unchanging."

Says McPhee: "Fundamentally, I'm a journalist, and I've got to get out and work."

Clarity foremost   More than any other type of article, the how-to depends on clarity for its effect. Indeed, most of these articles sacrifice other qualities of readability, the writer reasoning that attempting to inject reader interest through metaphor, alliteration, anecdote, and other literary devices is likely to affect clarity.

Depending on the amount of space allotted to the how-to article, the writer may proceed directly to the instructive information or may be able to provide a great deal of background on the subject. Consider these two excerpts from articles that appeal to the treasure hunter in all of us.

COMMENT

In this paragraph, the writer realizes that she has a limited time to capture the reader. She opens with a serious sentence, then begins to show the joy of spending an afternoon panning for gold. The sentence beginning "Or it can be" is important because it tells the readers that finding gold isn't easy.

As soon as the writer begins the paragraph she realizes that it's all business to the end of the story. Everything is written as plainly as possible, which is the best kind of style for a how-to-do-it.

It's important to realize that in writing a how-to-do-it story you must physically carry out all the operations necessary. If you fail to carry them out yourself, you will almost certainly leave something out. One critic of how-to-do-its, Holly Arpan, has said: "It *seems* to be so easy that its users forget

HOW-TO-DO-IT

Gold mining can be hard, back-breaking work that requires long hours of concentrated effort; cold, wet feet; and a lot of luck. Or it can be a marvelous way to spend a spring afternoon by the side of a streambed, soaking in the sun and the wildflowers in bloom. The difference is how hard you want to work for your find, whether it be a small glass vial filled with minute gold flakes or that fabulous 100-pound nugget. Old-timers contend that looking for gold is like any other gamble—there are those who strike it rich by placing the first bet and those who acquire wealth by building up their winnings slowly. The choice is yours.

Gold is one of the heaviest metals and, with proper care, will settle to the bottom of a pan with heavier black sand in your mixture. To pan for gold, submerge the pan in the riverbed by keeping the rim level with the top of the water, being careful not to lose any of the contents. Pick out the largest pieces of gravel with your fingers, stirring to break apart any clumps of clay or roots so that everything is soaked and moving freely about.

Then, hold the pan with your hands on either side, tipped slightly away from you but still under the water, and shake it with a quick clockwise and then counterclockwise motion, swirling the water to remove the lighter sand and coarse gravel over the rim of the pan. Repeat this several times, tapping the pan often to keep the gold from washing over the rim. Now hold the pan outside the river and give it the same clockwise-counterclockwise motion again.

Alternate dipping the pan and rotating it out of the water, each time settling the heavier black sand and gold at the bottom. Carefully tip the pan occasionally to let the pebbles and lighter sand wash over the side until only the fine black sand seems to remain.

the overriding necessity for extreme clarity of expression. Even professionals have a deplorable habit of leaving out one step in a process, or one detail, and somehow that omission always is the vital one, without which the whole process falls apart."

Because this writer went through the process before she wrote about it, she has carried through everything in her description.

Keep washing the mixture gently until most or all of the blonder sand is removed and the blacker sand is settled on the bottom of the pan. Use a magnet to remove the last of the black sand and expose the gold. . . .

How to Find Florida's Lost Treasure

COMMENT

Unlike most how-to articles, this one uses anecdotes and history. That is because this article is not a step-by-step explanation of how to carry out a process but a guide to lost treasure.

It is important to mention the Smithsonian quite early to establish authenticity. So many articles about buried and lost treasure are contrived that a respected institution like the Smithsonian is a valuable ally. Note, too, that the next paragraphs cover a buried treasure museum.

ARTICLE

An ambitious young map maker once set out to do his bit for mankind by listing the best sites for treasure hunters along the coasts of the United States. He started counterclockwise at Oregon, ran down the Pacific Coast, jumped across Lower California and Mexico, marked the X's on the coastal waters of Texas, Louisiana, Mississippi and Alabama—and quit work entirely when he hit Florida. There he went hunting for treasure himself.

This cartographer was a victim of the lure that eventually attracts every get-rich-quick schemer in the Sunshine State who doesn't go into the motel business. For Florida is to treasure hunting what Fort Knox is to gold.

Not only did Gasparilla, Lafitte, Blackbeard, John Rackham, and the other bloody-handed pirates who sailed the Florida mains cache gold and silver on the little islands that dot the sweeping Florida coast, but the storms that assault South Florida during the bad-weather seasons sent many a gold-laden galleon to the bottom. Now, thanks to modern underwater gear, the treasure is being brought to the surface.

Only a few months ago, the Division of Naval History of the Smithsonian Institution sent divers five fathoms deep off the Southern Coast to hit the richest historical jackpot in the annals of coastal treasure hunting. The treasure in this case was precious mainly to the Smithsonian: rare artifacts with a few coral-encrusted gold and silver coins. Far more important commercial finds have been made. But the 200-year-old shipwreck the Smithsonian located is important, too, because it shows that the stories are far from false and that tales of Florida gold are based on fact.

The Smithsonian find also demonstrated once again that Arthur McKee, who operates McKee's Museum of Sunken Treasure on Plantation Key in South Florida, should be the man to hold the floor when the discussion swings to underwater searches for gold and silver.

McKee, who was one of the four divers who went down to the wreck wearing only a helmet, has long been considered the foremost Floridian in the treasure-hunting division. Formerly a recreation director and underwater moviemaker, McKee was down in the waters of Florida's fabulous keys in 1949 shooting pictures when he found a sunken galleon and brought up three silver bars weighing 65, 70, and 75 pounds. He sold the 70-pound ingot to the Smithsonian for $1,000. Dr. Alexander Wetmore of the Institution offered to buy a second ingot on the same terms after learning the bars assayed at 99.36 percent pure silver, but McKee put them on exhibition in his museum instead.

A black flag emblazoned with the skull and crossbones flies over McKee's museum. Inside the $65,000 building are pieces of eight, doubloons, a 3,000-pound coral-laden cannon, bar shot, grapeshot—and ivory elephant tusks recovered from the wreck of a slave trader. Collecting such valuable memorabilia has been so profitable that the museum is incorporated.

The home for ship relics began on a much less lavish scale, but it is now far from the roadside stand type of vacation attraction. It has an observation tower 65 feet high that affords a view not only of the Atlantic Ocean and the Gulf of Mexico, but also of the Gulf Stream itself, the route followed by Spanish galleons returning to Madrid from the New World with treasure.

McKee, who is not a man to overlook the obvious, has taken a lease on the treasure hunting rights in the area off the key. The tower not only serves as a tourist-catching throwback to the days of the great sailing ships when crows' nests were in fashion, but also is a lookout to preserve the claim. The organization headed by McKee, thanks to the lease, is working a wreck in the staked-off area, and recently recovered two silver platters, pieces of eight, a silver cup and other objects.

The State of Florida issues treasure leases and these leases do double duty, for a hunter in shoal waters usually needs both kinds the state offers—exclusive and nonexclusive.

The nonexclusive permit, which costs $100, gives a bullion seeker a chance to search in waters that may cover four or five counties.

After looking around the large territory until he has pinpointed his treasure, the leaseholder is then ready to return to the Land Agent in Tallahassee and swap his nonexclusive permit for an exclusive right which also costs $100.

The exclusive permit limits the search to one acre but it's valuable because no one else can jump the claim during the year the permit is in effect.

By the terms of the permits, the applicant agrees to return 12¼ percent of the value of all treasure he finds to the state, if the find is within the territorial jurisdiction of Florida.

That's the official necessity, but, of course, the Land Agent is aware that many treasure hunters never bother to comply with the special statute. And of those who do follow the letter of the law and pay for permits, few admit their discoveries.

Again, no explicit how-to information is offered, but the next few paragraphs suggest avenues for prospective treasure hunters.

One method of determining which of the hundreds of sites would be best for an expedition is to check on the areas that have proved most popular with permit-buyers.

There is, of course, no single best site, but one of the most popular has always been the mouth of the Suwannee River on the Gulf Coast. One expedition or another is busy in this area at least every 10 years looking for an estimated $5,000,000 in gold coins. The money was part of the indemnity paid to Spanish subjects who were forced to move when the United States negotiated a large-scale real estate deal with Spain in 1820.

The $5,000,000 was carried first to Pensacola, far up the Northwest Florida Coast, then loaded aboard a Spanish schooner for the long trip around the tip of Florida to Havana. However, a storm separated the gold-filled vessel from its escort, the ship sprung a leak and the captain ordered a run for the beach. Instead, the craft landed on a sandbar and was pounded to pieces while the crewmen escaped to the mainland.

Is the fortune in gold still there? Professional treasure hunters insist that it is—and prove that they really believe it by fitting out elaborate expeditions.

At least $7,000,000 in silver bullion is awaiting the discoverer of the Spanish galleon *Santa Margarita*, which lies in only 15 or 20 feet of water. The problem: where is it exactly? All anyone is now certain of is that the ship went down near Sebastian inlet, north of Vero Beach, which is on the Atlantic Ocean side of the Peninsula State. . . .

In the first article, writer Rita Stollman wastes no space on the history or attractions of gold mining. By the second paragraph, she begins the how-to part of her article. In contrast, the writer of the second story devotes the first ten paragraphs to developing the readers' interest and to showing them through examples that sunken treasure can be found.

Aside from space allotments, another factor influences how much background information should be included in a how-to. How much knowledge will the average reader have about the subject? If you are writing an article for a sports magazine on how to improve your tennis serve, you can assume your readers are well acquainted with tennis. Likewise, if you are writing an article for a business magazine on how to play the stock market, you can expect your readers to know in general how the market operates. But suppose you are writing an article on the same subject for a general interest magazine. Then you would need to explain how the stock market works and what it is before you give any advice about how to invest money in it.

This student wrote a how-to-do-it about film composing. However, he failed to provide background information, and most readers would be confused by reading it. Read the first two paragraphs and notice the lack of description and detail:

When Chris Young is signed to score a film, the most common starting point is for him to sit down with the director or producer and view the movie. They will then discuss what type of music would be most appropriate and where music would best suit the film. Many times the version of the film that Young sees will have a "temp track," where music editors have laid down music from other films into the soundtrack to tell the composer what sound the director is looking for.

Young then returns to his studio, where he begins composing various themes on the piano. Usually he has no more than 12 weeks to compose up to 70 minutes of music. When the compositions are finished, he performs the basic themes for the director or producer and tailors them to fit their desires. The score is then recorded, often with Graunke Symphony in Germany, and then editors dub the music into the film.

The magazine market for how-to articles is large and reliable. It is worth the effort for a writer to master this form and to regard any piece as a prospective how-to.

Students should do plenty of research for their how-to articles. Research is necessary to add credibility to many how-to stories. Students should be careful when choosing topics for these kinds of articles: if you try to write a how-to about a subject such as facing a mid-life crisis, you will not have credibility if you're only a freshman in college.

Exercises

1. Write an informative article of approximately 1,500 words on a subject of your choice. Explain why you think the subject is a good one and which magazines might publish the article.

2. Write a short article on how to drive a car. Be sure to include every action a person would need to perform. Or choose another activity you have carried out yourself and write a how-to story telling your readers how to carry out the process.

3. Choose one magazine and examine six back issues to determine whether it publishes how-to articles and informatives. Then list five topics you think might be published in this magazine in either category and explain why. In addition, describe how you think the magazine would handle each article in terms of angle, organization, and visual display.

4. Here is a how-to exercise to do in class. Each student should write instructions on how to perform a simple task (such as tying one's shoes or making a peanut butter and jelly sandwich). Next, pass the pages of directions to the front of the class, and have one student at a time go to the front of the class, pick a seat of directions, and follow them. Is the student able to perform the task correctly? Were vital steps or details omitted from the directions?

SEVENTEEN

RESEARCH STORIES, ANALYSES, AND ESSAY-REVIEWS

The truth is never pure, and rarely simple.

OSCAR WILDE

ll articles require research, but those that depend on it entirely to answer a question or explain something are known as research stories. The question may be as (relatively) simple as "How do colleges decide which students to admit?" or as complicated as "How do people's votes in an election reflect their income, race, religion, and social class?" In attempting to answer such questions, writers must use many different research sources. The writer must know where to look for information and must go beyond the minimum research required to write the story.

Consider this excerpt from an article by Terry Anzur on how young people find jobs today. Note that she combined interviews, observation, and library research to produce the article. At the end of the excerpt, you will find a list of some of the sources she used.

COMMENT	RESEARCH ARTICLE
Although this story is about thousands of un-employed students, the writer realized that she needed to focus on one person at the beginning of the article. Jon Levin was interesting, so she went into his case in detail.	Jon Levin started out tracking wild cats and ended up tracking subatomic particles.

During fall quarter of his sophomore year, he checked the part-time employment listings in the financial aids office. He discovered that the Health and Safety Department was looking for a student to trap wild cats that have been breeding for generations in the steam tunnels under university buildings.

Jon met all the prerequisites—he was reliable, honest, and had a driver's license. He could earn $2.50 an hour and schedule work hours around his classes. He was interviewed and hired. |
| Note that the writer describes Jon's garb minutely, knowing that it was interesting. It would have been a mistake | Armored with a helmet, heavy work gloves, and coveralls, and armed with a flashlight, a $3\frac{1}{2}' \times 1'$ trap, and a can of cat food for bait, he entered the tunnel labyrinth through a manhole. He had to crouch to avoid bumping his head against the $4'$ ceiling. And he knew he shared the passageway with 400 to 1,000 wild cats. |

had she written something like "Jon was dressed like a wild cat hunter" and been content with that.

By giving herself the space to describe Jon's predicament and success, the writer presents the case of many of those who have succeeded despite difficulty.

Here the writer is beginning to introduce all the students who need jobs, meshing Jon's case with many others.

The writer deals deftly with these numbers by guarding against the piling of number upon number. Note that this paragraph starts with one number, then there's the rest of the sentence and a second sentence space, then a dash separates the next number from three numbers, and then there are many words before she uses the last two.

It is important that such an article present the university's problem as

He'll never forget the first one he caught: "It shook me up to suddenly realize that it wasn't a normal housecat. It was scrawny. It was vicious. It would just as soon have eaten my arm. And it would have, if it had been clever enough."

After three weeks of outsmarting wild cats, Jon quit the job to spend more time studying for final exams. His next job would be less dangerous, but just as challenging.

The Stanford Linear Accelerator Center (SLAC) advertised in the Physics Department for students who could help analyze data. Jon, a physics major, was hired. For the past year and a half he has been working 15–20 hours weekly, usually between 8 P.M. and 3 A.M. He traces the path of charged protons and electrons across a bath of cold, liquid hydrogen in a bubble chamber. He earns $3 an hour.

Jon was hired because of his interest and competence, not his financial need. "The experience is the most important thing," he says. "The job helps me understand what I want to do after I graduate and why I want to do it." Now a senior, he plans to do graduate work in physics.

Jon is one of 2,300 undergraduates who held jobs on campus during the academic year 1973–74. Students with demonstrated financial need are eligible to apply for on-campus jobs listed in the financial aids student employment office. This year 1,100 jobs are listed, representing about $800,000 in earning potential.

An estimated $1 million was earned in 1973–74 by students who found part-time work through the Student Employment Office of the Career Planning and Placement Center. The Student Employment Office has listings of all on-campus jobs not filled through the financial aids office, but its primary responsibility is off-campus employment. Last year 4,954 people—3,105 undergraduates, 1,548 graduate students, and 301 student spouses—indicated an interest in part-time work by registering at the Placement Center. According to Pam Evans, director of the Student Employment Office, they filled 3,314 jobs off campus and 924 on campus.

Although students who need jobs to meet the self-help requirements of their financial aid packages are given preference for on-campus jobs, it would be impossible for university departments to hire all students who need to work. Jobs account for only about 7.5 percent of the university's financial aid budget. About three-fourths of the total reaches students in the form of scholarships and grants. Gift aid to undergraduates has grown from $6.6 million in 1973–74 to $7.1 million this year.

But tuition is growing too. The Board of Trustees has approved a tuition increase from $3,375 to $3,810, effective next fall. Partly as a consequence of the 12.9 percent hike, the largest in the university's history, gift aid to students will pass the $8 million mark next year, not including $2 million in student jobs and loans.

During the past decade, the university has met all the demonstrated need of entering freshmen, based on a parents' confidential statement of financial resources. Aid packages usually are a combination of gift aid and self-help. Ac-

well as the students' difficulties. Too often, undergraduates write of this kind of problem from the viewpoint only of students. Terry Anzur manages to balance the sides admirably.

Note especially the many quotations used in this excerpt. Quotations interest the reader.

cording to Kenneth Kaufman, assistant director of financial aids in charge of loans, a typical freshman is asked to meet half of his or her self-help requirement with income from jobs. The rest may be taken out in interest-free or low-interest loans.

Lynne Mason, assistant director of financial aids in charge of student employment, estimates that the typical undergraduate works 8–10 hours per week at about $2.50 an hour to fulfill a self-help requirement. Aid packages are periodically reviewed and adjusted to align with changes in student family income and increases in the cost of their education. The aim is to assess the gap between the cost of an education and the student's ability to pay for it, and to fill the gap with an optimum combination of gift aid and self-help. "We will do our best to maintain the same level of financial aid support for a student throughout the undergraduate years," Kaufman says.

But it won't be easy.

"There's a limit to how much we can increase gift aid and the number of on-campus jobs," Ms. Mason points out. "More students will have to take out loans."

Kaufman predicts a large increase in the number of low-interest federally insured loans to students from middle-income families. "Tuition has risen to a point where it is impossible for a student to completely work his way through this university," he says. . . .

Research Sources for the Article

Job descriptions and employment listings, placement center and financial aids office.

Undergraduate student job wage scale descriptions, financial aid office.

University news release, 1/13/75, on placement center peer counseling.

Internship descriptions, City of Palo Alto Personnel Department.

Intramural Handbook by W. P. Fehring, director of intramurals.

Campus Report, 11/13/74, "Summer conferences here provide jobs, income—and some laughs" by Pat Black (p. 9).

Memo from Delmer Daves, '26, "History of Stanford Period: Jobs" (to be published in full in *Stanford Magazine*'s fall issue).

The Innocents at Cedro by R. L. Duffus.

The Making of a Reporter by Will Irwin.

The Memoirs of Ray Lyman Wilbur.

This excerpt from the beginning of her piece and the partial list of sources, which included more than thirty interviews, suggest the range of avenues this writer explored. What she had to do before she could begin to write her article is the same process any successful writer for the modern newspaper has learned to follow.

RESEARCH ARTICLES

Here are a few tips on writing good research stories:

> "Good prose is like a windowpane."
>
> GEORGE ORWELL

Use authoritative sources   To have credibility, your article must include information from sources that everyone would regard as authorities on the subject. If the source is a person, be sure to state his or her credentials (president of an organization, leading researcher in the field, and so on). The "man on the street" approach may be useful for providing examples, but the article must include information from a source that has an overall picture of the subject. If the source is a document, be sure that it contains the most current information available.

Present the information clearly   The more complicated your subject is, the more attention you need to give to clear, direct writing. That doesn't mean you sacrifice smooth, flowing prose; it does mean that you need to be concise in constructing sentences and precise in choosing words. In addition, the article must be well organized. One way to approach the problem of organization is to first jot down the basic elements of the story in no particular order. Next, group those that are related to each other. Finally, rank the groups and their individual elements in order of importance. The result is an outline that will help you organize the material.

Include only interesting quotations   Well-chosen direct quotations make the article more lively and readable; don't ever use a dull quotation. "That's very interesting" is an example of a dull quotation. It adds nothing. When you use a direct quotation, subject it to a test of justification. You should have a reason for including it. Perhaps it is an insightful comment on the subject. It may explain something better than you could by paraphrasing. It may reveal something noteworthy about the speaker. Or it may be unusual, witty, or eloquent. If the quotation doesn't pass one of these tests, discard it or paraphrase.

Write in an authoritative tone   Don't hide behind qualifiers such as "in some instances" and "it seems to be." Too many of these make your article weak and uncertain. Although you shouldn't make absolute statements about facts you are unsure of, the presence of many qualifiers in an article is usually a sign that you didn't do enough research. Confidence in your own grasp of the subject is the key to an authoritative tone.

Here is an excerpt from an article by Madeline Camisa about an initiative to limit the construction of high-rise buildings in San Francisco. Originally written during a course in magazine writing, the article was published in *San Francisco* magazine. It gives a detailed account of the history of the initiative, the political elements that are for and against it, how its passage or failure is likely to affect the city's future, the various provisions of the initiative, and similar laws and trends in other cities. But even in the few paragraphs presented here, the author's considerable research and good command of the subject show:

The famous French architect, Le Corbusier, designed an ideal city for the twentieth century. Above all, his utopia was a city of administration: "From its offices come the commands that put the world in order. In fact, the skyscrapers are the brain of the city, the brain of the whole country. Everything is concentrated there: the tools that conquer time and space—telephones, telegraphs, radios; the banks, trading houses, the organs of decision for the factories: finance, technology, commerce." The city was composed of glass and steel skyscrapers set in parks.

But one man's dream is another man's nightmare. The dense, centralized city may receive accolades from corporate leaders or clerical workers, but not from some environmentalists and urban dwellers. Certainly not from some San Franciscans. To a growing number of inhabitants of the City by the Bay, the "ills" of high-rises far outweigh their economic benefits. According to these urban dwellers, the negative impacts of the giant slabs on the environment are clearly visible: disruption of the skyline, increased traffic, less open space, loss of older buildings, greater density and congestion, and environmental pollution.

Recently this anti-high-rise sentiment led to an initiative that would limit height and density of buildings in the city's financial center. The initiative is slated for the November ballot.

Though some Eastern cities have limited the density and height of their downtown buildings through various means, San Francisco is the only American city that has used this ballot-box approach to urban design controls. It's little wonder, then, that Kenneth Halpern, director of the Mayor's Office of Midtown Planning and Development in New York City, wrote in his study of urban design in nine American cities, *Downtown USA:*

Concern with the special quality of San Francisco has led citizens to focus more seriously than any other American city on the question of height limitations.

With its natural and man-made beauties, San Francisco can truly be called a unique city. But some shudder at what has happened to its visual character in the last 30 years. John Elberling, one of the sponsors of the initiative, said:

San Francisco has turned into an office city. It's still the Bay in the hills, but it's become less distinctive and that kind of special feeling has been lost.

Perhaps local columnist Herb Caen best summed up the feeling of San Franciscans about the changing skyline when he addressed the American Institute of Architects, which met in San Francisco in early May 1973. Caen wrote:

You architects who have visited San Francisco before may wonder where the city has gone. It's here somewhere, cowering behind hills and down alleys that form the new skyline that is almost indistinguishable from Pittsburgh's, Houston's or Atlanta's.

This article leaves the reader feeling that the author knew much more than she wrote, but that she selected the most important and informative material for her story. Any good research story should create a similar impression.

ANALYSES AND ESSAY-REVIEWS

More than any other kinds of magazine articles, analyses and essay-reviews offer an opportunity for the writer to leave detached objectivity behind and present subjective opinion. Many welcome the chance to exercise their analytical and interpretive skills. It offers them the role of thinker as well as journalist, and many can hardly wait to set their great thoughts down on paper.

The danger is that beginners often become so preoccupied with the magnitude of their thoughts that they neglect their presentation. The writing in analyses and essay-reviews should be forceful and concise. Important points should be carefully developed and illustrated by well-chosen examples. The writer must exert tight control over any tendencies to use flowery language or to present opinions without supporting illustrations. As in other magazine articles and features, it is essential to show concretely rather than to tell in abstract terms. In short, all the discipline of good writing should be applied.

Analyses

Most analyses are background articles aimed at answering the question "What's it all about?" when a war, a social explosion, a political upheaval, or any other momentous event makes the headlines. Analyses are built primarily on prosaic fact and only secondarily on incidents, anecdotes, and personalities. Now that more newspapers are turning toward interpretive reporting and analytic writing, magazines are being pushed into developing analyses more carefully and thoughtfully.

Since most magazines run many analyses, the beginner naturally assumes that there is a ready market for his talent. There is—but with built-in obstacles. Analyses call for generous use of facts and figures. Most analyses also require firsthand reporting and intimate knowledge of the subject. Before he realizes it, the writer can be bogged down in numbers and in quotations borrowed from books, which make dull reading. The veteran writer surmounts this hurdle by larding her analysis with episode and anecdote.

This college student solved some of the usual problems of writing analyses by choosing a topic that he understood: dating in college. Also, his sources were informative and lent an authoritative tone to the piece. Read this analysis, aimed at asking the question "What's dating in France all about?":

France is light-years away from Taiwan when it comes to the passion that St. Thomas Aquinas once referred to as "nocturnal pollution." "We make love, while Americans have sex," says Alexandre Abadie, repeat-

> "The more we do our job of questioning accepted norms, the more we can be expected to be questioned."
>
> DAVID HALBERSTAM

ing the refrain that perhaps ranks second only to the national anthem in a French heart.

Abadie, who's studying operations research at Stanford, is from Paris, where dating habits are more liberal than in the rest of France. "When you date a girl in France, you expect something," says Abadie, halfway through his hour-long discourse on love.

So what do you expect, and when do you begin to expect it? Dating begins during high school, though not at the high school, which is typically single-sex. Abadie's long dating career—yes, it's almost a career—began when he was 14. His parents, like other upper-class Parisian parents, held a rallye, or coming-out party, where a tuxedoed Abadie wowed the little women. At that stage, going out with a girl meant kissing her, says Abadie. He means the "intense" French kiss, he says, drawing out his words almost to the length of the kiss.

Abadie remembers going to sunny beaches in the south of France in the summer holidays. Summer at the beaches is a permanent dating period. Boys and men hang out in a very excited mode, "in Brownian motion," while the women laze around, rarely in bikinis, mostly in monokinis, and in no kinis on certain beaches, says Abadie. But this scene of adolescent amour is not typical France.

In a *Teen* magazine interview, Guylaine Gaspart from France says that a young girl of 15 or 16 has to be chaperoned on a date. One-to-one dating begins at 18 or 19, she says. Not so for Abadie, who says he's been a "heavy-duty dater." Abadie shudders in distaste at the thought of taking his date for pizza. Candlelit dinners and gourmet cuisine is more his idea of dating. What's *not* his idea of dating is spending the night at home with his girlfriend. "At home" is the key phrase, says Abadie. According to him, it's fine to go away for the weekend with your lover, but taking her home is taboo, because kids live with their parents, and "it's the house of the parents, it's not your house." In fact, he says, a man will introduce a lover as just a friend to his parents.

At this stage, a one-syllable question formed in my mind: Why? According to Abadie, it's a combination of French subtlety, formality, the appearance-is-all attitude, and strong home and family ties. "Do whatever you want as long as no one knows it's you." So, Abadie will introduce his lover as his lover to his parents only when marriage bells start to ring. And until they start to peal, he wouldn't live with her in Paris.

The Essentials of the Analysis

Dissection   The central purpose of an analysis is to *examine*. In a profile of a scientist, for example, a writer might cover the scientist's chief theory fairly superficially and focus on other aspects of his or her life and work. But writing an analysis calls for shining a fierce light on the central matter—the scientist's theory—and dissecting it with words that reveal its components, values, and implications.

Anticipating arguments and questions   A thoughtful editorial writer anticipates the arguments that will be used to counter his or her viewpoint and counters them in the editorial. The writer of an analysis tries to present a balanced examination rather than an editorial, but here, too, the writer must anticipate arguments and questions.

Clarity and unity foremost   Like the how-to writer, the writer of an analysis must work for extreme clarity. Almost any analysis will be considered by some readers to be argumentative, which makes it essential that the writer be understood. To be persuasive, an analysis must be unified, sentences marching along decisively, major point following major point in a way that seems inevitable. These are the essential stylistic qualities, and the writer of an analysis will leaven his or her work with devices that lend color and flavor only if they do not impair clarity and unity.

Here is the beginning of a readable analysis written by a student, Michael Ann Arenas:

> At 200,000, the number of women selling Mary Kay skincare and makeup products exceeds, by some 30,000, the global payroll of the mammoth Exxon Corporation, Thomas C. Hayes wrote in a recent *New York Times* article.
>
> Last year, gross sales for the company exceeded $320 million. And company profits are not the only thing soaring at Mary Kay Cosmetics. In 1983, 166 sales directors earned at least $50,000, while the top 50 averaged more than $150,000. Chairman of the Board Mary Kay Ash boasted at a recent San Francisco convention visit that her company has more women earning $50,000 each year than any other in the country. She earned $325,000 herself last year and owns 1.7 million of the company's shares, worth an estimated $221 million. . . .

Essay-Reviews

The chief difference between an analysis and an essay-review is that a book (or movie or play or other work of art) is the center of the latter. In fact, the work of art is the reason the essay-review exists. But it is much more than a conventional review, which often consists merely of the reviewer's reaction. The essay-review of a book, for example, is usually approximately half-article, half-review, with the part that is article focusing on the general subject of the book but not on the book's particular treatment of that subject. The review, of course, does focus on the book's treatment of the subject, but reading a perceptive essay-review is much more like reading an analysis than it is like reading a conventional book review. In other words, the essay-review provides a larger context in which to consider the book.

When Walter Kerr was the drama critic for the *New York Times,* he would fashion his criticisms of plays late at night, just in time for his work to be included in the next day's paper. In the following review, Kerr works his magic:*

---

*Reprinted by permission of Walter Kerr.

"Carnival," which has opened at the Imperial Theater, is a world of shadows—wonderful to look at, as most shadows are, graceful and glancing and dancing lightly as smoke, and somewhat distant.

Gower Champion is the shadow-master. Sometimes the giant silhouettes are quite literally there, as this choreographer-director imagines a regretful love song for brassy Kaye Ballard while the magician she most admires weaves an enormous black pantomime over a stageful of gauzes. Sometimes the sudden, weaving profiles come as a shattering shock, most effectively when a sharp, angry parting between puppeteer Jerry Orbach and waif-like Anna Maria Alberghetti is roughly climaxed by a downpour of circus banners let loose from the

WALTER KERR

To help you appreciate good writing, here is an analysis of the preceding review by Walter Kerr:

Plot The review runs more than five hundred words long, but Kerr only touches on the plot. He deals with two sequences in some detail, but his purpose is to show the reason for his approving judgments; the story itself is left to unfold on the stage for any reader who wants to see it. One learns little more than that the play has to do with a wandering troupe, an angry parting, and a festival.

Judgments The play is not just pronounced good (with qualifications); it is characterized by "wonderful to look at," a "world of shadows," "somewhat distant," and "gentle splendor." Champion is a "shadow-master"; he directs with a "paintbrush." And note that Kerr does much more than simply approve of Orbach's performance. He sketches its most affecting moments.

Phrases Consider the effect of "painting on frosted glass," "an odd little circle of joy," "outlined like dawn against a wispy Paris sky." Notice, too, the judicious use of alliteration: "shattering shock" and "graceful and glancing."

Organization Kerr's reviews are usually notable for their unified construction, a quality that can be traced to transitions. See especially how he moves from the first paragraph, which ends on a discussion of the world of shadows, into the second, which is concerned with the director as a shadow-master. Then the second paragraph ends with "wispy Paris sky," and the third be-

gins, "And always the whisper. . . ." At the end of the review, there is a faint echo—but not a restatement—of the beginning: ". . . if the shadows are forever moving, the people are forever shadows." This ending does not, however, wrap up a too-obvious ending with a pink bow but provides a natural concluding judgment that is related to the lead and thus unifies the whole.

As the greatest drama critic of modern times, Walter Kerr began in an unlikely place: he taught drama at Catholic University in Washington, DC. Because he was a versatile writer, he became the drama critic of *Commonweal*. Noticing Kerr's flair for writing, the *New York Herald Tribune* hired him away from *Commonweal* in 1951. For fifteen years, he was *the* drama critic in New York until the *Herald Tribune* died in 1966. The combination of the New York *World Journal Tribune* tried to hire Kerr, but the *New York Times* won.

Working for the *Times* gave Kerr an ability to be well known outside New York. Not only did he continue to write drama criticism for the *Times*, Kerr also wrote well-received books: *How Not to Write a Play, Criticism and Censorship, Pieces at Eight*, and others, especially *The Silent Clowns*, which makes an unusual plea to reexamine unspeaking clowns.

Kerr is one whose ability to judge drama overshadows his wonderful knack to write sentences that draw laughter. Of the many Kerr wrote, here are two:

"'Hook 'n Ladder' was the sort of play that gives failures a bad name."

"The critic who attempts to reverse the judgment of an audience, to 'instruct' it in taste, is the critic who deals in lost causes."

heavens—leaving the lovers and their indifferent friends outlined like dawn against a wispy Paris sky.

And always the whisper in which a lonely, wandering, down-on-its-luck troupe eternally moves about the countryside is brilliantly intimated. From the time that Pierre Olaf's accordion lets loose its first longing wheeze, while a straggle of tumblers and trumpeters make their way between two leafless trees, till the time that the last tent comes down again and the matchstick Ferris wheel vanishes from view, Mr. Champion's paintbrush is unerringly in command.

The small, yearning, never-tell-the-truth story that Michael Stewart has derived from Helen Deutsch's striking film, "Lili," of a few seasons ago, does not always hide away shyly at the edge of the Imperial's proscenium arch.

Nothing is more fetching than the sneaky way in which Mr. Olaf, lately of "La Plume de ma Tante," and hopefully to remain with us forever and ever, first strains to see us through his old-fashioned glasses, clasps his hands passionately as he tries to remember Paris, bites his tongue just to get the circulation going, and then slowly begins to circle in an odd little circle of joy. Mr. Olaf does something very strange to the floor. He makes it go the other way, without interrupting his own spinning one foot clockwise in a manner the girls in the line—trailing him as dutifully as chicks might their mother—find it not altogether easy to imitate. Before he is through, a number called "Grand Imperial Cirque de Paris" is flooding stage and auditorium with irrepressible joy.

And attend to the wide-eyed sobriety Miss Alberghetti brings to a tiny festival with her marionettes, caroling out the three or four Bob Merrill tunes (very lively) that open the second act all the while.

Jerry Orbach is the player who has made himself invisible—but emphatically present—in the shadow-box beneath these tantalizing figures (and they owe him a lot, too, for the fire with which he batters out a ballad called "Her Face"). But they still seem to lead lives of their own as they fix their stern gazes on the ragamuffin at their feet, and lecture her. The walrus, his kitchen-mop mustache blowing in the wind, wishes always to be introduced as a walrus, so that the ignorant company will not make anti-walrus remarks in his presence. The fox, quite naturally, objects to the phrase "Tally-ho," no matter in what context it may be carelessly used. The sequence is enchanting.

With so much gentle splendor to offer, and with James Mitchell taking time out to slap and storm his way through a dandy bit of mummery entitled "Sword, Rose and Cape," why is the pictorially perfect evening a little remote in its emotional effects? The fact that Mr. Stewart's book does subside noticeably whenever comedy is asked for does not explain the fact that Lili herself leaves our hearts untugged, and the battle over her own heart is a rather formalized affair.

"Carnival" is something more than sheer showmanship. It is painting on frosted glass, done with a hand that cares. But it is also something less than the impeccable style of its mounting; if the shadows are forever moving, the people are forever shadows.

"Truth disappears with the telling of it."

LAWRENCE DURRELL

The Essentials of the Essay-Review

The essential elements of the essay-review are much the same as those of the analysis: dissection, anticipating arguments and questions, and clarity and unity. An important additional element, of course, is *opinion*—the writer's opinion of the work he is reviewing. And to present his or her opinion persuasively, the writer must provide examples and evidence. Although analyses and essay-reviews differ in tone along with the subjects they cover, it is likely that the writer of an essay-review can often do more than can the writer of an analysis to enliven an article with color and flavor.

Magazine editors usually assign essay-reviews to free-lancers or staff writers who are specialists in the field covered by the book. In such cases, the writer is likely to have a mind so well stocked with relevant facts, ideas, and insights that he need do little more than read the book he is assigned to review and then write. But many writers choose to research an essay-review in much the same way they would prepare to write a more conventional article.

It is important to realize that although essay-reviews are based largely on the opinion of the writer, she does not allow her presence in the article to overwhelm the subject she is discussing. Thus, Dena Dawson's opinions color this entire article, but she does not intrude on the subject by continually using "I."

Police Women: TV's Newest Heroes*

COMMENT

Note how the tone of the first two paragraphs informs readers that this is a review, not a straight news story.

By the third paragraph, the writer has already begun to discuss the shows in the larger context of society.

ARTICLE

The new TV season's creators seem finally to have grasped the plain fact that among the many million evening or prime-time viewers are several million non-WASP males, which they cleverly term "ethnics," and even a few dozen women.

Since the purpose of television is to SELL! SELL! as well as, of course, to provide Quality Entertainment, it's surprising that those feverish players of the Ratings game haven't turned their attention to the women in the audience until now. On the other hand, if the Hero represents the ideals of a culture, would Americans, whatever their genealogy or sex, accept a hero or Top Person belonging to the nondominant group? It seems they do. If the producers think they do—they do.

Not only is every ethnic group from Aborigine to Zulu represented in the new shows, *two* of the new weekly police programs star women. This can only mean one thing—that our culture symbols *are* changing—and that the long arm of the women's movement is reaching even here, into nine out of ten U.S. homes.

---

*Reprinted by permission of the author.

She does not digress for long and returns quickly to the topic of her story in the next paragraph.

Refusing to abandon the stock-in-trade of police and adventure stories—i.e., murder, rape, kidnapping, larceny, etc.—the "creators" of TV police shows give you a hard-hitting, sexy Hero-cop who brings all the bad guys to justice. Lately, this mythic figure has become more vulnerable and sensitive, at times even poetic.

This unusual development of the police-hero figure seems to be, at least partly, a result of a significant attitude change in the public towards the police of the 60's—remember Berkeley and Chicago. Throughout the world, it is common to fear and/or despise the police, but only here, I suspect, has the Word come down to make them lovable, or at least human.

At any rate, the trend toward humanization continues with the emergence of the police woman. If the steely automation is no longer tolerated in males, it would be unthinkable in females.

Having set the stage for her discussion, the writer then begins to review the two shows.

Well-chosen examples and quotations from the show are used effectively here to make a point. The writer believes her readers will get the message without being told directly.

The opening episode of "Police Woman" is characteristic of the new mode in which Hard-hitting is replaced by Tough-tender. As Sergeant Pepper Anderson ("Beauty, Brains and a Badge") and her partner arrive at the scene, a young policeman has been shot and is dying in the street. She kneels by him, reassuring him about the ambulance on its way. He looks youthfully and sadly into her face and says, "Will you hold me, please?" She cradles his head in her arms and lowers her cheek to his. He dies.

The next scene shows her going into the office and sobbing against the file cabinet. The boss, sympathetic and resigned, says, "It's part of the business Hon . . . but no way you get used to it."

This particular episode exists only to set up the character and has no connection with the main story of a team of bank robbers, two white males, a black female and a white female. Later, in the climactic scene, Sgt. Anderson, disguised as a bank teller, shoots and kills the black woman, to save an innocent person's life. But even this realistic note of violence does nothing to reduce identification with her.

Exercises

1. One of the key elements of writing analyses and essay-reviews is concise language. To increase your awareness of wordiness in commonly used phrases, edit the unnecessary words from the phrases below:

his other alternative
found strangled to death
its future prospects
was of an oblong shape

his advance predictions
will start off soon
a bald-headed man

Choose a single word to replace these phrases:

in the neighborhood of
owing to the fact that
have openly voiced complaints

at this point in time
lent a hand to the efforts of
in the majority of instances

2. Write a review of a movie, play, concert, or other performance. Explain who the readers of your review would be and why they would be interested in the items you have criticized. What publication might use the article, and why?

3. Bring to class an article by a reviewer whose writing you like and explain why his or her reviews are effective. Comment on the person's writing style, general approach to reviewing, knowledge about the general subject, and tone.

4. You are assigned a story on how inflation has affected the ability of young couples to buy houses. List the sources of information you would consult in order to research the article.

EIGHTEEN

WRITING LONG ARTICLES

*What no wife of a writer can ever understand
is that a writer is working when he's staring
out of the window.*

BURTON RASCOE

M any beginning writers have the mistaken impression that it is easier to write a short article than a long one. Experienced free-lancers often claim that it's really just the opposite. Of course, the rigors of precise language, tightly knit structure, and well-chosen quotes and anecdotes apply in both cases. In a short article, however, a writer cannot afford to include a single line or paragraph that is not essential to the story, and if the subject is broad or complex, the task of extracting the most important points without omitting any crucial ideas can be quite demanding.

And even in a long article, the writer is rarely free to loosen the reins and trot along at a leisurely pace. In order to keep the reader's attention from beginning to end, the writer may even want to quicken the pace somewhat. Smooth transitions are essential to keep readers moving from one paragraph to the next without losing their attention. Paragraphs are usually short, no more than four or five sentences; otherwise, the printed page begins to look like a mass of gray that is not only difficult to read but also unappealing to the eye. To maintain visual appeal, magazines and newspapers often break up long articles into sections and add subheadings or sidebars that are either interesting quotes from the article or summations of the main ideas.

Long articles are especially good barometers of whether or not the writer has done a thorough research job. It's not hard to tell when the author has used every last quote and every drop of information squeezed from other sources. Regardless of the length of a story, it is always better to have far more research material than you actually use. The surplus allows you to be selective, to choose the best quote rather than just the only one you happen to have on the subject. In addition, extensive knowledge about the subject gives the author feelings of confidence and authority that translate into sure, thoughtful prose.

Having a desk piled high with research material can itself be a problem for beginners. The difficulty lies in how to organize the material before you start and in how to use it as you go along. Writers' solutions to these problems are as individual as their styles; the best way is simply the way that works best for you. In this chapter, you'll learn how some experienced writers tackle the task. Try the methods that seem most appropriate for you.

Steve Ames, who writes often for sports magazines, has proposed some general guidelines on how to write long articles. Here are his suggestions:

1. Type notes double-spaced, reorganize them, number them, then cut and paste to insert new ideas.

2. Draw an outline from your reorganized notes. Suggested order:
Anecdote or general statement of fact
Main thought development
Quote as example
Underlying, or secondary, thought briefly stated
Example

3. Write a lead built around the ideas as you have organized them and decide whether an anecdote would be fitting to precede the lead.

4. Try writing at least a 1,000- to 2,000-word story nonstop. Writing is an artistic method of stringing words together. However, what it is not is an elongated newspaper story. It must have depth, background, color; write to one point of view. The author must completely submerge himself in the topic. Step away a bit, then write like an observer.

5. Come back to the writing after a brief time. Reread the story. Look over your notes and finish writing. Be selective. You owe nothing to anyone you have interviewed. Just because you have spent fifteen minutes or even two hours with someone who has produced nothing that will make an important contribution to your article doesn't mean that you have to include his name or anything he has said.

6. Come back a day or two later. Look at your story cold. Read it aloud or have someone else read it to you. Ask yourself, is it conversational?

7. After you have done some thinking about it—make that *critical* thinking—retype it.

8. Read it into a tape recorder.

9. Play back the tape. Check for transitions as the tape plays back. How do the words sound that you have strung together?

10. Rewrite for the final draft. And now, research your article. Are quotes transcribed correctly?

Here is a writer who knows about organizing and the sweet agony of writing. In writing about writing, here is what Gloria Steinem wrote:*

---

*Reprinted by permission of Gloria Steinem.

Writers are notorious for using any reason to keep from working: over-researching, retyping, going to meetings, waxing the floors—anything. Organizing, fund raising, and working for *Ms.* magazine have given me better excuses than those, and I've used them. As Jimmy Breslin said when he ran a symbolic campaign for a political office he didn't want, "Anything that isn't writing is easy." Looking back at an article I published in 1965, even when I was writing full-time and in love with my profession, I see, "I don't like to write. I like to have written."

That thought comes from "What's In It for Me," the subject on which *Harper's* had invited a group of writers to contribute. In fact, most of my reasons in that essay still hold.

> There is freedom, or the illusion of it. Working in spurts to meet deadlines may be just as restricting as having to show up at the same place every day, but I don't think so. . . . Writing about a disliked person or theory or institution usually turns out be worthwhile, because pride of authorship finally takes over from prejudice. Words in print assume such power and importance that it is impossible not to feel acutely responsible for them.

> Writing, on the other hand, keeps me from believing everything I read.

> Women whose identity depends more on their outsides than their insides are dangerous when they begin to age. Because I have work I care about, it's possible that I may be less difficult to get along with when the double chins start to form.

GLORIA STEINEM

When Gloria Steinem's book *Marilyn* was published by Henry Holt & Company in late 1986, readers were surprised. The book carried so many new observations of Marilyn Monroe that it became a best-seller. Here is an example of Steinem's reporting on Monroe:

> As an actress, she often objected to playing a "dumb blonde," which she feared would also be her fate in real life, but she might have attempted the "serious actress" appeal of playing Cecily, a patient of Sigmund Freud. After all, the director of this movie was John Huston and the screenwriter was Jean-Paul Sartre, who considered Marilyn "one of the greatest actresses alive." Ironically, Dr. Ralph Greenson, a well-known Freudian who was Marilyn's analyst in the last months of her life, advised against it, because, he said, Freud's daughter did not approve of the film. Otherwise, Marilyn would have been called upon to enact the psychotic fate she feared most in real life, and to play the patient of a man whose belief in female passivity may have been part of the reason she was helped so little by psychiatry.

Steinem had written of Monroe for *Ms.* magazine in 1972, writing that problems the actress had, such as guilt over not having children, also were felt by many women. Steinem's article led Henry Holt & Company to ask her to write a text on Monroe to accompany pictures of her taken by a photojournalist before her death.

Steinem said, "One aspect of writing about a woman like Marilyn is that you feel you're exploiting her all over again." But Steinem spends much time raising funds for women's causes, and she decided to donate her money from this book to a Marilyn Monroe Children's Fund. "Not to be presumptive, I thought Marilyn would like to see the money go to children's projects."

For me, writing is the only thing that passes the three tests of metier: (1) when I'm doing it, I don't feel that I should be doing something else instead; (2) it produces a sense of accomplishment and, once in a while, pride; and (3) it's frightening.

ESTABLISH THE THEME

Write to a title or at least to a thematic sentence. This practice is desirable because a writer must know where he or she is going; and a thematic statement, whether it is expressed in a title of a few words or in a complete sentence, will guide you. The absence of a thematic idea (many writers call it "the angle" or "the slant") is nearly always damaging. A writer may wander through sentences that add little to the thrust of the article or, worse, through sentences that are peripherally relevant; they seem central because they are fairly close, but they are the most voracious time-wasters imaginable.

Consider the danger of working without a theme: thousands of words *can* be written about almost anything. A simple room, a simple object, a simple person—an imaginative researcher-writer can explore any of these in paralyzing detail. Without a theme that states the salient features of a subject, the writer has no guide to tell her what to point up, what to ignore. Of course, a thoughtful writer has some vague notion of purpose without a theme because she has read extensively and because her own interest in certain aspects of the subject will guide her toward a proper emphasis.

What of Steinem's own money? Happily, Letty Cottin Pogrebin, her agent, sold at an auction in March 1987 proposals for two books at a total of $1,200,000. The first proposal at the auction was for Steinem's *Bedside Book of Self-Esteem*. Little, Brown outbid sixteen other publishers with an offer of $700,000. As for the second proposal, for a book about women from rich and powerful American families, Simon & Schuster outbid seven other publishers with a $500,000 offer. Pogrebin said, "Now maybe Gloria can grow old without worrying about having to go to the Feminist Old Folks Home."

Perhaps no one would have predicted this success for a teenager in blue-collar Toledo, Ohio, who was taking dance lessons as a means of "dancing my way out of the neighborhood." Steinem is a product of a working-class background. When she was nine, her parents separated. Steinem took care of her mother, who became an invalid; "her spirit was broken."

Everything Steinem has done as an adult—especially writing—has carried her forward and up.

Now, at fifty-six, Steinem must be satisfied with her life so far. She may think of a *New Statesman* review of one of her books, *Outrageous Acts and Everyday Rebellions*:

> The most engaging feature of this collection, apart from its maturity and humour, is Steinem's habit of turning the world outside-in at the stroke of a pen, in her own observations and in snappy anecdote. . . . In a collection that ranges widely and with brilliant clarity from articles on Linda Lovelace (a shocker) to Alice Walker (the best review of *The Color Purple* (BRD 1982) I've ever read), to pieces on the sexual politics of conversation, little facts are constantly popping up to surprise, horrify or amuse.

But this notion can be no better than vague unless the writer makes a conscious effort to state a theme specifically. Thus, it is not enough for a free-lancer to begin to write about the UCLA basketball team or the president of the United States *in general.* He must decide, for example, that he will write about the ruthless efficiency of UCLA, including the seriousness and rigor of the training that produced the team. Entire books could be written about the team, but the article writer needs a focus that will enable him to contain his piece in 3,000 to 4,000 words. The fact that he places his focus on UCLA's efficiency does not require that he ignore evidence of locker-room horseplay or practical jokes during travels to out-of-town games. If these sidelights exist, the writer would be dishonest to ignore them. Instead, he subordinates them, recounting an example or two to indicate that the players are not always serious.

What the focus on theme really means is that the writer has an instrument that will enable her to *select.* For example, the sequences in the UCLA article may seem, superficially, to be quite diverse—everything from the coach's religious training to the All-American guard's family life. The writer deals with the coach's background, however, because it is central to understanding why he runs the team as he does. The writer deals with the guard's home life not merely to make the point that the player is pleasant during the off-season and barely civil during the winter, but to show how one player reacts to the rigors of efficiency athletics.

Similarly, a story on the president (or almost any other subject) must be thematic. One can write volumes about the presidency in general, or even about the current president in particular. *What* about the president? Is this an article predicting that he will run for reelection? Is it about his sense of humor?

Asking and answering such questions is a commanding necessity in beginning an article. Most careful writers determine the theme at the beginning—while writing the query to the editor about writing the article or early in the research process. Themes that have been developed early sometimes change. Editors may suggest different themes, often in responding to queries from the author, sometimes when responding to a writer's progress report on research, and occasionally—unhappily—when they have read the article in the form that the writer fondly supposes to be final. Ideally, though, the writer shapes a captivating theme quite early, when the idea begins to emerge, and only if research yields new facts and thoughts that thrust forward a compelling new theme will the writer change that initial idea.

Even when the theme is in mind, many writers postpone putting words on paper and indulge in rituals that help them absorb the feel of a story. One writer becomes so wound up that he paces up and down the corridor outside his office. Another leaves her desk to walk around and sometimes digs out and reads similar articles she has written for the magazine at which she is aiming. A third broods about the form of his article while absently working in his garden. Eccentric though these activities seem, all are designed to search out the feel of the article. When you have captured the feel of your article, the writing will flow.

Even though the following article, which is about 4,500 words long, is not reproduced in its entirety, you can get a sense of how Mark Stephens, the writer, organized his material, determined a theme, and settled on an overall feel in shaping this article:

> Before dawn, up behind the Stanford University campus, Kim lies in the dark, listening to the birds and to the automatic sprinklers. Slowly, with as little extra movement as possible, her hand slides from under the covers to her throat, where it rests just above her carotid artery. Using the clock by her bed, she times the pulse in her neck (11 beats per minute) and then rises to write the figure under the day's date in her running log. Barefoot on the cold hardwood floor, at five foot six and 102 pounds, this 21-year-old is all legs and rib cage, with stomach and hips that fade to nothing. Kim's hair, long and dark, falls loosely in braids behind her model's neck, high cheekbones and large eyes. Her emaciated arms contrast sharply with her muscular legs. She looks like a dancer or a gymnast, not a runner. But Kim Schnurpfeil, on this autumn day in 1982, is the reigning American women's 10,000-meter track champion.
>
> Across the Stanford campus, near Palo Alto, California, half a dozen other young runners are going through the same pulse-taking and record-keeping rituals. With names like Regina, Cecilia, Alison, and Jessica, they could be an abstract of every expectant mother's wish book from 1961. The pulse rates of these slender, attractive young women are all in the low to mid 10s. By 7:00 A.M., as the hackers crawl in from long nights at the computer center and the hashers crawl out to serve breakfast in the dorms, three of these women are out running by themselves in the campus's oak-studded hills, while the other three have gone to one of the university pools for an hour of swimming laps. Somewhere nearby, a 30-year-old male writer with a resting pulse of 63 has turned over and gone back to sleep.
>
> Intercollegiate track and field was always a sport of men. Even at so-called "track schools" like Washington State, Oregon, Villanova, and Texas-El Paso the athletes were nearly all men. Until the mid-1970s, most colleges and universities had no competitive cross-country or track programs for women. Those programs that did exist mainly used volunteer or part-time coaches, offered no athletic scholarships to women, and often denied their women athletes access to equipment and training facilities essential to any varsity sport.
>
> It was sex discrimination, rationalized for the most part by the myth of no demand, to think that for some reason only male American college students wanted to run or throw or jump in competition. Women students were immune to the desire. . . .

I have rewritten— often several times— every word I have ever published. My pencils outlast their erasers.

VLADIMIR NABOKOV

WRITE AND REVISE

The following case study illustrates important ways of shaping articles.

Changing Yosemite

CRITIQUE

The first paragraph doesn't build to its point; the point is made in the middle of the paragraph. In the revision—right column—the paragraph builds to the point.

Publicity—the focus of the first sentence in the original draft—is far from noteworthy in itself. The first sentence in the revision creates suspense and, therefore, interest. It makes the reader ask, "What *is* the future of the place?"

One speaks of "amounts" of sugar, sand, and so forth; of "numbers" of people, bricks, trees, and the like.

Are there visitors who are *not* transient?

Test each use of "for example." If your next statement is quite obviously an example of a generalization you have just written, "for example" wastes words. If you must identify Yogi Bear with Jellystone, the point is lost. Instant recognition of his name is essential. "Pic-in-ic," on the other hand, asks too much of the reader.

This probably isn't contrary to what the reader would think. The friendly park bears are widely known. "Contrary" makes "rather than pleased" superfluous.

ARTICLE

Yosemite National Park has been widely publicized since its early history. In fact, just six years after the valley was discovered, the first tourist party was brought in by English adventurer James Hutchings in 1855. The terrible word "Commercialism" that has infiltrated so much of America during the last decade has regretfully not forgotten about Yosemite. Tucked away in the high Sierras, Yosemite National Park is now just five to seven hours' driving time from both San Francisco and Los Angeles.

Yosemite Valley, although still abounding in natural beauty, is evolving to keep up with the whims of modern America. Every summer, the amount of tourist inhabitants increases to a record number. Due to this alarming number of transient visitors, last year over one million, the valley has had to make some corresponding changes.

For example, no longer do the park rangers think it wise to let the entertaining bears conduct their nightly raids. This season, for the first time, nearly all of the bears were carted to the uplands of the park. Only two of the usual thirty were sly enough to avoid capture so that they could continue on their usual summer capers of robbing "pic-in-ic baskets," as Yogi Bear of Jellystone National Park fame would say.

Contrary to what the reader might think, this move disappointed rather than pleased the loyal Yosemite visitors who have been returning faithfully to the park for their allotted ten days of vacation every summer. The bears used to put on a nightly show at the valley

REVISION

Perhaps the future of Yosemite National Park was forecast at the beginning. Just six years after the Yosemite Valley was discovered in 1849, English adventurer James Hutchings brought in the first tourist party. Now, although Yosemite is tucked away in the High Sierras, it is just five to seven hours from both Los Angeles and San Francisco—and the commercialism that has tainted so much of America is slowly enveloping it.

The valley is still rich in natural beauty, but Yosemite is evolving with the whims of modern America. Every summer, the number of tourists sets a record; last year, Yosemite lured more than one million. And every summer the valley changes.

No longer will the park rangers allow the resident bears to conduct their nightly raids. For the first time last summer, the bears were carted away to the uplands. Only two of the thirty escaped the exodus and continued their amiable robbery of picnic baskets, Yogi-Bear style.

The disappearance of so many of the bears was a stark disappointment to regular Yosemite visitors. They can remember the years when everyone crowded around the valley garbage dump to watch the bears put on a nightly show.

The point about the limitation *by park officials* to ten days comes much later. The reader won't understand.

Few readers know what is meant by "Firefall." Don't use it until you define it.

Note that through this paragraph and the beginning of the next there's a slight drift away from the theme, almost as though the writer of the article had forgotten the point he was making and was beginning to offer general information. It's important for a writer to keep his theme in mind throughout. He may certainly bring in matters that may seem extraneous—bears, campsites—but only insofar as he can fit them into the framework of theme.

Now the left column is getting back to the theme. But recognize that the use of "so-called" precludes the use of quotes around *backwoodsman*. And note that the column at right makes clear the relevance of the theme to the change in campers.

This paragraph gets a bit heavy with sarcasm. Better a touch of subtlety.

garbage dump which drew an intrigued crowd of regular spectators every night. This event began the evening's entertainment program which was culminated by watching the Firefall.

In addition, late in the season, usually in September, every night after the Firefall precisely at 9:45, garbage can lids were heard to bang in every campsite as the bears began their nightly raiding parties. Some campers left a jar of food out by their campsites waiting for the bears to appear so they could get a close-up look.

But there are more than the bears to worry about feeding during the summer tourist season in Yosemite. Many campers forgot to bring the necessary food and supplies with them, and ultimately just two years ago another significant change occurred in the valley. A supermarket was built as the nucleus of a new shopping center right in the middle of American ex-wilderness. The new Yosemite Village also contains a bakery, barber shop, garage, filling station.

Another change in Yosemite is in its tourists and campers. It seems that the so-called "backwoodsman" type of camper gets more scarce every year. Now camping in Yosemite is like moving into your backyard. If it is too much effort for the tourist to set up his own tent, then all he has to do is move his family into one of Yosemite Valley's "pre-fab" tent towns already set up for the increasing number of visitors, who prefer, as the brochures say, "Less rugged living."

If this is still not enough of a homey touch to suit our friend "Joe Tourist," then he can rent a housekeeping cabin at Camp Curry. Of course, there are hot showers, a cafeteria, post office, gift shop, and heated swimming pool nearby, lest the hardy traveller need to indulge in "wilderness activities" missing at home.

And late in the season, precisely at 9:45, garbage can lids banged in every campsite, the signal of the bears' nightly raiding parties. Some campers left jars of food out beside their tents to bring the bears near enough for a close-up look.

Now, instead of wandering wildlife, Yosemite features all the comforts of suburbia. Since many campers forgot to go to the store before heading for the valley, the store has come to the campers. Two years ago, a supermarket went up—the nucleus of a shopping center. Yosemite, ex-wilderness, now has everything from a bakery to a barber shop.

And, of course, the character of the typical Yosemite camper is changing. The "backwoodsman" has apparently gone way back in the woods, leaving Yosemite Village to the backyardsman. If the new tourists don't feel like setting up camp, they can move into the "pre-fab" tent towns available to those who prefer, as the brochures say, "less rugged living."

The tourist who dies a little at the thought of any kind of tent can settle at Camp Curry, where hot showers, a cafeteria, a post office, a gift shop, and a conveniently located heated swimming pool are guaranteed to whisk away any vestige of wilderness fever.

First Draft, Second Draft, Third Draft

Should one write the first draft hurriedly or painstakingly? A writer may choose to blast ahead, giving little attention to phrases or sentence structure, trying to get the basic framework on paper in the first draft, saving deftness and polish for revisions. Or he can shape and polish as he goes, phrasing as vividly as his talent allows the first time through, smoothing one sentence before he moves on to the next. There can be no rule about such matters, of course, but most writers advise beginners to try to develop the habit of writing the first draft rapidly. Because the theme is likely to be nebulous and the process of worrying each sentence can lead the writer into dead-end paragraphs, it is far better to build a basic structure, however unwieldy, and polish everything in subsequent drafts. Resisting the desire to stop and polish is difficult for some writers. In fact, the author of this book sometimes finds that he cannot bear to leave a page without revising. He works at increasing his ability to run through a first draft rapidly, though, recognizing its value. For writers who have to fight the impulse to rewrite as they are putting a first draft on paper, marking portions to be rewritten in the margin and circling possible misspellings can help.

When the writer has rapidly written a first draft, what does she have? Usually a crude framework for an article. Converting this into publishable prose requires restraint, for the impulse to move directly to a final draft is strong. A better course is suggested by an experienced free-lancer:

> I've found that it pays to have each rewriting, each draft, serve a specific purpose. My article is barely hatched with the first draft. I compare it to my notes and other material and insert anything I've overlooked that will make the story stronger. I don't try to do too much refining in the second draft, which is longer than the first—and much too long for the editor. The third draft is the one in which I do the refining, cutting unnecessary paragraphs or sentences or even words, and often changing the position of sequences. This gets the manuscript down to length, and this is usually the semifinal copy. Now I begin sandpapering and polishing. You might call this a fourth draft, but it's probably just an upgrading of the third. It's overwhelmingly important, though. With *Roget's Thesaurus* and Rodale's *Word-Finder* at hand, I go through the entire manuscript looking for words I can upgrade to make the story more vivid or lively or moving. I try to replace static words with those that have action. It's amazing what refining a dozen to a score of words will do for a manuscript.
>
> It's especially important to rework the lead. If I rewrite a manuscript three to six times, or more—and I often do—I usually refine the first two or three paragraphs ten or a dozen times. And that's no exaggeration. I have about one minute flat to catch my editor and my reader with that first paragraph or two. So I try every combination of words and phrases that seem challenging. Often, I've tried a few of these combinations before I start to write the first draft. If I can hit the right one, it's a guideline when I'm doing the first draft. The probability is that I'll distill out a better one when I finish the first draft.

The target in distilling out a lead is to make every word say exactly what you want it to say. If a word or a phrase doesn't say enough in the right way, then you have to find a better one. This process of making words say exactly what you mean goes for the rest of the story as well as the lead. It's the difference between sharp writing and fuzzy writing.

MEMOS FROM EDITORS

> "Advice is seldom welcome, and those who want it the most always want it the least."
>
> EARL CHESTERFIELD

When a free-lancer or staff writer has completed a long article and submitted it to an editor, the learning process may be just beginning. For this much is certain: perceptive editors have much to teach writers who will listen. Contrary to the beliefs of some disgruntled writers, an editor is not hired to make the life of a staff writer miserable and the life of a free-lancer impossible. The chief responsibility of most magazine editors is to produce successful magazines, so they discover and cultivate writers who can provide the articles that make a magazine successful. The point is that helping writers helps editors. The excerpts in this chapter from editors' letters and memos show how they try to help with sharp, but friendly, criticism. These excerpts should also demonstrate some of the techniques important in writing magazine articles.

Study Your Magazine Before You Write for It

Thank you for letting me see "The Anatomy of the Shark Scare," which I return herewith. Like all your work, this is extremely well-written, with considerable flavor. It is not, however, the kind of article we would use. It is subjective and literary, whereas our pieces are more apt to be objective and factual.

To write successfully for the national magazines, the writer must aim each article at a specific magazine. He must familiarize himself with the kind of article used by that magazine by long reading and study of its pages. No longer—perhaps unfortunately—can the writer simply write an article and then send it out to be published.

You will see that preparing such an article entails a great deal of work—preliminary as well as final. It is altogether different from writing a newspaper story: long and careful research is necessary, and then great attention to content, construction and writing. Our successful contributors sometimes spend much more time on preparing an outline than the average writer spends in writing a finished article for other magazines.

Stick to Your Theme

There should be only one main theme in your article—i.e., the fact that the police are unpopular and why. This would include both the themes mentioned in your letter, that hooligans have been making violent attacks on police, and that the police are unpopular with the general public. Naturally, the piece would go on to tell what is being done constructively about the problem in various cities. But if you go too much into techniques of handling crowds, for instance, you get away from the main theme. Remember that the article came out of our conversation which was devoted to the two closely connected points: *Why* do we have this wave of attacks on the police? and *What* can be done to stop it? Naturally, you are going to describe such attacks, using your most dramatic case histories. I feel sure you can put the piece together solidly, so that it will have the coherence and unity to make it convincing.

Tell Only One Story at a Time

The Boss asked me to write you about "Lazybones Gardening Is for Me," which we have concluded is a darned good subject, but not "as is." The problem, we think, is that you have tried to tell two stories in one: (a) how gardening has become a lazy man's job for you and (b) how others developed various gadgets and chemicals that help the gardener become lazy.

Honestly, we think the first story is the best one, the most widely appealing one—and while the other relates to it, you have let it more or less take over, which, in addition to the effect it has on the story organization, also throws too much emphasis on particular products.

What we would like to have is a fairly straight story about lazy man's gardening from your own experience and that of your gardening friends. It should be told with a light touch, of course, but shouldn't strain to be humorous; we think there is an extensive interest in gardening that will welcome a fairly serious, informative article. There are a lot of puzzled gardeners, caught between the traditional back-breaking systems, and the plethora of new plant foods, fungicides, insecticides, soil conditioners, and the array of gadgets. We can't, of course, do a how-to-do-it guide, but certainly you can tell how you and some other gardeners have licked this dilemma. Keep the focus on the lazy gardener—the kind we all hope to be.

Personalities Make Your Story Come Alive

The chief trouble with this piece is that it comes out a rather dull piece of copy. Somehow it becomes largely a catalogue of philanthropies in the field of conservation and seems to be done at arm's length. It just doesn't have the breath of life in it. And of course this is the most difficult of all rewriting problems to solve, but it will have to be solved somehow if we are to have an acceptable article.

I think one element, now missing, that would help would be to give us some personality stuff on your character—how he works, what kind of guy he is, maybe a few more quotes from him about people and problems he deals with in this work. In the present manuscript, he seems to be only a shadowy figure in the background. Is he really a self-effacing character, or does he just come out this way in your article?

One thing I think you should *not* do in trying to get more life into the article is to make it more breezy and slangy. You have a bit too much of that kind of writing in the manuscript now. This technique is all right for a lighter vein piece, but it doesn't seem to belong in a serious article like this one.

Enliven with Examples

Your Indian girl story arrived this morning—and you are going to be just as disappointed in my report on it as I was in reading it. To put it bluntly, the story misses the mark entirely. I am extremely puzzled by this, because there is wonderful material here for a striking and memorable piece. I find myself wondering whether you have really read our magazine carefully, studying the articles to familiarize yourself with the kind of things we use.

I still believe, however, that you *can* write for us successfully, and that you will do so in the future. Anything I can do to help, I shall gladly do. But I think it would be wise for you not to attempt any more articles until we have had a chance to sit down and discuss matters of technique again. Why don't you wind up your story investigations when convenient and come back to New York? Then we can go over everything carefully, and you can write the other pieces you have in hand when you get home. Working together more closely, I have every hope that they will end up in the magazine. I hope you don't mind me writing thus frankly to you, pulling no punches. That is the only way I know how to talk to someone I like and whom I want to help.

As to detailed criticism of the Indian girl piece, I shall list some of its failings. In the first place, it lacks anecdotes. There are really only two good ones in the whole article—the lead story of finding the little girl, and the story of Marie-Yvonne picking a thief to guard the Red Cross goods. As I have pointed out before, a successful article must be constructed almost entirely of anecdotes, a series of short narratives vividly representing particular events and places. In your article, you *tell* the reader about Marie-Yvonne's life in general terms; what you must do is show the reader the most interesting events of that career in anecdotes and narrative.

You tell the reader that Marie-Yvonne is accustomed to do this and that when she visits the Indians. How much more effective this section would be if it were the narrative of one specific trip, one specific scene around the campfire, with actual quotes of her conversation. You write: "When her father was with her on similar expeditions, he made it a point to tell them his history, and how he had adopted and raised her. It always made them like him better." This is an indirect and passive presentation of what could be a most interesting point—you are asking the reader to take your word for an opinion. But write that scene as an actual occurrence—the half-naked savages around the campfire, the white man standing before them, the Indian girl trying to make the two understand each other, the shadows, the jungle, etc.— and you will have the kind of effective anecdote that makes a moving piece.

Perhaps you are writing too much for yourself, and not enough with the reader in mind. This is never a successful approach for us, except by accident. Our articles are written for a calculated effect on specific readers—the successful magazine writer never loses sight of that. He must say to himself continually, "Is my reader still with me? Am I losing him? Would this interest him more than that? Now I shall make him laugh, now I shall make him choke up," and so on. And the way to do this is to give the reader a continuing narrative, formed of a series of memorable anecdotes. General exposition and leisurely description do not make a good magazine piece.

Part of this calculated effort to interest the reader is of course the presentation of pictures, sharp images. In the lead of your article, for instance, the only description you give of your heroine is that she was a "two- or three-year-old girl, showed marks of severe mistreatment, and she was terrified." Well, what did she look like? Was she fat or thin? Was she clothed or naked? If clothed, with what? Black hair? Color of eyes? As a matter of fact, nowhere in the whole article do you tell us what Marie-Yvonne looks like, either then or later. Of course there should be two descriptions—of the tiny savage found in the jungle, and of the civilized young woman twenty years later. But you do not even tell the reader the color of her skin, whether she is short or tall, how she dresses, what her figure is like, or the sound of her voice.

Dr. Vellard's first glimpse of the child, in the jungle, should be one of the highlights of the story. You hardly mention it, merely quoting from the doctor's diary. Compare the lead of your article—which is written in general terms—with the detailed, vivid picture of the same scene which could be written. You say that Dr. Vellard and his Indian guides were walking through the jungle under constant attack by unseen Guayaki Indians with bows and arrows, that two of the guides fled, and that on September 23, "a strange thing happened." In transcribing from his notes later, Dr. Vellard made this simple entry in his journal. "Our fugitive Indian guides returned. On the way they found a small Guayaki camp, two women and a child." But nowhere do you *show* us the "constant attack with bows and arrows"—you merely tell us that it occurred. There is no description of the guides, or even of the "small Guayaki camp, the two women or the child." Yet think how effective and memorable could be a vividly painted scene of savages in the jungle, arrows quivering in trees, and Dr. Vellard stepping out into the small clearing, here and there a hut or two, the naked women lamenting and crying, the tiny child, and so on. This could be an extraordinary scene; it must not be thrown away with a noncommittal quotation from a diary. This is such a dramatic story that it is begging to be written. I know that I am going to be writing you my hearty congratulations one of these days. I look forward to that day.

Omit Slang, Please

I am sorry to say that your piece needs more work. Your material is good, and I am sure you will be able to produce an acceptable article, but, to state the matter candidly, we think the writing is pretty darned bad in the present version. In revising the manuscript, the following matters will require your attention.

We don't like your excessive use of slang in this article. Slangy writing may be all right with some subjects, such as sports or perhaps Hollywood characters, but it seems out of place when you are writing about a great university and its president. Even in this sort of article, we don't object to an occasional slang expression, but you have loaded the whole piece so heavily with this type of writing that it gives the effect of being overly cute and kittenish. I haven't gone through the manuscript and marked these too-slangy spots, because there are some on virtually every page.

There are also a number of fuzzy, unclear spots in the manuscript. I have marked most of these marginally. These places need careful recasting and clarification and in some cases additional information. A particularly bad example is the section telling what Stanford is doing to develop its large land-holdings into profitable property through residential and industrial developments. It is simply impossible to tell what is going on from reading the present manuscript.

In rewriting the piece, I think you need to bring the biographical material about Sterling's earlier career up much closer to the front of the article. As it stands now, you merely hint at some of his previous experiences, then launch right into the job he has done at Stanford. I think his work at Stanford will be much more meaningful to the reader if you first give us a good glimpse of the man himself. Your present lead, the piano-playing incident, makes a good beginning. After that, you should state briefly, in a paragraph or two, that Sterling has done a remarkable job of reviving Stanford. Then, it seems to me, you should tell the story of his earlier life and give us a good picture of the man. After that could come your detailed story of his accomplishments at Stanford. And, finally, your present ending, giving some nice personality glimpses of the man, is okay.

Make Your Piece Move

I have messed up your manuscript, in an attempt to make it more dramatic. If this piece is to be successful for us, it must really be the exciting and breathless account of an extraordinary occurrence. Everything leisurely or inconsequential must be pared away from it, so that the piece moves with the utmost speed from beginning to end. Short, staccato sentences will help, and short paragraphs, too.

I have cut out a number of the more leisurely descriptions in an attempt to speed things up. What I have not succeeded in doing is to add to the piece the idea that Rummel, having been shot point-blank twice, should have been mortally wounded or at least thought he was. Perhaps you can get this in at several places. Did Rummel fall down when he was shot? Or was he still standing up; one wonders why he didn't stagger over to the car and empty the gun into Clark. Perhaps he was unable to walk? Have you any information as to how many bullet holes were found in Clark's car afterward? Was Clark himself hit?

I think the lead is pretty good as edited—at least as far as construction is concerned. You get right into the story quickly, and it moves. Indeed, I think the construction of the whole piece is sound— the framework. But I do feel that it will need some "sheer writing" and that, of course, is up to you. You can throw aside all restraint on this one, and really let yourself go. You might get the idea of your title into the piece at several places—the fact that Rummel had three lives. When he finally gets out of the car after its turning over, you might say that for the third time that night he had brushed by death.

Why You Can't "Dash Off an Article"

Your article, "Ten Ways to Cut Your Medical Bills in Half," which I return herewith, is a beginning—but it is far from being the finished article we would require. Writing a magazine piece is considerably different from knocking out a newspaper story—as I can assure you from my own experience. The articles we buy are most thoroughly and carefully researched, sometimes for months; then are checked and re-checked; and are written and re-written. When finished, you and I both should be able to say that the article is just as comprehensive, just as perfect, as it can be made. It is because we demand such a high standard that we pay generously for the articles we accept.

You have an excellent idea for your article, and some of it reads well as it stands. But the piece gives the impression of being hastily put together, and it is by no means complete and comprehensive enough. As the piece now stands, there is a tendency to jump around from subject to subject; whereas we prefer to have everything on one subject brought together logically. Each section of the text needs careful thinking out before it is written.

Incidentally, we do not use the newspaper style of one-sentence paragraphs which you have used in this piece. It might be a good idea for you to read ten or twelve of our medical articles published over the last year or so, to give you an idea of the way in which we handle articles of this kind.

I hope you will spend at least an additional month on revising the article. Every section should be checked carefully with authorities to be sure that it is as complete as it can possibly be made. Would it not be a good idea to ask the directors of a number of hospitals what ways they can suggest in which people can cut their medical bills? And a number of other doctors as well? After all available material has been assembled, the article should be carefully constructed from start to finish. Finally, the writing itself should be done with great care.

You have an original and promising idea here, and it should make a fine article. I know you can make it just that if you will devote plenty of effort to it.

Detail Makes the Story Vivid

I wish you would have another go at this piece. The main trouble is lack of detail, clear pictures of what went on, and ease of understanding. It is better to write in detail, clearly and completely, about a certain number of events than it is to skim over many more. We like the easily understandable narrative style, which consists of a series of sharp pictures. Your opening paragraphs are excellent examples of this. It is also advisable to remember that the average American has little knowledge of foreign words and phrases and even less of remote geography; therefore, when using any such references, they must be explained; it is better to avoid them when possible.

Perhaps a good example of what I mean by the detailed narrative approach is afforded by your account of the capture of Riyadh. Rarely, in this account, does the reader get a clear picture of what went on. The town itself is not described, except to say that it has 50,000 inhabitants and has a wall and a moat around it. Yet, to make this important incident memorable to the reader, it will be necessary to give him a vivid picture of the town, the scene of the struggle, the fighters on either side—nowhere is there a word as to how they are dressed or armed—and so on.

Perhaps you have been trying to condense the article as you wrote it. But this is a handicap—you should forget all about condensation, leaving that to us, and simply write your story as vividly and as interestingly from the reader's point of view as you can. The more detail, the more color, the more pictures there are, the easier it is for us to make a lively condensation. I suggest you read a number of the biographies and adventure stories in recent issues and note the unusual amount of colorful detail you will find in each. All these pieces, it should be remembered, were three or four times as long when originally written.

Make Your Writing Clear

As it stands, the piece takes for granted too much ready comprehension on the part of the reader. For a large audience, it is necessary to spell things out somewhat more than you have done. We try, first of all, to make each of our articles crystal-clear to every reader. Just keep in mind the reader who doesn't know the West, or anything accurate about Indians, or ranching, or the country you describe. If you can make the story easily comprehensible to him, you will have achieved what I have in mind.

I feel that the piece reads too much like fiction. I think you can help this by introducing some facts and figures. This information is needed to complete the story. How many students has the Indian school graduated or placed in jobs? How long has it been in existence and how many students does it normally accommodate? What are the buildings like, the teachers, etc.? Is there some outstanding personality connected with the school who is responsible for its success? If so, can't we have a short profile of him? In brief, the normal data of a non-fiction article, inserted here and there throughout your present script, would make the piece more realistic, with less of the sound of fiction.

The Eager Market for Humor

Thank you for letting us have a look at the piece on the perils of remodeling an old house, which I return herewith. I read it with personal, as well as professional, interest—for I am similarly entrapped. I wish I could give you encouragement on this article, but I fear I cannot. In the first place, the subject is not a fresh one, it having been treated many times in different ways. And then I think you have set down approximately what actually happened in your case, whereas a successful humorous article of this nature should be *based* not only on actual experience, but also built up of the purely imaginary. The whole thought of the writer should be entertaining the reader, and not of reporting what has happened in real life to the writer. This requires a great deal of creative effort. You certainly have the gift of humor in your writing, and if you would give your imagination free play—forgetting the facts—I should think you could bring off some very amusing pieces. As usable humor is the hardest thing for a magazine editor to find, there is always an eager market for it. But it has to be very good, quite fresh and original.

Exercises

1. Choose two long magazine articles from any current publication, one of which is interesting and the other of which is not. Then analyze the structure, style, and content of the articles, and decide how these elements contribute to each article's overall impact on the reader.

2. Select a subject you think would be suitable for a long article. Then make a list of topics and subtopics you would expect to cover in the article and organize them into an outline. Finally, develop an alternative structure for the article by rearranging the outline. Discuss the differences that would result and the reasons you might choose one outline over the other.

3. Read again the letters from editors of magazines and list the most important things you have learned from these letters. Turn in your list to the instructor at the next class meeting.

NINETEEN

LAWS, ETHICS, AND ETIQUETTE

The unexamined life is not worth living.

SOCRATES

Playwright Lillian Hellman was persuaded by author John Hersey of Yale's Pierson College to teach writing to a group of freshmen. "I've got a recommendation for you students," said Miss Hellman as she commenced the course. "All young people make things simple. But there ain't nothing that is."

Journalists' work involves hundreds of decisions each day. In the course of their normal activities, they must decide what to write about, whom to interview, which information to use in the story, what order to present the information in, what kind of story to write, what words to use, and so on. Many of these choices affect only the final product, so writers are free to act on their judgments about what will produce the best story. But many decisions affect things other than the story itself, such as writers' relationships with their sources or editors, their relationships with other writers, or their professional standing in the publishing world. Such decisions often involve issues of law, ethics, and etiquette.

No writer can expect to practice the craft without having to confront situations that demand such choices be made. It is therefore reasonable for writers to acquire a practical knowledge of the laws that not only protect their work but also limit their use of other people's work. In addition, they should be familiar with the legal incentives society provides for writers to publish accurate and truthful statements about their subjects. They should also be aware that their ability to protect the confidentiality of their sources is not absolute.

Beyond the areas of journalism that are regulated by law are territories governed solely by ethics. Decisions involving ethical choices are often more difficult to make than those involving legal choices because of the absence of absolute guidelines. Should you allow a source to read an article before it is published? Suppose that person asks for changes? Are you obligated to make them? Is it all right to submit articles to several magazines simultaneously? Suppose two magazines want the story. Should you sell to the highest bidder? What if you stumble across a story that someone doesn't want made public? How can you decide whether or not to go ahead with the article? These kinds of decisions can be made only on the basis of an individual's standards of professional conduct. The standards you choose can greatly influence your standing among your peers.

Finally, the unwritten code of publishing etiquette should guide a writer's activities. Who pays for what in a relationship between writer and source, or writer and magazine? How much revision should an editor expect a writer to do on an article without a guaranteed payment? How much revision of an article by a magazine's editorial staff should a writer accept before claiming that his or her work has been substantively altered? And when that does happen, how should the writer handle the situation?

Recognizing that many practices are not covered by statute—and that legal action is often so cumbersome and expensive that it is all but useless in many cases—the American Society of Journalists and Authors (ASJA) has developed a code of ethics and fair practices. The code, reprinted in Appendix A, is excellent for spelling out pivotal matters affecting the relationships between writers and editors. This code is not entirely satisfactory for the purposes of this book because it is largely limited to writer-editor relations and is designed for professionals, who take for granted many points that are perplexing to beginners.

The code is limited in another respect. Although the ASJA is a healthy organization having nearly 700 members, many other writers make agreements with editors that do not conform to the code, and members of the society are sometimes unable to persuade editors to conform.

Whether editors observe the code is their decision. If many of their best writers insist that their assignments be governed by the provisions of the code, editors are likely to acquiesce. So many editors have backgrounds as free-lancers that sympathy for the code is apparent, even in magazine offices where editors find it difficult or impossible to live up to its provisions.

Thus, the code is both a set of practical guidelines and an ideal to be attained. In this chapter, we cite some of the provisions of the Code of Ethics and Fair Practices—in the context of discussing questions that are important to beginners as well as to professionals.

LAW AND THE WRITER

"Love truth but pardon error."

VOLTAIRE

No matter what its constitution states, nearly every society restricts free expression. The basic restrictions take the form of laws to protect individuals or groups against defamation, copyright laws to protect authors and publishers, statutes to protect the community standard of decency, and statutes to protect the state against treasonable and seditious expression. Volumes have been written about these laws. A short work that writers find valuable is Paul Ashley's *Say It Safely*. Much larger and more complete books are *Mass Communication Law* by Donald M. Gillmor and Jerome A. Barron and *Law of Mass Communications* by Harold L. Nelson and Dwight L. Teeter, Jr. Writers interested in the laws governing communication are referred to such books for full discussions. In this chapter, we will consider some of the highlights of the laws governing a writer's career.

Libel

A libelous statement is a false statement, written or broadcast, that causes anyone to suffer public hatred, contempt, or ridicule; to be shunned or avoided; or to be injured in business or occupation.

In 1964, the United States Supreme Court decided in *New York Times Co.* v. *Sullivan* that even false statements tending to injure public officials must be protected by law unless facts were deliberately misstated or unless there were reckless disregard of the question of truth or falsity. In 1971, the Court decided in *Rosenbloom* v. *Metromedia* that private individuals who are involved in matters of public or general concern also should be severely limited in their ability to recover damages in libel actions. Like public officials, they must prove that they are the victims of actual malice or "calculated falsehood" to sue successfully, no matter how great the damage. The Court upholds a broad umbrella to protect writers who attempt to present facts about public issues—even if the writers are mistaken and the "facts" turn out to be false.

In presenting opinion, writers have long enjoyed the privilege of "fair comment and criticism." This means that people, measures, and social institutions that seek public approval are fair game for the writer's judgments. The judgments may be cruel—as when a critic wrote in a scathing review, "'Sing Until Tomorrow' had two strikes against it. One was the fact that you couldn't hear half of it. The other was the half you could hear"—but they are fully protected.

There is much more to the law of defamation, and every writer should study it. In public affairs journalism, the writer who takes due care to present facts rather than distortions and does not write maliciously avoids the principal dangers. In most states, if a defamatory publication is true, the injured person cannot recover damages except in highly unusual circumstances. But the writer must prove that the statements are true if a suit is filed. Studying the laws of libel should be an important part of the education of every public affairs journalist.

Privacy

Here, too, the writer's freedom has been growing; the courts support the public's right to learn about their fellow citizens. This does not mean that a writer is free to invade privacy at will. It means that the courts weigh the public interest against the interest of the person who believes that his or her privacy has been invaded. Where it can be shown that issues or matters of general concern are involved, the courts tend to rule in favor of publication. Courts sometimes go much further. In a famous case, a one-time child prodigy named William Sidis was the subject of a profile in the *New Yorker.* Repelled by the publicity that had enveloped him when he was a child, Sidis, who had lost his passion for mathematics and was leading an obscure life as a bookkeeper, sued on the grounds that the *New Yorker* had invaded his privacy. But the court ruled that he had been a public figure and still was.

Since the majority of magazine articles are written with the cooperation of those who are prominently featured, few writers have been threatened with suits based on the right of privacy. Writers who become defendants in such suits usually recognize while researching an article that danger looms, and this gives them time to seek legal help. There are enough exceptions to these rules of thumb, however, to suggest that writers should study the passage covering privacy in one of the books on communications law cited above, or in *Rights and Writers* by Harriet F. Pilpel and Theodora S. Zavin.

Copyright

How can I protect my work from being stolen? This is a question that worries beginning writers much more than it should. Since January 1, 1978, when the Copyright Revision Act of 1976 went into effect, a writer's article has been protected by federal copyright laws from the moment it is written. Even if the article is never published or, for that matter, never leaves the author's desk, it is subject to copyright restrictions for the author's lifetime and for fifty years afterward. Two criteria must be met for a work to be copyrighted: (1) it must be original, and (2) it must be "fixed in a tangible form." Magazine articles that are the unique work of an author clearly meet these specifications.

Another source of comfort to beginners should be that the cost of the text material represents a small fraction of the total cost of *any* magazine. *Playboy* pays $3,000 for some articles, but producing and distributing a single issue costs hundreds of thousands of dollars. The publisher of a down-at-the-heels journal who can afford to pay no more than 3 cents a word may begrudge the $90 he lays out for a 3,000-word article, but he is certain to grieve more over the thousands of dollars that must go for other expenses. The outright theft of a manuscript makes so little sense that the editor who risks a lawsuit by stealing one should have his sanity questioned.

The "Theft" of Ideas

Some dangers do exist, but there are many fewer than the fearful beginner imagines, and most of them are subtler than thievery. If 100 free-lancers each submit an article to a magazine tomorrow, one can bet confidently that no article will be stolen outright. It will be almost as unlikely—but not a certain bet—that a magazine staffer will steal a passage or a paragraph from any of the articles. But just as it is not safe to assume that college students will neither cheat on exams nor plagiarize in writing term papers, fresh thoughts are so important in the magazine world that assuming that nothing will be taken is risky. Perhaps a young staffer eager to impress his superiors will appropriate a title or a phrase—or perhaps the article he is evaluating carries an anecdote that would sparkle in the article he is writing. The culprit need not be a beginner. A seasoned editor may be captivated by an article idea but may think that the article itself is not up to her standards and that the writer is not likely to revise successfully. She may then reject the article and assign the subject to one of her regular writers. These kinds of thievery need not be conscious. Human frailty is such that one can easily rationalize until guilt disappears. It is especially easy for a staffer to persuade himself after some time has passed that he originated the title, the phrase, or the idea.

Unfortunately, ideas are not subject to copyright laws. Only their expression in a certain form is protected. Thus, there is no legal recourse for a writer who feels that a magazine has stolen his or her article idea. Because the magazine world places such a premium on new ideas, or good ideas, this situation sometimes causes problems for writers and editors. The American Society of Journalists and Authors has proposed some guidelines on this subject in its Code of Ethics and Fair Practices:

> An idea shall be defined not as a subject alone, but as a subject with an approach to the handling thereof. A writer shall be considered to have a property right in such an idea. Under ordinary circumstances he shall have priority in the development of it. When an editor likes an idea, he normally is bound to permit the writer who presents it first to proceed with it.

These guidelines reflect the spirit of the federal law, which distinguishes between ideas and their form of expression.

Magazines and Copyright Law

Published magazines are protected by copyright laws, as are the individual articles they contain. This does not prevent a writer from asserting his right to separate copyright because he is regarded by law as the first owner. Although individual registration with the copyright office is not mandatory, a writer cannot sue for infringement without having registered, nor can she collect damages or attorney's fees for any infringement that occurred before the article was registered.

In general, when a magazine buys an article, it purchases specific rights to publish the article or to authorize others to publish or reprint the article. Some magazines give reprint royalties to writers, but others do not. It is important for free-lance writers to understand exactly what they are selling when they sign contracts and receive payments for articles.

A writer who produces an article while working under contract to a magazine is considered to have written a "work made for hire." In such cases, the magazine is considered the "author" for copyright purposes and is thus entitled to initial ownership of the copyright. Staff writers also work under this condition.

Since most publishers are fair-minded and since so few articles have a life beyond first publication, it seldom pays an author to register the copyright for his or her own work or to worry about which rights he or she is giving up. Once most articles have been published, rights to them are no more valuable than used theater tickets. But enough authors have had cause to rue the cost of their once-careless habits to suggest that knowing the law and reading contracts carefully can be important. Consider this excerpt from a magazine contract:

> In consideration of the sum of $_____ (in payment of which we herewith enclose our check), the author grants to _____ Publishing Com-

pany, its licenses and assigns forever, all rights in and to the material and all rights of copyright and renewal of copyrights therein, including, but without limitation, the exclusive right to publish the material in magazine, newspaper and book form, and to use it in dramatic, motion picture, radio and television productions anywhere. The rights herein granted include the right: to edit, revise, abridge, condense and translate the material; to publish the same in one or more installments; to change the title thereof; to use the author's name, biography and likeness in connection with the publication, advertising and promotion of the material; and to make such other promotional use of the material as _____ Publishing Company may determine.

Copyright Law and the Doctrine of Fair Use

Most magazine writers find that protecting themselves is less significant than how they use the copyrighted work of others—sometimes quotations from other articles, more often quotations from books. How much can I quote? This question centers on the doctrine known as "fair use," and, as one panel of distinguished judges pointed out, "The issue of fair use . . . is the most troublesome in the whole law of copyright."

The courts have developed the doctrine, which is imprecise at best. No fixed rules have emerged to tell a writer how much he or she may quote. In some desperation, most book publishers tell their authors that they must seek permission to quote any substantial amount of copyrighted material, and that in any case the author must obtain permission to quote a passage as long as 300 words—or 400, or 500, varying with the publisher. Seldom does anyone fear that quoting a sentence or a paragraph will infringe on copyright. But if mere length were the criterion, one might freely quote four lines from an eight-line poem. The pivotal question is whether the quotation represents substantial use—and especially whether quoting, whatever the length, may prejudice the sale or diminish the need for the original work.

Some magazines and books carry notices that not a word may be reproduced. The *Reader's Digest* masthead states, "Reproduction in any manner in whole or in part in English or other languages prohibited." This is nonsense. Publications cannot pass their own laws. Those that issue such warnings are as subject as others to the rules of fair use.

Writers should also know that general facts cannot be copyrighted, and a writer can paraphrase almost at will. Copyright is not a prison for ideas or reports of events; it protects the sequence of ideas, words, phrases, and the phrasings themselves. Conceivably, copyright can be infringed by paraphrase—if the writer paraphrases at length and so deftly that a court might rule unfair use—but that danger is remote.

Copyright Infringement

Infringement of copyright is illustrated by the case brought by writer Gene Miller of the *Miami Herald* against Universal City Studios, Inc., American Broadcasting Companies, and Post-Newsweek Stations Florida, Inc. In 1971, Miller covered the story of the kidnapping of Barbara Mackle, who was abducted from an Atlanta hotel and buried alive in a coffin for five days before she was rescued. Miller and Mackle agreed to write a book together about her experience called *83 Hours Till Dawn.* A producer for Universal Studios subsequently saw the book, decided it would make a good movie for television, and gave a copy of it to a screenwriter. The producer offered to purchase the rights to the book from Miller, but Miller wanted more money than the producer was willing to pay.

Universal went ahead with the movie, called *The Longest Night.* Miller then sued on the basis of infringement of copyright, and in 1978 the case was decided in his favor. The decision was based largely on the fact that the movie script contained a number of similarities to material in the book that was not available in other accounts of the kidnapping, including some factual errors. The decision was that Miller's research—that is, those facts he discovered through his own effort during 2,500 hours of interviews and digging— was subject to copyright restrictions. It was evidence of the originality of his work and its form of expression. In its opinion, the court stated the following:

> To this court it doesn't square with reason or common sense to believe that Gene Miller would have undertaken the research involved in writing *83 Hours Till Dawn* (or to cite another more famous example, that Truman Capote would have undertaken the research required to write *In Cold Blood*) if the author thought that upon completion of the book a movie producer or television network could simply come along and take the profits of the books and his research from him. In the age of television "docudrama" to hold other than research is copyrightable is to violate the spirit of the copyright law and to provide to those persons and corporations lacking in requisite diligence and ingenuity a license to steal.

Magazines and Copyright Infringement   Magazines often seek to protect their own legal interests by inserting provisions in their contracts in which the writer guarantees various aspects of his or her work. The following paragraph is an example of this kind of protection:

> You represent and warrant originality, authorship and ownership of said contribution, that it has not heretofore been published, that its publication will not infringe upon any copyright, proprietary or other right and that it contains no matter which is libelous, obscene, or otherwise contrary to law.

Copyright Law and U.S. Government Publications

Few writers are aware that the law holds that "no copyright shall subsist . . . in any publication of the United States Government. . . ." Like all other works that are not protected by common law or statutory copyright, government documents are in the public domain and may be quoted freely. There can be questions about particular works because the Copyright Act does not define "government publication," but the only practical danger is that a government publication may reprint copyrighted material. This does not transform the reprinted work into a government publication. A copyrighted magazine article reprinted in the *Congressional Record* is still protected under copyright law.

Access to Government Information While federal law permits one to quote freely from government documents, writers sometimes have trouble getting at them. Government secrecy is an old story.

As we are all now well aware, secret dealings have been common in every presidential administration. For example, some members of Congress were as disturbed by governmental secrecy during the Eisenhower administration as were spokespersons for the mass media. They began in 1955 to work for an amendment to the Administrative Procedure Act. It was a laborious process. Representative John E. Moss's Subcommittee on Government Information held 173 public hearings and investigations and issued seventeen volumes of hearing transcripts and fourteen volumes of reports, all of which documented widespread secrecy. By 1966, both houses of Congress had passed an amendment to the public information section of the Administrative Procedure Act. But by the time the amendment became the law known as the Freedom of Information Act, nine categories of information had been exempted:

1. Information specifically required by executive order to be kept secret in the interest of national defense or foreign policy.
2. Information related solely to internal personnel rules and practices of any agency.
3. Information specifically exempted by statute from disclosure.
4. Trade secrets and commercial or financial information obtained from any person and privileged or confidential.
5. Interagency or intraagency memorandums or letters that would not be available by law to a private party in litigation with the agency.
6. Personnel and medical files and similar files the disclosure of which would constitute a clearly unwarranted invasion of personal privacy.
7. Investigatory files compiled for law enforcement purposes except to the extent available by law to a private party.
8. Information contained in or related to examination, operating, or condition reports prepared by, on behalf of, or for the use of any agency responsible for the regulation or supervision of financial institutions.
9. Geological and geophysical information and data (including maps) concerning wells.

Understandably eager to promote and protect their own policies and programs, officials often hide and manipulate information. As the American public learned during the revelations of the Watergate scandal during the second half of the Nixon administration, sometimes their purpose is shady. In one relatively innocuous example, the commander of the Military District of Washington, DC, once attempted to withhold a letter that pressured liquor lobbyists and wholesalers to provide free drinks for 1,200 guests at an army party. He tried to justify his action by citing the first exemption to the Freedom of Information Act, which protects national security information.

Despite its flaws, the Freedom of Information Act has enhanced access at the federal level. More than half of the states have passed laws that provide access to state, county, and municipal records and require open meetings of public bodies. These laws, too, are flawed by exemptions. But it seems clear that the writer's freedom to find facts in the labyrinths of government is improving.

ETHICS AND THE WRITER

"Feigning invariably fails."

MALCOLM S. FORBES

The writer should understand the distinction between plagiarism and the unfair use that is copyright infringement. Plagiarism is not necessarily illegal (although it is certainly unethical). That is, one might steal a few sentences or a few paragraphs by passing them off as one's own. This act is one of failing to give credit, but it does not necessarily infringe copyright.

A writer may satisfy the courts that he or she has not infringed copyright and thus settle the legal question. Whether he can satisfy his conscience—or, in the absence of a conscience, whether he might be able to satisfy a jury of other writers—poses the ethical question. Although it is easy to rationalize and explain away plagiarism, anyone who has the intelligence to write for publication *can* tell when she is failing to give appropriate credit. It is unnecessary, of course, for the writer to try to trace down the origin of every captivating phrase. The person who coined "credibility gap" to describe one of the problems and failings of the president of the United States would probably like to be credited every time the phrase is used, but that would be absurd.

It is not at all absurd, however, to give credit for a sentence. One worth using should be clothed in quotation marks and attributed to its author. (Not, for most magazines, with the footnoting that is common in scholarly journals—but in a smooth note in the text: "As James Thurber pointed out in . . ." or "Gunnar Myrdal's *An American Dilemma* cites. . . .") If the phrasing of a sentence a writer wants to use is limp but the idea is attractive, the writer should paraphrase and give credit.

These guidelines are not rigid for the writer who uses them sensibly. For example, an article on the crushing troubles that afflict New York City must deal with financial problems and air pollution. The writer might take facts and figures from an article or book and accurately feel that he owed no credit because dozens of articles and books carry the same information. He must ask himself in each case: did the person who wrote this have to work for it—dig—or are these facts widely known and readily available? This criterion can apply in almost any situation. Facing it squarely and answering it honestly will suggest whether giving credit is necessary.

When honest answers to such questions result in paragraph after paragraph of attribution to others, a writer should not assume that she is spreading credit too liberally. Rather, like the bad scholar who leans so heavily on other scholars that she does little more than move bones from one graveyard to another, the writer is merely rehashing.

In one dark area, many writers and sources (not to mention editors) seem to be united against readers. This may be a harsh judgment of the practice of sources who try to promote favorable articles by arranging free travel and other expensive assistance for writers. But seldom are readers informed that the writer of the glowing article on Oahu was able to explore the island because someone with an interest in promoting tourism there paid the bill. In some cases, the editors are not told of the arrangement. Normally, however, editors know or can guess, if only because they are paying a $400 fee to a writer whose expenses were $750.

The fact that an interested party paid the bill is not the essential point. The ethical question springs from the fact that the reader is not fully informed that the article may have been biased.

Simultaneous Submissions

Should a free-lancer submit an article to more than one publication at a time? If the world of magazines observed the rules of the retail marketplace, the answer would be "Of course." But editors make a vociferous case for single submission. They point out that an editor may devote hours, even days, to reading and evaluating a manuscript. A staff conference involving a dozen editors may be given over to discussing an article. If an editor of *Cosmopolitan* sends a four-page letter suggesting revisions, many hours and hundreds of dollars are wasted if the writer responds that *McCall's* bought the article the day before.

This does not mean that there are no reasonable exceptions. When a writer has an idea or an article so timely that waiting for an editorial decision may jeopardize it, some editors consider simultaneous submission appropriate. The cardinal rule in such cases is that all editors must be informed.

Beginners sometimes reason that their articles have so little chance of acceptance at major markets that they can safely submit to four or five simultaneously on the off chance that one will buy. This is usually a safe assumption because few beginners *can* publish in a major magazine without serving the apprenticeship of writing first for minor magazines. But even a beginner jeopardizes his or her future by submitting simultaneously without informing each magazine.

Double-Duty Articles

Imaginative writers can make one research project go a long way—perhaps far enough for three or four articles. Should they? It is easy to pose an example that clearly suggests an affirmative answer. Certainly, a slow journey down the Mississippi can yield the material for a profile of the river, a profile of a port city, an article on a riverboat, and another on a riverboat captain. In fact, given the time, energy, and ingenuity, a capable writer might fashion a hundred articles for a hundred different magazines from a single trip. If passages in the articles do not duplicate one another, and the information in each article is substantially different, the ethical question disappears.

But there are questions in this area that must be examined closely. For example, what of writing on one entertainment personality for different magazines? Two factors are now pivotal: the similarity of the articles and the similarity of the magazines. If the articles are similar, the magazines must be different. If the magazines are similar, the articles must be different. Thus, one might write an article for a magazine circulated in the Southwest and a similar article for a magazine circulated in New York. One might also write a profile of an entertainment personality for one magazine and barely mention that he loves to cook and, for a similar magazine, base an article on the same man's prowess as a gourmet cook.

The requirement that either the articles or the magazines be quite different is easy to understand. If readers of *Harper's* and the *Atlantic* were to find one month that an author had written similar articles on Edward Kennedy for both magazines, many would feel cheated because they subscribe to both. If the articles were quite different, though, the readers of both magazines would probably feel only that that was a bit too much Kennedy. If similar articles by one writer are published in magazines that have quite different sets of readers, clearly no harm is done.

Whatever the writer believes about the similarities and differences in magazines and audiences, he should inform the editors. Their judgments may not square with hers. The author of this text once agreed to write for a magazine a 3,500-word essay-review of three books. A short time later, he agreed to write a 900-word review of one of the books for another magazine. The reviews were so strikingly different in substance and tone as well as length that he did not trouble to inform the editors. When the 900-word review was published, the other editor called long distance to say that its appearance had ruined his day.

Informing everyone who is centrally involved is also essential when a writer wants to sell once again an article purchased by a magazine that died without publishing it. The writer should get a letter of permission from the publisher of the defunct magazine and show it to any editor interested in the article.

ETIQUETTE AND THE WRITER

Points of etiquette have been treated generally in earlier pages of this book, but several that are important to the free-lancer and the staff writer are discussed specifically here.

Writer and Source
One of the most important points of etiquette arises from the fact that many articles are built on massive research. If the writer interviews widely and gathers much more information than he can use—and he should—how does he explain to his sources why he ignored their contributions? Explaining

should begin not after an article is published but during interviews. A writer should tell her sources that she is interviewing not only for quotations but also for background information. This is, of course, quite true, and very few interviews yield *nothing* of value. It is true also that many interviews do not show up in articles because space in that issue of the magazine was limited. Most interviewees are mollified by one explanation or the other, even though they may not be happy. Sources who are quoted as well as those who are not are often gratified by thank-you notes from writers, just as most are pleased when a writer calls for an appointment and arrives punctually.

With few exceptions, writers should take sources to lunch, not the other way around. It is easy to overemphasize the point that in many cases, the source is likely to benefit at least as much as the writer (introducing a note of sticky piety where it does not belong), but the writer should not yield to that easy rationalization. A writer who establishes businesslike re-

ELIE WIESEL

"All the world's roads, all the outcries of mankind, lead to this haunted place unlike any other. Here is the kingdom of night, where God's face is hidden and a flaming sky becomes an accursed graveyard for a vanished people," Elie Wiesel wrote in his article for the *New York Times Magazine* titled "Pilgrimage to the Country of Night."

This vivid description of Auschwitz, where he and his family were prisoners, continues: "The red flames that lick the sky inspire neither fear nor memory." This is a sample of the Nobel Peace Prize–winner's writing that is found in his six books depicting the plight of Jews.

For his books, *Night, Dawn, The Accident, The Town Beyond the Wall, The Gates of the Forest,* and *The Jews of Silence: A Personal Report on Soviet Jewry,* Wiesel has received numerous honors in addition to the Nobel Peace Prize, including the National Jewish Book Council Literary Award in 1965 and the Jewish Heritage Award in 1966.

Wiesel was born on September 30, 1928, in Sighet, Romania, to Shlomo and Sarah Wiesel. He became the authority on the plight of the Jew after surviving as a prisoner of a Nazi concentration camp, where he saw his family die. His experiences are described while he depicts aspects of Judaism in his first five books, in which he is the main character.

"Loneliness is the key word that evokes, that describes the Jewish experience during World War II. . . . The fact remains that today there are 6,000 Jews in Poland. Before the war, there were 3,500,000." Wiesel tells about concentration camps like Auschwitz, Treblinka, and Birenau from firsthand experience in a quest to let the truth be known.

Much of his writing is done to heighten awareness about the tragic happenings during World War II. He wrote: "When obscene propagandists are trying to 'prove' that Auschwitz never existed, what can be more urgent than attracting as many visitors as possible to the site?"

In an interview with a writer from *Contemporary Authors,* Wiesel stated: "What torments me most is not the Jews of silence I met in Russia, but the silence of the Jews I live among today." He wishes for them to "cry out, cry out, . . . enlist public opinion, . . . turn to those with influence, . . . involve the governments—the hour is late." His purpose in writing *The Jews of Silence: A Personal Report on Soviet Jewry* was to get their voices heard.

Another purpose in his writing is to help victims of oppression everywhere in the world. He serves as a voice for those whose freedom is infringed on, such as the Cambodian boat people, Soviet Jews, and Arab refugees.

"It is by freedom that a man knows himself, by his sovereignty over his own life that a man measures himself," Elie Wiesel wrote for *Parade* magazine one year after winning the Nobel Peace Prize. "To violate that freedom, to flout that sovereignty, is to deny man the right to live his life, to take responsibility for himself with dignity."

—Sue Kown

lationships is not likely to find someday that his or her sources will expect too much.

Here is a writer of great power who is the gentlest of men. Elie Wiesel is a man who can use words that will explode in the minds of many people. Nonetheless, he is a humble person, even after winning the Nobel Peace Prize in 1986, which included $287,769.78. Wiesel writes about his teachers:*

> I would like to talk to you about one exceptional teacher. His name was Saul Liebermann, and he was one of the great Jewish Talmudic scholars of the last few generations.
>
> Twice a week, I would go to his library in the Jewish Theological Seminary to study for three hours at a stretch under his direction. It was he who led me to discover the inherent beauty in exploring ancient texts.
>
> Studying became an adventure.
>
> Professor Liebermann was both teacher and friend. I did nothing without consulting him. Before publishing work, I would show it to him. It was he who officiated at my marriage in the old city of Jerusalem. And it was he who gave my three-year-old son his first Hebrew lesson. Our bond lasted seventeen years. I often think of it with sadness and longing.
>
> Then, one day, this relationship ended. He was leaving for Israel one afternoon. As for me, I had to set off for Yale, where I would teach.
>
> As usual, our session began at eight a.m. and ended at eleven. We stood up and embraced. I wished him a good journey.
>
> We were both sure we would be resuming our sessions before long. He walked with me to the door, opened it, and then closed it again. "Come back," he said. "We still have a little time."
>
> We went on reading until noon. It was getting late. I stood up once again and held out my hand to him. He walked with me to the elevator. I was already inside it when he drew me toward him: "Come," he said. "We still have a little time."
>
> Once more, we opened the thick Talmudic treatise and dove into its dazzling world. At one o'clock, we reluctantly broke off. Now it was really getting late. He had to catch his plane, and I had my class at Yale. We embraced for the third time, and I left him. I never saw him again. He died less than twelve hours later, in his sleep, aboard the plane taking him to Jerusalem.
>
> A friend told me the news. I was not surprised. Without daring to admit it, I had expected this. During our reading, I had looked up and noticed that his work table, usually in hopeless disorder, had been thoroughly tidied and was almost bare.
>
> A Talmudic saying came to mind: The Righteous are warned of their imminent departure, so that they may prepare themselves for it.
>
> A certain law commands the disciple to go into mourning upon the death of his teacher. This law answers a need—the need to express one's sorrow. The need, also, to remain attached to the one who is gone.
>
> I miss my teachers.

---

*Reprinted by permission of Elie Wiesel.

Writer and Revision

The knottiest problem of etiquette in the writer-editor relationship is revision. It poses questions like these:

1. How much rewriting should an editor be able to ask a writer to do without guaranteeing that the article will be bought and published?
2. To what degree should an editor be allowed to rewrite an article?
3. What recourse has the writer who thinks that editing has ruined an article?

The code of the ASJA states:

> No writer's work shall be rewritten without his or her advance consent. If an editor requests a writer to rewrite his manuscript, the writer shall be obliged to do so. Alternatively, he shall also be entitled to withdraw the manuscript and offer it elsewhere.

Although this provision falls far short of covering all questions, it offers useful guidelines. Like the rest of the code, however, it is designed for the established writer. It assumes that writer and editor have settled on an article fee beforehand. This is unlikely for the beginning writer. What should a writer do if an editor asks for an extensive revision but does not promise to pay for the result?

As always, circumstances alter each case. If the writer thinks the revision will improve the article (and make it more salable elsewhere), he or she might simply revise as suggested. But if the revision requires extensive research and rewriting, the writer might ask for a guarantee. The rankest beginner is justified in asking for a guarantee when a revision is requested in a way that suggests that the editor is strongly interested in the article and is optimistic about publishing it.

If it seems too elementary to advise that manuscripts should be neat and easy to read, the many that arrive in magazine offices looking as though they have endured a bad trip suggest that it is not. Editors face stacks of manuscripts every day. Are they likely to enjoy those that writers have edited heavily in pencil, those that are typed in purple on yellow paper, those that are creased and dog-eared? Genius or great talent is welcome in whatever form it arrives. Editors will not reject articles they want because the writer is a slovenly typist. But writers who are not geniuses or great talents—those who must compete with thousands of others—must submit manuscripts that eye-weary editors can read without groans. (See the example of standard form for a manuscript at the end of this chapter.)

The most considerate writers mail their manuscripts flat and put them in folders before inserting them in manila envelopes. (Folders are essential when pictures accompany an article. Pictures should be protected between two pieces of corrugated cardboard held together by rubber bands.) Because most editors like to work with loose pages, manuscripts should be paper clipped, never stapled.

A stamped, self-addressed envelope should accompany query letters and manuscripts until the writer is established as a professional *or* until a relationship with a particular magazine is established. A beginner who has received a highly favorable response to a query need not enclose an envelope when submitting an article. A writer who has come close to selling ideas or articles to a magazine and receives encouraging letters also need not.

Whether a covering letter should accompany an article depends on the reason for the letter. *Never* should a letter be written to explain the article. If the rows of words that make up the manuscript fail to do their own explaining, a letter will do no more than mark the writer as an inept amateur. Covering letters are always in order when writer and editor have corresponded extensively about an article.

IN SUMMARY

Laws regarding communications vary somewhat from state to state. Precepts of ethics and points of etiquette are likely to vary at least slightly from magazine to magazine—and on some publications from editor to editor. Such variations make it impossible to describe exactly how writers and editors should behave in all cases. The principles set forth in this chapter, however, sketch the central bodies of law, ethics, and etiquette. The wise writer will give them as careful attention as he or she gives to fashioning evocative sentences.

Exercises

1. You have discovered that a young woman enrolled at your school is a former star of a popular television series. According to your source, she has had a nervous breakdown because of the pressures of Hollywood and has come to escape being a celebrity. Her activities are closely monitored by the dorm supervisor, and he refuses to help you arrange an interview, stating that she wishes to be left alone. You know that an article about her would be a good one for a magazine, but you have not figured out how to get an interview. What should you do?

2. A national magazine has responded favorably to one of your queries. The articles editor who writes back to you says that the magazine will give you the assignment on spec and will pay you $1,000 for the article if it is published, zero if it is not. You write the article, then wait anxiously for a month to hear from the magazine.

   Finally, you get a phone call from the articles editor. Your article has been accepted, but the editor in chief feels that the magazine should pay only $500 for it because you are a new writer. The articles editor apologizes profusely and reminds you that you can refuse the offer and try to sell the piece elsewhere. If you demand $1,000 as agreed, the magazine will simply reject the story. What should you do?

3. You have written a profile for a national magazine published in New York, and it has been accepted. One day, you get a phone call from an editorial assistant at the magazine saying that she has spoken to the person you wrote the article about and has been told that your story is riddled with factual errors. Your research for the piece included conducting a two-hour recorded interview with the person, reading a book written by her, and reading numerous articles in which she is mentioned. You did the interview when you happened to be passing through the city where the person lives, and you have not spoken to her since then. What should you do?

Standard form for a
manuscript.

Your Name   Approximate Word Count
Your Address   Rights Offered
Your Telephone Number   © 19___ Your Name
Your Social Security Number

TITLE OF ARTICLE

by

Your Byline

Type the title in capital letters about one-third down the page to leave room at the top for the editor's instructions to the printer. Begin your manuscript two double spaces after your byline. The manuscript should be double spaced to facilitate easy reading and to leave room for editing marks between lines.

The second and all succeeding pages should carry your last name, a dash, and the page number in the upper left or right corner. Leave two double spaces between this line and the following lines of manuscript, and leave margins of about 1¼ inches on all sides. On the final page, type "The End," centered, three double spaces after the last line of your manuscript.

Use pica or elite type (never script or other unconventional type). Black type on white paper is preferred, and only one side of the paper should be used.

Where possible, end a page at the end of a paragraph. This has several advantages, among them the fact that in writing memos to other editors or to the writer, an editor can refer to "the last paragraph on 5" rather than to "the paragraph that begins on 5 and ends on 6."

American Society of Journalists and Authors Code of Ethics and Fair Practices

Preamble

Over the years, an unwritten code governing editor-writer relationships has arisen. The American Society of Journalists and Authors has compiled the major principles and practices of that code that are generally recognized as fair and equitable.

The ASJA has also established a Committee on Editor-Writer Relations to investigate and mediate disagreements brought before it, either by members or by editors. In its activity this committee shall rely on the following guidelines.

1. Truthfulness, Accuracy, Editing

The writer shall at all times perform professionally and to the best of his or her ability, assuming primary responsibility for truth and accuracy. No writer shall deliberately write into an article a dishonest, distorted, or inaccurate statement.

Editors may correct or delete copy for purposes of style, grammar, conciseness, or arrangement, but may not change the intent or sense without the writer's permission.

2. Sources

A writer shall be prepared to support all statements made in his or her manuscripts, if requested. It is understood, however, that the publisher shall respect any and all promises of confidentiality made by the writer in obtaining information.

3. Ideas

An idea shall be defined not as a subject alone but as a subject combined with an approach. A writer shall be considered to have a proprietary right to an idea suggested to an editor and to have priority in the development of it.

4. Acceptance of an Assignment

A request from an editor that the writer proceed with an idea, however worded and whether oral or written, shall be considered an assignment: (The word "assignment" here is understood to mean a definite order for an article.) It shall be the obligation of the writer to proceed as rapidly as possible toward the completion of an assignment, to meet a deadline mutually agreed upon, and not to agree to unreasonable deadlines.

5. Report on Assignment

If in the course of research or during the writing of the article, the writer concludes that the assignment will not result in a satisfactory article, he or she shall be obliged to so inform the editor.

6. Withdrawal

Should a disagreement arise between the editor and writer as to the merit or handling of an assignment, the editor may remove the writer on payment of mutually satisfactory compensation for the effort already expended, or the writer may withdraw without compensation and, if the idea for the assignment originated with the writer, may take the idea elsewhere without penalty.

7. Agreements

The practice of written confirmation of all agreements between editors and writers is strongly recommended, and such confirmation may originate with the editor, the writer, or an agent. Such a memorandum of confirmation should list all aspects of the assignment including subject, approach, length, special instructions, payments, deadline, and kill fee (if any). Failing prompt contradictory response to such a memorandum, both parties are entitled to assume that the terms set forth therein are binding.

8. Rewriting

No writer's work shall be rewritten without his or her advance consent. If an editor requests a writer to rewrite a manuscript, the writer shall be obliged to do so but shall alternatively be entitled to withdraw the manuscript and offer it elsewhere.

9. Bylines

Lacking any stipulation to the contrary, a byline is the author's unquestioned right. All advertisements of the article should also carry the author's name. If an author's byline is omitted from a published article, no matter what the cause or reason, the publisher shall be liable to compensate the author financially for the omission.

10. Updating

If delay in publication necessitates extensive updating of an article, such updating shall be done by the author, to whom additional compensation shall be paid.

11. Reversion of Rights

A writer is not paid by money alone. Part of the writer's compensation is the intangible value of timely publication. Consequently, if after six months the publisher has not scheduled an article for publication, or within twelve months has not published an article, the manuscript and all rights therein should revert to the author without penalty or cost to the author.

12. Payment for Assignments

An assignment presumes an obligation upon the publisher to pay for the writer's work upon satisfactory completion of the assignment, according to the agreed terms. Should a manuscript that has been accepted, orally or in writing, by a publisher or any representative or employee of the publisher, later be deemed unacceptable, the publisher shall nevertheless be obliged to pay the writer in full according to the agreed terms.

If an editor withdraws or terminates an assignment, due to no fault of the writer, after work has begun but prior to completion of the manuscript, the writer is entitled to compensation for work already put in; such compensation shall be negotiated between editor and author and shall be commensurate with the amount of work already completed. If a completed assignment is not acceptable, due to no fault of the writer, the writer is nevertheless entitled to payment; such payment, in common practice, has varied from half the agreed-upon price to the full amount of that price.

13. Time of Payments

The writer is entitled to payment for an accepted article within ten days of delivery. No article payment should ever be subject to publication.

14. Expenses

Unless otherwise stipulated by the editor at the time of an assignment, a writer shall assume that normal, out-of-pocket expenses will be reimbursed by the publisher. Any extraordinary expenses anticipated by the writer shall be discussed with the editor prior to incurring them.

15. Insurance

A magazine that gives a writer an assignment involving any extraordinary hazard shall insure the writer against death or disability during the course of travel or the hazard, or, failing that, shall honor the cost of such temporary insurance as an expense account item.

16. Loss of Personal Belongings

If, as a result of circumstances or events directly connected with a perilous assignment and due to no fault of the writer, a writer suffers loss of personal belongings or professional equipment or incurs bodily injury, the publisher shall compensate the writer in full.

17. Copyright, Additional Rights

It shall be understood, unless otherwise stipulated in writing, that sale of an article manuscript entitles the purchaser to first North American publication rights only, and that all other rights are retained by the author. Under no circumstances shall an independent writer be required to sign a so-called "all rights transferred" or "work made for hire" agreement as a condition of assignment, of payment, or of publication.

18. Reprints

All revenues from reprints shall revert to the author exclusively, and it is incumbent upon a publication to refer all requests for reprint to the author. The author has a right to charge for such reprints and must request that the original publication be credited.

19. Agents

According to the Society of Authors' Representatives, the accepted fee for an agent's services has long been ten percent of the writer's receipts, except for foreign rights representation. An agent may not represent editors or publishers. In the absence of any agreement to the contrary, a writer shall not be obliged to pay an agent a fee on work negotiated, accomplished, and paid for without the assistance of the agent.

20. TV and Radio Program

The writer is entitled to be paid for personal participation in TV or radio programs promoting periodicals in which the writer's work appears.

21. Indemnity

No writer should be obliged to indemnify any magazine or book publisher against any claim, actions, or proceedings arising from an article or book.

22. Proofs

The editor shall submit edited proofs of the author's work to the author for approval, sufficiently in advance of publication that any errors may be brought to the editor's attention. If for any reason a publication is unable to so deliver or transmit proofs to the author, the author is entitled to review the proofs in the publication's office.

On "Work Made for Hire": A Statement of Position Announced April 28, 1978*

It has long been the established practice for responsible periodicals, in commissioning articles by free-lance writers, to purchase only one-time publication rights—commonly known as "first North American rights"—to such articles, the author retaining all other rights exclusively and all revenues received from the subsequent sale of other rights reverting to the author.

This practice is affirmed by the Code of Ethics and Fair Practices of the American Society of Journalists and Authors (ASJA), the national organization of independent nonfiction writers. The philosophy underlying this tradition has been further reaffirmed by the Copyright Law of 1976, which took effect in January of 1978 and states explicitly that copyright is vested in the author of a work and commences at the moment of creation of that work. "Copyright" is, literally, the "right to copy"—i.e., to publish in any form; that right is the author's, transferable only by written agreement and only to the degree, and under the terms, specified by such agreement.

It has come to the attention of the ASJA that certain periodical publishers have recently sought to circumvent the clear intent of the law by requiring independent writers, as a condition of article assignment, to sign so-called "all rights transferred" or "work made for hire" agreements. "All rights transferred" signifies that the author, the recognized copyright owner, transfers that ownership—and the right to all future revenues that may accrue therefrom—to the publisher. A "work made for hire" agreement specifically relegates the independent writer, so far as the article under consideration is concerned, to the status of an employee and creates a mythical—but nonetheless presumably legally binding—relationship in which the author agrees to function as a hired hand, while the publisher assumes the mantle of "creator" of the work, with all the rights of ownership vested in the creator under the law.

Both types of agreement clearly presume that the work being produced has an inherent value beyond one-time publication. Both the law and the ASJA Code of Ethics recognize that presumption, and it is the intent of both documents that the transfer of any rights beyond one-time publication take place only as the result of negotiation that assigns a monetary value to each such specific right a publisher seeks to acquire. Both types of agreement described above deny the author's basic role as owner and creator and seek to wrest from the writer, even before work has been produced, all future interest in revenues that may derive from that work.

This effort, subverting the intent of the law and contrary to ethical publishing trade practices, is condemned by the American Society of Journalists and Authors. The demand for blanket assignment of all future right and interest in the article or other creative work simply *will not be met* by responsible independent writers. Publishers who persist in issuing such inequitable agreements in connection with commissioned works will find that they have done so at the certain risk of losing a healthy flow of superior professional material. The result, for those periodicals, is likely to be a sharp and inevitable decline in editorial quality—an erosion and debasement of the standards on which periodicals must rely in order to attract readers and maintain their own reputations.

Suggested Letter of Agreement

Originating with the writer (to be used when publication does not issue written confirmation of assignment).

EDITOR'S NAME & TITLE
PUBLICATION
ADDRESS

Dear EDITOR'S NAME:

This will confirm our agreement that I will research and write an article of approximately NUMBER words on the subject of BRIEF DESCRIPTION, in accord with our discussion of DATE.

The deadline for delivery of this article to you is DATE.

It is understood that my fee for this article shall be $ AMOUNT, payable on acceptance, for which sum PUBLICATION shall be entitled to first North

American publication rights in the article.[1] If this assignment does not work out after I have submitted a completed manuscript, a kill fee of $ AMOUNT shall be paid to me.

It is further understood that you shall reimburse me for routine expenses incurred in the researching and writing of the article, including long-distance telephone calls, and that extraordinary expenses, should any such be anticipated, will be discussed with you before they are incurred.[2]

It is also agreed that you will submit proofs of the article for my examination, sufficiently in advance of publication to permit correction of errors.

This letter is intended to cover the main points of our agreement. Should any disagreement arise on these or other matters, we agree to rely upon the guidelines set forth in the Code of Ethics and Fair Practices of the American Society of Journalists and Authors.

Please confirm our mutual understanding by signing the copy of this agreement and returning it to me.

Sincerely,

(signed)

WRITER'S NAME

PUBLICATION

by ――――――――――
NAME AND TITLE

Date ――――――――――

Notes*

[1] If discussion included sale of other rights, this clause should specify basic fee for first North American rights, additional fees and express rights each covers, and total amount.

[2] Any other conditions agreed upon, such as inclusion of travel expenses or a maximum dollar amount for which the writer will be compensated, should also be specified.

Glossary of Newspaper and Magazine Terms

Newspaper Terms

Ad   An advertisement.

Advance   A news story about an event to occur in the future.

AM   Morning newspaper.

Angle   A slant or special aspect of a story.

AP   Associated Press.

Art   General term for all newspaper illustrations, including photographs.

Backroom, Backshop   Mechanical section of a small newspaper plant.

Banner   A headline stretching across a page; also known as a streamer, a line.

Beat   An exclusive news story; also, a reporter's regular run, as "City Hall beat."

BF   An abbreviation for bold-face or black-face type.

Body type   The small type, usually 8-point, in which most news stories are printed.

Box   News material enclosed by line rules.

Break   To become available for publication.

Bulldog   The earliest edition of the newspaper.

Bulletin   An urgent last-minute news brief.

Byline   Signature of a reporter preceding a story.

Caps   Capital letters.

Caption   Cutline; explanatory material that accompanies art.

CLC   Capital and lowercase letters, as in headlines.

Clip   A newspaper clipping.

Cold type   Characters set through a photographic or computerized process without use of Linotype machine or metal type.

Color story   A feature story that plays up the descriptive elements of a news event.

Copy   All news manuscript.

Copy desk   The desk where copy is edited and headlines are written.

Copy reader   A newsroom employee who reads and corrects copy and prepares heads.

Correspondent   An out-of-town reporter.

Cover   To get all the available news about an event.

CRT   Cathode ray terminal, also video display terminal (VDT), on which an editor may view and edit copy entered into a computer by a reporter or wire-service machine.

Cut   Metal plate bearing a newspaper illustration.

Dateline   The line preceding an out-of-town story giving the date and place of origin.

Deadline   The last moment to get copy in for an edition.

Deck   A section of a headline.

Dummy   A drawing or layout of a newspaper page.

Ears   Small boxes of type on either side of the newspaper name plate (flag) on page 1.

Edition   All copies of a newspaper printed during one run of the presses.

Editorialize   To inject the writer's opinion into a news story.

Engraving   Same as *cut.*

Exclusive   A story printed by only one paper; a scoop.

Extra   An edition other than those regularly published.

Feature   (1) To give special prominence to a story; (2) the most important or interesting fact in a story; (3) also, human interest or magazine type of story.

File   To send a story by wire.

Filler   A short, minor story to fill space where needed.

Flag   Front-page title of a newspaper; also known as a name plate.

Fold   The point at which the front page is folded in half.

Follow-up   A story presenting new developments of one previously printed; also known as a second-day story.

Fotog   Photographer.

Galley   A shallow metal tray for holding type as it comes from a composing machine.

Graph (or Graf)   Paragraph.

Guideline   A slug or title given each news story as a guide to both copy editor and printer.

Handout   Piece of publicity material.

Head   Headline.

Hold for release (HFR)   News not to be printed until a specified time or under specified circumstances.

How-to-do-it   A story that explains in minute detail how to perform some activity.

HTK   Head to come; endorsed on copy indicating the headline will follow.

Human interest   Emotional appeal in stories; a story with emotional appeal, as contrasted with straight news.

Insert   New material inserted in the body of a story already written.

Italic   Type in which letters and characters slant to the right.

Jump   To continue a story from one page to another.

Jump head   Headline carried over continued portion of jumped story.

Kicker   A small, short overline over the headline.

Kill   To strike out or discard part or all of a story.

LC   Abbreviation for lowercase.

Lead   (1) Introductory sentence or paragraph of a story; a tip that many lead to a story. (2) Thin metal strips used to space out lines of type; the process of spacing out.

Leg man   Reporter who gathers information and telephones it in to a rewrite man or woman at the office.

Linotype   A keyboard-operated machine that sets type in the form of a metal slug.

Localize   To stress the local angle of a story.

Makeup   Arrangement of news matter and pictures on a newspaper page.

Masthead   An editorial page box giving information about the paper.

ME   Managing editor.

More   Word put at the bottom of a page of copy meaning "more to come."

Morgue   Newspaper library for clippings, photos, and reference material.

Must   Designation on copy ordering that it be used without fail.

New lead   A new or rewritten item replacing a lead already prepared; new lead usually contains new developments.

News feature   Tied to a news event, the story is approximately halfway between the straight news story and the feature story.

Obituary   (Obit) A death story or a biography of a dead person.

OCR   Optical character recognition (or reader). A device that interprets typewritten copy for a computer or typesetting machine.

Overline   Same as *kicker.*

Pad   To make a story long by padding it out with words.

Personal   News brief about one or more persons; local item.

Personality sketch   A feature story that portrays a person, generally designed for emotional appeal.

Pix   Pictures.

Playup   To give prominence to.

PM   Afternoon paper.

Policy   Story written to suit the publisher's point of view.

PR   Public relations.

Privilege   Right granted press by the Constitution to print with immunity news that might otherwise be libelous.

Proof   An impression of type taken on paper on which to make corrections.

Quote   Quotation.

Rewrite man   Staff member who rewrites but does not cover news.

Rim   Outer edge of a copy desk where copy readers work.

Roundup   Comprehensive story from several sources.

Running story   Fast-breaking story written in sections or takes.

Scoop   An exclusive.

Seasonal story   A feature pegged to the occurrence of an annual event, often a holiday.

Sidebar   Usually a feature story that is subordinate to the main news story.

Slant   To emphasize a phase of a story.

Slot   The inside of a copy desk, where the chief sits.

Slug   A guideline set in type; notation placed on a story to identify it or specify disposal.

Straight news   A plain recital of new facts written in standard style and form.

Sub   Substitute.

Subhead   A small head inserted in the body of a news story to break up long stretches of type.

Summary lead   A lead summarizing high points, usually including "who, what, where, when, and why."

Suspended interest   News story with climax at end.

Take   A portion of copy in a running story, often one page.

Teletypesetter (TTS)   Trademark applied to a machine that transmits and sets news into type automatically.

Thirty (30)   The end; placed at the last of the copy to signify end.

Tie-in   Tie-back; information previously printed and included in a story to refresh the reader's memory.

Tip   Information that may lead to a story.

UPI   United Press International.

Magazine Terms

Analysis   An article that is a critical examination, usually designed to explain an event.

Angle   An aspect or emphasis played up by a writer, as in "woman's angle," emphasizing elements that will interest women.

Art   Any illustration.

Assignment   A writing or editing task.

Back of the book   Last section of a magazine, usually made up of materials that appear after the main editorial section.

Blackite   Black and white pictures.

Bleed   Running a picture to the edge of a page.

Blurb   A short, appreciative description of a story or article.

Book   Generally, a synonym for magazine.

Caption   Synonymous with *cutline*.

Center spread   The two facing pages printed on a single sheet.

Color   (1) To enliven writing; (2) to exaggerate and falsify.

Copy   Any written material intended for publication.

Copy reader   One who edits and otherwise processes copy.

Cover   (1) To gather facts; (2) the outer pages of a magazine. The outside front is the first cover; the inside is the second cover; the inside back is the third cover; the outside back is the fourth cover.

Cover plug   Special emphasis on the first cover for one or more stories.

CTC   Copy to come.

CTG   Copy to go.

Cut   (1) An engraving; (2) to shorten copy.

Cutline   The text accompanying art.

Dateline   Printing of date on any page.

Deadline   Last minute for turning in copy or art.

Department   A regular column or page.

Descriptive   The article given to describing, usually a place.

Dirty copy   Written material heavy with errors or corrections.

Double-page spread   Two facing pages of text or pictures or both.

Double truck   An editorial or advertising layout covering two pages made up as a single unit.

Dress   The appearance of a magazine.

Dummy   The draft of a magazine showing positions of elements. A diagram dummy is careful and complete. A hand dummy is roughly drawn. A paste-up dummy is made up of proofs of elements pasted in their positions. A positive blue dummy shows blueprints in rotogravure form.

Duotone   Art in two colors.

Edition   All identical copies.

Ed page   Editorial page.

Essay-review   A feature article that reviews a book, a movie, a play, and so on, within the larger context of the subject of the book, movie, or play.

Fat   (1) Oversize copy; (2) type that is too wide.

Feature   (1) To play up or emphasize; (2) an article, usually human interest, related to news but not necessarily news.

Filler   Copy set in type for use in emergencies.

Format   The size, shape, and appearance of a magazine.

Free-lance   An unattached writer or artist.

Front of the book   The main editorial section.

Galley proof   An impression of type that is held in a shallow metal tray, or galley. Also, first proofs of typeset matter.

Ghost writer   One who writes for others without receiving public credit.

Gutter   The space between left- and right-hand pages.

Hack   A writer who will work on any assignment for any publication.

Handout   Publicity release.

Head   Name, headline, and title of a story.

Headnote   Short text accompanying the head and carrying information on the story, the author, or both.

Hokum   Overly sentimental copy or art.

Hold   Not to be published without release; HFR, or "hold for release."

House ad   An advertisement for the magazine in which it appears or for another issued by the same publisher.

House magazine   (also known as house organ or company magazine) Internal house publications are issued for employees; external house publications may go only to company-related persons (customers, stockholders, and dealers) or to the public.

HTK   Head to come: a note to the printer that the headline is not accompanying the copy but will be supplied later.

Human interest   Feature material designed to appeal to the emotions. Also called personality sketch.

Impure pages   Those carrying commercial *puffs*.

Indicia   Mailing information data required by the post office.

Informative   A feature article that informs readers, normally about a place or a process.

Island   Position of an advertisement surrounded by reading matter.

Jump   (1) Running a story from one page to another, (2) the portion jumped.

Jump head   The title or headline over the jumped portion.

Jump lines   Short text matter explaining the destination or course of the continued text.

Jump the gutter   Titles or illustrations that continue from a left- to a right-hand page.

Layout   Positioning of text and art on layout sheets.

Legend   Explanation of an illustration.

Makeup   Planning or placing elements on a page or a group of pages.

Markup   A proof on which changes are indicated.

Masthead   Information, usually on the editorial page, on publishing, company officers, subscription rates, and the like.

Must   Copy or art that must appear.

Name plate   (also known as flag) The publication's name on the cover.

Narrative   A feature article that is story-telling in that the events are tightly transitional.

Outline   The gist of an article.

Pad   To increase length.

Page-and-turner   Text running more than a page.

Page proof   An impression of type that makes up a page.

Personal experience   A first-person feature article that relates the writer's experience.

Pic   Picture.

Piece   A synonym for story.

Pix   Pictures.

Play up   To emphasize.

Policy   A magazine's viewpoint.

Position   Where elements of a magazine appear.

Profile   A feature article that describes a person.

Puff   Praising publicity release.

Pulps   Magazines printed on coarse paper stock.

Punch   Vigor in writing or editing.

Query   A letter summarizing an article idea and asking whether the manuscript might be considered for publication.

Rejection slip   A printed form accompanying a manuscript returned to its author and rejected for publication.

Reprint   (1) To print a story that has appeared in another publication; (2) a separate printing of an article after publication.

Review   A magazine carrying literary stories, critical articles, and commentary.

Running foot   Identifying information (magazine title, date, and so forth) appearing in the bottom margins in some magazines.

Running head   Same as the running foot except that it appears in the top margins.

Shelter books   Magazines that focus on housing or related subjects.

Slant   Generally, synonymous with *Angle*.

Slicks   Magazines printed on glossy paper and having large (usually mass) circulation.

Slug   Word or words placed on copy as a guide to the printer.

Slushpile   The mass of unsolicited manuscripts received by magazines.

Spread   A long story, often with many illustrations.

Standing head   A title regularly used.

Tail-piece   A small drawing at the end of a story.

Tight   An issue with little space left for additional material.

Trim   To shorten.

Typo   A typographical error.

Vignette   A very short sketch or story.

When room   Copy or art that can be used at any time.

Wide open   An issue with plenty of room for additional material.

INDEX